*Interpreting*Davidson

CSLI Lecture Notes
Number 129

*Interpreting*D avidson

edited by
Petr Kotatko
Peter Pagin
Gabriel Segal

CSLI
PUBLICATIONS
Center for the Study of
Language and Information
Stanford, California

Copyright ©2001
CSLI Publications
Center for the Study of Language and Information
Leland Stanford Junior University
Printed in the United States
05 04 03 02 01   1 2 3 4 5

Library of Congress Cataloging-in-Publication Data

Interpreting Davidson / [edited by] Petr Kotatko, Peter Pagin, Gabriel
Segal.
    p. cm. – (CSLI lecture notes ; no. 129)
    Includes bibliographic references and index.
    ISBN 1-57586-356-1 (pbk. : alk. paper) – ISBN 1-57586-335-9 (cloth :
alk.paper)
    1. Davidson, Donald, 1917—Congresses. I. Kotátko, Petr. II. Pagin,
Peter, 1953- III. Segal, Gabriel. IV. Series.

B945.D384 I59 2001
191–dc21   2001037823

∞ The acid-free paper used in this book meets the minimum requirements of
the American National Standard for Information Sciences – Permanence of
Paper for Printed Library Materials, ansi z39.48-1984.

Please visit our web site at
`http://cslipublications.stanford.edu/`
for comments on this and other titles, as well as for changes
and corrections by the authors, editors and publisher.

Contents

Contributors

LARS BERGSTRÖM: Department of Philosophy, Stockholm University, 106 91 Stockholm, Sweden.
lars.bergstrom@philosophy.su.se

DONALD DAVIDSON: Philosophy Department, University of California, Berkeley, CA 94720-2390, USA.
davidson@socrates.berkeley.edu

PASCAL ENGEL: UFR de Philosophie, Université de Paris-IV-Sorbonne 1 rue Victor Cousin 75230 Paris cedex 05 F, France.
engel@poly.polytechnique.fr

KATHRIN GLÜER: Institut für Philosophie, Humboldt-Universität zu Berlin, Unter den Linden 6, D - 10099 Berlin, Germany.
kathrin.glueer@rz.hu-berlin.de

SAMUEL GUTTENPLAN: Philosophy Department, Birkbeck College, London, UK.
s.guttenplan@bbk.ac.uk

PAUL HORWICH: Department of Philosophy, The Graduate Center, City University of New York, 365 5th Avenue, New York, NY 10016, USA.
phorwich@gc.cuny.edu

ERNIE LEPORE: Center for Cognitive Science & Lab of Vision Research Rutgers University - New Brunswick, Psych Bldg Addition, Busch Campus, 152 Frelinghuysen Road, Piscataway, NJ 08854-8020, USA
lepore@ruccs.rutgers.edu

KIRK LUDWIG: Philosophy Department, Box 118545, University of Florida, Gainesville, FL 32611-8545, USA.
kludwig@phil.ufl.edu

JOHN MCDOWELL: Department of Philosophy, University of Pittsburgh, Pittsburgh PA, 15260, USA.
jmcdowel@pitt.edu

STEPHEN NEALE: Department of Philosophy, Davison Hall, Douglas College, Rutgers University, New Brunswick, NJ 08903, USA.
neale@ruccs.rutgers.edu

PETER PAGIN: Department of Philosophy, Stockholm University, 106 91 Stockholm, Sweden.
peter.pagin@philosophy.su.se

BJÖRN RAMBERG: Department of Philosophy, University of Oslo, Box 1024 Blindern, N-0315 Oslo, Norway.
b.t.ramberg@filosofi.uio.no

PIERS RAWLING: Department of Philosophy, University of Missouri-St Louis, St Louis, MO 63121, USA. From fall 2001 at Department of Philosophy, The Florida State University, Tallahassee, FL 32306, USA.
piers@umsl.edu

FREDRIK STJERNBERG: School of Humanities, Växjö University, 351 95 Växjö, Sweden.
fredrik.stjernberg@hum.vxu.se

FOLKE TERSMAN: Department of Philosophy, Stockholm University, 106 91 Stockholm, Sweden.
folke.tersman@philosophy.su.se

Foreword

The words 'Interpreting Davidson' might be read as a play on the title of Donald Davidson's famous collection *Inquiries Into Truth and Interpretation*. What the editors actually have in mind is more straightforward: it is the plain fact that interpretation of Davidson's work is an exciting task which, if pursued seriously, leads to substantial and sometimes surprising philosophical insights. Davidson has, more than anybody else, insisted that interpretation in everyday communication is a creative enterprise that cannot be reduced to the subsumption of an utterance under shared rules or standards known prior to the communication itself. By the same token, it would be hopeless to try to subsume Davidson's philosophy under a few slogans or categories—such as 'nominalism', 'pragmatism', 'anti-representationalism' or 'externalism'—in order to get an interpretative key to his philosophy. For instance, when he famously suggested that one could replace talk of meanings with talk of interpretative *theories* of speakers, and then argued that such theories could have the form of (modified) Tarski-type theories of truth, it was not a mere philosophical thesis. Rather, it opened a space both for highly subtle and creative work in the field of semantic analysis and for a substantial debate about conditions under which ascription of truth-conditions to utterances can be interpretative, about the relation between interpreting speech and interpreting behaviour and so on. It is Davidson's systematic, constructive work—rather than his supposed subscription to nominalism, anti-representationalism or anti-conventionalism—that led him to develop a theory of meaning that has no need for meanings as entities, or a substantial relation of reference or a role for linguistic conventions. The same systematic, creative and positive approach characterises his work in philosophy generally.

In September 1996, an international group of about twenty philosophers gathered in the Bohemian spa, Karlovy Vary, to participate in the immensely exciting and enjoyable entreprise of interpreting and criticising Davidson. A selection of their papers, together with Davidson's opening paper 'Externalisms', are presented in this book. The participants greatly appreciated Davidson's careful replies to all the papers, and the editors are happy that Davidson's reactions, included in the last chapter of this volume, will now also be available to the public. The succinctness, comprehensiveness and systematic structure of Davidson's concluding essay make it unnecessary to try to characterise in this Foreword Davidson's philosophical views or the topics discussed in this book.

Although Davidson's article is structured by topics rather than persons, one name does appear in a subtitle: not surprisingly, it is Quine's. The relation between Davidsonian and Quinean philosophy is a fascinating issue and one much discussed; as such it appears in several articles collected in this volume. Willard Van Orman Quine was among the participants of the Karlovy Vary symposium on Davidson's philosophy and contributed substantially to the discussion. He would undoubtedly have had a lot to say about the views expressed in this book. Sadly enough, he will not be among its readers.

There are four persons, apart from the contributors themselves, that the editors wish to thank especially for help with bringing about this volume: Dagfinn Føllesdal, Oslo and Stanford, John Perry, Stanford, and Gunnar Svensson and Henrik Ahlenius of the department of philosophy at Stockholm University.

Petr Kotatko
Peter Pagin
Gabriel Segal

1

Externalisms

DONALD DAVIDSON

Our beliefs are objective, not, of course, in being unprejudiced and formed in the light of all the evidence, but in the sense that they are true or false, and that, with few exceptions, their truth depends on matters independent of us. Our other thoughts and attitudes, in so far as they have a propositional content, are also objective: it is an objective question whether or not our intentions or desires will be fulfilled, whether our hopes or fears are realized, whether our suspicions are justified, whether our orders will be obeyed, whether we will find what we seek.

Thought is objective, and we know that it is. But it is not obvious what it is about thought that makes this possible. This question is not, in itself, epistemological. It is not the question how knowledge of the world is possible, or what justifies the beliefs we have. Skeptics think beliefs are objective, that is, that they are objectively true or false, for unless at least some of our beliefs were objectively true or false, there would be nothing to doubt. What skeptics doubt is whether we have good reason to hold those of our beliefs that happen to be true, that is, whether we have knowledge. If we cannot justify our beliefs, the skeptic maintains, then we must question whether the world is at all like what we believe it to be.

If we are not to be skeptics about the possibility of knowledge of the external world or other minds we must reject the view that all knowledge of the world depends on objects or phenomena that are directly present in in-

1

dividual minds, objects such as sense data, impressions, ideas, raw feels, or propositions, objects that might be just as they present themselves to us even if the world were very different than it is. I do not deny that such objects and phenomena exist; it hardly matters. What matters is whether such objects are taken as epistemically basic, and therefore as epistemic intermediaries between our minds and the rest of the world, the messengers on which we must depend for all news of what goes on outside. Such theories are not only individualistic, but also subjectivist; according to such a theory, each person's world is constructed from material available in consciousness, material connected only indirectly, if at all, to the world. Empiricism is a form of subjectivism insofar as it claims that the ultimate evidence for beliefs about the external world is something nonconceptual that is directly given in experience. This empiricist dogma should not be confused with the harmless doctrine that the *source* of all empirical knowledge is the senses.

The only alternative to subjectivism is externalism, a view that makes the connection between thought and the world intrinsic rather than extrinsic—a connection not inferred, constructed, or discovered, but there from the start.

There are two major species of externalism: *social externalism,* which maintains that the contents of our thoughts depend, in one way or another, on interaction with other thinkers; and *perceptual externalism,* which holds that there is a necessary connection between the contents of certain thoughts and the features of the world that make them true. The form of social externalism I find the most interesting is one Saul Kripke tentatively promotes in the name of Wittgenstein: someone is said to have grasped the truth conditions of a sentence if one uses the sentence in situations relevantly similar to the situations in which others would, or do, use that sentence (Kripke 1982). The form of perceptual externalism I find most defensible is one to which I have myself long subscribed, and which has more recently been well stated and defended by Tyler Burge (Burge 1988). Both of these forms of externalism suffer, however, from one or another defect or omission, at least as marshaled in response to the demand for an understanding of objectivity.

Kripke's suggestion—or Wittgenstein's, if it is his—valuable as it is, is not satisfactory as a solution to my problem. One reason is that Kripke does not even attempt to give an account of the contents of particular thoughts; at best, he explains when two thoughts are the same (or when two utterances have the same meaning). Part of the reason for the failure to give an account of the contents of thoughts is due to the fact that Kripke dwells almost exclusively on mathematical examples, and so cannot connect the contents of thoughts with the empirical circumstances of speech behavior.

Furthermore there is the question how the content, however it is determined, is recognized as the same from one occasion of utterance to another,
for Kripke's answer leaves us with another question. Kripke's answer is that
an agent goes on in the same way as before (that is, means what he did before, or is following the same 'rule') if he goes on as others do or would.
The further question is Warren Goldfarb's: he asks, if we can't tell when a
single speaker's replies constitute his going on in same way, how can we
tell when the replies of one speaker are relevantly like those of another
speaker (Goldfarb 1985). Perhaps it will be said in Kripke's defense that we
must take the notion of similarity for granted. The question was not, the
defense continues, when one response of a speaker is like his previous responses, but rather what makes some responses *correct* and others not. A
series of responses by a single speaker just shows that that person has one
disposition or another; the notion of correctness or incorrectness has no
application in such a situation. But when we add other speakers we have
added a radically new element and with that addition we can say that correctness is defined as going with the crowd.

But this, too, seems unsatisfactory. For how can the simple fact that
two or more people have gone on in the same way introduce the distinction
between following a rule and just going on in one way or another? All the
sunflowers in the field turn together to face the sun: are they following a
rule? Surely not in the required sense; they have no concepts and so cannot
misapply concepts. Simply adding further creatures with identical dispositions cannot turn dispositions into rule-following. Doesn't Kripke himself
show he is aware of the point when he quotes Wittgenstein as saying '...no
course of action could be determined by a rule, because every course of action can be made to accord with the rule'(Wittgenstein 1953:20)? It seems
clear that this difficulty remains no matter how many creatures follow the
same course of action. What is missing is something to satisfy what Kripke
calls the 'basic requirement' for a rule, namely that the rule should *tell* the
speaker what he ought to do in each new instance (the word 'tell', italicized,
is Kripke's). Or, more strongly still: 'The relation of meaning and intention
to future action is *normative*, not *descriptive*' (Kripke 1982:37).

But then, is it clear that Kripke has solved his own problem? For why
ought I to go on as others do? What makes their behavior my norm? It does
not answer this question to say that the teacher, or society, tells me. They
can punish me if I fail to toe the line, but fear of punishment can't, in itself, give me the idea that there is anything more wrong with my action
than that others don't like it. What is missing, one might say, is the idea of
understanding. Introducing more than one creature does add something basic to the situation with one creature, for with the possibility that their ac-

tions may diverge we have introduced the gap needed to make sense of the notion of error. But the mere possibility of divergence, even when combined with sanctions to encourage conformity, does not introduce the sort of norm needed to explain meaning or conceptualization. However, despite these unanswered problems, I am persuaded that the basic idea is right: only social interaction brings with it the space in which the concepts of error, and so of meaning and of thought, can be given application. A social milieu is necessary, but not sufficient, for objective thought.

Perceptual externalism, as described by Burge and others, supplies one of the elements missing in Kripke's Wittgensteinian account by suggesting how particular contents can be assigned to our perceptual beliefs, and so explains in part how thought and language are anchored to the world. But there are serious lacunae in Burge's account of perceptual externalism. There is, first, the problem of the content of perceptual beliefs. According to Burge, it is the 'normal' cause of a perceptual belief that determines the content of the belief. But what is the normal cause? It could be anything from the stimulation of nerve endings to the original big bang. Clearly, we need a way to isolate the right cause.[1] Second, Burge gives no serious account of error, and without an account of error, there is no way to distinguish between having a concept and simply having a disposition. How do we identify a mistake as a mistake? In other words, Burge's account fails to solve, or even address, the Wittgensteinian problem.

These are both problems about relevant similarity. Fake cows are in one way relevantly similar to real cows—that's why we make mistakes. But in another way, fake cows aren't at all like cows—they don't fall under the concept cow. It is because we occasionally mistake fakes for the real thing that we can be said to have concepts, to classify things, and so sometimes classify them wrong. There's nothing amiss with a concept that includes the fakes with the reals—that's why it's hard to say what makes it possible to go wrong. It takes only a thoughtless disposition to distinguish cows from other things; it takes only another mindless disposition to treat cows and fake cows alike. What is difficult is to explain what is going on when someone *thinks* a fake cow is a cow, for that requires having the *concept* of a cow.

The problem of relevant similarity comes up also in connection with the idea that the content of a perceptual belief depends on its common or usual cause. Even to approach the question, we must have some idea which causes are being gathered together. Since any set of causes whatsoever will

---

[1] Quine quite properly raised this question (in conversation) in connection with my original suggestion that the content of an observation sentence was its 'common cause'. By this I then meant, not its cause for *various* speakers, but for one. I had not yet appreciated the importance of the social element.

have endless properties in common, we must look to some recurrent feature of the gatherer, some mark that he or she has classified cases as similar. This can only be some feature or aspect of the gatherer's reactions (perhaps these are verbal reactions), in which case we must once again ask: what makes these reactions relevantly similar to each other? Wittgenstein's problem once again.

It would not surprise me if, at this point, someone were to say in exasperation, but of course we just do react in similar ways to certain stimuli: we shy away from extreme heat, we shrink from loud sounds, we smile when smiled at. It is a brute fact that we class certain things together in these ways. Of course it is easy for *us* to describe the stimuli and the responses, since we are among the creatures that naturally make these classifications. So of course we have predicates—concepts—that reflect these characteristics of ours. If we are going to describe anything, we have to use the equipment we have. None of this shows that it isn't true that creatures like us naturally classify things as we do.

This is, of course, right, and it points us in the direction of Kripke's Wittgensteinian answer to the problem of rule following. It is a brute fact—a fact about each brute, including you and me—that each reacts to stimuli as it does; but it is a suggestive fact that many of these brutes react in more or less the same ways. It is a suggestive fact, but what exactly does it suggest? As we just noticed, mere crowd behavior in itself can't explain conceptualization; it can't even explain error. What it can do, however, is *make space* for something that can be called error: room for error is created by cases in which one individual deviates from a course of action when the crowd does not. For example, when a fake cow is introduced among the real cows, the crowd ceases to mutter 'Cow' while the deviant individual persists in saying 'Cow'. This is not enough, as we remarked just now, to justify an attribution of error; we can still say there simply are two different dispositions at work. Room has been made for error, but error itself has not been explained. What must be added in order to give an account of error is something that can count as recognition or awareness, on the part of the those who share reactions, of each other's reactions.

The basic situation, as now set forth, contains a minimum of three elements: two creatures and a world of objects, properties and events the creatures can discriminate in perception. Of course the social environment would typically be more numerous, but it will simplify the story if we can for the moment stick to this irreducible triad. Each of the creatures is carrying out its habitual inductions, whether learned or inherited. This means that for each creature there are stimuli which can be classed together by virtue of the similarity of the responses. There will be cases that fit this de-

Triangulation
2 speakers and
a world of objects

scription: creature A displays responses similar to its past responses at the same times and in the same places that creature B displays responses similar to its past responses. (The responses of A may or may not be similar to B's responses; A may run, while B cowers.) We can then ask what stimuli plausibly cause these repeatedly correlated responses. This common cause will typically be some objective feature of the environment.

Nothing in this story suggests the necessity of thought, conceptualization, or error, even if the creatures occasionally fail to act in concert. No doubt we can say, looking on with our conceptual advantage, that one of the creatures has gone wrong when it reacts, perhaps verbally, to the fake cow as it does to real cows. The problem is to put the creatures in a position to think this. Something must be added which will make the difference between the cases where the creatures act in unison, and the cases where they do not, available to the creatures themselves.

This can be done by adding a further element of association or natural induction: each creature associates the other creature's responses with stimuli from the shared world. (Perhaps this does not have to be learned in some cases.) Let us assume that our two creatures, A and B, can often observe one another when both can observe cows. Now suppose that creature A responds to cows by uttering the sound 'Cow'; creature B then associates cows with the utterances of 'Cow' by A. Creature B similarly associates cows with A's utterances of 'Vache'. A and B are now each in a position to notice occasions on which the responses of the other differs from the other's usual responses (perhaps one is badly placed for seeing a cow; or one has better eyesight or a keener sense of smell). When I speak of responses differing, I mean: A's responses are not taken by B to be the same as A's earlier responses, while B's responses *are* the same as B's earlier responses. The basic triangle is now complete: there are causal connections between cows and our two reacting creatures, by way of perception, and there are causal connections between the creatures, also by way of perception. Finally, these two sets of connections are correlated, for each creature associates cows with the cow-reactions of the other creature, except, of course in the relatively rare case of error.

Take an example. I observe a lioness stalking a gazelle. I describe this situation in this way by correlating two aspects of the situation: gazelle behavior and lion behavior (the lioness changes course to intercept the gazelle; the gazelle changes course to evade the lioness). I can confirm my theory that the gazelle is the object salient for the lioness by (among other possibilities) noting the responses of other lionesses to gazelles on other occasions. But even this further evidence leaves it up to me to decide what the object of the lioness's attention is; I decide on the basis of what catches *my* attention. If a second lioness joins the first in pursuit of the gazelle, I can eliminate such complete dependence on my own choice of salient object in this way: I class together the responses of lioness A with the responses of lioness B in the same places and at the same times. The focus of the shared causes is now what I take to be the salient object for both lionesses. I no longer have to depend on my own choice of the relevant stimulus of the lionesses' behavior. In the exceptional case where responses differ *I* can say: one of the lionesses has erred. The challenge is to put the lions in a position to distinguish these cases. To do this we have to eliminate the dependence on my arbitrary (or interested) choice of relevantly similar responses on the parts of the lionesses. A further element enters when the lions cooperate to corner their prey. Each watches the other while both watch the gazelle, noting the other's reactions to the changes of direction.

Here is my thesis: an interconnected triangle such as this (two lionesses, one gazelle) constitutes a necessary condition for the existence of conceptualization, thought, and language. It make possible objective belief and the other propositional attitudes. It fills in the gaps in social and perceptual externalism, at least the versions, due to Kripke and Burge, that we have been discussing. It clearly incorporates the essential element in Kripke's 'solution' to the problem, which requires that we distinguish between a mere disposition and rule following. That element is provided by the second creature, who stands for society. The simple model I have described does not, to be sure, suggest where the norm lies when the creatures differ in their responses; but neither does Kripke's account of the matter. The point is not to identify the norm, but to make sense of there being a norm, and this has been done if we can point to the difference between the preponderance of cases where the creatures respond alike and the deviant cases where they diverge. I insisted that it is not enough that a third party be able to observe or describe these two cases; I claimed it was necessary that the existence of the contrast be available to the creatures themselves. This essential element enters the triangle when the creatures observe each other's reactions to the very phenomena they are both observing.

The triangle also makes plain, what Kripke's mathematical examples could not, the role perception plays in the social establishment of a ground for objective thought. It does this in two ways: first, it allows the creatures involved to observe each other's reactions. But it also makes (partial) sense of the idea that there is a single focus for the joint reactions. Mathematical examples simply ask us to assume there is a common focus; in the case of perceptual objects, while shared reactions help locate the focus.

Our triangular model thus makes a step toward dealing with another troublesome feature of Burge's perceptual externalism, the indeterminate nature of the contents of perceptual beliefs. That difficulty arose because there seemed to be no way to decide the location of the objects and features of the world that constitute the subject matter of perceptual beliefs; Burge told us only that the content was given by the 'usual' or 'normal' cause. But this did not help choose between proximal and distal stimuli, or anything in between, in the causal chain. By introducing another perceiver, it is possible to locate the relevant cause: it is the cause common to both creatures, the cause that prompts their distinctive responses. Both creatures observe a cow. They do not share the neural turbulence that stirs in their brains, nor their retinal stimulations. They do not share photons streaming in, but the cow is mutually sighted and perhaps otherwise sensed. We can call it a form of triangulation. In the case of sight, it is quite literally a matter of triangulation: the lines of sight converge on the shared stimulus. It would not count as triangulation if there were no signal passed between the observing stations, but we have provided for this by requiring the observation of each other's responses to the shared stimulus by the creatures involved.

I have emphasized at a number of points the way the notion of relevant similarity can play an essential role without being noticed: thus Kripke, in the attempt to say when a creature's subsequent response was relevantly similar to an earlier response, helped himself to the notion of the relevantly similar responses of another creature. Burge helped himself to the idea of relevantly similar stimuli. The reason it is so natural to avail ourselves of such concepts is, of course, that they are ours. The trouble is, we move in a circle when we appeal to what is natural for us in order to explain conceptualization itself—to explain, in other words, what is natural for us. Triangulation faces the problem in the only way it can be faced, by introducing the interaction of classifying agents. The difference is the difference between an external commentator slipping in his categories to make sense of an isolated creature, and a participant observing another participant doing his or it's thing. The social scene provides a setting in which we can make sense of the transition from mere dispositions to conceptualization.

I mentioned earlier the fact that by using mathematical examples, Kripke deprived himself of one apex of the triangle, the apex occupied by the shared perceptual object. This left no way of determining the potential content of the purported rule, no observable object external to the learner and the teacher to be objective about. But here I was not entirely fair to Kripke: he does mention two examples which bring in external objects or features of the world. After saying that it is a 'brute fact' that people go on in the way they do rather than in some other way, he asks,

> Can we grasp how someone could be presented with a number of green objects, and be told to apply the term 'green' just to things 'just like these', and yet apply the term learnt as if it meant 'grue'? It would

seem that if we find our own continuation to be inevitable, in some sense we cannot (Kripke 1982:98).

This is the case of our acting as detached observer: no interaction is involved. The following is closer to the situation I have been describing:

> A child who says 'table' or 'That's a table' when adults see a table in the area (and does not do so otherwise) is said to have mastered the term 'table': he says 'That's a table', based on his observation, in agreement with the usage of adults, based on their observation. That is, they say, 'That's a table' under like circumstances, and confirm the correctness of the child's utterances (Kripke 1982:99).

Perhaps this is a correct interpretation of Wittgenstein; I do not know. But it still seems to me an incomplete statement of the nature of mastery of a word or concept. All that this analysis demands of the child is that he have acquired a certain habit, a disposition, a disposition that matches that of the adults. This is a disposition which (aside from the inessential fact of saying 'table' instead displaying some other distinctive form of behavior) the child might have had independent of any training or even learning. Mastery of the word or concept requires in addition, I believe, that the child understand that error is possible, that 'That's a table' expresses a judgment that has a truth value independent of its merely being uttered. It may be that to add this condition is to fail to grasp Kripke's or Wittgenstein's point that nothing purely internal, no feeling, attitude, or intention should feature in the explanation. But to rule out awareness of truth conditions, or of the possibility of error, is to reduce mastery of a word or concept to aping the behavior of others. To suggest that this is exactly what accepting a 'way of life', using words as others do, comes to is to miss the difference between two senses of use. In the sense in which use might be claimed to be meaning, two people may use a word in the same way when one is prepared to apply it in a certain situation, and the other is not. This is not mere aping. The fact that someone has grasped the distinction between following the crowd and being right is not without observable behavioral fallout; one such fallout is willingness to change one's mind (and therefore what one says), not because one differs from others, but because the change fits better with further observations. I will return to this general theme presently, but first I want to describe another precursor of my triangulation thesis, a precursor which has had a large influence on me. The precursor is Quine's account of radical translation.

Quine has always been a sort of externalist, though this is not easy to see. Part of the reason it is—or was—not easy to see is that Quine long claimed that all empirical content rested, in the end, on something entirely private, what he called 'stimulus meaning'. It is true that stimulus meaning was defined in terms of physical events at our nerve endings; but as far as epistemology is concerned, stimulus meanings could as well have been classes of sensations or sense data. This was in fact what Quine wanted: a scientifically respectable substitute for sense data, or whatever else provided the basis for the various forms of empiricism, such as Carnap's, Russell's, or C. I. Lewis's. The result was that the ultimate 'input', or 'evidence', or 'data' (these are Quine's words), all that (according to Quine) we have to go on in building up a picture of the world, was private. The subject matter of our utterances, and the contents of our thoughts, was determined by the world beyond our skins only as mediated by some sort of unconceptualized 'evidence'. If the impacts of the world on our skins were unchanged, but the world very different, we would never know it. This is a form of skepticism that did not trouble Quine, in part, perhaps, because he seemed, at least at times, to view material objects as mere 'nodes' or 'posits' in a scheme of which all that could be demanded was that it successfully predict sensory input. In this respect Quine was no worse off than other empiricists, at least empiricists who, like Quine, hold that all our 'information' or 'data' about the world can be characterized in terms of patterns of sensory stimuli or sensations, percepts, some uninterpreted 'given'.

Quine has modified his views on meaning in recent years, and stimulus meaning in particular no longer plays the role it did (Quine 1995; Quine 1996). But his epistemology remains resolutely individualistic; though he allows that society provides obvious gains in precision and the amassing of knowledge, there is no reason in principle why we could not win an understanding of the world on our own. This is not a position which can get a grip on the objective character of thought. Nevertheless, there has always been a strong externalist element in Quine's theory of meaning, and therefore also in his overall view of the contents of the propositional attitudes. Although the meaning of each person's utterances of observation sentences was at one time determined by the proximal stimulus (i.e., patterns of sensory stimulations), the only clue Quine provided to this content was by way of a comparison with other people's patterns of stimulation. This comparison was put into practical effect by the translator noting when, and under what circumstances, the speaker to be translated was prompted to assent to or dissent from a sentence; the translator was then to translate the speaker's sentence by the sentence the translator would assent to under the same circumstances. The Quine of *Word and Object* and many later works says the criterion of correct translation is a matching of stimulus meanings—of patterns of stimulation. But in fact, of course, no ordinary, or even extraordinary, translator has any idea what the patterns of stimulation of someone else, or of himself, are; he will in fact translate on the basis of what he perceives in the world and that he assumes the speaker also perceives. There is then, a certain ambivalence in Quine's position. On the one hand, the epistemology is empiricist, based on private 'evidence'; on the other hand, the theory of meaning, as implemented by the process of radical translation, is basically social. Disposed from early days to distrust empiricist foundationalisms, I chose the social, and therefore externalist, position from the start.[2]

If we make this choice, Quine's picture of radical translation satisfies the conditions for triangulation I have been describing. We have two interacting people, their interaction mediated by the external objects, situations, and events they mutually observe. This is how Quine has recently described radical translation (Quine 1996). It is not clear how this form of externalism fits with Quine's epistemology, which maintains that our perceptual beliefs are based on something private and given to the senses. Nevertheless, Quine teaches us that what a speaker means by what he says, and hence the thoughts that can be expressed in language, are not accidentally connected with what a competent interpreter can make of them, and this is a powerfully externalist thesis.

Let me now go back over some of the ground we have covered, taking things in the natural order of increasing complexity, following what may be the history of the development of thought in each individual. I mentioned first a single animal, isolated in the sense that its relations to other animals do not supply any of the necessary conditions of propositional thought. Such an animal could, at least in theory, come equipped from the start to cope with endless contingencies, and could learn more. We are familiar with machines which give us the idea, without having to suppose they are capable of thought or conceptualization. We, observing and describing such a creature (or machine), say that it discriminates certain shapes, objects, colors, and so forth, by which we mean that it reacts in ways we find similar to shapes, objects, and colors which we find similar. But we would be making a mistake if we were to assume that because the creature discriminates and reacts in much the way we do, that it has the corresponding *concepts*. The difference, as I keep emphasizing, lies in the fact that we, unlike the creature I am describing, can, *from our point of view*, make mistakes in classification. We judge, come to believe, on looking, that something is a table, and *that* the table is brown and rectangular. The creature is reacting appropriately; it is not judging.

---

[2] In adopting Quine's radical translation to my radical interpretation, I opted from the start for the distal (external) stimulus as the basis for interpreting what Quine called 'observation sentences', rather than Quine's proximal stimulus meaning. See Truth and Meaning (1967) and Semantics for Natural Languages (1970), both reprinted in (Davidson 1984). I emphasized this difference only later (Davidson 1983).

It does not add anything important to suppose that our creature responds to the behavior of other creatures, the way fish or birds swim or fly in formation. But it does make a significant difference if the creature associates the responses of other creatures with aspects of the world to which it also responds, for it then has a double take on the world. This double take benefits the creature in that it is now able to respond to threats or opportunities it does not independently sense; and it puts us in a position to note that the basic triangle is in place which is necessary if anything is to count as error, and to locate the features of the world to which the creatures are responding. Certain primates, for example, make easily distinguished sounds when different predators appear: one sound for eagles, one for snakes, one for lions. Other members of the group, though they may not have seen the danger, react to the appropriate threat by hiding, running, or climbing a tree. A more elaborate case is this: there is a species of bird in Africa which craves honey, but cannot break into a hive. When such a bird discovers a hive, it will fly over human honey-hunters indicating, by the direction and length of the segments of its flight, the location of the hive, correcting the course of the human hunters as necessary. When the human hunters have broken open the hive, they share its contents with the bird. For all the amazing sophistication of the bird's behavior, there is nothing in this story to suggest that we ought to attribute propositional attitudes like intention, belief, or desire to the bird; the bird follows a set pattern, but there is no reason to suppose it has the idea of a failure to carry out an intention, or for a belief to be false, or a desire misguided.

But although we are not in a position to speak of conceptualization, many of the conditions for conceptualization and thought are present. To recapitulate once more, these are:

1) With two creatures in general responding in characteristic ways to distal stimuli, we can speak of the *focus* of their responses, the common cause of the most frequent cases.

2) If thought were present, this would provide an obvious indication of the *content* of the thought.

3) There is a space for the concept of *error*, which appears when there is a divergence in normally similar reactions.

4) Finally, and perhaps most important, since this is what we are most apt to miss: we have moved the reliance on our notion of relevant similarity into the realm of animal interests, where it surely belongs. We have accomplished this, not by projecting thought-like distinctions onto inanimate nature, as Plato and Aristotle both did in their ways ('dividing at the joints'), but rather by seeing the relevant similarity of one animal's responses through the eyes of another animal. We have embraced the Witt-

gensteinian intuition that the only legitimate source of objectivity is intersubjectivity.

Mere similarity of response is obviously not enough for thought, however, not even when one animal's responses to events and features of the world serve to touch off responses appropriate to those same events and features in other creatures. This triangular arrangement is a necessary, but not sufficient condition, of thought. What must be added to make the conditions sufficient? If we could answer this question we would have an analysis of thought. It is hard to think what would satisfy us which did not amount to a reduction of the intentional to the extensional, and this, in my opinion, is not to be expected. What further progress we can make will be in the direction of theory building within the realm of the rational, not reduction of that realm to something else.

What must be added to the basic triangle of two or more creatures interacting with each other through the mediation of the world if that interaction is to support thought? The unhelpful answer is that the relation between the creatures must include linguistic communication. For unless the creatures can communicate, unless they can engage in the exchange of propositional contents, there is no way they can take cognitive advantage of their ability to triangulate their shared world. They must, in other words, recognize each other as embodied minds with a location in a common space and time. The reason this answer is not very helpful is that it assumes what was to explained. Of course if there is language there is thought, so it cannot be easier to explain the former than the latter. Nevertheless, it is useful to recognize the somewhat surprising fact that the social element that is essential to language is also essential to thought itself. What makes this relation between thought and language useful in the present context is that it makes it possible to study thought by studying language.

We exploit this possibility when we think of the case where the basic triangle is complete except that our two creatures do not understand one another. Each, we may suppose, has learned a language in a social setting, and has the general knowledge of the world and of people that this presupposes. We simply drop the assumption that the languages are the same. Each creature then has the task of coming to understand the other's language without the help of a bilingual informant or a dictionary. What makes understanding in such a situation radical is that since thought depends on language, our would-be interpreters cannot assume without circularity that they can fathom the thoughts of the other independently of understanding their speech. This is the problem of how radical interpretation is possible, and I believe it can, in outline, be solved.

There is an intermediate stage which deserves independent discussion, the stage at which a person is first introduced to the world of thought and reason, the stage of language acquisition. In this situation society is the teacher, whether deliberately or not, for even if a child has only one teacher, that teacher was taught by another, and so on back until we reach a stage at which no one is more a teacher than another. Foregoing speculation on how it might all have begun, let us consider how it begins for someone joining the society of those who are already seasoned speakers.

For an individual, the process must at some early point involve the learning, through ostension, of words and concepts for the most easily observed and discriminated objects, events, and features of the learner's environment. We come into the world equipped to recognize faces, colors (even when reflected wavelengths and saturation vary according to amount and character of light), shapes (even when distance and perspective greatly alter what reaches the retina), and objects (though again, under many aspects, from many angles and under varied illumination). We are probably better, at least at first, in lumping together cow or rabbit appearances than in lumping together appearances of the same cow or rabbit after an interrupted viewing. What matters, in any case, is that for starters we learn words for what we preverbally discriminated; we learn from creatures very like ourselves, and could not learn from creatures very unlike ourselves.

I spoke just now of learning words and concepts. This is, of course, the goal of the process. But something else must come first. At the start, the teacher has language and the concepts that come with it, the beginner does not. What comes first for the beginner is simple conditioning of sounds to sights (or whatever is otherwise perceived). 'The origin and the primitive form of the language game is a reaction; only from this can more complicated forms grow. Language—I want to say—is a refinement. "In the beginning was the deed"' (Wittgenstein 1993:395). This remark of Wittgenstein's is in the same vein as his remark that '*The basic form* of our game must be one in which there is no such thing as doubt' (Wittgenstein 1993:377). What we are describing is on the road to speech and conceptualization, but it is not yet there. Once one has mastered a concept, or words that express it, one can always doubt whether it applies in a given case. But one cannot doubt the application from the start.

Here is a way of putting this central point. Someone who is consciously teaching a beginner the use of a word may think of herself as simply passing on a meaning that already attaches to the word. But from the learner's point of view, the word—the sound—is being *endowed* with a meaning. This is why doubt makes no sense at the start. The first examples, the first things ostended, must, from the learner's point of view, belong to the application of the expression. This is so even if the teacher is at fault from society's point of view, whether because the teacher does not know how others use the word, or because the teacher has mistaken fake cows for real ones. From the learner's point of view, any mistakes or doubts must come later. If we know what the objects are to which the learner associates the learned sound, then to the extent that we are like the learner, we know (i.e., can reasonably induce) what the learner, when he is capable of meaning anything, will mean by the learned sound. The question what others besides the learner, even his teacher, means by the sound is irrelevant; the sound has been given a meaning by the learning process itself, and we will misinterpret the learner if we assume that for him it has any meaning not connected with that process. This is a large part of the lesson of externalism, and we must never lose sight of it, for it is the reason it is impossible to be generally mistaken about the aspects of the world we have learned to conceive through ostension.

I have been talking all along as if learning a first language depended on natural induction. I am aware that Chomsky and those in his thrall resist the application of this notion on the ground that basic grammar is wired in, and that early language acquisition is too rapid to count as learning or to require anything like induction. Let it be so. But whether or not we call acquiring them learning, we are not born knowing the words of Bantu or Armenian. It may well be that one hearing is enough in many cases to give us all we need in order to 'go on' in the right way. This cannot change the point I am making, provided the one hearing is in the presence of an ostender who is ostending an appropriate object, event, property, or state of affairs.

We must remember, of course, that if going on in the right way means only going on as the teacher does, this is not enough in itself to constitute mastery of word or concept; there remains the grasp of truth conditions, the awareness of the possibility of error. Nor will punishing or correcting what the teacher sees as error suffice, for the same reason. We can say that in the potential gap between how the learner goes on and how the teacher goes on there is room to introduce the idea of error, not only in the mind of the teacher, for we are assuming it is *there*, but also in the mind of the learner. But how that room gets filled it is probably beyond our powers to tell. Our failure to provide an analysis of the concept of error or, as we could as well say, of the concept of objectivity, or of thought itself, does not mean there is something hopelessly mysterious about these concepts; it only reflects the fact that intentional phenomena cannot be reduced to something simpler or different. Nor does our failure mean that true grasp of concepts as opposed to mere following of routines does not reveal itself in behavior. What we cannot do is say, in non-intentional terms, in what the difference consists.

References

Burge, T. 1988. Individualism and Self-Knowledge. *Journal of Philosophy* 85:649-63.

Davidson, D. 1983. A Coherence Theory of Truth and Knowledge. *Kant oder Hegel*, ed. D. Henrich., 423-38. Stuttgart: Klett-Cotta.

Davidson, D. 1984. *Inquiries into Truth and Interpretation*. Oxford: Oxford University Press.

Goldfarb, W. 1985. Kripke on Wittgenstein on Rules. *Journal of Philosophy* 82:471-88.

Kripke, S. 1982. *Wittgenstein on Rules and Private Language*. Oxford: Oxford University Press.

Quine, W. V. 1995. *From Stimulus to Science*. Cambridge, Mass.: Harvard University Press.

Quine, W. V. 1996. Progress on Two Fronts. *Journal of Philosophy* 93:159-63.

Wittgenstein, L. (1953). *Philosophical Investigations*. New York, MacMillan.

Wittgenstein, L. (1993). *Philosophical Occasions 1912-1951*. Cambridge, U. K.: Hackett Publishing Co.

2

Davidson's Objections to Quine's Empiricism

Lars Bergström

1 Introduction

There are many similarities between Donald Davidson's philosophy and W. V. Quine's, but there are also differences. One difference has to do with Quine's empiricism. As everyone knows, Quine has argued that the notorious 'two dogmas of empiricism' should be abandoned, but he himself is definitely still an empiricist (see Quine 1953). Davidson, on the other hand, has drawn attention to a 'third dogma of empiricism', which he attributes to Quine among others. Davidson has argued that this third dogma should also be given up, and he suggests that when it is gone there is nothing left to call empiricism (Davidson 1973-74). In this paper I shall describe this apparent disagreement between Davidson and Quine in more detail, and I shall argue that Quine's empiricism is not really undermined by Davidson's arguments.[1]

---

[1] I am grateful to Donald Davidson, Roger Gibson, Sören Häggqvist, Peter Pagin, W. V. Quine and Folke Tersman for helpful comments on earlier versions of this paper.

2   The third dogma of empiricism

What Davidson refers to as the third dogma of empiricism is a certain 'dualism of scheme and content', which occurs in the work of many philosophers. Davidson claims that such a dualism is a presupposition of all forms of conceptual relativism. Roughly speaking, the third dogma is that conceptual schemes—which can be identified with languages or with sets of intertranslatable languages—are used to organize or give structure to something which constitutes the raw material, as it were, for our beliefs and theories (Davidson 1973-74:7). For an empiricist, this raw material is empirical content. According to Davidson, empirical content 'is in turn explained by reference to the facts, the world, experience, sensation, the totality of sensory stimuli, or something similar' (Davidson 1973-74:11). This dualism of conceptual scheme and empirical content is the target of Davidson's criticism. He writes:

> I want to urge that this [...] dualism of scheme and content, of organizing system and something waiting to be organized, cannot be made intelligible and defensible. It is itself a dogma of empiricism, the third dogma. The third, and perhaps the last, for if we give it up it is not clear that there is anything distinctive left to call empiricism (ibid.).

Davidson claims that Quine accepts this dualism of scheme and content, the third dogma of empiricism. Personally, I am not so sure, but this is mainly because I am not sure what the dogma says. If it only says that *there are* these two elements, scheme and content, then it seems clear that Quine accepts it. Quine's empiricism can be summarized in the two theses that 'whatever evidence there is for science is sensory evidence', and that 'all inculcation of meanings of words must rest ultimately on sensory evidence' (Quine 1969:75; italics in original have been removed here). Moreover, he identifies sensory evidence with the triggering of sensory receptors (Quine 1992:2). It seems clear that Quine admits the existence of both conceptual scheme (language, theory) and empirical content (sensory evidence, i.e. the triggering of sensory receptors).

But presumably the third dogma also says that schemes 'organize' or 'fit' the relevant content. Davidson writes:

> The images and metaphors fall into two main groups: conceptual schemes (languages) either *organize* something, or they *fit* it [...] The first group contains also *systematize*, *divide up* (the stream of experience); further examples of the second group are *predict*, *account for*, *face* (the tribunal of experience) (Davidson 1973-74:14).

The question, then, is what is meant by this. Quine believes that there is an interesting relation between language (or theory) and sensory evidence. In fact, the main purpose of his naturalized epistemology is to study this very relation. But would he claim that language 'organizes' or 'fits' sensory evidence (in the sense that Davidson finds objectionable)—or that it ought to do so? That is hard to say.

3 Quine's view of the third dogma

Quine has replied to Davidson's paper (Quine 1981). In this reply, he makes a distinction between two different interpretations of the third dogma. On one of these interpretations, he accepts the dogma; on the other, he rejects it. He writes:

> If empiricism is construed as a theory of truth, then what Davidson imputes to it as a third dogma is rightly imputed and rightly renounced. [...] As a theory of evidence, however, empiricism remains with us, minus indeed the two old dogmas. The third purported dogma, understood now in relation not to truth but to warranted belief, remains intact. It has both a descriptive and a normative aspect, and in neither do I think of it as a dogma. It is what makes scientific method partly empirical rather than solely a quest for internal coherence (Quine 1981:39).

So Quine accepts a certain 'dualism of scheme and content'. As an empiricist, he believes that our beliefs about the world are, and should be, based upon experience—where, for him, 'experience' is identified with the triggering of sensory receptors (surface irritations). At the same time, he also accepts Davidson's argument against a different kind of dualism, namely an empiricist theory of truth. According to such a theory a sentence is true, roughly speaking, if it is entailed by a theory which fits the totality of possible sensory evidence (Cf. Davidson 1973-74:15; and Bergström 2000). Quine takes Davidson's argument against the third dogma to be directed against an empiricist theory of truth.[2]

This might leave the reader with the impression that there is no disagreement between Quine and Davidson on these matters after all. But I believe such an impression would be mistaken. Let me explain.

It seems that empiricism may take one or more of at least three different forms. These may be referred to as empiricist theories of *truth*, empiricist theories of *evidence*, and empiricist theories of *meaning*. I myself have argued elsewhere that there is some support in Quine's writings for an empiricist theory of truth (Bergström 1994 and 2000). Quine has rejected this suggestion. However, it seems clear that he is an empiricist with respect to

---

[2] See Quine 1981:39, where he writes: 'Against the purported dogma he argues that "the notion of fitting the totality of experience, like the notion of fitting the facts, or being true to the facts, adds nothing intelligible to the simple concept of being true ..."'

evidence and meaning.[3] Davidson, on the other hand, appears to reject all three kinds of empiricist theories. I believe he would say that they are all unacceptable, since they all contain the third dogma of empiricism. So there is still disagreement between them.

4 Proximal and distal theories of meaning

Let us now consider their disagreement concerning meaning. (I will return to the question of evidence in section 10 below.) In his paper 'Meaning, Truth, and Evidence', presented at the St. Louis conference on Quine's philosophy in 1988, Davidson makes a distinction between proximal and distal theories of meaning and evidence. He writes:

> Our knowledge of the world depends directly or indirectly on elaborate and perilous causal sequences that originate with events like a rabbit scurrying by, or a spasm in the stomach, progress through the nervous system, and terminate in beliefs. Where, in the chain of causes and effects, do we come across the items that give our beliefs their particular contents and our words their meanings? [...] A clever compromise brilliantly advocated by Quine is to tie meaning and content to the firings of sensory nerves (Davidson 1990a:68).[4]

The firings of sensory nerves—the triggering of sensory receptors—is called the proximal stimulus (in the causal sequence), and Quine's theory of meaning is therefore a *proximal* theory. Davidson wants Quine to abandon this theory, and he points out that this 'would mean relinquishing what remains of empiricism after the first two dogmas have been surrendered' (ibid.). However, Davidson also claims that there is another account of meaning in Quine's work, which ties meaning and evidence to more distal stimuli in the causal sequences, namely to 'the very events and objects that the sentences are naturally and correctly interpreted as being about' (Davidson 1990a:72). The distal stimuli in Davidson's example are the scurrying of the rabbit and the spasm in the stomach. The resultant theory of meaning, which is the one that Davidson accepts, is a *distal* theory (Davidson 1990a:73).

It is not quite clear to me whether the proximal and distal theories are exclusively concerned with the meaning of observation sentences. For simplicity, we may assume that they are. Maybe they can later be extended to cover more theoretical sentences as well. There is some indication that Da-

---

[3] Compare the two theses that 'whatever evidence there is for science is sensory evidence', and that 'all inculcation of meanings of words must rest ultimately on sensory evidence' quoted in section 1 above.

[4] The 'compromise' referred to here is between external things, on the one hand, and internal 'raw material of thoughts' such as sense data, on the other.

vidson takes a distal stimulus to be publicly or intersubjectively observable (Davidson 1990a:72-73). On the other hand, a spasm in my stomach is hardly publicly observable, so maybe the distal theory is also concerned with theoretical sentences.

Davidson refers to causal sequences which 'originate' in distal stimuli, such as a rabbit scurrying by. Surely, however, the causal sequences go much further back. So maybe Davidson's point is that we need not go any further than the distal stimulus, where this is defined as *what the sentence is about*. If so, however, we may not have to bother about causal sequences at all. If we already know what a given sentence is about, why do we want to consider the causal sequence which leads up to the utterance of it? In general, it is not clear to me why there must be *any* particular item in the actual causal sequence leading up to a belief which 'gives' the belief its particular content and the words in the corresponding sentence their meanings. (Another thing is, of course, that interpretation may often involve or depend upon assumptions about causality.)

A more plausible alternative is that the distal stimulus is defined, not as what the corresponding sentence or belief is about, but as the closest event in the causal chain which is publicly observable and also *salient* in the situation. In one place, Davidson says that '[w]hat narrows down the choice of the relevant cause is what is salient for speakers and their interpreters' (Davidson 1990a:77). On the distal theory, this salient cause is what determines the meaning of an observation sentence.

5   Quine's proximal theory of meaning

What determines the meaning of an observation sentence according to Quine? How, more precisely, does the triggering of sensory receptors 'give our beliefs their particular contents and our words their meanings' (as Davidson puts it)?

For Quine, 'the central problem of the theory of meaning' is to define meaning in non-intensional terms (Quine 1977:226). The way to start is to define sameness of meaning or (cognitive) synonymy. If this can be defined, we may simply say that the meaning of the sentence S is the set of all sentences, including S itself, which have the same meaning as S (see e.g. Quine 1995:76). So the problem is to define sameness of meaning.

However, one and the same sentence may have different meanings for different persons and for the same person at different times. Therefore, sameness of meaning cannot be taken as a simple two-place relation. On the other hand, it is usually assumed that one sentence may have the same meaning for a certain person as another sentence (or the same sentence) has for some other person. This is perhaps a presupposition of translation and communication. Consequently, we must also distinguish between intrasubjective and intersubjective sameness of meaning.[5]

Quine can be said to be both a verificationist and an empiricist about meaning, since he takes the meaning of a sentence to be at least roughly the same as the empirical evidence on which the sentence may be assented to or dissented from. In one place, he writes the following:

> The statement of verificationism [...] is that 'evidence for the truth of a sentence is identical with the meaning of the sentence'; and I submit that if sentences in general had meanings, their meanings would be just that. It is only holism [...] that tells us that in general they do not have them (Quine 1986a:155).

In general, classical verificationists hold that the meaning of a sentence can be identified with the observations which would confirm or disconfirm the sentence (see e.g. J. Dancy and E. Sosa eds.:263). For Quine, the 'observations' which would confirm or disconfirm an observation sentence are global sensory stimulations, which consist in the triggering of sensory receptors. Consequently, he introduces the notion of stimulus meaning. The stimulus meaning of an observation sentence for a person is the range of stimulations (triggered receptors) associated with it for that person, affirmatively or negatively (see e.g. Quine 1992:3, and Quine 1960:32-3). Consequently, we may say that two observation sentences have the same meaning for a person at a time if and only if they have the same stimulus meaning for the person at the time. Intrasubjective synonymy of observation sentences over time can be handled in the same way.

So far, so good. However, it is hard to see how intersubjective sameness of meaning could be defined in terms of stimulus meaning.[6] The reason is that stimulus meanings are private; a stimulus meaning in Quine's sense is an ordered pair of sets of sensory receptors belonging to a given person. Therefore, stimulus meanings cannot be shared. But distal stimuli can be shared. Presumably, this is at least one of the reasons why Davidson prefers the distal theory of meaning.

(This last point may be questioned on the ground that Davidson, in his argument against the proximal theory, seems to take it for granted that stimulus meanings can be shared. He imagines a case where two persons have the same patterns of stimulation, but where these are caused by different distal stimuli, and he says that this supposition 'is not absurd' (Davidson 1990a:74). He also says that, '[o]n the proximal theory ...

---

[5] This is also pointed out in Davidson 1990a:73.

[6] Quine himself says that stimulus meaning 'is no part of the intersubjective business of semantics' (Quine 1993:114n).

sentences have the same meaning if they have the same stimulus meaning' (Davidson 1990a:73). But I do not think that he himself would defend the view that a sentence may have the same stimulus meaning for different persons. Surely, no one would defend this view.)

On the distal theory—if I understand it correctly—we may say that an observation sentence used by one person has the same meaning as some (possibly different) observation sentence used by another person if and only if 'identical events, objects or situations cause or would cause assent and dissent' (ibid.). For example, in radical translation, my sentence 'That's a rabbit' and the native's sentence 'Gavagai' have the same meaning if our particular acts of assent to and dissent from them, are caused or would be caused by the same distal stimulus.

However, it seems that the proximal theory might also be able to handle interpersonal synonymy. In the case of radical translation, we may think of the field linguist's hypothesis that 'Gavagai' in the jungle language means the same as 'That's a rabbit' in the linguist's own language somewhat as follows: If I (the linguist) were to learn the Jungle language of my informant—in the sense that I acquired the capacity to converse with him fluently and predict his actions on the basis of his utterances, and so on—then 'Gavagai' and 'That's a rabbit' would have the same stimulus meaning for me.[7] Of course, in order to support a hypothesis like that, the linguist might still have to use arguments which refer to distal stimuli, but this should not be inconsistent with a proximal theory of meaning.

What about intersubjective synonymy in ordinary dialogue (in English, for instance)? Quine says that this is no problem for observation sentences, since 'concurrence of witnesses is already a defining condition of observationality' (Quine 1995:81). But it is not obvious how this solution can be combined with a proximal theory. On such a theory one might wish to say that observation sentences have different meanings for different speakers, even though there is perhaps complete concurrence of witnesses, on each occasion. But that would be very strange. Surely, if you and I use the sentence 'It's raining', say, in exactly the same way on all occasions, it may be assumed that we use it with the same meaning. Can a proximal theory give this result?

I think it can. A plausible proximal theory should not *identify* meaning with stimulus meaning. Rather, it should say that the stimulus meaning an observation sentence has for a person *determines* the meaning the sentence has for the person. The meaning itself can be identified with the person's disposition to assent to, and dissent from, the sentence on various occa-

---

[7] Quine exploits the possibility of bilingual speakers to handle radical translation in Quine 1995:78.

sions. If this sounds odd, we might say instead that the meaning of a sentence (for a person) is *its* disposition to be assented to or dissented from (by the person) on various occasions. In any case, if two people have the same disposition to assent to and dissent from the sentence on all occasions, the sentence has the same meaning for them.

My suggestion may also be put as follows. Meaning is use. So, if two persons are disposed to use an observation sentence in exactly the same way, it has the same meaning for them. But a person's disposition to use an observation sentence is fixed by the stimulus meaning it has for him or her. Consequently, the proximal theory is right in saying that meaning is determined by proximal stimuli.

6 Objective and immanent meaning

So far, I have only considered the meaning of observation sentences. The meaning of observation categoricals—i.e. general standing sentences of the form 'Whenever X, Y', where X and Y are observation sentences—can be taken to be determined by the meaning of the relevant observation sentences. This seems acceptable on both distal and proximal theories.

Theoretical sentences have meaning, according to Quine, in so far as they have empirical content (see e.g. Quine 1992:53). The empirical content of a sentence can be identified with the set of observation categoricals implied by it (see Quine 1992:17 and also Quine 1980:80). But since theoretical sentences in general do not imply any observational sentences, Quine concludes that they do not, taken in isolation, have any (empirical) meaning at all. Some theoretical sentences, notably some fairly long conjunctions of theory formulations, have meanings of their own, but most theoretical sentences do not. Quine writes:

> Unless pretty firmly and directly conditioned to sensory stimulation, a sentence S is meaningless except relative to its own theory; meaningless intertheoretically (Quine 1960:24).

However, as this quotation indicates, Quine seems to operate with two different notions of 'meaning'. First, there is objective or intertheoretic meaning, which is the same as empirical content. Second, there is 'immanent' or intratheoretic meaning, a meaning which a sentence has 'relative to its own theory'. I take it that the immanent meaning of a sentence is the same as the truth condition of the sentence; truth, for Quine, is also immanent to theory (see e.g. 1986b:367). For example, the sentence 'It's raining' means that it is raining. This is as it should be.

Now, I believe Davidson is right in saying that Quine accepts a proximal theory of meaning, but I would add that this theory is exclusively concerned with objective meaning. When it comes to immanent meaning, Quine's position may be more like Davidson's. In one place, Quine writes:

> Davidson calls his position a distal theory of meaning and mine a proximal one. Actually, my position in semantics is as distal as his. My observation sentences treat of the distal world, and they are rock-bottom language for child and field linguist alike. My identification of stimulus with neural intake is irrelevant to that (Quine 1993:114n).

Here, it might seem that Quine rejects the proximal theory. However, on my interpretation of Quine, observation sentences have both proximal (empirical, objective) and some kind of distal (immanent) meaning. Theoretical sentences have distal or immanent meaning, but in most cases they do not have any proximal or empirical meaning of their own.

7 Possible differences between immanent and distal meaning

It is not quite clear, however, that Quine's immanent meaning is precisely the same as distal meaning in Davidson's sense. Quine seems to think that it is, but I am not so sure. In particular, there are two problems with the distal theory that do not seem to arise in connection with Quine's view.

The first problem has to do with the use of one and the same observation sentence on different occasions. It is natural to say, that the sentence 'It's raining' has the same meaning for me when I assent to it on two separate occasions (yesterday and today, say). On the proximal theory, this is quite possible. The stimulus meaning the sentence has for me—as well as my corresponding disposition to use the sentence—may be the same on both occasions. So the empirical meaning is the same.

However, the distal theory seems to imply that the meaning is different on the two occasions. For, surely, the distal stimuli are different. Yesterday's rain is not the same as today's rain. Davidson writes:

> Meanings are shared when *identical* events, objects or situations cause or would cause assent and dissent (Davidson 1990a:73. My italics.)

It is hard to see how this allows for sameness of meaning from one occasion to another. And if observation sentences have a new meaning on every occasion, it is hard to see how a person can learn their meaning. Maybe there is some way to handle this, but I have not been able to think of one.

A natural move might be to say that a sentence has the same meaning on two different occasions when assent to it is caused by the same *kind* of event on both occasions. However, we are then faced with the problem of deciding when two events are of 'the same kind'. We might say that events are of the same kind if we react to them linguistically in the same way, but if so, meaning would be determined by our verbal dispositions rather than by external events. Besides, it seems two reactions should be reckoned as linguistically the same, in the relevant sense, only if the linguistic expressions involved have the same meaning, so this proposal does not really help us to define sameness of meaning.

The second problem with the distal theory has to do with observational mistakes. Suppose, for example, that I am looking through the window and think I see rain outside. My sensory receptors are triggered in a way which disposes me to assent to the observation sentence 'It's raining'. But, in fact, there is no rain. Instead, someone is watering the lawn outside the window.[8] Clearly, I am mistaken. The distal stimulus, in this case, is not what I think it is. But it does not follow from this that the meaning of my sentence is not what I think it is. The meaning of the sentence remains the same in deviant cases, where assent to it is caused by events which are not correctly described by it. As far as I can see, the distal theory cannot account for this.

So maybe we should conclude that there is a difference between Davidson's distal theory and Quine's view after all. When Quine says that his position in semantics is as distal as Davidson's, I think what he means is only that observation sentences 'treat of the distal world' and not of proximal stimuli. But I can find no indication in Quine's work that the immanent meaning of a sentence—i.e. what is says—is somehow determined by distal elements in the chain of causes leading up to beliefs or utterances in particular cases.

On the other hand, there is some indication that actual chains of causes are not are not really decisive for Davidson's theory of meaning either. In one place, he says that

> a distal theory connects meaning directly to the conditions that make sentences true or false (Davidson 1990a:75).

If this is taken as the central idea of Davidson's distal theory, it seems that meaning in his sense could be much the same as what I have called 'immanent meaning' in Quine's theory. It should be remembered, however, that both Quine and Davidson are actually quite sceptical concerning the existence of 'conditions that make sentences true or false'. I take it that such conditions, if they existed, would be 'facts'. Neither Quine nor Davidson believes that there are such things (see e.g. Quine 1960, and Davidson 1990b:303-4).

---

[8] This particular example was suggested to me by Burton Dreben.

8   Davidson's argument against the proximal theory

Let us now go back to what I take to be Quine's proximal theory of meaning. As we have seen (in section 5 above) Davidson's main argument against the proximal theory—viz. that it leads to 'truth relativized to individuals, and skepticism'—assumes that sentences may have the same stimulus meaning for different people (Davidson 1990a:76). Consequently, this argument does not apply to (my interpretation of) Quine's theory. But Davidson also has another argument, which may seem more effective. It goes as follows:

> One might think to rescue the proximal theory, for example, by counting as stimulus-synonymous sentences to which assent was prompted by different patterns of stimulation—different patterns for different people, according to the way that their nervous systems were variously arranged. The difficulty is that your pattern of stimulations and mine are guaranteed to prompt assent to distally intertranslatable sentences only if those patterns are caused by the same distal events. Such a theory would be a distal theory in transparent disguise, since the basis for translating your sentences into mine (and hence for comparing our sensory stimulations) would depend on the shared external situations that caused both our various stimulations and our verbal responses.(Davidson 1990a:76-7)

The question, then, is whether Quine's theory—as I understand it—is really a distal theory in disguise. My suggestion was that one observation sentence A has the same (empirical) meaning for one speaker S_1 as another observation sentence B has for another speaker S_2 if and only if the stimulus meanings of A for S_1 and of B for S_2 are such that S_1 and S_2 tend to assent to (dissent from) A and B, respectively, on the same occasions. (This, I take it, is what Quine has in mind when he writes about 'concurrence of witnesses'.) Now, Davidson might object to this by saying that the reference to stimulus meanings plays no essential role here; and he might say that, when this reference is dropped, what is left belongs to a distal theory, not a proximal one.

As far as I can see, this objection is not decisive. Of course, we may say that sentences have the same meaning for different speakers when the speakers tend to use them in the same way.[9] But there is nothing particularly distal about this formulation. Sensory receptors are not mentioned, but neither are distal stimuli. A proponent of the proximal view may still insist that what *determines* the way a speaker uses an observation sentence is the stimulus meaning the sentence has for him. The various causal chains that

---

[9] Compare the following statement in Quine 1992:38: 'There is nothing in linguistic meaning beyond what is to be gleaned from overt behavior in observable circumstances.'

lead up to the triggering of sensory receptors in different situations do not determine the meaning of the sentence. The distal causes may change—e.g. in the case of observational mistakes—even though the meaning of the sentence remains the same.

9   The conflict between distal and proximal meaning

On Quine's view, as I understand it, proximal meaning—i.e. meaning understood in accordance with the proximal theory—is something that most sentences lack. What has proximal meaning is primarily observation sentences holophrastically construed.[10] In order to illustrate the conflict between the distal and proximal theories, let us consider such a sentence in the following thought experiment.[11]

Suppose a person has learnt to use the observation sentence 'That's red' in the usual way, by conditioning. Then something happens in his environment, which results in a dramatic change: he now assents to 'That's red' when the rest of us dissent from this sentence and see green things in his visual field. If the distal theory is right, we should say that the meaning of 'That's red' has changed for him. It should now be translated into our language as 'That's green'. On the proximal theory, such a translation may be mistaken. On the proximal theory, the question is whether the stimulus meaning of 'That's red' has changed. Let us assume that it remains the same as before, but that the relevant stimulations are now caused by green instead of red objects. This assumption is far-fetched, but it does not seem impossible. Perhaps a certain kind of spectacles could have this effect. Then, on the proximal view, we should say that the meaning of 'That's red' remains the same for him, but that something in his environment (his glasses, perhaps) makes him have false beliefs about the color of green things.

In short, the assumption is that green things cause 'red' stimulations in him, but 'green' stimulations in us. Now, if this is possible—i.e. if we can establish that the very same stimulations that have always disposed the person to assent to 'That's red', and which used to be caused by red objects, are now caused by green objects—then I suggest that the natural thing to say is that the meaning of the sentence remains the same, but that he is now systematically mistaken about the color of green objects. In other words, the proximal theory yields a more plausible verdict than the distal theory.

---

[10] For the distinction between holophrastic and analytic construals of observation sentences, see e.g. Quine 1992:50.
[11] This thought experiment was suggested to me by Folke Tersman.

What would happen if there were a 'change' which made *all* of us call green things red? It is natural to say that this is inconceivable, on the ground that, if all of us call these things red, they *are* red. Perhaps this is not necessarily so. If our scientific theories imply that green color is correlated with certain other properties, we may want to retain these theories in conjunction with the hypothesis that our sense of color has changed so that green things now look red to us. This may be tempting for some proponent of the proximal view. On a distal theory it may be more correct to say that a change of meaning has taken place. But a more plausible description is that something has happened which forces us to modify our theories. The properties that used to be correlated with green color are now correlated with red instead. The meaning of 'That's red' then remains the same on both the distal and the proximal view.

I do not wish to exclude the possibility that there are cases, of the kind sketched here, in which the proximal and distal theories give different answers to the question of whether there has been a change in meaning or a change in belief. However, it seems to me that the proximal theory is at least as plausible as the distal theory in such cases, but in a Quinean spirit I would add that the disagreement between the two theories in such cases does not concern any real fact of the matter.

10 Empiricism and skepticism

At this point, let us leave the theory of meaning and return instead to epistemology. In particular, let us return to the third dogma of empiricism mentioned in sections 2 and 3 above. Davidson's main argument against this dogma—and thereby against empiricism—has to do with its emphasis on an intermediate epistemic level between the world and our theory of the world. This intermediate level consists of empirical content; in Quine's case it is the triggering of sensory receptors. Davidson claims that the introduction of such an intermediate epistemic level leads to skepticism. In a talk in Stockholm in 1993 on Quine's philosophy, he recalled his early reaction to 'Two Dogmas', and its 'distinction between a non-propositional content given in experience and a conceptual scheme, language, or framework which organizes that content'. And he went on:

> This distinction, characteristic both of Kant and many empiricists, spells trouble only if the 'given' element is assigned a subjective epistemic role; in that case, there is an epistemic intermediary between the world which (we assume) causes our sensations and our conceptualization of the world. The trouble I see in such an epistemology is that it leaves no escape from skepticism of the senses, for we can always wonder whether the world is the way we imagine it to be or whether we're just getting the impressions we would be getting if the

world were that way. [...] A completely familiar problem; but wasn't
Quine hinting that he would be satisfied with the 'as if' position by
calling physical objects 'posits'? (Davidson 1994:187)

And again, a few pages later:

Unless we are willing to settle for the skeptical view that success in
predicting our future (observational) beliefs is all there is to having a
true view of the world, we need a theory of meaning and an epistemology that somehow ties the contents of speech and thought to the situations and objects we take those contents to be about (Davidson
1994:190).

But the skeptical question Davidson imagines of 'whether the world is
the way we imagine it to be or whether we're just getting the impressions
we would be getting if the world were that way' is, I believe, ruled out by
Quine's naturalism. It seems that this question makes sense only if there is
a higher tribunal of truth than science, but the existence of such a higher
tribunal is precisely what Quine's naturalism rules out. Truth, for Quine, is
immanent. Facts are also immanent (see e.g. Quine 1986b:367). There is no
Ding an Sich which is forever beyond the reach of science (Quine 1981:22).
The only way in which we can be mistaken about the world is the way in
which science itself sometimes shows us that we are mistaken.

In the quotation above, Davidson also refers to 'the skeptical view that
success in predicting our future (observational) beliefs is all there is to having a true view of the world'. He seems to imply that this is not Quine's
view. However, I believe, on the contrary, that something like this is indeed Quine's view, and I also believe that this view is not a skeptical one.
Let me quote a few passages from Quine, which seem to support this interpretation:

[...] systematization of our sensory intake is the very business that
science itself is engaged in (Quine 1995:15).

The scientific system, ontology and all, is a conceptual bridge of our
own making, linking sensory stimulation to sensory stimulation (Quine 1981:20).

From impacts on our sensory surfaces, we in our collective and cumu-
lative creativity down the generations have projected our systematic
theory of the external world. Our system is proving successful in predicting subsequent sensory input. [...] Not that prediction is the main
purpose of science. [...] Prediction can be a purpose too, but my present point is that it is the *test* of a theory, whatever the purpose (Quine
1992:1-2).

Our scientific theory can indeed go wrong, and precisely in the familiar way: through failure of predicted observation. [...] Our overall scientific theory demands of the world only that it be so structured as to

assure the sequences of stimulation that our theory gives us to expect (Quine 1981:22).

These quotations indicate that Quine accepts the view that the world is, in a sense, a human construction or projection (a 'posit'). But this view does not have any skeptical implications. On the contrary, the very idea that the world is a human construction rules out the possibility that we may be massively mistaken about the world. The nature of the world is specified in our theories, and there is no truth independent of these theories. As mentioned above, truth, for Quine, is immanent; but this immanence of truth is no limitation.

> Within our own total evolving doctrine, we can judge truth as earnestly and absolutely as can be; subject to correction, but that goes without saying (Quine 1960:25).

It is not just that our judgments concerning what is true have to be made from the perspective of our total evolving doctrine; truth itself is determined by this doctrine. The term 'the world' (or 'reality') has no meaning outside our total system of the world. We must 'recognize "real" as itself a term within our scientific theory' (Quine 1994:504). Accordingly, there is no truth and no reality independent of this system; 'it is within science itself, and not in some prior philosophy, that reality is to be identified' (Quine 1981:21).

11 Sensory evidence

However, Davidson would still insist that it is illegitimate to assign an epistemic role to sensory stimulation. He agrees that sensory stimulation plays a *causal* role in the production of beliefs, but he does not accept Quine's view that 'whatever evidence there is for science is sensory evidence'. Davidson writes:

> [...] our experimentation bears no epistemological fruit except as it *causes* us to add to, cling to, or abandon our beliefs. This causal relation cannot be a relation of *confirmation* or *disconfirmation*, since the cause is not a proposition or belief, but just an event in the world or in our sensory apparatus. Nor can such events be considered in themselves to be evidence, unless, of course, they cause us to believe something. And then it is the belief that is properly called the evidence, not the event (Davidson 1982:486).

It is not clear to me why it would be improper to use the term 'evidence' for some event—such as proximal stimulation—in the causal sequence leading up to belief. Maybe this use is not very common, but Quine for one does seem to use the term this way, for example in the following passage:

> The stimulation of his sensory receptors is all the evidence anybody has to go on, ultimately, in arriving at the picture of his world (Quine 1969:75).

However, it might be argued that Quine has changed his view in his more recent writings. For example, Roger Gibson, who is one of the leading interpreters of Quine, has said that on Quine's 'new view', observation sentences are causally but not epistemically related to neural inputs (Gibson 1994:458). On an earlier occasion, Gibson said that (for Quine) '[t]he stimuli related via conditioning to the observation sentences constitute their evidence' (Gibson 1988:54-5). This indicates that Gibson believes that Quine has changed his mind on this point. Personally, I am not so sure. In one fairly recent answer to Davidson, Quine says of surface irritation that its proper role is as 'a basis not for truth but for warranted belief' (Quine 1981:39).

Anyway, the substantial question is whether or not proximal stimuli can play an epistemic role in addition to their causal role. It seems to me that they can. I suggest that Quine might still be willing to accept some principle like the following:

> (E) *A person P is justified, ceteris paribus, in assenting at t to observation sentence S, if P at t has the capacity to use S in a competent way, and if P is subject to neural input which is included in the (affirmative) stimulus meaning of S for P at t.*

I suggest that (E) is an element of Quine's empiricism. It seems to me that (E) may be the very point at which Quine and Davidson differ—if they differ. Davidson would certainly reject (E), but Quine might accept it. This is what makes Quine an empiricist and Davidson an anti-empiricist.

Moreover, I believe that (E) is one of the grounds for the special status of observation sentences in Quine's philosophy. (The other ground is the intersubjectivity of observation sentences.) For Quine, observation sentences play a role 'as vehicles of evidence for our knowledge of the external world', as follows:

> We are not aware of our neural intake, nor do we deduce anything from it. What we *have* learned to do is to assert or assent to some observation sentences in *reaction* to certain ranges of neural intake. It is such sentences, then, thus elicited, that serve as experimental checkpoints for theories about the world. Negative check points (Quine 1993:110-11).

Of course, the ceteris paribus clause in (E) is essential, for a person may have good theoretical reasons for dissenting from an observation sentence even though he is subject to stimulation which belongs to its (affirmative) stimulus meaning. But observation sentences have an epistemologically privileged status.

By contrast, according to Davidson, if I understand him correctly, observation sentences have no special privileged status; in particular, we are not justified in assenting to them simply because we are subject to the appropriate stimulation. Davidson writes:

> In my view, erasing the line between the analytic and synthetic saved philosophy of language as a serious subject by showing how it could be pursued without what there cannot be: determinate meanings. I now suggest also giving up the distinction between observation sentences and the rest. [...] Accordingly, I suggest we give up the idea that meaning or knowledge is grounded on something that counts as an ultimate source of evidence (Davidson 1986:313).

In particular, then, knowledge is not grounded on sensory evidence. Davidson is a coherentist, and 'the coherentist will hold that there is no use looking for a source of justification outside of other sentences held true' (Davidson 1986:312). For Davidson, neural input is not an ultimate source of evidence. It is not a source of evidence at all.

12 The justification of observational beliefs

On Davidson's coherentist view, you may of course have evidence for observational beliefs; in other words, you may be justified in holding true, or assenting to, observation sentences. But, on a coherentist view (of Davidson's type), the evidence for an observational belief can only be some other belief or beliefs (Davidson 1986:310).

In other words, Davidson is an internalist about justification and evidence, while Quine—if I understand him correctly—is an externalist.[12] For Davidson, all the evidence you can have for a belief is internal to your system of beliefs. For Quine, much evidence is indeed internal to your system of beliefs, but there is also an external source of evidence: the triggering of your sensory receptors.

In order to illustrate the external position consider the following thought experiment. I am sitting in my office looking out through the window. As it happens, there is no rain outside. However, unknown to me, someone is manipulating my nerve endings by some kind of remote control in such a way that I get a stimulation which is included in my positive stimulus meaning of 'It's raining'. So I believe that it is raining. Now it seems that, in this case, *I am justified* in believing that it is raining, even though I am mistaken. I have been educated in the use of the sentence 'It's raining', and the education has been completely successful. I am a fully

---

12. For the distinction between externalism and internalism, see e.g. Dancy and Sosa eds. 1993.

competent user of the sentence, and there is nothing wrong or blameworthy about my use of it in this particular situation. It is only that the situation has been rigged in a way that fools me. But from an epistemic point of view, I have made no mistake. My belief is justified. This fits well with (E).

Compare this with a situation where someone manipulates, not my nerve endings, but the interior of my nervous system. Now the stimulation I get is not included in my positive stimulus meaning of 'It's raining', but the end result is the same: because of the manipulation, I believe that it is raining. In this case, it seems that my belief is *not* justified. The reason is that in this case the manipulation affects me in such a way that I am no longer a competent user of the sentence. My very competence is lost. Hence, my belief is unjustified. Again, this fits well with (E).

In the case of observation sentences, truth conditions and assertability conditions seem to coincide. However, we should distinguish between two kinds of assertability conditions: recognizable and physiological. (The latter are objective physical states of the speaker's organism.) When I learn the sentence 'It's raining', I acquire the practical ability to recognize the conditions under which this sentence is true. I also learn that the conditions under which the sentence is true are conditions under which I am justified in asserting or assenting to the sentence. These conditions are *recognizable.* They are also immanent to my language.

However, there are also *physiological* (objective) assertability conditions. Surely, I am justified in assenting to 'It's raining' when I have learnt to use the sentence correctly—by having gone through a suitable and successful conditioning process—and my sensory receptors are stimulated in a relevant way. In such a case, my assent is justified, but what I assent to may be false. The principle (E) ties my personal state of justification to the social learning process which explains my disposition to use the sentence in question. When I have learnt to use the sentence 'It's raining' correctly, i.e. to the satisfaction of my peers, I am justified (ceteris paribus) in assenting to it on those very occasions on which I do assent to it. This is precisely what successful learning results in.

At later stages in my education, when my theory of the world has grown into a more mature and sophisticated system, I may also be able to justify my belief that it is raining, on a certain occasion, in more indirect ways, namely by inferring it from certain other beliefs that I have. For example, I may be able to infer it from beliefs concerning my subjective cognitive states, the reliability of my sensory organs, the relation between my cognitive states and my sensory organs, and beliefs about what would be the best explanation of certain cognitive states. Moreover, with greater sophistication I will also learn that my immediate assent to observation sentences is sometimes mistaken. I learn that there are sometimes theoretical reasons for rejecting observation sentences which would otherwise be appropriate on a given occasion. But these complications are quite compatible with principle (E).

In conclusion, then, I want to side with Quine when he replies to Davidson that '[t]he third purported dogma [of empiricism], understood now in relation not to truth but to warranted belief, remains intact. [...] It is what makes scientific method partly empirical rather than solely a quest for internal coherence' (Quine 1981:39).

References

Bergström, L. 1994. Quine's Truth. *Inquiry* 37:421-35.

Bergström, L. 2000, Quine, Empiricism, and Truth. *Knowledge Language and Logic*, ed. A. Orenstein & P. Kotatko, 63-79. Dordrecht: Kluwer Academic Publishers.

Dancy, J. & E. Sosa (eds.) 1993. *A Companion to Epistemology*. Oxford: Blackwell.

Davidson, D. 1973-74. On the Very Idea of a Conceptual Scheme. *Proceedings and Addresses of the American Philosophical Association* 47:5-20.

Davidson, D. 1982. Empirical Content. *Grazer Philosopische Studien* 16/17:471-89.

Davidson, D. 1986. A Coherence Theory of Truth and Knowledge. *Truth and Interpretation: Perspectives on the Philosophy of Donald Davidson*, ed. E. LePore, 307-19. Oxford: Blackwell.

Davidson, D. 1990a. Meaning, Truth, and Evidence. *Perspectives on Quine*, eds. R. Barrett & R. Gibson, 68-79. Oxford: Blackwell.

Davidson, D. 1990b. The Structure and Content of Truth. *Journal of Philosophy* 88:279-328.

Davidson, D. 1994. On Quine's Philosophy. *Theoria* 60:184-92.

Gibson, R. 1988. *Enlightened Empiricism*. Tampa: University of South Florida Press.

Gibson, R. 1994. Quine and Davidson: Two Naturalized Epistemologists. *Inquiry* 37:449-63.

Quine, W. V. 1953. Two Dogmas of Empiricism. *From a Logical Point of View, 20-46*. Cambridge, Mass.: Harvard University Press.

Quine, W. V. 1960. *Word and Object*. Cambridge, Mass.: The M.I.T. Press.

Quine, W. V. 1969. Ontological Relativity. *Ontological Relativity and Other Essays, 26-67*. New York: Columbia University Press.

Quine, W. V. 1977. Review of *Truth and Meaning*, eds. G. Evans & J. McDowell. *Journal of Philosophy* 74:225-241.

Quine, W. V. 1980. The Nature of Natural Knowledge. *Mind and Language*, ed. S. Guttenplan, 67-81. Oxford: Clarendon Press.

Quine, W. V. 1981. On the Very Idea of a Third Dogma. *Theories and Things, 38-42.* Cambridge, Mass.: Belknap Press.

Quine, W. V. 1986a. Reply to Roger F. Gibson, Jr. *The Philosophy of W. V. Quine*, eds. E. Hahn & P. Schilpp, 155-7. La Salle, Illinois: Open Court.

Quine, W. V. 1986b. Reply to Robert Nozick. *The Philosophy of W. V. Quine*, eds. E. Hahn & P. Schilpp, 364-7. La Salle, Illinois: Open Court.

Quine, W. V. 1992. *Pursuit of Truth*. Revised edition, Cambridge, Mass.: Harvard University Press.

Quine, W. V. 1993. In Praise of Observation Sentences. *Journal of Philosophy* 91:107-16.

Quine, W. V. 1994. Reply to Hookway. *Inquiry* 37:502-4.

Quine, W. V. 1995. *From Stimulus to Science*. Cambridge, Mass.: Harvard University Press.

3

Is Truth a Norm?

PASCAL ENGEL

1   Introduction

A familiar theme—indeed a sort of slogan—in contemporary philosophy is that meaning and mental content are 'normative' or have a normative dimension. One of its origins is in Wittgenstein's rule-following considerations: to understand the meaning of a word, or to possess a certain concept, is to be able to appraise correct or incorrect uses of it. This feature is often held to be the main obstacle to a naturalistic analysis of meaning and intentional concepts. Davidson is equally skeptical about such an analysis, since he has long held that the 'constitutive ideal of rationality' which governs our concepts of propositional attitudes have no 'echo' in physical theory and in naturalistic concepts in general. One of his main arguments for this view is that 'the concepts we use to explain and describe thought, speech and action are irreducibly normative' (Davidson 1999:460). In a previous article (Engel 1999[1]), I have tried to elucidate in what sense we can say

---

[1] That paper was a descendent of the one I read at the Karlowy Vary conference on Interpreting Davidson in 1996. The present paper is an attempt to answer Davidson's reply (Davidson 1999) and to further the discussion that I have initiated in Engel 2000 and Engel *forthcoming*. I have been much influenced, while writing this paper (especially the second section), by Paul Boghossian's article 'The Normativity of Content', read at the Summer School on Normativity and reason in Parma (July 2000). Boghossian is, of course, in no way responsible for the mistakes and misunderstandings of his views that might be present in this paper.

that, for Davidson, mental concepts have a normative dimension, and I have suggested a reading of this claim, which, I thought, he could at least partly agree with: that the normative dimension in mental content resides in the specific norms attached to concepts, along the lines of conceptual role accounts and theories of concept possession, and in a general norm of truth attached to the concept of belief, which is central among the propositional attitudes. But Davidson disagrees. He sees little promise in conceptual role accounts of concepts, and bluntly rejects the second suggestion: 'Truth is not, in my opinion, a norm' (Davidson 1999:461). Since he has taught us that what matters in interpretation (including the interpretation of philosophers) is more understanding than agreement, I shall leave aside here the first suggestion, and shall try to articulate better the second, in the hope of furthering this dialogue with him. In the first part of this paper, I try to spell out what is at stake in the claim that truth is a norm and why Davidson could have grounds to oppose this claim. In the second part, I try to argue that there is a reasonable sense in which we can, and must, say that truth is a norm of belief, and that most of our epistemic norms are grounded in this one.

2

What does it mean to say that truth is a norm, and what is at stake in such a claim? There are, basically, two strands in this debate, although they are intimately connected. One strand is with the analysis of the concept of truth and of the meaning of the word 'true', which opposes, in contemporary philosophy, two camps. A number of philosophers hold that truth is a 'robust' property, to be analyzed in terms of such 'substantive' notions such as correspondence, coherence, or perhaps along pragmatist lines. A number of other philosophers hold that truth is a 'thin' property, which does not contain more than what is expressed by the disquotational feature of the truth predicate or by the trivial equivalence 'It is true that P iff P', and propose 'deflationary' or 'minimalist' conceptions.[2] For a philosopher of the second persuasion, any attempt to read into the concept of truth more than these trivial or formal features, would be an attempt to 'pump more content in the concept of truth' than a minimalist theory should allow (Davidson 1996:310). Thus, when Crispin Wright (1992), following to a large extent Dummett (1959), claims that a deflationary theory of truth should be 'inflated' in order to accommodate the fact that truth is 'a norm of our assertoric practice' and of belief, this claim is rejected by one of the main con-

---

[2] There are, of course, a number of different versions of 'minimalism' about truth. But for the purposes of the present discussion, I shall largely ignore these differences.

temporary proponents of the deflationary theory, Paul Horwich (1998).[3] The second strand concerns the question whether truth itself is a norm, or a value, which should be pursued for its own sake: is truth a goal or an ideal of our inquiries? Is there any sort of ethical command to search after the truth? Some pragmatist philosophers, such as Peirce, believe that there is; other pragmatists, such as Rorty (1986, 1995) or Stich (1990), disagree. They do not see why we would be aiming at truth, more than utility or pragmatic value. And the connection between the two strands seems to be this: in claiming that truth is a norm or an ideal, we reintroduce the idea that truth is a grand or robust notion, which, according to minimalist theories, it is not.

Where does Davidson stand in these debates? With respect to the issue of robustness vs. minimalism about truth, it seems quite obvious that he sides with the second camp, although he does not accept Horwich's version of deflationism, and does not hope to give any general definition of truth along this or other lines (Davidson 1996). So it seems that his denial that truth could be a norm is based on his suspicion that any attempt to read more into the concept of truth than the familiar formal features would be an attempt to define or to explain further this fundamental and essentially 'indefinable' concept. With respect to the second issue, he is equally clear: 'I do not think it adds anything to say that truth is a goal, of science or anything else. We do not aim at truth, but at honest justification' (Davidson 1999:461). His reason for this claim is this: 'There must be cases of fully justified beliefs where the fact that they are false will never come to be known. I cannot see that cases of the last kind are more desirable than cases of the first kind' (ibid.). The point, presumably, is this: if truth were a goal of inquiry or of science, then in some sense truth should be essentially knowable and justifiable, the concept of truth would coincide with the concept of justification and truth would have to be an epistemic concept. But this implies a form of anti-realism about truth, and an attempt at 'humanizing truth by making it basically epistemic' (Davidson 1990:298). On the other hand, the goal of belief is justification, but there is no point in linking justification intrinsically to truth, as the claim that truth can be a norm of belief and knowledge seems to imply. So theories of truth, which like

---

[3] Other writers who have advocated the idea that truth is a norm include Hornsby (1997 and 1998). She defends this claim in the context of her own version of the 'identity theory of truth': 'The conception of truth which the identity theory brings with it allows truth to be a *sui generis* norm, in play where there are rational beings who may go right or wrong in their thought and speech' (Hornsby 1997:22). I have myself defended the view that truth is a norm in Engel 1991, in the context of the philosophy of logic, and along more general lines in Engel 1998.

Peirce's, or Putnam's, tie truth to rational acceptability at the 'limit' of scientific inquiry and which make truth a goal of inquiry, are equally guilty of epistemologizing truth.

Here, Davidson's position seems to be quite close to Rorty's, who, in a paper targeted at Wright's claim that truth is a norm of our assertoric practice (Rorty 1995), has also denied that truth could be a goal of inquiry, on behalf of a 'Davidsonian' conception of truth. In spite of Rorty's tendency to try to read more (and more Rortian theses) into Davidson's views than Davidson himself would allow, it is useful to briefly go over Rorty's account of these issues.

Crispin Wright (1992) basically agrees with minimalism about truth that truth is a 'metaphysically lightweight' notion, which contains not much more that the usual platitudes attached to it (namely that 'P' is true iff P, that our statements are true if things are such as they say they are, or that every true statement has a negation).[4] But he denies, contrary to what is claimed by pure deflationism, that the whole meaning of the word 'true' is exhausted by the 'Disquotation Schema':

(DS) 'P' is true if an only if P

Wright claims that deflationism is subject to a characteristic tension, since the acceptance that (DS) says all there is to say about truth, associated to the acceptance of the platitude about negation:

(Neg) Every statement P, has a negation, not P

entails inconsistent claims about the relations between truth and assertibility. Both are, according to Wright, norms of assertoric discourse, in the sense that in making an assertion, we aim at truth, and aim at making assertions that are warranted or justified. So (DS), according to Wright, says *more* than simply the fact that 'P' and 'it is true that P' are equivalent. It also says that if we have a reason to say that P is true we have thereby a reason to assert or to accept it. DS entails that 'true' and 'is warranted assertible' or 'justified' coincide in 'normative force': to think that P is true is to think it warrantedly assertible, and conversely. In this sense deflationism is committed to granting the 'normativity' of the truth predicate. Now if deflationism holds that DS exhausts what there is to say about truth, it should also deny that truth and warranted assertibility are *distinct* norms of assertion. But these are distinct norms, since the predicate 'is true' and 'is warrantedly assertible' diverge in their extension. For it follows from (DS) and (Neg) that :

---

[4] Wright calls his own view 'minimalism', but he intends to dissociate it from other varieties of minimalism, in particular from Horwich's (1990) deflationary conception.

(1)   'It is not the case that P' is true iff it is not the case that P

and contraposing on DS :

(2)   It is not the case that P iff it is not the case that 'P' is true

and by the transitivity of the biconditional:

(3)   'It is not the case that P' is true iff it is not the case that 'P' is true

But replacing 'true' by 'is warrantedly assertible' in (3) is incorrect: for if P nor the negation of P are warrantedly assertible, it may be that neither 'P' nor 'It is not the case that P' are warrantedly assertible.

It should be noted that Wright's argument, to the effect that truth is a *distinctive* norm of assertion in no way implies the *coincidence* of truth and warranted assertibility or justification. On the contrary, the argument trades on the difference between a statement being true and our being warranted in asserting it. So in Wright's hands, the thesis that truth is a distinctive norm of assertoric practice does not amount to making truth an essentially epistemic concept.

Now, of course, Wright's argument rests upon the claim that truth *is* a norm of our assertoric practice, or at least a norm of belief, and someone who denies the existence of such a norm would immediately reject it as question begging. But is this claim so controversial? It seems to amount to the familiar idea that the concepts of belief, of assertion, and of truth are intrinsically interconnected: to assert that P implies (or at least implicitates) that one believes that P, and to believe that P is to believe that P is true (hence the oddity of utterances such as those which give rise to Moore's paradox: 'P, but I believe that not P'). Now, why should Davidson deny this obvious point? Has he not repeatedly claimed that the concept of belief and the concept of truth are intimately connected, that the basic attitude which lies behind belief and which is evidence for it is the 'holding-true' of sentences? And has he not emphasized that the indispensability of the Principle of Charity amounts to the claim that 'belief is by nature veridical'?

But Rorty urges us *not* to interpret this basic conceptual link between belief and truth as implying that there is a distinctive norm of truth:

> To say, as Davidson does, that 'belief is in its nature veridical' is not to celebrate the happy congruence of subject and object but rather to say that the pattern truth makes is the pattern which *justification to us* makes (Rorty 1995:286).

This, according to Rorty, is not alien to Davidson's emphasis on the 'normative character' of meaning and intentionality. But this character does not amount to the recognition of the distinctive normative nature of truth itself:

> The pattern that truth makes is, in fact, indistinguishable from the pattern that justification to us makes—so it might be best to say simply

> that 'most beliefs held by anybody are justifiable to us' rather than
> 'most beliefs held by anybody are true'. [...] The former expression
> seems to me the clearest way to exhibit the force of Davidson's claim
> ... that the guiding principles used in detecting this pattern 'derive
> from normative considerations' and to bring out the importance of his
> reference... to 'the norms that govern our theories of intentional attri-
> bution'. The need to justify our beliefs and desires to ourselves and to
> our fellow-agents subjects *us* to norms, and obedience to these norms
> produces a behavioural pattern which we must detect in others before
> confidently attributing any beliefs to them. But there seems no occa-
> sion to look for obedience to an *additional* norm, the commendment
> to seek the truth. (Rorty 1995:287).

In a sense, Rorty does not deny that there is, for our beliefs, a norm, in the
sense that any interpretation of a being as having beliefs derives from certain 'guiding principles': precisely those that Davidson calls 'norms of rationality' governing our attributions of beliefs and other propositional attitudes to agents. Truth, in the form of the principle of charity as a principle
of veridicality (the other half of the principle being a principle of coherence)
may well be such a 'norm'. But there is no point in taking this 'norm' to
be different from the norm according to which our beliefs have to be *justified*. But 'justified' here does not mean *objectively justified*, for there are as
many ways of justifying our beliefs and our actions as there are human interests, and there is no way in which these interests could be subsumed
under a single interest or goal. This would come up to reintroducing into
truth the very metaphysical weight that deflationism or 'quietism' about
this notion have gotten rid of. This is why, according to Rorty, talking of a
'norm of truth' as distinctive, and attempting to read it into our very concept of belief, is highly misleading. On his view, pragmatism, in the form
advocated by Dewey and by himself, does recognize this fact, as does (according to Rorty) Davidson's own version of 'pragmatism':

> If Dewey and Davidson are asked 'What is the goal of inquiry?' the
> best either could do would be to say that it has many different goals,
> none of which has any metaphysical presupposition: for example, get-
> ting what we want, the improvement of man's estate, convincing as
> many audiences as possible, solving as many problems as possible,
> and so on. Only if we concede to Wright that 'truth' is a name of a dis-
> tinct norm will metaphysical activism seem desirable. For Dewey and
> Davidson, that is an excellent reason not to view it as a
> norm (Rorty 1995:298-299).

It seems to me that Rorty gets Davidson right on the negative side, and that
his reasoning is quite close to the one which underlies the latter's refusal to
consider truth as a distinctive norm of belief. On the positive side, however, it is less obvious to me that Davidson would subscribe to the so-
called 'pragmatist' idea that inquiry has as many different goals as one

might want to have, and that there is some essential relativity in these goals. For he says, as we have seen, that 'we aim at honest justification', and I do not see how this could imply that there are as many justifications that it might please to us, as 'Dewey-and-Davidson''s view seem to imply. I other words I do not see why Davidson would agree with what 'pragmatism', according to Rorty, implies, i.e. that justification cannot be objective, but is purely subjective or context–relative.

Be it as it may, is the negative part of this reasoning correct, and are Rorty and, for that matter, Davidson, right in denying that there is any interesting sense in which we can call truth a norm? In order to see whether it is the case, we should try to spell out a little more what this talk of 'norm' and 'normativity' amounts to.

3

The above description of the debate about the normativity of truth suffers, just as do the debates about the normativity of meaning and mental content, from serious ambiguities. Indeed both claims are far from clear.[5] When we talk about the 'normative' character of truth are we saying that its normative property or (properties) *exhaust* the concept, or are *essential* to it, or are we merely saying that truth has, among other (non-normative) properties, some normative properties as well? And if there are any such properties, do we want to say that they enter this concept *directly* or that they enter merely *indirectly*? If truth is 'normative' what *kind* of norm is it, and in what sense is this norm attached, or implicated, by the very concept of truth? There are plenty of norms: ethical, legal, social, culinary, architectural, and so forth, relative to a whole range of human activities. Truth is presumably a norm of the cognitive kind, and not a norm pertaining to certain actions. But then in what sense is it normative?

We have encountered above two senses of 'norm' which may be relevant for answering these questions: (a) truth is a norm of belief and of assertion, in the sense that it is *constitutive* of belief and assertion that 'belief aim at truth' and that asserting something is asserting something that one takes to be true; (b) truth is a norm of belief, in the sense that it is the *goal* of inquiry or of our epistemic enterprises. The celebrated phrase 'belief aims at truth' seems to imply both senses, and in fact to conflate them, and since it has been used by Dummett (1959) and by Williams (1971), it has been the source of many confusions. On the one hand, saying that belief 'aims at truth' seems to say something about what belief *is*, namely that the concept

---

[5] I have tried to spell out further what these claims mean in the case of meaning and mental content in Engel 2000 and *forthcoming*.

of belief has to be defined, or at least understood, through the concept of truth, and this points in the direction of the sense (a) of the notion of norm. On the other hand, saying that belief 'aims at truth' seems to indicate what belief is *for*, and to suggest that aiming at belief is a conscious, or unconscious goal of all believers, or that it is something desirable or a value. Rorty's discussion of Wright on this point explicitly moves from the first to the second, when he claims that taking truth to be constitutive of assertoric practice implies that there is some 'duty' to attain the truth (Rorty 1995:288). But certainly there is no such direct implication, and the two senses are distinct. For instance the fact that 'being an unmarried person' is constitutive of the concept of bachelor does not imply that there is any special value in being an unmarried person, or some duty attached to having this status.

Still, it is often claimed that there is some element of normative appraisal, or some action-guiding implication, in the concept of truth itself. For it is often said that one of the ordinary uses of the word 'true' is an *endorsing* use: saying that something is true, or adding to a given assertion: 'And that's true', seems to imply that the speaker praises his assertion, and enjoins his hearer to believe it or to take it as worth asserting. This idea often underlies what is called the 'performative' theory of truth: saying 'It is true that ...' is the performance of a sort of illocutionay or perlocutionary act. This, indeed, is but one version of the deflationary conception.[6] But it is not clear that this meaning of the word 'true' exhausts all the possible uses of it, and it is even less clear that this kind of use implies that the speaker invokes some sort of duty, on the part of his hearer to believe or to assert what he claims is true. Certainly there are uses of 'true' which are, at least *prima facie*, purely descriptive, and which carry no sort of commitment. And there are truths that we do not even dream of asserting or of believing, and hence for which we do not feel any sort of obligation to believe or to assert them. Hence saying that 'truth is normative' needn't commit us to some performative conception of truth.

In order to get a clearer grip on the normative implications of the concept of truth, let us try first to spell out different senses of the word 'norm' in ordinary parlance. A number of theorists who have dealt with the meaning of 'norm' in moral philosophy and in law have long remarked that there

---

[6] The view is often attributed to Strawson (1950), but it lies also behind Rorty's own version of deflationism: 'Truth is but a little tap that we do on the shoulders of the beliefs that we like'. Strawson himself has later rejected his previous view. See his note at the end of the reprinting of his 1950 paper in Blackburn and Simmons eds. 1999.

are, basically two main kinds of normative vocabulary or of normative concepts:[7]

(a) concepts of the 'deontic' kind or normative concepts proper such as: ought, obligation, norm, requirement, permission, regulate, correct, *rectified, etc.* Such concepts are action-guiding, in the sense that they are such that they imply that an appropriate response to what they prescribe, permit, or prohibit is a voluntary or intentional action: *ought* implies *can*;

(b) concepts of the evaluative kind such as : *good, valuable, desirable, worth, etc.* The appropriate responses to judgments involving such concepts are not actions performed by the agents, but feelings or psychological attitudes.

This is a very rough characterization, but it is enough for our purposes here. We can ask the question: if truth is a norm of belief or of assertion, and if saying or believing something true involves something 'normative', does it involve a norm of the first kind or of the second kind, and if so in what sense does it involve it?

Let us suppose first that it involves a norm in the first, deontic sense. The idea would then be that in ascribing truth to certain statements or beliefs, we are in some sense speaking 'oughts', or implicitly relying on certain imperatives about what one ought to believe or assert. The plausible sense in which we could cash out imperatives, prescriptions, or permissions from the application of the predicate 'true' to a sentence or a belief would presumably be by issuing conditionals of the following form:

(1) If it is true that P, then one ought to believe (assert) that P.

For instance:

(1') If it is true that snow is white, then one ought to believe (assert) that snow is white.

And if truth is a norm of belief, or of assertion, such conditionals must be issued not simply for some particular truths, but also for *any* particular truth, including those that we do not even dream of believing or of asserting, either because they are so trivial that they do not merit consideration (for instance the truth that there are presently 10 264 blades of grass on the piece of lawn before me), or because we could never figure out any one of them. But this is absurd, for nobody is in the position to believe *every* truth whatsoever. So general conditionals of the form:

---

[7] I am indebted here to a talk given in Paris in March 2000 by Peter Railton. Since then, I have heard from Kevin Mulligan that Brentano had a similar kind of classification.

(2) For any P, if it is true that P, then one ought to believe (assert) that P

are absurd. Certainly we are under no such obligation. Given that 'ought' implies 'can', and that there is no possible way in which we can perform this obligation (or even the corresponding permission), the claim that truth could be a norm in the deontic sense (a) is absurd. There is a further reason, if our characterization of norms of type (a) is correct, why truth could not be a norm in this sense. It is that we are supposed to conform ourselves to such norms through *actions*. It may be that believing that P, or coming to believe it, in the sense of accepting it, or judging it, is a form of action, as is asserting it. But belief *per se*, the state of believing that P, is not voluntary, and it cannot be an action (in the sense of Williams 1971, but more on this below). Hence belief could not be subject to an 'ought' of the deontic kind.

Could it be, then, that the norm involved in truth ascriptions is a norm of the second kind? The idea would then be that the truth of a particular belief or assertion would imply that it is in some sense valuable, or that it merits appraisal, or that it provokes in us some positive feeling. This time, the response to the norm would not be a voluntary action, and it would be plausible to say that it could be an involuntary state such as a belief. But the idea is equally hopeless. For consider:

(3) If it is true that snow is white, then it is valuable to believe that snow is white

or possibly:

(4) If it is true that snow is white, then one appraises, or feels well about believing that snow is white

and by generalizing:

(5) For any P, if P is true, then it is valuable to believe that P.

This is absurd for the same reason as above, since even on the reading of 'norm' as 'value', it makes no sense to say that we value all true beliefs whatsoever. So it makes no sense to say that the norm of truth consists in a form of intrinsic value of truth.

So, on the supposition that our two senses of 'norm' exhaust the possible senses of this notion, the claim that truth is a norm of belief is obviously false. It may be what Davidson and Rorty are aiming at when they declare that truth is not a norm, and not a goal of belief or of inquiry. For what the remarks above suggest is that it is not simply truth *in general* which interests us, but, so to say, *interesting* or *relevant* truth. And, to pursue this line, what kinds of truth are interesting depends upon our explanatory interests, which may vary from context to context. In some contexts, certain truths are interesting or valuable, and should be attended to, and others are not, and are not worthy of consideration (for instance a climber will be interested in the truth that the rock on which he is leaning is friable, but a tourist who contemplates the cliff from below has no such interest). We are not interested in truth as such, but in *knowledge*, in so far as knowledge is relative to our human interests (just as we are not interested in believing any truth whatsoever, we are not interested in knowing anything whatsoever). And in so far as knowledge is justified true belief (whatever that means), what we are interested in is, as Davidson says, 'honest justification'.

On this much, then, and in so far as the notion of 'norm' is cashed out in such conditionals as (2) or (5), I quite agree with Davidson and Rorty that truth is not a norm, in any interesting or important sense. But is this the sense which we want to put forward when we say that truth is a constitutive norm of belief, or a norm of assertoric practice? Certainly it is false to say that 'belief aims at truth' if truth is conceived as the goal, conscious or not, of belief, or as a form of obligation to believe everything that is true. But this is not what one ordinarily means when one says that truth is the norm of belief. What one means, rather, is that the concept of truth is constitutive of the concept of belief, in the following sense: if one has good reasons (is justified) to believe that P, then one has thereby good reasons (is justified) to believe that P is true. The concept of truth goes with the concept of good reason, or of justification for belief. Reason or justification for belief is reason or justification for *truth*. Certainly saying that a belief is justified does not entail that it is true, and justification is not truth, but saying that a belief is justified is *a prima facie* reason for thinking that it is true.

Now the concepts of 'reason', of 'good reason', or of 'justification' are certainly normative concepts, if there are any. They are relevant to whether it is *correct* to believe something. So we can try to cash it out in terms of conditionals of the preceding form. But (to use only deontic concepts of the first type) the correct form of the conditional should not be (2) or (5) but the following :

(6)   For any P, one ought to believe that P only if P.

And this makes perfectly respectable sense. The claim is not, like (5), that if something is true then one ought to believe it, but that one ought to believe only what is true. This does not have the implication that we should believe everything that is true. This imperative, in a sense, is quite obvious, for it amounts to saying that claims to belief are claims to *true* beliefs. It is in this sense that truth is the fundamental norm of belief, since someone who would not recognize the truth of this imperative would not understand the very concept of belief.

But here again, one may object that it is not right. May it not be the case that someone can find it valuable, desirable, or even pressing or obligatory, to believe something that is false and that he recognizes as such? After all, cases of self-deception, as they are analyzed by Davidson (1985) are precisely cases where an agent believes that P is false but nevertheless believes that P, as a result of his desiring or wanting to believe that P. And the self-deceived person seems to reach the latter belief on the basis of some action that he performs. We could add, in the vein of James' *Will to Believe* that there are cases where it may be desirable to believe things that one believes to be false, if it is otherwise desirable, or useful to believe such things, in spite of all the evidence that one has against their truth, or in spite of having insufficient evidence for believing them. And a 'pragmatist' of the Rortyan stripe would certainly press this point.

Such cases, or such *prima facie* exceptions, might well be exceptions to the claim that truth is the goal of belief, or that, in *this* (intentional) sense belief 'aims at truth'. If we agree with James that truth in itself may sometimes not be valuable, or that the epistemic value of truth may be overridden by other personal or subjective values that an agent happens to have, or that epistemic reasons alone may not be sufficient for belief, or that there may be advantages to willful belief, then certainly one will not agree that truth is a norm of belief in the sense of an exceptionless goal. So I grant to Rorty, and to Davidson – if such considerations underlie his claim – that *in this sense* truth is not uncontroversially a norm of belief or of assertion.

But once again, this is not the sense in which I want to claim that truth is a norm. The fact that truth is a constitutive norm of belief, in the sense that I intend to promote, is in no way refuted by the fact that we may sometimes (and possibly justifiably so) want to believe what is not true, and succeed in doing so. The point is familiar from discussions about the possibility of believing 'at will'.[8] Suppose that someone wants to believe that, say, the Dalai Lama is a Living God, because he has a special interest in believing this (he praises the value of religious belief, or he is paid a large sum of money for believing this), and moreover that he succeeds in acquiring this belief (admittedly not immediately, 'just like that', but by some indirect means, such as a drug or self-indoctrination). But he could not at the same time want to believe that the Dalai Lama is a Living God *and* succeed in performing an action which would result in his believing this, for the very fact that he wants to believe this shows that he *does* not believe

---

[8] I have reviewed these arguments, which stem from Williams 1971, in Engel 1999a.

it in the first place. Hence, if he succeeds, he would be in a state both of believing that the Dalai Lama is not a living God and (as a result of his success in realizing what he wants) of believing that the Dalai Lama is a Living God. The situation is reminiscent of Moore's paradox and of the case of self-deception (although I am not saying that wishful thinking and self deception are the same). Whether or not someone can succeed in being in such states, and whatever is their proper etiology, the reason why they are paradoxical and the reason why we hesitate to attribute to the agent both the belief that P and the belief that not P is that when someone has a belief that P, he thereby has the belief that P *is true*. If he comes to believe (consciously, at the same time) that his belief that P is false, then either he does not have either one belief, or he is not really, with respect to these contents, in a state of belief. So even someone who, for any reason, is not moved by an interest for truth, or who rejects the idea that it can be a goal for his beliefs, has to recognize that truth is what his beliefs are aiming at, *in virtue of their being beliefs*. Otherwise he does not understand the very concept of belief, or us, the ascribers, are at a loss in attributing to him such a state. Deciding to believe what is false is to undermine the very possibility of believing.

This is the sense in which we are entitled to say that truth is a norm of belief, and that 'beliefs aim at truth'. Although it can be formulated in terms of 'oughts' like in (6) this norm is not a norm in the deontic or in the evaluative sense: rather it is definitional of the state of belief and of our concept of this state. The same point is often put by saying that beliefs have a certain 'direction of fit' ('mind to world') and that desires have an opposite direction of fit ('world to mind'). This is why there is no corresponding norm for desires: having a desire carries no implication that the desire should be satisfied. I am claiming that it is what grounds the truth of conditionals such as (6). And the important point is that this norm is in place even when one does *not* take truth to be a goal of our inquiries, or of science, or whatever. It is essential to what we understand by the notion of belief. It is a *conceptual* norm.

Does the recognition of this norm entail, as Rorty thinks (1995:298), that truth itself is the 'fixed' goal of inquiry, and that we should subscribe to the metaphysical (realist) picture which underlies this view? No, for it is one thing to say that our concept of belief is such that they *purport* to be true, and quite another thing to say that there really *is* something in which their truth consists, a sort of real essence underlying all our belief claims.[9]

---

[9] Cf. Wright 1996:914: 'It is one thing for an expression to be used in the making of a distinctive kind of normative judgment; quite another matter for there to be such a thing as a bearer *really deserving* a judgment of that kind'.

In this respect I do not see why the notion of a norm of truth, in the sense defended here, would be inconsistent with a minimalist conception of truth. For a minimalist conception says that we cannot define truth through some explanatory or essential feature over and above the platitudes which characterize this concept. And the idea that truth is a norm of belief *is* such a platitude, although it is an important one.

The upshot of this is that there are, with respect to truth, two quite different notions of norm: a conceptual norm, which goes with the notion of belief, and perhaps with the concept of assertion,[10] and a cognitive norm, which has to do not with what belief is, but with the value or with the requirements of belief. I have claimed that there is no reason to think that admission of the first norm automatically entails admission of the second, in the sense in which truth would be the general goal of inquiry, and *vice versa*. But the fact that these notions are different should not lead us to think that they are unconnected, and that what I have called the conceptual norm of truth does not underlie the cognitive norm of truth. For suppose that one says, like Davidson, that what we aim at is not truth, but justification, whatever way we are to analyze justification (as evidential support, probabilistic nor not, or as coherence, or reliability, and so forth). If this is so, we ought to believe that P only if P is justified, or is believable to a high degree, etc. But I do not see how our grounds for taking P to be justified could not be also grounds for taking P to be true, even if it turns out that P is not true. Justification and truth are not the same thing, but it is difficult to see how aiming at the first would not be aiming at the second. More, of course, is needed in order to establish that truth is the main, or the only, cognitive value, and that a form of pragmatism which, like Rorty's, flatly denies this, is false. But this form of pragmatism seems to me to be self-defeating when it denies that truth is a norm of belief.

---

[10] I say 'perhaps' because I do not want to commit myself fully to Wright's view that truth is a norm of 'assertoric practice', and to the linguistic expression of belief, but only to the corresponding claim about belief and thought. It is not clear that there is a norm of asserting what is true in the same sense as the one in which there is a norm of believing what is true. Lying does not undermine the possibility of assertion as deciding to believe what is false undermines the possibility of belief. (I am here again indebted to Paul Boghossian).

References

Blackburn, S. and Simmons, K. eds. 1999. *Truth*. Oxford: Oxford University Press.

Boghossian, P. 2000. The Normativity of Content. Paper read at the Summer School on Normativity and reason, Parma, July 2000, unpublished.

Davidson, D. 1985. Deception and Division. *Actions and events: Perspectives on the Philosophy of Donald Davidson*, eds. E. Lepore and B. McLaughlin, 138-48. Oxford: Blackwell.

Davidson, D. 1990. The Structure and Content of Truth. *Journal of Philosophy* 87:279-328.

Davidson, D. 1996. The Folly of Trying to Define Truth. *Dialogue and Universalism 6:39-53*. Reprinted in *Journal of Philosophy* 94:263-78. Reprinted in Blackburn, S. and Simmons, K. eds. 1999, 308-22. Page references to the second reprint.

Davidson, D. 1999. Reply to Pascal Engel. *The Philosophy of Donald Davidson* ed. L. Hahn. La Salle: Open Court 1999:460-61.

Dummett, M. 1959. Truth. Proceedings of the Aristotelian Society, LIX, 141-62. Reprinted in *Truth and Other Enigmas*, 1978m 1-24. London: Duckworth.

Engel, P. 1991. *The Norm of Truth*. Hemel Hemstead: Harvester Wheatsheaf and University of Toronto Press.

Engel, P. 1999a. Volitionism and Voluntarism about Belief. *Belief, Cognition and the Will*, ed. A. Meijers, 9-25. Tilburg: Tilburg University Press.

Engel, P. 1999b. The Norms of the Mental. *The Philosophy of Donald Davidson*. L. Hahn, ed, 447-59. La Salle: Open Court.

Engel, P. 2000. Wherein lies the Normative Dimension in Mental Content? *Philosophical Studies* 100:305-21.

Engels, P. Forthcoming. Intentionality, Normativity and Community.

Hornsby, J. 1997. Truth: the identity theory. *Proceedings of the Aristotelian Society* XCVII:1-24.

Horwich, P. 1990. *Truth*. Oxford: Oxford University Press.

Horwich, P. 1998. *Meaning*. Oxford: Oxford University Press.

Rorty, R. 1986. Pragmatism, Davidson and Truth. *Truth and Interpretation*, ed. E. LePore, 333-55. Oxford: Blackwell.

Rorty, R. 1995. Is Truth a Goal of Inquiry? Davidson vs. Wright. *Philosophical Quarterly* 45:281-300.

Stich, S. 1990. *The Fragmentation of Reason*. Cambridge, Mass.: MIT Press.

Williams, B. 1973. Deciding to Believe. *Problems of the Self*, 136-51. Cambridge: Cambridge University Press.

Wright, C. 1992. *Truth and Objectivity*. Cambridge, Mass.: Harvard University Press.

4

Dreams and Nightmares: Conventions, Norms, and Meaning in Davidson's Philosophy of Language

KATHRIN GLÜER

1 Introduction

Donald Davidson has famously denied that linguistic communication requires convention. At the same time, the philosophy of language has been echoing with the Kripkean slogan 'meaning is normative'. Rarely, however, have the two claims been brought together.[1] The issue here is lexical or semantic normativity, and while I agree with Davidson's view that communication neither requires the conventional assignment of the *same* meanings across speakers and times, nor individually over time, I also think that such Davidsonian anti-conventionalism leaves open a more basic question about meaning determination. If we look at recent discussions about the so-called normativity of meaning, it might seem as if the relation between the meaning of an expression and its use might be determined by norm or convention even if conventional assignment of the *same* meaning over time is not required. I am going to argue, however, that this is not the case; on a Davidsonian account of meaning, there is no room for the so-called normativ-

---

[1] Exceptions are Davidson 1992 and Bilgrami 1992, 1993.

ity of meaning. Moreover, or so I am going to suggest, it is a mistake to conceive of this relation as essentially normative at all.

I shall proceed as follows. In the second section, I shall give a sketch of Davidsonian anti-conventionalism and its underlying approach to linguistic meaning. In the third section, I shall present such readings of the normativity thesis as would *prima facie* be tenable even in the face of Davidsonian anti-conventionalism. The normativity thesis usually runs two claims of normative determination together that it is helpful to distinguish: These are the claim that meaning has normative consequences for the use of expressions and the claim that meaning itself is determined normatively, i.e. by rules, conventions, or norms. In sections 4 and 5, I shall discuss the question whether meaning has normative consequences for the use of expressions. Being concerned with semantic normativity, such consequences could either follow directly from meaning (section 4) or be argued for from the idea that meaning itself is normatively determined (section 5). In the last section, I shall make use of Wittgenstein's own analogy with games to suggest that it is a mistake to conceive of the relation between meaning and use as essentially determined by norms or conventions at all; the meaningful use of linguistic expressions lacks characteristic features required of activities essentially governed by rules or norms.

2   Davidson's Anti-Conventionalism

In 'Communication and Convention', Davidson quotes David Lewis, who wrote: 'It is a platitude – something only a philosopher would dream of denying – that there are conventions of language' (Lewis 1975:7). But isn't that really one of the secret dreams of any philosopher: To show that something everybody thought was too trivial to dispute actually is highly problematic? In 'Communication and Convention' and subsequent writings, Davidson made such a dream come true.

What Davidson tries to make us see is that it is anything but a platitude that there are, or have to be, conventions of language. Rather, this is a philosophical thesis loaded with theoretical content. To expose the supposed platitude not only as highly theoretical, but moreover as false, Davidson suggests two seemingly slight but actually momentous modifications to our basic approach to language. First, he shifts the focus of attention from the concept of *a language* to that of *communication by language*. What we have to realize when we take this stance is the great deal of abstraction implicit in even the seemingly most innocent talk about meaning and language. Not only is it highly theoretical to talk about the meanings of words but the same goes for the meanings of sentences: 'In the end', Davidson says, 'the sole source of linguistic meaning is the intentional production of tokens of sentences. If such acts did not have meanings nothing would' (Davidson 1993:298). What is meaningful, that is to say, are utterances, i.e. particular actions by particular speakers at particular times. And even at this characterization, we must not stop. For the concept of meaning itself is a theoretical concept. 'The notion of meaning', Davidson says elsewhere, 'depends entirely upon successful cases of communication' (Davidson and Glüer 1995:81). Meaning, therefore, is of a fundamentally intersubjective nature; what is meaningful is first and foremost utterances whose intended meaning is actually understood by their interpreter. It is successful communication that concepts like meaning, language, word or sentence are used to explain.

The second step, then, is to identify the philosophical nature of such explanation. To be philosophically interesting, the 'conventional platitude' needs to be invested with a certain necessity; it needs to be read as the claim that communication by language is *essentially* conventional. The philosophically interesting question here is not the empirical one of whether people in fact talk to each other in fairly conventional ways; rather, the question is whether conventions are necessary for communication by language.

As is well known, Davidson answers this question by arguing that 'convention does not help explain what is basic to linguistic communication' (Davidson 1982:280) regardless of the theoretical level at which convention is supposed to do its work. Here, however, we shall look at the lexical or semantic level only. Davidson himself considers the question whether 'the meaning of a word is conventional, that is, that it is a convention that we assign the meaning we do to individual words and sentences when they are uttered or written' (Davidson 1982:276). From a Davidsonian point of view, it clearly is not necessary for communication that there are *shared* conventions governing the assignment of meanings to words (and sentences). That is, for two speakers communicating with each other, it is not necessary that there is a convention assigning the *same* meaning to an expression regardless of which of the speakers utters it. It is not necessary that there is a convention to this effect since it is not necessary that the same meaning is assigned to an expression across speakers at all, no matter what the nature of the assignment is. All that matters for successful communication is that, regarding a specific utterance, the hearer assigns the meaning that the speaker intended.

Neither is it necessary that there is a convention to assign the same meaning to an expression whenever a particular speaker utters it. What the speaker intends the hearer to interpret him as meaning with a particular expression does not have to be the same whenever he utters it. On a Davidsonian account, such variation in literal meaning is perfectly possible as long as the hearer can plausibly be expected to understand what the speaker is doing. Understanding and being understood, on such an account, are holistic enterprises in which the parameters meaning, belief, desire and intention are mutually interdependent. Understanding and making oneself understood, in other words, involve too many interdependent parameters for it to be necessary that the connection between expression and meaning be held stable by convention. And again, that convention is not necessary follows, on this account, from it not being necessary that that connection be stable at all, no matter how stability might be effected.[2]

However, conventionality of this type shall not be my main topic here. What I am interested in is not so much the question whether there have to be conventions to the effect that the *same* meaning is to be assigned to expressions, regardless of whether across speakers and times or individually over time. It seems to me, for Davidsonian reasons, that that is not the case, but I also think that this leaves open a more basic question about meaning determination and conventions. For even if conventions to the effect of assigning the *same* meaning to an expression over time are not necessary for communication, it might still be the case that meaning is determined by convention.

3   Is Meaning Normative?

At this point, I think, it is instructive to bring in recent discussions about the so-called *normativity* of meaning. That meaning is normative has these days become as natural a platitude as conventionalism once was. This undoubtedly is due to Kripke and the rule-following boom his *Wittgenstein* initiated in the recent philosophy of language. Nabokov once called 'numbers and rows and series – the nightmare and malediction harrowing pure thought' (Nabokov 1969:450); and Kripke's meaning skeptic may provide an illustration of what he might have had in mind in saying this. Normativity, however, is part of what Kripke describes as our intuitive conception of meaning, moreover, normativity is that part of this conception that he ultimately makes responsible for the alleged impossibility of meeting the skeptic's demands; normativity, thus, is the ultimate reason for nightmares here.[3] Commentators accordingly agree that normativity is an essential feature of meaning and has to be part of any straight solution to Kripke's prob-

---

[2] Note, however, that anti-conventionalism does not have to take this form. For even if regular assignment of meaning would be necessary for communication, be it across times or across times and speakers, there would still be room for denying the essentially conventional nature of the regularity.

[3] Thus Kripke about the 'various philosophical theories as to what the fact that I meant plus might consist in. There will be many specific objections to these theories. But all fail to give a candidate for a fact as to what I meant that would show that only "125", not "5" is the answer I "ought" to give' (Kripke 1982:11).

lem. Apart from that, however, there is considerable lack of agreement about what the normativity of meaning might exactly amount to.

Still, most of its proponents seem to agree on the following: The normativity of meaning resides in the relation between the meaning of an expression and its use. This relation is one of normative determination in a double sense: It combines the idea that meaning has normative consequences for the use of expressions with the idea that meaning itself is determined normatively, i.e. by rule, convention or norm. On a use-conception of meaning, meaning determining norms simply *are* norms for the use of expressions, that is, they do double duty: they determine both the use of an expression *and*, thereby, what meaning it has. Thus, two relations of determination fuse into the two directions of an equivalence relation. In assessing the normativity thesis, however, the distinction should not be forgotten.

Proponents of the normativity of meaning often take for granted that such norms require regular use over time, that is, that they require use of the same expression according to the same rule over time, but this does by no means follow immediately. The idea to be pursued here, then, is the following: Even if there don't have to be conventions of using expressions with the same meaning over time or across speakers, it might still be the case that there have to be conventions (or other norms) determining how to use an expression *if* it has or is intended to have a particular meaning (at a particular time and for a particular speaker).

Let's start by casting a look at that passage in Kripke that has become the *locus classicus* of the normativity thesis in recent literature. Kripke says:

> Suppose I do mean addition by '+'. What is the relation of this supposition to the question how I will respond to the problem '68 + 57'? The dispositionalist gives a *descriptive* account of this relation: if '+' meant addition, then I will answer '125'. But this is not the proper account of the relation, which is *normative*, not descriptive. The point is *not* that, if I meant addition by '+', I *will* answer '125', but that, if I intend to accord with my past meaning of '+', I *should* answer '125'. (...) The relation of meaning and intention to future action is *normative*, not *descriptive* (Kripke 1982:37).

In the context of our discussion, a couple of points should be noted: First of all, the normativity thesis here is formulated in terms of the individual speaker. So far, nothing is presupposed about what his speech community means by the plus-sign. So far, that is, there is no conflict with the Davidsonian claim that meaning does not presuppose *shared* languages, conventions or rules. Secondly, the proviso in the formulation of normativity needs to be noted: '*if I intend to accord with my past meaning of* "+", I should answer "125"'. The normativity that Kripke initially invokes places no restrictions on what a speaker intends to mean by some specific expression, but tells him what to do *if* he has a certain intention. The norm here is, in Kantian terms, a 'hypothetical norm'. So far, therefore, there is no conflict with the Davidsonian claim that a speaker under certain conditions very well might intend to mean something idiosyncratic by a certain expression. And thirdly, Kripke makes an interesting connection in summing up his normativity thesis: 'The relation of meaning *and intention* to future action is normative'. This can be read in two ways: either, he is saying that both meaning and intention are normative for future action, or else it is meaning *in combination* with intention that is normative. If we take the proviso seriously, only the last interpretation makes sense.

Thus, the relation Kripke is characterizing as normative seems to fit nicely with what we were looking for: It is a relation between expressions, the meaning a speaker intends them to have at a time and their use at that time.[4] Moreover, the normativity Kripke is talking about derives from the intended meaning itself; it does not need any other source. To see how exactly normativity might be seen to derive from (intended) meaning, it is instructive to look at Boghossian's reconstruction of Kripkean normativity.[5] Boghossian argues as follows:

> Suppose the expression 'green' means *green*. It follows immediately that the expression 'green' applies *correctly* only to *these* things (the green ones) and not to *those* (the non-greens). The fact that the expression means something implies, that is, a whole set of *normative* truths about my behaviour with that expression: namely, that my use of it is correct in application to certain objects and not in application to others. This is (...) a relation between meaning something by it at some time and its *use at that time* (Boghossian 1989:513).

According to this reading, the normativity of meaning 'turns out to be (...) simply a new name for the familiar fact that, regardless of whether one thinks of meaning in truth-theoretic or assertion theoretic terms, meaningful expressions possess conditions of correct use' (Boghossian 1989:513).

Now, it is hardly deniable that meaningful expressions do possess such conditions. If Boghossian is right, however, then it is equally undeniable that meaning is normative; the one cannot be divorced from the other. That

---

[4] Much of this changes with the skeptical solution. In particular, meaning loses its individuality and becomes a community affair instead. Accordingly, what is salvaged of the initial normativity becomes a matter of community-wide *regularity* over time. But I shall not be concerned with the skeptical solution here.

[5] Kripke himself characterizes this normativity in a rather mystifying variety of ways; he for instance describes it in terms of 'justification' (1982:11), of telling the speaker what to do (1982:24), of what one 'should' do or 'ought to' do, and what one is 'compelled' (1982:11) or what it is 'inevitable' (1982:40) to do. How all this is supposed to go together, he does not tell us, however; there seems to be tension at least between the ideas that what follows from the intended meaning is how one *should* use an expression and the idea that, given the intended meaning and some other conditions, it is *inevitable* to use it in a certain way. For more discussion see Glüer 1999a, chapter 4, and Glüer 1999b.

meaning is normative, or so Boghossian suggests, simply means that conditionals like the following are true:

(G)   For any speaker s, and any time t: if 'green' means *green* for s at t, then it is correct for s to apply 'green' to an object x iff x is green at t.

Again, the relation that is characterized as normative fits nicely with what we are looking for; it is a relation between expression, meaning and use at a time and for a speaker and, moreover, it is clear that correctness conditions are determined by meaning. What is less clear, however, is in what sense, if any, conditionals like (G) are normative.

As stressed above, this question can be read in two different ways. These are usually combined, and, possibly therefore, not always sufficiently distinguished. On the first reading, the question would be whether (G), by itself, has normative consequences for the use of 'green', given that 'green' means *green*. Both Kripke and Boghossian answer this question in the affirmative; both quite naturally proceed to interpret correct use in deontological terms as use that *should* or *ought to* be made of the expression. More generally, the question is whether any hypothetical imperatives and/or evaluations of actions in a strong, normative sense immediately follow from conditionals like (G). In other words: Do they, by themselves, have any action-guiding or action-appraising force?

On the second reading, meaning itself is determined normatively, that is, the relation between the meaning of an expression and its use, here, its correct use, is conceived of as established by norm or convention. This question can be put in terms of *truth or validity*; is (G) true because there is a norm or convention to that effect? Note, that an affirmative answer to the first question does not imply an affirmative answer to the second. Even if hypothetical imperatives or appraisals were to be derived from (G), this would not necessarily mean that (G) itself was 'true by convention'. Note, too, that the converse does not hold, either; even if (G) was true by convention, it would not follow that it, by itself, had to have any action-guiding or action-appraising force. I think that both claims actually are false; conditionals like (G) are neither true by convention nor do they have any purely semantic action-guiding or action-appraising force. I shall argue against these claims in reversed order. In the next section, I shall take issue with the idea that possession of correctness conditions *directly* implies normative consequences. In section 5, possible arguments for the normative force of correctness conditions from the idea that meaning is, or has to be, determined by rule or convention will be discussed. And in section 6, I shall mobilize Wittgenstein's own analogy with games to argue that conditionals like (G) are not true or valid by rule or convention.

4 Correctness and Deontology

Do correctness conditions directly imply normative consequences? I shall mainly discuss this claim in its prevalent deontological form; however, as will be noted later, the main results of this discussion apply to a reading in terms of strong evaluation or appraisal as well.

On the suggested reading of the normativity thesis, normativity resides in the incontrovertible fact that meaningful expressions possess conditions of correct application. Simon Blackburn once put this as follows: 'The topic is that there is such a thing as the correct and incorrect application of a term, and to say that there is such a thing is no more than to say that there is truth and falsity. (...) It is not seriously open to a philosopher to deny that, in this minimal sense, there is such a thing as correctness and incorrectness' (1984:281f). That is surely true. However, normative consequences can only be derived on the following additional assumption: 'It is an essentially normative judgment that we are chasing. It is the judgment that something is correct or incorrect' (Blackburn 1984:286f). And this, it seems to me, is perfectly controvertible, not the least so where semantic evaluation is concerned.

Correct use, on this reading, is *semantically* correct use. What semantically correct use amounts to, however, depends on the choice of basic semantic concept. If it is truth, semantically correct use is true use, if it is justification, it is justified use. (G) is formulated in terms of 'correctness' precisely in order to be neutral between these options; 'correct' here is some kind of variable, to be replaced by your favored basic semantic concept. Read as a 'normative' truth, however, 'correctness' in (G) is understood not only as a semantic, but also as an already *deontologically contentful* concept. This might well be owing to equivocation.

Conditions of semantic 'correctness' are first and foremost conditions for the application of the basic semantic concept. They make semantic evaluation possible, but what needs to be noted here is that, as far as semantics is concerned, this does not have to mean anything beyond the possibility of *categorizing* utterances, of *sorting* them into true (or justified) and false ones. That we also tend to view truth or justification as values is a different matter; since we do not do that for semantic reasons it needs to be abstracted from in our context. In consequence, however, talk of 'correctness conditions' might turn out to be deontologically completely innocent as far as semantics is concerned. What should be clear, therefore, is that normative consequences do not follow *directly* from correctness conditions. Additional argument is needed to show that semantically correct use at the same time already is prescribed use; what is lacking so far is precisely the *source* of this supposed prescriptive force.

It should also be clear that any step from correctness conditions to evaluations in a strong sense, i.e. to appraisals or real value judgments, is as indirect and in need of motivation as that from correctness conditions to prescriptions. No doubt, we do tend to conceive of semantic correctness as a value, but for merely semantic purposes, values are not required. What semantic 'evaluation' does require is semantic categorization, and in this normatively innocent sense we could, if we like, call (G) a 'standard of correctness'. What we must not forget, however, is that in this sense, *any* concept is a standard of correctness. The 'standards' of semantic evaluation therefore could be completely without normative consequences; semantic evaluation does not necessarily come in a package with action-guidance or action-appraisal.

5   Whence Normative Force?

The next question to consider is whether the missing normative force could be derived from the idea that the prescriptions or strongly evaluative standards in question are themselves what determines meaning, from a combination, that is, of both readings of the normativity thesis.

The first point to note is that prescriptive force cannot be derived by considerations like the following: (G) tells us how to use 'green' in order to mean *green* by utterances of 'green'. It doesn't. We don't have to *follow* (G) in order to mean *green* by 'green'. It is perfectly possible to mean *green* by 'green' and to apply it incorrectly at the same time; otherwise, any semantically incorrect application would have been turned into a change or loss of meaning. It would not even be possible to use 'green' for the expression of an empirical mistake, and, consequently, 'green' would have lost its correctness conditions, would have lost its meaning.[6]

However, the defender of meaning determining imperatives does not have to identify semantically correct use with use with a specific meaning. Thus, Sellars once remarked, only seemingly paradoxically, that 'ordinary empirical judgments can be correctly made without being true' (Sellars 1956:166). And we find the same point in Moore: 'It is obvious that you may use language just as correctly when you use it to assert something false as when you use it to assert something true' (Moore 1954:80). Both obviously do not identify the correctness they are after with semantic correctness. However, we do not have to bring two different notions of correctness into play, and if we are interested in saving meaning determining imperatives, imperatives, that is, that determine the conditions of semantic correctness, refraining from this seems wise. Instead, we can distinguish be-

---

[6] For this, I have argued in more detail in Glüer 1999b.

tween *following* a rule and its being *valid*. This, moreover, seems entirely natural; the idea of violating a rule depends just as much on its nevertheless being valid as the idea of saying something empirically false depends on one's words nevertheless retaining their meaning.

Based on this distinction, the defender of meaning determining imperatives could argue that the meaning of the expression 'green' could well be determined by a prescription like the following:

(PG)   Apply 'green' to objects iff they are green.

This prescription would not have to be followed in order to mean *green* by 'green'; rather, 'green' would mean *green* exactly as long as (PG) is *valid* or *'in force'* for a speaker.[7] Other questions regarding the possibility of prescriptions to utter nothing but truths aside,[8] the main problem with this suggestion in our context is that it does not seem necessary that meaning is determined this way. Of course, if (PG) is valid or in force, then 'green' is correctly applied to objects iff they are green. But why should the converse hold? In order for semantic evaluation of utterances of 'green' as meaning *green* to be possible,

(CG)   It is correct to apply 'green' to an object x iff x is green

has to be *true,* but so far, nothing has been done to show that (CG) has to be true because (PG) is in force.[9]

It is in Dummett that we find passages out of which an argument to this effect can be reconstructed, an argument to the effect that there would not be any correctness conditions if speakers did not have a 'prescriptive attitude' towards the language they are speaking. He writes:

> [A]ny speaker beyond the initial stages of mastering language must have some conception of what language he is speaking and hold himself responsible to that. (...) Using language and playing a game are not like doing one's hair and taking a bath. One may do either of the last two things as one likes and still be doing it. But, if the game ceases to have rules, it ceases to be a game, and, if there cease to be right and wrong uses of a word, the word loses its meaning (Dummett 1991:85).

Reconstructed in our terms, Dummett is not claiming that words must be used correctly in order to have meaning, but that they would not even have correctness conditions if correct uses would not be regarded as prescribed by the speakers. Thus, no correctness conditions without prescriptions regarded to be in force by their subjects. But why?

---

[7] This suggestion is due to Peter Pagin. See Pagin 1987. See also Glüer and Pagin 1999.

[8] But see Glüer 1999b and Wikforss 2001 on this.

[9] Again, it should be clear that the same holds for the idea that (CG) is true because a strongly evaluative standard for the appraisal of applications of 'green' to green objects is in force.

Dummett again: 'The paradoxical character of language lies in the fact that while its practice must be subject to standards of correctness, there is no ultimate authority to impose these standards from without' (Dummett 1991:85). The standards of semantic correctness, Dummett seems to be saying, are, somehow or other, of our own making; language is paradoxical in the sense that we, by practicing it, at the same time set the standards for practicing it. Their validity depends on our attitude towards them, and if we didn't regard them with a prescriptive attitude, they would vanish or change. On the basis of what we have argued so far, we can distinguish two steps in this line of argument: Dummett claims, first, that the standards of semantic correctness are set by us, and that that means that they are valid by norm or convention. And, second, that these norms or conventions have to be prescriptions.

However, Dummett's first claim does not sufficiently motivate the second; even if we agree that language is paradoxical in Dummett's sense, the 'standards' of semantic correctness might, as far as semantics is concerned, still be merely classificatory. Of course, one might challenge the claim that it is us who conventionally set the correctness conditions for our concepts, and I shall do so in the next section. What interests us here, however, is that even if this were true, there still would be no argument for the claim that correctness conditions have to be set by prescriptions (or, for that matter, strongly evaluative standards). Conventional agreement on the truth of merely classificatory claims would seem to be at least as good a candidate. Before we go on, I would therefore like to inspect one last argument for the essential prescriptivity of semantic correctness, an argument to the effect that even classificatory standards would not be valid unless they were, by and large, actually followed.

Above, we made much of the fact that an expression like 'green' does not necessarily have to be applied correctly in order to express the concept *green* with it. But from this it does of course not follow that 'green' could *always* be applied incorrectly without losing this meaning. Arguing in a familiar Davidsonian way, this does not only not follow, it actually seems false. For if someone apparently never applied an expression correctly, what reason would we have to think that we had even interpreted that expression correctly? Such an outcome would rather give very good reason to think that we had come up with the wrong interpretation, that we had assigned the wrong correctness conditions to that expression as used by our speaker. This is simply part of the *principle of charity* which, in turn, on a Davidsonian account is a condition on the possibility of meaning. Thus, by and large correct use of an expression, correct use, that is, according to the interpretation intended by the speaker, seems to be a condition on that expression's having correctness conditions at all, even though for any particular utterance it holds that it might be incorrect. Davidson himself has in more recent writings been putting considerations like these into terms of 'practices'; he says, for instance: 'meaning something requires that by and large one follows a practice of one's own, a practice that can be understood by others' (Davidson 1994:15f).

Given the obvious Wittgensteinian connotations of the term 'practice', passages like these might seem to support claims to the effect that in order to be interpretable, a speaker *should* use his expressions by and large correctly. Analogously, our claim that the 'standards' of semantic correctness might simply be classificatory, and not prescriptive, could be countered by arguing that unless they were at least by and large actually followed such standards would not even be valid.

This line of argument is mistaken. Consider a Davidsonian model of understanding. Here, it is important to remember the distinction we made at the beginning of this paper, the distinction between requirements to use one's expressions regularly, i.e. with the *same* meaning over time, and requirements as to how to use an expression if it is to have a particular meaning at a particular time. Using an expression by and large correctly means using it by and large correctly with respect to one particular meaning, which, in turn, of course means to use it with the same meaning on all the respective occasions. Thus, it might now seem as if the requirement to use an expression by and large correctly if it is to have particular correctness conditions undermines our distinction, thus overriding earlier anti-conventional arguments to the effect that regularity in the first sense is not necessary for meaning. This, however, is not the case.

On a Davidsonian account, there is no general requirement that any particular expression, if it is intended to have a particular meaning at a particular time, has to be by and large used correctly (with respect to that meaning) over time.[10] It is not even required that it be used over time at all. It might be used only once. It might even be used only once and to express an empirical mistake. Seen from the speaker's side of the interaction, what he can understandably do or what the best means of making the interpreter understand him is, depends on the various other intentional and non-intentional parameters of the situation. These are most radically restricted if I am a 'radical speaker', that is, trying to make myself understood to a radical interpreter. Then, I can be pretty sure that I won't succeed if I frequently try to switch the meanings of the expressions I use. And there will be trouble for the interpreter, too, if I am making tons of empirical mistakes. With an old friend, on the other hand, who knows a lot about me and my odd sense of humor, it might be perfectly reasonable to expect him to come up with the right interpretation even if I use an uncommon expression only once. And this even holds when I use it for expressing an empirical mistake – as long

---

[10] This is also stressed by Bilgrami, see Bilgrami 1993.

as my friend can be expected to know what belief I am expressing. Thus, on a Davidsonian approach, there is no general requirement regarding particular expressions to be derived from the principle of charity.

Secondly, even if this were the case, it would not follow that the speaker *should* use his expressions correctly. It would not follow, in other words, that what is required is not only that an expression actually is used by and large correctly but that this, moreover, has to be the result of following a rule or doing what a prescription requires one to do. Even if regularity in this sense were necessary for meaning, that is, it might be mere regularity in behavior, without being rule-following at all. Thus Davidson asks Dummett: 'what magic ingredient does holding oneself responsible to the usual way of speaking add to the usual way of speaking?' (Davidson 1994:8).

Finally, and quite independently of a Davidsonian approach, it should be noted that for a standard of semantic correctness to be valid or in force it is of course *not* required that the expression it is a standard for is applied by and large correctly. What needs to be applied by and large correctly is the standard itself. What is required therefore is conventional agreement on judgments of semantic correctness and we have found no convincing argument to consider these as judgments with intrinsic normative import for the use of signs. In the next section, I would like to round off this discussion by using Wittgenstein's own game-analogy to suggest that it is a mistake to conceive of the relation of meaning and use as obtaining by norm or convention at all, that it is at least very misleading to spell out what Dummett calls the paradoxical character of language in terms of rules, norms or conventions.

6   Games, Constitutivity and Arbitrariness

Wittgenstein treated activities like applying a predicate with a particular meaning to objects, activities we might well call 'semantic practices' in terms of the game-analogy, that is, as in certain respects analogous to paradigmatically rule-governed activities. I am going to argue, however, that especially if seen in terms of the game-analogy, we find reasons *against* regarding 'semantic practices' as essentially rule-governed activities. They are in illuminating ways like such activities but without themselves literally being such activities.

It is instructive here to look at a characterization of what Wittgenstein calls the 'rules of grammar' from his middle period when he actually did identify using language with using a calculus according to rules. For it is here that he explicitly brings out the specific characteristics that the rules of essentially rule-governed activities possess. And this is, as far as I can see, not a matter about which he changes his mind later. In *Philosophical Grammar*, we for instance find the following:

> Why don't I call cookery rules arbitrary, and why am I tempted to call the rules of grammar arbitrary? Because I think of the concept 'cookery' as defined by the end of cookery, and I don't think of the concept 'language' as defined by the end of language. You cook badly if you are guided in your cooking by rules other than the right ones; but if you follow other rules than those of chess you are playing another game; and if you follow grammatical rules other than such and such ones, that does not mean you say something wrong, no, you are speaking of something else (Wittgenstein 1969a: X, 133).

Games are the paradigm cases of essentially rule-governed of rule-constituted activities. Their rules do not depend on natural laws prior to and independent of anyone's being guided by them in cooking or other activities. On the contrary, the rules of games clearly are 'human creations, made, not found' (Baker and Hacker 1985:63). They are *arbitrary* in just this sense. And we can come up with endlessly many different sets of rules, endlessly many different games; there is nothing like the right game, or the right set of rules. The second main characteristic of essentially rule-governed activities like playing chess is that it not only is impossible to play chess *without rules*, but impossible to play chess without the *rules of chess*. Such activities are *defined or constituted* by their rules; if you change the rules, you automatically change the activity. Taken together, or so I shall argue, these two characteristics, arbitrariness and constitutivity, make it impossible to regard the relation between meaning and use as rule-constituted.

Of course, there is an analogy here; as Wittgenstein says: 'if you follow grammatical rules other than such and such ones, that does not mean you say something wrong, no, you are speaking of something else' (Wittgenstein 1969a: X, 133). What has puzzled commentators about this remark is why Wittgenstein takes a change in rules to amount to talking of something else rather than to playing a different game (cf. e.g. Schulte 1989:116). The upshot of the analogy usually is taken to be this: If you follow rules different from the ones established for your language you speak a different language. It then follows that if you want to speak a specific language, say, English you have to follow the rules for English.

However, this is not the conclusion Wittgenstein himself draws. If he who follows different rules is merely taken to speak a different language it is not at all clear why he automatically would be talking about something different as well. To relinquish the possibility of talking about the same things in different languages that easily would be careless, indeed. But since Wittgenstein emphasizes the difference in what is talked about rather than in the language that is spoken, it looks as if he were concerned with different rules in a deeper sense. A little earlier, Wittgenstein explains the relation a specific expression and the rule for its use stand in as follows: 'without these rules the word has as yet no meaning; and if we change the rules, it now has another meaning (or none), and in that case we may just as well change the word too' (Wittgenstein 1969a: X, 133). Obviously, he does not take rules to be individuated by the expression that is used according to them. Rules therefore cannot be taken to necessarily vary with difference in language where a language consists of a list of words plus rules for their use. In particular, simply exchanging those words for different ones does *not* mean changing the rules. Changing the rule according to which one and the same expression is used, however, does amount to a change in meaning and, in this sense, to talking about something else. In other words, the rules Wittgenstein talks about are not rules for the use of specific signs in a specific language but rules that determine or constitute a relation between a specific meaning, a specific use and any expression whatsoever, given that they are valid for this expression.

For this very reason, neither a prescription like (PG) above, nor a conditional like (CG) can do duty as a meaning constituting norm or standard. Of course, (PG) and (CG) are *arbitrary* insofar as the specific expression they are bound to is arbitrary. Trivially, any other expression whatsoever could have been used for expressing the concept *green*. In our context, however, this is exactly what creates the problem. For even though (PG) or (CG) would confer the meaning *green* upon any sign substituted for 'green', they are bound to 'green'. Therefore, these rules are changed by the substitution of another sign for 'green'. The activity to be constituted, however, the activity of expressing the concept *green* or of meaning *green*, remains the same. Consequently, neither (PG) nor (CG) are constitutive for that activity.

Trying to come back on this by arguing that the constituted activity should not be identified as meaning *green*, but rather as meaning-*green*-by-'green' does not seem helpful. Neither does suggesting meaning-*green*-in-English. Put in terms of the game-analogy, this would be like talking about the rules of chess-played-with-a-specific-set-of-chess-figures. This is clearly not the level at which the analogy is intended or illuminating; given that we can play chess with any set whatsoever (and even without) and that we can express the concept *green* in different languages, the rule we are after is a rule *establishing* a relation between the meaning *green* and the correctness conditions given in (CG) for any sign it is valid for. For remember, this rule is not only to be constitutive, it is also to be *arbitrary*; it must not rely on any relations existing prior to its being valid or in force for any specific sign. Neither (CG) nor (PG) however, do this, and they cannot be made to, either, for they do not tell us anything about the meaning or concept to be expressed. Rather, both (CG) and (PG) presuppose that a determination relation already holds between correctness conditions and meaning.

Rectifying the level on which the rule we are looking for works thus sends us back to

(G)   For any speaker s, and any time t: If 'green' means *green* for s at t, then it is correct for s to apply 'green' to an object x iff x is green at t.

(G) formulates a relation between meaning, expression and correctness conditions that can easily be read in terms of variable expressions and that is clearly constitutive for the activity of expressing the concept *green*. But is (G) arbitrary? A standard true by convention? Does (G)'s validity depend on anyone's attitude towards it, on anyone's putting it into force or regarding it as valid? I tend to think that the answer to these questions is 'no'; relations like the one given in (G) are not arbitrary in any sense that would make it illuminating to conceive of them in terms of norms, rules, or conventions.[11]

In order to see why, we should first try to get a better understanding of what such arbitrariness would exactly amount to. Let's therefore look at the game analogy again and try to understand the sense in which the rules of games are arbitrary. The first thing to note is that arbitrariness must *not* amount to the possibility of *changing* the relation established by the rules as we can, for instance change the law determining the appropriate punishment for murder; it is as impossible to change the rules for moving the

---

[11] Note, that *prima facie* it might look as if a more traditional conception of constitutive rules would not fall prey to these criticisms. According to a tradition having its roots in Wittgenstein, and elaborated especially by philosophers such as Midgley 1959, von Wright 1963, Shwayder 1965 and Searle 1969, constitutive rules are understood as rules for action very different from prescriptions. Such rules, as von Wright puts it, 'neither describe nor prescribe, but determine something' (von Wright 1963:6), for instance *what it is* to play a certain game. According to Searle, their typical form is this:

(S) Doing X in context C counts as doing Y (Searle 1969:35).

Such rules do not tell us what we *should* do; rather, they tell us *how* to perform an action of a specific type in a specific context. Applied to meaning, such a rule would tell us, for instance, that

(SG) Uttering 'green' in C counts as expressing the concept *green*.

However, even though rules like (SG) bring in the concept to be expressed, they are clearly bound to particular expressions, and, therefore, not constitutive of the activity of expressing the concept in question. If 'red' was substituted for 'green' in (SG), and (SG) true or valid, the rule would have changed, but not the activity constituted; then, uttering 'red' would count as expressing the concept *green*. Moreover, rules like (SG) are in fact as guilty of presupposing the relation they are supposed to establish as rules like (CG); for even though (SG) mentions the concept *green* and the use of the expression 'green', the conditions for semantically evaluating such use are not specified. Again, a prior relation between concept or meaning and correctness conditions is presupposed. For more on this, see Glüer 2000.

king of chess, for instance, without thereby changing the game as it is impossible to change correctness conditions without thereby changing meaning. Read thus, no rule could be arbitrary and constitutive with respect to the same type of action at the same time. Moreover, this is exactly what is analogous between rules of games and the relation of meaning to use, as Wittgenstein makes quite clear. Arbitrariness in this respect therefore cannot be what he has in mind when the analogy is tempting him to call the rules of grammar arbitrary. Note, however, that he explicitly calls this a *temptation* – thus strongly suggesting that it should be resisted.

In what sense, then, *are* the rules of games arbitrary? In the passage quoted above, Wittgenstein draws another comparison, a comparison with rules that are *not* arbitrary in the sense he is talking about, the rules of cooking for instance. Rules of cooking are what von Wright later would call 'directives' (von Wright 1963:9ff); directives tell us by what means to reach certain ends given the underlying facts of nature, the underlying natural laws. Directives clearly owe their validity, their action-guiding and action-evaluating force to relations obtaining prior to and independently of any hypothetical imperatives being derived from them: the laws of nature. Such, however, is not the case for the rules of games. They are arbitrary in the sense that their validity does not derive from relations existing prior to and independently of them. And this holds for the rules of games as well as, for instance, the laws of state.

Of course, it is tempting to think analogously about concepts or meanings. They are, after all, *our* concepts, *our* meanings. Nevertheless, I think this is a temptation that should be resisted; if not for Wittgensteinian, then for Davidsonian reasons. The analogy between the rules of games and the basic relations constitutive of our concepts, or so I should like to urge, breaks down in decisive respects: There are different games we can play, but there is only one system of concepts. And, consequently, the rules of games can be 'switched on and off' while those of grammar cannot.

There is no alternative to the rules of chess, we said, if we want to play chess. However, if all we want to do is play some game, there are a lot of games to be chosen between. But from a Davidsonian point of view, there is no alternative to our system of concepts. It does not even make sense to speak of (radically) different systems here (cf. Davidson 1974).[12] From the

---

[12] But doesn't Davidson himself stress the normative nature of meaning or content determination? He says, for instance:

> The reason mental concepts cannot be reduced to physical concepts is the normative character of mental concepts. Beliefs, desires, intentions and intentional actions must, as we have seen, be identified by their semantic contents in reason-explanations. The semantic contents of attitudes and beliefs determine their relations to one another and to the world in ways that meet at least rough standards of consistency and correctness. Unless such standards are met to an adequate degree, nothing can count as being a be-

lief, a pro-attitude, or an intention. But these standards are norms – *our* norms – there being no others (Davidson 1987:46).

It is not completely easy to understand what this talk of norms and normative character exactly amounts to. Discussing the question whether such basic standards or principles are to be considered as normative or descriptive, Davidson doubts 'that there is an interesting way of understanding that distinction' (Davidson 1985a:89) to be drawn in this context; in some respects they are normative, but not in others. Using the example of 'some sentential operator in the speaker's language that when applied to a sentence always converts assent to dissent and vice versa' (Davidson 1985a:91), Davidson says that the interpreter's best guess is to interpret the operator as negation. However, such a principle is *not* normative 'in that no alternative strategy is available for deciding what the speaker means' (ibid.). For an intentional creature, there is no alternative to these basic standards; holding them to be true or valid is a condition on being an intentional creature (cf. Davidson 1985b:351). Moreover, as stressed above, by and large conforming to them is such a condition as well (cf. for instance Davidson 1985a:90). In this respect, the respect salient for my discussion, Davidson thus clearly agrees that these basic standards are not normative.

But then, in what sense are they normative? Interpreting the operator in the example as negation, Davidson goes on to argue, 'is normative in this respect: it imposes a small part of the interpreter's logic on the speaker, for it interprets him as inferring that a sentence is to be held to be false if it is the negation of a sentence held to be true' (Davidson 1985a:91). It is this part that I confess to find difficult to understand. Is the normativity in the imposing? In this case, I don't understand what would be normative about that, given that there is no choice. Or is it that what is imposed on the speaker is acceptance of something normative, i.e. acceptance of a normative standard?

If the latter, what would 'normative' exactly mean here? That the standard has normative consequences for the speaker's judgments? Above, I have argued that conditionals like (G) are not essentially normative in this sense, at least not for reasons of meaning determination. I think that this generalizes to content determination. The principles or basic standards of content determination are not normative in the sense of determining *how to act or judge*. More precisely, they are not normative in this sense exactly *because* they are the basic principles of content determination. In the most basic cases, there simply is *no room* for any norm telling us what to do. Take for instance the belief that a sentence s is true, interpreting ¬ as the negation sign and the belief that ¬s is false. If there were room for a norm here, a norm telling us how we *should* judge or what it is to judge rationally, it would have to be possible to be in the former states without being in the latter. But this is exactly what the basic 'norms' of content determination prevent. Failing to have the last belief is not violating some norm; rather, it is impossible to attribute holding s true to a speaker and interpreting ¬ as the negation sign if he doesn't hold ¬s to be false. That intentional creatures in fact to a very large degree do accord with the basic standards of content determination is a condition on their being intentional creatures, a condition on being able to follow and accept norms, not something induced by the acceptance of basic norms.

Of course, we can say that these principles are 'standards' in the deontologically innocent sense that they determine conditions of correctness, conditions of correct inferring and judging. These are, on a Davidsonian account, as content or meaning determining as conditionals like (G) discussed above, but, as for (G), this does not mean that it follows directly that they are essentially *evaluative in a strong, normative sense*, i.e. in terms of real value judgments, either. As in the case of semantic evaluation, the standards of content evaluation give the conditions of application for basic intentional concepts like rational inference or judgment, and even though we in fact tend to see these as values, these conditions are by no means intrinsically deontological or appraising. For reasons of content determination, this point of view of the radical interpreter, no one can be counted as meaning anything or having any intentional states at all unless these are interpretable in terms of our concepts. Of course, we can discover that a creature lacks certain concepts, but those that it has nevertheless have to be interpretable in terms of ours. Having concepts therefore basically is having our concepts. It is these very concepts that are a condition on having any intentionality, any beliefs, desires, intentions and the means of expressing them through language at all. They are, consequently, also a condition on playing or inventing any games, and a condition on making decisions like the one now to play some chess or to stop playing chess now and play checkers instead. Put in terms of games, there therefore is no sense in which we could play any other 'game' than the intentional; this is the one 'game' we cannot but play, no matter what we do. But then the question is, of course, how illuminating it is to conceive of this as a game at all.[13]

This difference can also be brought out in terms of the validity of the rules in question. Rules of games tell us what to do, they tell us how the king of chess is to be moved, for instance, or that spearing is not allowed in ice-hockey. On the most general level, such rules enable some sort of evaluation or classification of actions; moving the king thus and so is a move allowed in chess, spearing is a violation of the rules of ice-hockey and will be punished, a player's having possession of the ball in the opponent's end zone while a play is in progress is scoring a touchdown in football. Outside the context of the game in question, the rule does not apply; if no game of chess is on, moving *this* little wooden figurine called 'king of chess' does not constitute making a move of chess, no matter whether it is in accordance with the rules or not. Searle once remarked that it is possible that twenty-two men go through all the physical movements as gone through by two teams playing football, but if there were no rules of football, there would be no sense in which their behavior could be described as football. The mere *existence* of the rules, however, is hardly more than a necessary condition for those movements actually being a game of football. Another condition is that a game is actually on. And this can, as Peter Pagin (1987) has suggested, be put in terms of the rule's being in force: A

---

seems superfluous. As far as I can see, there is therefore no good reason, from a Davidsonian point of view, to conceive of the basic constitutive principles or standards of intentionality as norms at all.

[13] Wittgenstein's stand on this issue is not completely easy to understand. Like Davidson, he clearly maintains the necessity of agreement for communication but it is not quite clear whether he excludes the possibility of languages that we could not understand. He e.g. says: 'If a lion could talk, we could not understand him' (Wittgenstein 1953: II, xi). This seems to imply that there could be languages that we cannot understand (see also Wittgenstein 1969b, e.g. 375). However, there are also passages which seem to point in the opposite direction, e.g. Wittgenstein 1953: 207.

game of chess is on if the rules of chess are in force.[14] Deciding to start a game of chess thus can be understood as 'switching on' the rules of chess, as deciding, that is, that they do apply to subsequent relevant actions, for instance, movements of specific wooden figurines on a checkered board. Basic conceptual relations, however, are something that we already have to presuppose if we consider a physical movement as an action at all. Unlike the rules of games, basic conceptual relations cannot be 'switched on or off'. Rather, their validity is a condition on the possibility of meaning and intentionality and, as such, *sui generis*; the basic 'rules of grammar' neither owe their validity to underlying laws of nature as the rules of cooking do, nor are they arbitrary in the sense the rules of chess are.

We have to conclude, I think, that on a Davidsonian account there is no room for the so-called normativity of meaning. Neither have we found good reasons to conceive of meaning as essentially normative at all – neither in the sense of meaning intrinsically having normative consequences for the use of linguistic expressions nor in that of meaning itself being normatively determined. Somewhat ironically, the analogy with games, paradigm cases of essentially rule-governed activities, breaks down at characteristic features of such activities.[*]

References

Baker, G.P. and Hacker, P.M.S. 1985. *Wittgenstein, Rules, Grammar, and Necessity.* Vol. 2 of *An Analytical Commentary on the "Philosophical investigations".* Oxford: Basil Blackwell.

Bilgrami, A. 1992. *Belief and meaning.* Oxford: Basil Blackwell.

Bilgrami, A. 1993. Norms and meaning. In *Reflecting Davidson,* ed. R. Stoecker, 121-44. Berlin/New York: DeGruyter.

Blackburn, S. 1984. The Individual Strikes Back. *Synthese* 58:281-301.

Boghossian, P. 1989. The Rule-following Considerations. *Mind* 98:507-549.

Davidson, D. 1973. Radical Interpretation. *Inquiries into Truth and Interpretation,* 125-39. Oxford: Clarendon Press (1984).

Davidson, D. 1974. On the Very Idea of a Conceptual Scheme. *Inquiries into Truth and Interpretation,* 183-98. Oxford: Clarendon Press (1984).

Davidson, D. 1975. Thought and Talk. *Inquiries into Truth and Interpretation,* 155-70. Oxford: Clarendon Press (1984).

Davidson, D. 1982. Communication and Convention. *Inquiries into truth and interpretation,* 265-80. Oxford: Clarendon Press (1984).

Davidson, D. 1885a. A New Basis for Decision Theory. *Theory and Decision* 18:87-98.

---

[14] For more on this, see also Glüer and Pagin 1999.

[*] For valuable comments on earlier drafts of this paper I would like to thank Åsa Wikforss and Peter Pagin.

Davidson, D. 1985b. Incoherence and Irrationality. *Dialectica* 39:345-355.

Davidson, D. 1986. A Nice Derangement of Epitaphs. *Truth and Interpretation. Perspectives on the philosophy of Donald Davidson*, ed. E. LePore, 433-46. Oxford: Basil Blackwell.

Davidson, D. 1987. Problems in the Explanation of Action. *Metaphysics and Morality*, ed. P. Pettit, R. Sylvan and J. Norman, 35-49. Oxford: Basil Blackwell.

Davidson, D. 1992. The Second Person. *The Wittgenstein Legacy. Midwest Studies in Philosophy*, vol. XVII, ed. P. French, T.E. Uehling, and H. Wettstein, 255-67. Notre Dame, IN: University of Notre Dame Press.

Davidson, D. 1993. Locating Literary Language. *Literary Theory after Davidson*, ed. R. W. Dasenbrock, 295-308. University Park, PA: Pennsylvania State University Press.

Davidson, D. 1994. The Social Aspect of Language. *The Philosophy of Michael Dummett*, ed. B. McGuiness and G. Oliveri, 1-16. Dordrecht: Kluwer Academic Publishers.

Davidson, D. and K. Glüer. 1995. Relations and Transitions. An interview with Donald Davidson. *Dialectica* 49:75-86.

Dummett, M. 1986. 'A Nice Derangement of Epitaphs': Some Comments on Davidson and Hacking. *Truth and interpretation. Perspectives on the Philosophy of Donald Davidson*, ed. E. LePore, 459-76. Oxford: Basil Blackwell.

Dummett, M. 1991. *The Logical Basis of Metaphysics*. Cambridge: Harvard University Press.

Glüer, K. 1999a. *Sprache und Regeln. Zur Normativität von Bedeutung*. Berlin: Akademie Verlag.

Glüer, K. 1999b. Sense and Prescriptivity. *Acta Analytica* 14:111-128.

Glüer, K. 2000. Bedeutung zwischen Norm und Naturgesetz. *Deutsche Zeitschrift für Philosophie* 48:449-68.

Glüer, K. and Pagin P. 1999. Rules of Meaning and Practical Reasoning. *Synthese* 117:207-227.

Kripke, S. 1982. *Wittgenstein on Rules and Private Language*. Cambridge: Harvard University Press.

Lewis, D. 1975. Languages and Language. *Language, Mind, and Knowledge*. Minnesota Studies in the Philosophy of Science 7, ed. K. Gunderson, 3-35. Minneapolis: University of Minnesota Press.

McDowell, J. 1984. Wittgenstein on Following a Rule. *Synthese* 58:325-363.

Midgley, G.C.J. 1959. Linguistic Rules. *Proceedings of the Aristotelian Society* LIX:271-90.

Moore, G.E. 1954. Wittgenstein's lectures in 1930-33. *Mind*:63-64.

Nabokov, V. 1969. *Ada or Ardor: A Family Chronicle*. New York: Vintage.

Pagin, P. 1987. *Ideas for a Theory of Rules*. Doctoral diss., preprint from Stockholm University.

Schnädelbach, H. 1990. Rationalität und Normativität. *Zur Rehabilitierung des animal rationale. Vorträge und Abhandlungen* Vol. 2, 79-103. Frankfurt a. M.: Suhrkamp (1992).

Schulte, J. 1989. *Wittgenstein. Eine Einführung.* Stuttgart: Reklam.

Searle, J. 1969. *Speech Acts. An Essay in the Philosophy of Language.* Cambridge: Cambridge University Press.

Sellars, W. 1956. Empiricism and the philosophy of mind. In *Science, perception and reality*, 127-196. Atascadero, Ca: Ridgeview Publishing Company (repr. 1991).

Shwayder, D. 1965. *The Stratification of Behaviour.* New York: Humanities Press.

Wikforss, Å. 2001. Norms and Dispositions. *Philosophical Studies*, forthcoming.

Wittgenstein, L. 1953. *Philosophische Untersuchungen, Werkausgabe* Vol. 1. Frankfurt a. M.: Suhrkamp (1984).

Wittgenstein, L. 1956. *Bemerkungen über die Grundlagen der Mathematik Werkausgabe* Vol. 6, ed. G. E. M. Anscombe, R. Rhees, and G. H. von Wright. Frankfurt a. M.: Suhrkamp (1984).

Wittgenstein, L. 1969a. *Philosophische Grammatik. Werkausgabe*, Vol. 4, ed. R. Rhees. Frankfurt a. M.: Suhrkamp (1984).

Wittgenstein, L. 1969b. *Über Gewißheit. On Certainty.* Ed. G. E. M. Anscombe and G. H. von Wright, New York: Harper and Row.

von Wright, G. H. 1963. *Norm and Action.* London: Routledge and Kegan Paul.

5

By Quantifying over Events

SAMUEL GUTTENPLAN

1 Introduction

The topic of my paper is the form of words found in such sentences as:

(1)   He poisoned the inhabitants by replenishing their water supply.

(2)   She signaled the troops' arrival by waving her arms above her head.

(3)   Jones ruined his suit by washing it in water.

(4)   Davidson solved the problems of logical inference in respect of action sentences by quantifying over events.

I should like to say that my topic is the form of words:

x Φ-ed by Ψ-ing,

but this would be inaccurate. There is a lot going on in this way of speaking, and any proposal which claims to give a unitary account, much less an 'analysis' of it, seems certain to be mistaken. Or so I shall argue.

'By'-sentences, as I shall call them from now on, have played a complicated role in philosophical and linguistic discussion. Given what is after all only a way of speaking—and one not available in the same form in languages such as French and German—'by'-sentences have been surprisingly prominent. Weaving in and out of metaphysical and semantic discussions of the identity and individuation of events and actions, the 'by'-sentence construction has been taken as evidence in favour of what are otherwise radically opposed positions. Bennett, whose own proposal will be a target of my later remarks, describes it as a 'vigorous and powerful form of speech' (Bennett 1994:29). This is perhaps reasonable given how much of his own view of events he finds supported in his account of the 'by'-locution, but I shall be more cautious. Indeed, I am sufficiently embarrassed by the underlying message of this paper that I feel it best to get it out into the open immediately. Having tried from time to time to get to grips with the 'by'-sentence locution, and not wholly succeeding, I have come to think my partial failure philosophically more important than any success I had originally hoped for. In essence, I shall argue that we can learn more about events and actions, as well as about semantics, from a less than exhaustive account of these sentences, than by any procrustean attempt to give what Bennett is happy to call an 'analysis'.

2

Anscombe never mentions the 'by'-relation in the section of her book *Intention* that is a locus classicus for the so-called *Anscombe–Davidson thesis* about act-identity. The identity thesis insists that, in appropriate circumstances, we can treat different descriptions of actions as in fact different descriptions of one and the same act. And it is surprising that Anscombe does not include the word 'by' when presenting her central example because many have tended to assume that the availability of 'by'-sentences constitutes some kind of support for that thesis. In that now familiar fantasy, she describes someone who aims to poison a group of party chiefs regarded by him as a threat to peace and decency. The poison is slow-acting, certain and undetectable, and the poisoner introduces it into the water supply. For reasons that are never made clear, he then tells what he has done—and why—to the worker whose job it is to pump water supplying the house where the party chiefs are meeting. We are then to imagine that:

> This man's arm is going up and down, up and down. Certain muscles with Latin names which doctors know, are contracting and relaxing. Certain substances are getting generated in some nerve fibres—substances whose generation in the course of voluntary movement interests physiologists (Anscombe 1957:37).

And so on. After a discussion of some other issues, Anscombe comes to ask:

> Are we to say that the man who (intentionally) moves his arm, operates the pump, replenishes the water supply, poisons the inhabitants, is performing *four* actions? Or only one (Anscombe 1957:45)?

Her answer, which I shall not quote in full, is of course that there is only one action which is differently described in each case. However, she reaches this conclusion without ever mentioning the 'by'-relation. She does not say that there is only one action because the agent poisons *by* replenishing, or replenishes *by* pumping or pumps *by* moving his arm, even though, as noted, this use of 'by' is often appealed to in support of the identity thesis. I was at first puzzled by this reticence, but, in due course, I shall suggest what might have been her reason for it.

Davidson, in the other locus classicus of the identity thesis, does actually mention the 'by'-locution, but not in the course of discussing the identity conditions of actions (Davidson 1980). The context is instead his discussion of Kenny's treatment of the variable polyadicity problem (Kenny 1963:ch.VII). Davidson wonders whether there can be any principled way to see action verbs as predicates with an indefinite numbers of places, rather than with some fixed number including agent, patient, time, place, manner and instrument. It would suit his own view if a principled yet indefinite kind of expandability were possible, so he finds congenial Kenny's suggestion that we can appeal to sentences such as:

(5)   Jones buttered the toast by holding it between the toes of his left foot,

to show how to effect such expansion. The idea here is that there seems to be no limit on the kinds of thing that can be introduced by 'by', so we cannot treat 'buttered' as a predicate whose number of places is fixed in advance. However, Davidson is not so sure. He is attracted to the idea, but notes that the 'by'-clause adds a place to the predicate only if it differs in meaning from 'while holding it between his toes' and he adds: 'it is not clear that this is so' (Davidson 1980:107-8).

3

In *A Theory of Human Action*, Goldman is explicit about the 'by'-relation, and his is perhaps the first use of it in connection with the identity thesis (Goldman 1970). But, as is familiar, he appeals to it, not in support of the thesis, but as a knock-down argument against it. The argument is straightforward. First one observes that typical 'by'-sentences do not allow reversal of causal order. Thus, we can say that Jones ruined his suit by washing it, but not that he washed his suit by ruining it. But, according to Goldman, if each side of a 'by'-sentence was merely a different description of one and the same action, then such reversal should both make sense and yield truths. By *reductio*, he concludes that the identity thesis is false.

When I first read this argument of Goldman's its 'mistake' seemed clear, as it had to many other commentators: the 'by'-sentences he cites do indeed seem asymmetrical, but, in them, the preposition 'by' does not relate two expressions which *refer* to events or actions. In particular, the first clause in a 'by'-sentence—the one containing the finite verb phrase—does not even have the appearance of a singular referring term. Indeed, if Davidson is right, this clause has an implicit existential quantifier whose range is events. As to the second, participial clause, things are less clear, and I shall consider its proper function later.

At the time—and initially unrelated to the 'by'-sentence argument of Goldman—I was puzzled by a second difficulty for Davidson's treatment of action sentences, one noted by many commentators. It is a difficulty which arises when the identity thesis is mobilized in the context of Davidson's proposals for the semantics of adverbial modifiers. Very briefly, if we treat:

(6)   Bill killed the tyrant with a revolver.

as:

(7)   ($\exists$x) [Killed (Bill, the tyrant, x) & With (a revolver, x)],

and if we agree that Bill did it by pulling a trigger with his finger, which comes out as:

(8)   ($\exists$x) [Pulled (Bill, the trigger, x) & With (his finger, x)],

then we can derive the misleading (at best) consequence:

(9)   Bill killed the tyrant with his finger,

and the much more difficult to swallow claim about Bill's dexterity that:

(10)   Bill pulled the trigger with a revolver.

The unwanted consequences (9) and (10) are the direct result of treating the act of pulling as one and the same as the act of killing—thus, allowing us to switch around the conjunctions between (7) and (8)—and this identification certainly seems to be demanded by the Anscombe–Davidson thesis. However, noting that the preposition 'with' functions in quite different ways in various adverbial phrases, I wondered whether one could defuse both Goldman's 'by'-relation objection and the 'with-a-revolver' problem by seeing a connection between them.[1] The key to such a connection would be the obvious fact that 'with' functions in quite different ways, and that one of them consorts with the 'by'-relation. Thus, compare:

(11)   Mary showered with a sponge.
(12)   Mary showered with a friend.

It seemed pretty obvious that the 'with a sponge' modifier means something like 'by using a sponge', whereas, unless circumstances are very odd indeed, 'with' in (12) functions quite differently. If, as I then hoped, a suitable account could be given of 'by'-phrases, then my feeling was that we could deal with the problem caused by modifiers such as 'with a revolver' by translating them into their more perspicuous 'by'-relation form. This

---

[1] In 1978, I sent a paper suggesting this to *Analysis*, but I am now not sorry that it was rejected. What was wrong with it (in my view) was that its account of the 'by'-relation was inadequate, though I continue to think that there is something in the connection of the two issues.

would then leave the other sort of 'with' modifier—that exemplified in (12)—to be handled by Davidson's proposal. This would work because, as seems obvious enough, we just do not get the possibility of an awkward shuffling of modifiers in cases like (12). (Assuming that Mary's showering is her washing, or her soothing her nerves, if the first is done 'with a friend' then so are the others.)

Recasting 'with a revolver' so that it was no longer handled as a predicate of an action in the conjunctive style recommended by Davidson seemed reasonable at the time given that, even on his own account of adverbial modification, certain exceptions need to be made, and certain awkwardnesses tolerated. Various verb-dependent attributivities forced Davidson to admit (I think wrongly) that slow journeys to Calais seemed unlikely to be fast swimmings of the Channel, even when the journey to Calais was a swimming of the Channel. And he has suggested that we must face with stoical calm the fact that his construal of 'Smith flew to the moon' entails that there is a 'to the moon' event.

I am not here arguing for, or even defending, my hunch about the connection between the 'by'-sentence objection to the identity thesis and the problem of adverbial modification. Indeed, I shall not say anything more about adverbs of action sentences in this paper. However, it was this hunch which got me interested in 'by'-sentences, even before they came to be generally fashionable.

4

My aim was very simple: find some way to understand 'by'-sentences which is: (a) faithful to the kind of quantification over events that Davidson saw in their initial clause; yet (b) tells us how to construe appropriately the participial 'by'-clause; and, finally, (c) defuses any threat to the Anscombe–Davidson identity thesis.

My very first thoughts revolved around what seems to be a clear division among 'by'-sentences into those that are causal and those that are noncausal. It is difficult not to be struck by the difference between 'Jones ruined his suit by washing it ' and 'Jones signaled by waving his arms'. The event that has Jones washing his suit causes changes in the suit that, in the circumstances, counts as its being ruined. But the waving does not cause a signal; it is one. Still, for reasons that I have only come much later to appreciate, this led nowhere.

More promising was the suggestion that the participial clauses in 'by'-sentences do not point to particular actions or events at all, but instead function as a sort of verb modifier. In the wholly familiar way that the category of *red things* can be adjectivally restricted, as when we say speak of *shiny red things*, perhaps we sometimes want to restrict ruinings to those done in a certain manner. And to achieve this should take ourselves to speak about 'ruinings by washing', rather as we speak of 'death by hanging', or 'lying by omission'. That this might even be a way forward that Davidson would sanction is hinted at, albeit tangentially, by his concluding remark about Kenny's proposal. When Davidson wondered whether 'by holding it between his toes' is simply a way of saying 'while holding it between his toes', he seems to imply that we can resist seeing the 'by'-clause as a way of expanding the places in the action verb 'butter'. And of course one way of doing so would be by treating 'while holding it between his toes' as a modifier of the main verb.

Of course, merely counting the 'by'-phrase as a predicate of the action event is not enough get us out of trouble. For if in turn we treat this predicate of events in the usual conjunctive style, then we are back where we began. The killing by pulling the trigger ends up as an event which is both a killing and a pulling of the trigger. If we treat 'with a revolver' as 'by using a revolver', then the multiplicity of conjunctive predicates at our disposal can be unhelpfully shuffled by the inference rules of simplification and conjunction to give the unwanted result that some event was a pulling of the trigger with, or by using, a revolver.

In view of this, one obvious thing to do is to treat 'by'-clause modification, not as apt for conjunctive treatment, but as some kind of predicate modifier. This detracts somewhat from the simplicity of the original Davidsonian idea, but many have thought that attributive adjectives will have to be handled as predicate modifiers in any case. So, perhaps there is no harm in treating action sentences as allowing a mix of conjunctive predications and predicate modifiers. On this view, a sentence such as:

Jones ruined his suit last Monday in the launderette by washing it.

would come out roughly as:

(13) ($\exists$x) (Washing-Ruining (Jones, the suit, x) & On (last Monday, x) & In (the launderette, x)).

In spite of these hopeful thoughts, I have come to think that the predicate modifier view of 'by'-clauses does not work. My reasons for this—only summarised here—were initially based on technical difficulties with the proposal, but I have come to think that these are only indicative of the essential misguidedness of the project.

As has been well-documented, predicate modification is syntactically very appealing, even natural, but giving such constructions a proper semantics is appallingly difficult. Gareth Evans' struggles to treat 'large' as a predicate modifier required him at one point to move this adjective into the semantic metatheory, so that he ended up saying such things as:

x satisfies 'is a large elephant' iff x is a large satisfier of 'elephant' (Evans 1976:203).

What sounds odd in connection with the attributive 'large' comes out even more peculiar when 'by'-clauses are at issue. Do we want to countenance such things as:

x satisfies 'ruins his suit by washing it' iff x is a by-washing-it satisfier of 'ruins his suit'?

Perhaps something could be said in favor of this way of speaking; in philosophy we are used to sacrificing bits of common language for the greater good of some theory. But the apparently technical problems do not stop here. The participial clauses in 'by'-sentences, unlike ordinary attributive adjectives like 'large', can themselves be modified *ad lib*. Thus, we can say that:

Jones ruined his suit by washing it vigorously in the launderette in hot water.

The consequence of this is not simply the strangeness of 'by-washing-vigorously in-the-launderette satisfiers', but the more serious one that special arrangements will have to be made for inference involving 'by'-clauses. For example, we will have to decide whether and how we can go from the above to any of:

Jones ruined his suit by washing it vigorously in the launderette.

Jones ruined his suit by washing it in hot water.

Jones ruined his suit by washing it in the launderette.

Jones ruined his suit by washing it.

Even without a detailed demonstration, it is clear enough what a nightmare this task is. Intensional logic will certainly have to figure as, for example, we probably wouldn't want to count 'washings' as simply a superclass of 'vigorous washings', since perhaps Jones's vigour did the ruining and not merely his washing. But even then we are not home free. Handling predicate modifiers such as 'large' requires that we deal with a semantically fixed unit. But 'by' would be indefinitely variable in its content, and I have seen nothing to suggest that we can manage this.

Nor should we try. For if the possibility of increasing specificity in this case of a 'by'-clause suggests anything, it is that we are not dealing with something intrinsically general. True enough, there are deaths and there are deaths by hanging. These seem to be different types of event, the second a subclass of the first. Here if anywhere the predicate modifier view seems appropriate. But, though I cannot prove it, it seems that the 'by'-clause in the Jones sort of case is more about that specific thing that an agent, Jones, did at a particular time. It is related in all its particularity to Jones's having ruined his suit, and is not merely a gesture towards a type of ruining. And it is this use of the 'by'-relation that I had been interested in, and which still seemed elusive.[2]

5

Assuming as I then did that the predicate modifier view was on the wrong track as a general account of 'by'-clauses, though it did seem appropriate for some specific examples, I came up with another idea. Unfortunately, I discovered quite quickly that, whilst it handled the Jones case, and many others like it, there seemed to be other examples to which it wasn't, so to speak, suited. I now think that my rejection was too hasty, but before describing it, I should like to put on the table another more recent proposal of Bennett's. The reason for this somewhat coy way of proceeding is that Bennett's work stimulated me to re-think my own proposal, and, more importantly, a comparison with his proposal makes it easier to appreciate the virtues of my own. Here then is a brief account of Bennett's suggestion, put together from his own words:

> In every plainly acceptable 'by'-statement of the form 'He φed by πing', the initial clause for which the 'He φed' stands means something of the form:
>
> Some fact about how he behaved had relational property RP.
>
> The relational property may be quite complex, ...however I skip the complexities and stress the phrase 'some fact'. These sentences all imply an existential quantification over the facts about how the person behaved.
>   The remainder of the analysis is startlingly simple. The initial clause says that *some* fact about how the person behaved had relational property RP, and the gerundial phrase says what...Thus,
>
> He broke a promise—by—coming home late.
>
> analyzes into
>
> Some fact about his behavior conflicted with a promise he had made earlier—namely the fact that—he came home late.
>
> Similarly, 'He overcooked the stew [by leaving it on the fire for too long]' says that some fact about his behavior causally led ... to the stew's being overcooked, and 'by leaving it on the fire for too long' says what (Bennett 1994:36).

---

[2] See Hornsby 1980 for the suggestion that the 'by'-relation should be understood in terms of predicate modification, though no worked out formal details are actually given. Hornsby sees the same connection as I did between the 'by'-relation and the problems of Davidson's conjunctive account of adverbial modification.

The key elements here are:

(i)   The insistence on treating both clauses in 'by'-sentences as fact-involving. The first, finite verb clause, quantifies over facts and the second refers to one.

(ii)   The role of the preposition 'by' is specification. It is said to name (as in 'namely') a fact only hinted at in the initial clause.

(iii)   The unsystematic nature of the supposedly recoverable facts that are imputed to the initial clauses in 'by'-sentences. (As well, of course, as the implicit quantification over facts said to lie hidden in that clause.) 'He broke a promise' becomes 'Some fact about his behavior conflicted with a promise he had made earlier', whereas, 'He over-cooked the stew' becomes 'Some fact about his behavior causally led to the stew's being overcooked'. These 'paraphrases' are very far from the original, and each new sentence presents a new challenge for such paraphrase.

Bennett is quite unapologetic about the looseness of connection between the actual words of the initial clause and his account of what such clauses mean. He notes that he will have to tell 'a separate story for each of the millions of them' but insists that this is only a reflection of the complexity of our language (Bennett 1994:37). Brave words, but surely this admission must undermine the claim that what he offers is an *analysis* of 'by'-sentences. At best what he says is something true, when, as it happens, a particular 'by'-sentence is itself true. However, whilst I don't think he is right even about this, my detailed criticisms must wait upon a discussion of my own earlier attempt to get to grips with the 'by'-relation. As noted, seeing the two views side-by-side seems to me the best way to see why, in spite of my initial misgivings, I think now that I was on to something.

6

If Bennett is right, then 'by'-sentences provide no support either for Davidson's suggestion that action sentences involve quantification over acts or events, or for the Anscombe–Davidson view about the identity of acts. This is not because of minor problems with this or that way of putting either proposal. It is much more radical than that. As he says, given his account of 'by'-sentences, 'the act concept is nowhere to be seen' (Bennett 1994:33).

It was this consequence of Bennett's view that I found implausible and which stimulated me to look again at my earlier view. What I had wanted, as part of dealing with the Goldman argument about the 'by'-relation, was a way of allowing a quantificational treatment of the initial finite verb clause in a 'by'-sentence, whilst also recognising that the participial 'by'-clause has some relation to a particular act or event. Treating it as a complex predicate modifier, for technical reasons, didn't really count as an option, and also it just didn't feel right for all cases. So, leaving the participial clause on one side, I tried to focus first just on the preposition 'by'.

Fairly obviously, 'by' seemed to suggest amplification or precisification of the initial clause. Bennett's suggestion that 'by' is something like 'namely' comes close to what I had in mind, but, in contrast to Bennett, I didn't think that this amplification was an attempt to answer the question 'How?'. Admittedly, in many cases, the 'by'-clause does provide an answer to that question, but I thought that something more general, perhaps less focussed on the causal, was going on. What I came up with was the idea that 'by' suggested the specific way in which the initial—supposedly quantificational clause—was made true. Hence, my construal of the 'by'-sentence:

(14)   Jones ruined his suit by washing it.

came out as:

(15)   The event of Jones's washing his suit makes-true: '(∃x) Ruin (Jones, his suit, x)'.

This sounded oddly right, but it seemed far-fetched to think that 'by' was in any way metalinguistic. After all, what I had wanted was a sentence close enough to the original to count as giving its truth condition. And if proposals about names, beliefs and many other constructions have taught us anything, it is that going metalinguistic undermines such aspirations. In any case, what does it mean to say that something 'makes-true' a certain existentially quantified sentence? It was the answer to that question—obvious as it is—that gave me some pause.

To say that some item, call it *a*, makes-true a sentence of the form '(∃x) Fx' is really just a fancy way of saying what comes out in the material mode as 'F*a*'. Surely, I thought, when this is read back into the case at hand, only nonsense will result. But I was wrong. For allowing a certain natural shift in pronouns, the original sentence (14), when treated in the manner of (15) and then rendered back into the material mode, comes out as:

(16)   Jones's washing his suit ruined it.

This is perfectly intelligible, and has the general form 'F*a*', given, of course, the assumption that the original finite verb clause is an existentially quantified sentence built with the predicate 'F'. Moreover, it seemed plausibly to give the truth conditions of 'Jones ruined his suit by washing it'. Judgments of synonymy are not always reliable, especially when one's own proposal is under test, but no one I asked could hear any semantic difference between: 'Jones ruined his suit by washing it', and 'Jones's washing his suit ruined it' when these were used in the circumstances imagined earlier.[3]

Pursuing this idea, I came to see that 'by' does not function primarily as a provider of causal answers to 'How?' questions, though *de facto* it does give such information in certain cases. Nor, of course, is it metalinguistic, though, a consequence of its work can be the re-arrangement of certain elements in sentences. Perhaps the best way of putting it, is to say that the 'by'-construction allows us to shift a special kind of nominal clause from its subject position. 'Jones's washing his suit' is replaced as the subject by 'Jones', and the nominal clause is then re-introduced via the 'by'-preposition. I leave it to those who know more about grammar than I do to judge, but it seemed that there was a certain parallel between this subject-shift and that which takes place in passives, and this seemed a plausible explanation for the two construction's using the same preposition. (No one, I take it, would suggest that the use of 'by' in a passive sentence is metal-inguistic, even though its use entails a re-arrangement of elements in the active sentence to which the passive can be linked. My suggestion about 'by' sees the connection between (16) and (14) as something like the active-passive relationship, at least in regards to the metalinguistic issue.)

Before worrying about drawbacks, I began to add up the advantages of my account. First, it seemed to offer support of yet another kind for Davidson's proposals about the quantificational nature of certain action sentences. Indeed, it convinced me of something that I, and many others, had found forced in Davidson's original proposal. When he suggested that 'Brutus killed Caesar' actually involved an existential quantifier, many were—and continue to be—ready to accept this because it is logically useful in various ways. But even those who agree with Davidson do not find it simply *obvious* that such sentences have a quantificational structure. Yet in the construction forced on me by my naive thoughts about 'by'-sentences, one can actually see the place for such quantification over events. The addition of the 'by'-clause seems to force us to notice an event place in otherwise innocent looking two-place predicates such as 'ruined' or 'killed'.

Thoughts about the Anscombe–Davidson identity thesis followed next. One of the two main arguments that Davidson appealed to in support of

---

[3] There are of course at least two ways of taking (14): it could suggest a single trip to the launderette in which a catastrophic washing took place; or, it could suggest a repeated and careless washing of a 'Dry Clean Only' suit which eventually results in complete ruin. As it happens, this ambiguity is perfectly matched by that of (16). Nonetheless, the circumstances of the case considered in the text is one in which the washing (and the ruining) are wholly particular things which happened. Yet in pointing to the equivalence of (14) and (16) I am certainly not suggesting that this specificity follows just from availability of the 'by'-sentence. After all, I have already admitted that some 'by'-sentences are of the 'death by hanging' sort. To repeat, I do not aim to offer a single analysis of all 'by'-sentences, but simply that one kind of case seems to consort well with talk of particular acts or events.

this thesis is based on the logic of certain sorts of excuses: the kind we come up with when we admit to having actually done some act, though not under a description that forces us to accept blame. He writes:

> The logic of this sort of excuse includes, it seems, at least this much structure: I am accused of doing b, which is deplorable. I admit that I did a, which is excusable. My excuse for doing b rests upon my claim that I did not know that a = b (Davidson 1980:109).

In my example, Jones stands accused of ruining his suit, but he admits only to washing it. His excuse for ruining it is that he didn't know that the washing was ruining. However, it has been pointed out by many commentators, that Davidson's argument here is less than conclusive. For example, it is open to someone who denies the identity thesis to explain Jones's excuse as his not knowing that the one action, his washing, would cause another, the ruining. The excuse doesn't seem to need the identity.

I have always been suspicious of these attempts to get around the Davidsonian argument: in some cases, it is natural enough to speak of one action causing another, even when they are, as it were, done together. However, in other cases, the natural form of words used as an excuse is difficult to re-interpret in this way. If Mary intentionally sticks out her arm, and if in the circumstances she inadvertently signals a turn, then, after the ensuing accident, she may correctly say that she didn't know that sticking out her arm was signaling. In an attempt to maintain that the arm gesture is distinct from the signal, an opponent of Davidson might construe the excuse as something like this: Mary didn't know that her arm gesture counted as signaling, where 'counted as' is non-causal. After all, her arm gesture didn't cause her signaling. But on the most natural reading of the phrase 'counted as' we have something awfully close to an admission of the identity thesis. Trying to avoid these words only underlines the unnaturalness of attempts to read a denial of the identity thesis into the language of excuses. Is it plausible to interpret Mary as saying: I didn't know that my arm gesture conventionally level-generated the signal? If we are willing to swallow this as an interpretation of what she meant, it is surely only because talk of 'generation' illicitly hints at causality, and thus reminds us of the more plausible ruining case (this talk of 'level generation' is found in Goldman 1970).

On my account, the words of both Jones and Mary can be taken quite literally: Jones didn't know the washing *was* ruining, and Mary didn't know the arm gesture *was* signaling. But in both cases, the copula is not that of identity but of predication. Neither Jones nor Mary believed that something of the form 'F*a*' was true. Understood in this way, we do not need to reinterpret the form of words used in giving excuses; no need to mention knowledge of what causes, or generates, what, nor any need to appeal to identity. But as I originally hoped, the identity thesis is not far

away. For, in the circumstances described, we happen to be correct in thinking that there was one and only one ruining, and one and only one signaling. And these facts, together with the uniqueness of the washing and the
gesturing guarantee the identity that Davidson was aiming at, even though,
as I now think, too immediately. They guarantee it by a simple piece of
logic. Knowing that, in the circumstances of each case, there is a unique F
(a ruining, a signaling), that *a* refers to a unique event (Jones's washing,
Mary's gesturing) and also that F*a* (Jones's washing ruined the suit, Mary's
gesturing signaled the turn), we can infer that there is nothing for that
unique F-event to be except *a*. So, we end up with the very identity that the
Anscombe–Davidson thesis predicted. Yet we only get this result by having
some independent reason to accept the uniqueness of F. Merely knowing
the truth of 'Jones ruined his suit', or of 'Mary signaled a turn' is not
enough, since if Davidson is right—and I am sure he is—these sentences
are merely existentially quantified. In and of themselves, they give no hint
that their quantification is restricted to a single instance. However, knowing
from the background stories that Jones's self-inflicted loss was the only one
involving the suit, and that Mary's accident was the result of a uniquely
disastrous gesture, we can argue our way through to the identity thesis.

It was this construal of the standard form of words in an excuse that
gave me a hint as to why Anscombe had been so reticent about appealing to
the 'by'-locution. From the truth of S does A by doing B, no identity follows unless you have *additional* reason to think appropriate things about
the uniqueness of A and B. However, in the literature on action, there does
seem to be an argument around which provides exactly this extra reason on
a case-by-case basis. Known sometimes as the 'no further effort' argument,
it has had a long and sometimes confusing history, especially in the context
of assigning temporal locations to events. (The argument comes roughly to
this: if S does A, and makes no further effort to do anything else, and S is
said both to have done B and done A by doing B, then there is every reason
to think that A is B. Thus, if I throw a brick, and do nothing further, then
if I am also said to have broken the window and done so by throwing the
brick, there is every reason to think that my throwing the brick is my break-
ing the window.)

Here I simply note that if you accept my account of the 'by'-relation
and, in a given case, find that circumstances support the no further effort
thesis, then certain things about the uniqueness of actions follow. And they
are just the extra which you need to add to a 'by'-sentence to get the identity thesis. Perhaps Anscombe's continued reluctance to appeal to 'by'-
sentences in her dealings with, amongst others, Goldman, results from her

recognition of the only *indirect* connection between the identity thesis and 'by'-sentences.[4]

A final thought, which at the time seemed further confirmation of my view, concerns yet another kind of sentence, one with a scarcely remarked on resemblance to those using 'by'. When we say that Jones ruined his suit by washing it, we cannot say that Jones washed his suit by ruining it. The asymmetry of 'by'-sentences was of course noted by Goldman, though, as I see it, its explanation is no more complex than the asymmetry of subject and predicate in a sentence. However, there *is* a way to change things around; we can say:

> Jones washed his suit, thereby ruining it.

It is no more obvious what 'thereby' is doing here than 'by' does in its context, but what I have said about 'by' might give us a clue. In 'thereby'-sentences we have reversal of clauses and an exchange between participial and finite verb forms. In effect, a 'thereby'-sentence allows us to change the emphasis of a 'by'-sentence, perhaps because, as in this example, the speaker wants to highlight the washing event. But how can such a reversal work, given that, on Davidson's account, there is a semantic change of role forced on us by the grammatical shift in verb forms? After all, in the initial clause of the 'thereby'-sentence we are quantifying over washings rather than referring to one. Here is how: first note, as seems plausible, that the function of the demonstrative 'there', which clearly refers back to the initial

---

[4] Bennett 1988 gets this wrong when he 'catches' Anscombe using a sentence which is as close to a 'by'-sentence as she ever gets. Anscombe writes:

> Do I say that John performed one act? We quickly guess from his discussion that Goldman means: in a case where he did do all that just by what it is rather natural to call one act (Anscombe 1979:224).

And she goes on to say of this case:

> When it is taken as Goldman intends, the identity of the act is assumed in giving a lot of different descriptions (ibid.).

Bennett demurs, insisting:

> Goldman could agree that John did all that by one act, while denying that 'all that' constitutes just one act. The force that Anscombe tries to give her 'by...one act' characterization presupposes the point that is at issue, namely that if John moved his Queen by moving his hand then his hand motion and his chess move were one act (Bennett 1988:123-4).

But, if I am right, Bennett has missed Anscombe's point. She wasn't suggesting that the appropriateness of the 'by'-locution was itself enough to show the presupposition she attributed to Goldman. It was the uniqueness of a certain act, together with a predication that was both true of that act and itself uniquely instantiated. (She calls it a 'description.') If someone says that there was only one act of moving the Queen, and it was a moving of a hand (a predication), and also that there was only one moving of a hand, then it follows, according to the pattern of inference described in the text, that the chess move and hand move are one and the same. Think about the force of the word 'just' in what Anscombe says.

clause, is both to suggest that a single washing event took place and to refer to it. Next see the 'by' part of this word as having the same function as it does in any 'by'-sentence. But, given that the demonstrative points backwards to the event of washing, recognize that we are invited to tack 'by' onto the washing event and not the ruining. If this is right, 'thereby' would preserve the assertion made by the original 'by'-sentence, whilst allowing us to reverse the order of the clauses. (Incidentally, you might think that the finite verb 'washed' in the 'thereby'-sentence tells against this proposal. But this is a mistake. I am not denying here that the finite verb phrase should be interpreted existentially; I am merely suggesting that 'thereby' invites us to see the quantification as uniquely satisfied. A lot more could be said about 'thereby', but my only interest here is finding some support for my view of 'by'.)

7

Now for the bad news. The predicational account of 'by'-sentences seemed too good to be true when I first thought of it, and it is. On the one hand, there are many 'by'-sentences it either doesn't handle well, or at all. Here is a sample:

(17)   Jones murdered the tyrant by shooting him.

(18)   Harry fished for trout by putting his nets across the river.

(19)   Gretchen bid for the painting by putting her hand up.

And, on the other hand, there is a problem about the participial clause that cannot go without mention any longer. I have been treating this clause as if it were a way of referring to an event, but, as many have pointed out, there is some reason to believe that this form of words is fact-, rather than event-, invoking.

These difficulties are closely intertwined with Bennett's account of 'by'-sentences, so in this section I shall finally be in a position to discuss the two proposals together. I begin with the worry about my treatment of the participial clauses.

As Bennett notes, there is a special form of participial clause most naturally used in 'by'-sentences. Sometimes called the 'imperfect nominal', this construction, as Vendler originally observed, has a verb 'alive and kicking in it' (Vendler 1967:125). For example, contrast the perfect nominal:

(20)   a vigorous washing of his suit,

with the 'by'-clause nominal:

(21)   by washing his suit vigorously.

The perfect nominal can be quantified, is adjectivally modified and uses the genitive form of direct object—all features which suggest that a genuine count noun is in play. In contrast, the imperfect nominal does not invite quantification, is modified adverbially and has, so to speak, 'direct' direct objects. It seems, in short, more a verb phrase than a noun. This, in turn, encourages Vendler, Bennett and others, to see imperfect nominals as fact-invoking. To give a typical example, a sentence using an imperfect nominal such as:

—(22)   John's singing the aria softly surprised us.

is apparently paraphrasable as:

—(23)   That John sang the aria softly surprised us.

And, of course, the verbal 'that'-clause in this paraphrase is assimilable to the explicit fact-stating:

—(24)   The fact that John sang the aria softly surprised us.

Having decided in this way that the 'by'-clause is fact-invoking, and having noted the amplificatory nature of the preposition 'by', it is easy to understand why Bennett is moved to interpret the finite verb phrase in 'by'-sentences as itself fact-invoking. If you understand:

by washing his suit,

as:

namely, the fact that he washed his suit,

it is perhaps reasonable to see the initial phrase as an existential report of some fact. The whole then becomes:

Some fact about Jones's behavior resulted in his suit's being ruined, namely the fact that he washed it.

Starting from the contrast between perfectly and imperfectly nominal-ized participial clauses, Bennett sees the need to transpose talk about events and acts into talk about facts. And of course after such transposition, the Anscombe–Davidson thesis, as well as Davidson's proposal to handle ac-tion-sentence inferences by quantifying over events, become invisible. Also, from his perspective my proposal is inadequate, in not handling all of the 'by'-sentences one can think of, and is misleading in requiring an eventive reading of what he regards as fact-invoking, participial phrases.

8

Having myself long-since noted that my 'by'-sentence proposal was less than general, my first reaction to Bennett's conclusions was one of resigna-tion. But that didn't last long. Initially, I wondered what Bennett would say about the sentence:

—(16)   Jones's washing his suit ruined it.

I had proposed that this was, in essence, what a 'by'-sentence reported, but leave that on one side. Given Bennett's insistence on the fact-reporting nature of imperfect nominals, he would construe this as:

(25)   The fact that Jones washed his suit ruined it.

and this struck me as odd. Facts don't ruin suits. Of course, Bennett would be quick to point out that this is somewhat unfair—that the second part of the sentence should be transposed into fact talk to give:

(26)   The fact that Jones washed his suit resulted in the fact that it was ruined.

Other examples seemed less congenial to Bennett. For instance, what would Bennett make of:

(27)   Mary's sticking her arm out of the car window signaled a turn?

Much more could be said against, rather than for, the following renditions:

(28)   The fact that Mary stuck her arm out of the car window resulted in the fact that a turn was signaled.

(29)   The fact that Mary stuck her arm out of the car window is the fact that a turn was signaled.

Clearly, the eventive reading 'Fa' is more natural and it handles effortlessly both causal cases of ruining and non-causal cases like conventional signalling. But, of course, this reading still seems to violate the distinction between perfect and imperfect nominals.

It was at this point that I began to wonder whether this distinction could bear the weight that Bennett had put on it. First of all, it is less clearcut than Bennett would have us believe that the perfect/imperfect divide matches that of event/fact. Secondly, and leaving this contentious issue on one side, it should be noted that the sentences given above, and 'by'-sentences themselves, can be framed using *perfect* nominals. It is slightly more awkward, but certainly acceptable to say:

(30) Jones's vigorous washing of his suit ruined it.

and:

(31) Jones ruined his suit by his vigorous washing of it.

Nonetheless, even without the support of the perfect/imperfect distinction, Bennett's fact-invoking analysis of 'by'-sentences stands or falls on its apparent ability to handle those cases which mine does not. And as I have admitted, there are 'by'-sentences which sound distinctly odd when rendered in my way.

Typically, one prefers analyses that hold more generally, but I suggest that the present case is atypical. My account yields transparent truth conditions for a large range of 'by'-sentences, and, in doing so, directly supports

Davidson's quantificational proposals and, indirectly, the identity thesis. In contrast, for all his use of the word, Bennett's proposal should not count as an 'analysis'—as a proposal for systematically uncovering the truth conditions of a particular construction. For, as he frankly admits, we have to tailor what we say to each 'by'-sentence, and the account offers us no systematic help with this task. But there is a more important point to be made, and this is part of my conclusion. In failing to handle certain 'by'-sentences, I suggest that my account reflects something significant, which, in giving a uniform treatment to all 'by'-sentences, Bennett's account actually conceals.

The facts are familiar enough to need only a brief summary. There are lots of things which we bring about that are, or are the result of, events we initiate, whether intentionally or not. Using the familiar example, Jones ruined his suit—unintentionally—by his intentionally washing it. And, as proposed, we can say that the event of his washing his suit ruined it. Further, the example would work just as well if the ruining was intentional. In non-causal cases, matters are no more complicated: Mary signaled by sticking out her arm. We can say here that event of Mary's having stuck out her arm signaled the turn, whether the signal was itself intentional or not. However, there are also things we bring about, not by some event we initiate, but more directly. One way to put it would be to say that some things done can only be done by agents. It is things done in this direct way that do not fit my proposal as it stands. Mary bid for the painting by nodding her head, but we cannot say that Mary's nodding her head bid for the painting.

It seems then that there is a distinction between verbs which can take events *or* agents as subjects and those which only take agents. Moreover, this distinction has little to do with deliberateness or intention, though it is certainly central to how we think about human action. Independently of my own account, I suggest that we would want this distinction to be reflected in whatever we came to say about 'by'-sentences. That is, I would expect any serious proposal for the truth conditions of 'by'-sentences to reflect the fact that some do, and some do not, allow of what it is reasonable to call the 'subject-predicate transformation'. In giving a uniform 'analysis' of 'by'-sentences, Bennett fails to capture this difference, and that strikes me as a fatal weakness. Not only is Bennett's recourse to facts not mandated by the grammatical demands of 'by'-sentences, it actually stops him seeing something central to our talk of action. I offer here no suggestion as to exactly what is going on in agent-only 'by'-sentences, but whatever we end up saying, it should give us a hint as to why they are different from agent-event examples.

9

The other part of my conclusion concerns imperfect nominals. Getting around Bennett's worries, it was sufficient to note that we can avoid the factive reading of imperfect nominals in disputes about 'by'-sentences. But I do think that 'by'-clauses, even those using the imperfect nominal form, refer to events and not facts, and I would like to end with a suggestion as to what is going on.

Particular objects are relatively easy to refer to demonstratively. We can ordinarily speak of 'this' or 'that' *thing* because things hang around long enough to be re-identified with minimal background information. With the particular events that Davidson and others appeal to in semantics, impermanence makes such ostension more difficult. To be sure, we do use sortals—sometimes perfect nominal participial clauses—to refer to them, and, in some particularly notable cases, we have proper names for events. Yet, given their ephemerality, it is reasonable to regard particular events as, so to speak, 'demonstratively challenged'. It is less easy to imagine the word 'this' straightforwardly effecting reference to them, except in very special circumstances. And it is here that imperfect nominals figure. Without insisting that they *always* do so, I suggest that they *sometimes* have a demonstrative role, albeit of a rather special sort.

Consider the adage from traditional grammar which, if I remember correctly, goes like this:

Nouns stand for persons, places or things, and verbs express actions.

This distinction between the job of nouns and verbs has always puzzled me. What after all could it mean for certain sorts of word—verbs—to *express* actions? Though I do not have a general answer to this—and I am by no means convinced that this bit of grammatical lore should be taken too seriously—there is a hint of an answer in the above suggestion about the demonstrative-like role of imperfect nominals. The basic idea is simple enough. We often have occasion to bring some event or action to the attention of our audience. If this event or action is important enough, it probably has its own proper name (as in 'The Battle of Hastings'). Or, even if it lacks such a name, if it is an event of an important enough kind, the chances are there will be a sortal noun that we can adapt to the occasion (as in 'Tuesday's thunderstorm'). But it can happen that we are not in a position to use either of these methods to effect reference. Yet a straightforward use of the demonstrative 'this' is not likely to be of use, given the ephemeral nature of events. So, what we might attempt instead is a kind of evocation of the action. Rather than referring (strictly speaking) to some action, we use words as if presenting the action to our audience. Such a use is rather like our saying:

(32) 'Imagine seeing this: Jones washing his suit vigorously in the launderette street'.

What makes the imperfect nominal in (32) so fit for purpose in this context
is its very imperfectness as a nominal. What Jones did is more reasonably
thought of as expressed in this sentence than referred to. (Note that in (32),
it is the perfect nominal that would sound odd.) My concluding, and
highly speculative suggestion, is that in a certain range of 'by'-sentences,
the imperfect nominal has the role of bringing an event to our attention in
pretty much the way effected in (32).[5]

References

Anscombe, G.E.M. 1957. *Intention*. Oxford: Basil Blackwell.

Anscombe, G.E.M. 1979. Under a Description. *Noûs* 13:219-33.

Bennett, J. 1988. *Events and Their Names*. Oxford: Oxford University Press.

Bennett, J. 1994. The 'Namely' Analysis of the 'By'-locution. *Linguistics and Philosophy* 17:29-51.

Davidson, D. 1980. The Logical Form of Action Sentences. *Essays on Actions and Events*, 105-22. Oxford: Oxford University Press.

Evans, G. 1976. Semantic Structure and Logical Form. *Truth and Meaning*, eds. G. Evans and J. McDowell, 199-222. Oxford: Oxford University Press.

Goldman, A.A. 1970. *A Theory of Human Action*. Princeton: Princeton University Press.

Hornsby, J. 1980. Verbs and Events. *Proceedings of the Keele Conference on Logic and Language*, ed. J. Dancy, 88-111. Keele: Keele University Press.

Kenny, A. 1963. *Action, Emotion and Will*. London: Routledge and Kegan Paul.

---

[5] I do realize that a friend of facts could accept my speculation, but insist that what is evoked
or expressed is some particular fact, not some event. Clearly, I do not intend my remarks
about imperfect nominals and 'by' to settle the titanic struggle between events and facts, but I
would hope that a neutral would find, in this case at least, for events.

6

Deflating Compositionality

PAUL HORWICH

What kind of assumptions about a foreign speaker would put us in a position to interpret anything he might say, and how could such assumptions be verified? Like Quine, Davidson supposes that the answers to these questions will constitute a more-or-less complete philosophical account of meaning. However, unlike Quine, who took for granted that the hard issue here was confined to the second question—Can determinately correct translation manuals ever be found?—Davidson focussed equal attention on an aspect of the first one—How could interpretations of the infinitely many complex expressions of a language be derived (as they surely must be) from finitely many assumptions about the meanings of the primitive terms?[1] What form would our hypotheses about the meanings of someone's words and sentences have to take in order that the latter be deducible from the former? And for that matter, how does the understanding we have of our *own* language derives from our understanding of its basic elements.

Davidson's positive proposal was ingenious and appealing—we should solve the problem by piggy-backing on Tarski's work on truth.[2] For Tarski

---

[1] For Quine's account of meaning and translation see Quine 1960; for Davidson's views see the essays in Davidson 1984—especially 'Truth and Meaning' (Davidson 1984b).

[2] To the other problem—that of how we might *verify* a given interpretation—Davidson's solution is similar to Quine's. The method based on his Principle of Charity differs only in detail from Quine's strategy of radical translation

showed how the truth conditions of various formalised sentences could be deduced, in predicate logic, from premises specifying the referents of names and simple predicates, and from further premises specifying, for each connective, how the referent (or truth-value) of any complex that is formed with it depends on the referents (or truth-values) of the connected expressions. Therefore, if we identify a sentence's possessing the meaning it does with its having a certain truth condition, and if we identify a word's possessing the meaning it does with its having a certain referent (or, in the case of a connective, with the fact about how the truth-values/referents of the complexes formed with it depend on the truth-values/referents of the connected expressions), then Tarski-style deductions of truth conditions become precisely what we were looking for: namely, derivations of sentence-meanings on the basis of assumptions about word-meanings.

Consider for example how to arrive by such means at an interpretation of the Italian sentence 'Gira Marte'. We would begin with the three semantic premises:

The name 'Marte' refers-in-formal-Italian to Mars[3]

The predicate 'gira(x)' is true-in-formal-Italian of k $\leftrightarrow$ k rotates

The result of applying a predicate to a name is true-in-formal-Italian $\leftrightarrow$ the predicate is true-in-formal-Italian of the referent-in-formal-Italian of the name.

And we also have the syntactic premise

The result of applying 'gira(x)' to 'Marte' is 'gira(Marte)'

From these assumptions we would infer that

'gira(Marte)' is true-in-formal-Italian $\leftrightarrow$ Mars rotates

Then we would have to invoke the fact that

The formal Italian, 'gira(Marte)', gives the meaning of the ordinary Italian sentence, 'Gira Marte'

which puts us in a position to conclude that,

'Gira Marte' is true-in-Italian $\leftrightarrow$ Mars rotates.

More generally, Davidson conjectured that for *every* sentence of a natural language we could deduce and explain why it means what it does by explaining, along Tarskian lines, why its logical formalisation (or regi-

---

[3] The route through 'formal Italian' is necessary because Tarskian deductions of truth conditions can be carried out only for sentences in some logically regimented (i.e. formalised) part of the language. Other sentences may then be dealt with by attributing to them the same truth conditions as their formalisations.

mented equivalent) has the truth condition that it does. And this idea became widely accepted, instigating several decades of 'normal science' in
semantics.

The research projects engendered by the Davidsonian paradigm fell into
two groups. First it became necessary to show how the strategy could be
applied to *all* sentences, including those built with devices that Tarski did
not investigate. How for example might we deduce the truth conditions of
sentences containing adverbs, or that-clauses, or attributive adjectives, or
conditional-probability constructions, on the basis of premises concerning
the referents of their words? To that end, how could such sentences be formalised in first order predicate logic? Over the last thirty years, ingenious
solutions have been found to several problems of this sort, although many
still remain intractable.

The second set of issues that needed to be addressed included various
foundational questions. For instance, does the truth condition of a sentence
in fact suffice to determine its meaning? In other words, is there any reading
of 's is true *if and only if* p' in which it will be strong enough to entail 's
means that p'? Considerable efforts to find or devise such a construal have
not yet produced an acceptable one.[4]

Moreover, does a natural language sentence in fact have the same meaning as the best formulation one can give of it in predicate logic? For example, is it plausible that 'John might win' has just the same meaning as
'$(\exists x)[\text{PossWorld}(x)\ \&\ \text{Wins}(\text{John}, x)]$', and that the sense of 'Mary is walk-
ing slowly' is identical to that of '$(\exists x)[\text{Walking}(x)\ \&\ \text{By}(x, \text{Mary})\ \&\ \text{Slow}(x)]$'? No doubt the members of such pairs necessarily have the same
truth value; but are they really exact synonyms of one another?

The expectation that these technical and foundational difficulties will
eventually be overcome derives largely from the conviction that there is no
decent alternative to the Davidsonian truth-theoretic perspective, and there-

---

[4] One sometimes hears it said, on behalf of Davidson, that he was not really attempting to
analyse, or even to explicate, 's means that p', but rather to get along without this obscure
notion and to make do with the relatively unproblematic 's is true if and only if p'. But remember that the problem he set was to specify which assumptions about a person would
enable us to tell what beliefs his assertive utterances are expressing—i.e. to say what he
means. So if the answer, roughly speaking, is that these assumptions must concern the truth
conditions of his utterances, then it is obligatory to face up to the challenge of articulating
precisely what sort of truth-conditional claim about a sentence would amount to a view of
what it means. It seems clear that Davidson himself *does* face up to this challenge, and that
he is responsible for some of the attempts to meet it. For example, there is the idea that 's is
true if and only if p' be understood as 'It is a law of nature that (s is true $\leftrightarrow$ p)', or that it be
understood as 'It follows from any truth theory satisfying the Principle of Charity that (s is
true $\leftrightarrow$ p)'. A problem with all such construals—which take the form '$\Box$(s is true $\leftrightarrow$ p)'—is
that if the analysans is satisfied, and if we can find some 'q' (as we always can) not synony-
mous with 'p' yet such that $\Box$(p$\leftrightarrow$ q), then even though s does not mean that q, we can
nonetheless infer that $\Box$(s is true $\leftrightarrow$ q).

fore that it *must* be more-or less right. It seems to me, however, that there *is* a good alternative—whose correctness would undermine the purpose of the Davidsonian research program and make it unnecessary to swallow its various implausible commitments.

This alternative is deflationary, for its basic idea is that Davidson's problem (of how we might derive interpretations of complex expressions) has a trivial solution. This solution assumes the principle of compositionality (that the meaning of a complex is determined by the meanings of its elements and by its syntactic structure); but it involves no explication of meaning (e.g. in terms of truth conditions) and hence no explanation of *why* the principle of compositionality holds.

For illustration, look again at how we might reach an interpretation of 'Gira Marte'. We might begin with premises specifying the meanings of its primitives:

> 'Marte' in Italian means the same as *our* 'Mars'
>
> 'gira_' in Italian means the same as *our* '_rotates'.

Then, from the principle of compositionality, we can infer

> The result of applying 'gira_' to 'Marte' in Italian means the same as the result of *our* applying 'rotates' to 'Mars'.

And finally, given the syntactic facts

> The result of applying 'gira_' to 'Marte' = 'Gira Marte'.
>
> The result of applying '_rotates' to 'Mars' = 'Mars rotates',

we can deduce the interpretation

> 'Gira Marte' in Italian means the same as *our* 'Mars rotates'.

And in general, whenever some foreign expression is constructed by imposing a certain combinatorial procedure on certain words with (including schemata), then we can interpret it in our language with the expression that results from imposing exactly the same procedure on synonyms of those words.[5]

If this sort of approach will do, then Davidson's program, and all its attendant difficulties, can be put behind us. We can abandon the desperate struggle to find a conception of 'truth condition' sufficiently strong to capture meaning. We will then be able to avoid the problematic commitment

---

[5] Notice that although inter-translated expressions must have the same structure (i.e. they must result from the same combinatorial procedure), that is not to say that they must, in every sense, be 'syntactically' similar'. In particular, the order of synonymous words need not be the same. For the basic elements of a language include *schemata* (e.g. 'gira_' and '_rotates'). Therefore word-order will partially derive from where the 'slots' in these schemata are located. Thus an identity of combinatorial procedure (required for inter-translatability) is quite consistent with difference of word-order.

to cram every natural language construction into the narrow mould of predicate logic. And in that case there will be no need to claim, rather implausibly as we have seen, that the predicate logic formalisation of a natural language sentence will perfectly preserve its meaning. What a relief!

But *will* the deflationary approach do? Davidson himself was always well aware of it. So it is worth our while to examine his reasons for rejecting the idea and to consider how persuasive they are.

In the first place, he argues (in his essay 'Radical Interpretation') that a manual of translation does fully not convey meanings, and so cannot amount to an interpretation. For one can be told that two expressions should be intertranslated—i.e. that they have the same meaning as each other—without being given any understanding either one of them (Davidson 1984:129-30).

However, the problem we were set was to specify the assumptions we might make that would enable us to interpret a foreign language. And one good answer is that a correct manual of translation will do the trick. Granted, the information it provides will suffice only given an unexplained further fact—namely that we understand our own language. But notice that no alternative account—no alternative view of which explicit assumptions will yield interpretations of foreign speech—could escape something like this critique. For any such assumptions would need a language for their articulation—a language which would have to be understood. So, for example, the explicit assumption that 'Marte' refers to Mars requires that we already understand some term that refers to Mars—and this understanding remains unexplained. The obvious moral to draw is that we can understand a language only if we have available to us certain terms (possibly within a different language) whose meanings we know *implicitly*—that is, not in virtue of *articulated assumptions* about those terms, but in virtue of *facts* about what they mean, i.e. facts concerning how they are deployed. But leaving that moral aside until later, the point remains that although a translation manual can supply interpretations only relative to our understanding of our own language, the same can be said of any alternative view one might have of which explicit assumptions would work.

But, for the sake of argument, let us bow to Davidson's objection—at least to the letter of it—and take up his challenge to specify what knowledge (whether explicit or implicit) would suffice to understand a language (whether someone else's or one's own). This creates no particular difficulty for the deflationary strategy, because it is a simple matter to present the approach in terms of meaning-facts rather than translation-facts. We can begin by adopting the convention that each capitalised English expression be the name of the meaning of the original uncapitalized expression: thus 'Mars' means MARS, '_rotates' means ROTATES(x), 'Mars rotates' means MARS ROTATES, and so on. Then we can invoke the principle of compo-

sitionality in a peculiarly *Fregean* form—namely, that the result of applying one term to others (to produce a complex) *means* the result of applying
the meaning of the first term to the meanings of the others. In that case, we
can infer that both 'Mars rotates' and 'Gira Marte' mean the result of applying the function ROTATES(x) to the argument MARS, therefore that these
sentences mean the same thing, and therefore—since, by our convention,
'Mars rotates' means MARS ROTATES—that 'Gira Marte' means MARS
ROTATES.

At the beginning of 'Truth and Meaning' Davidson dismisses this particular way of trying to give a

> ... useful account of how the meanings of sentences depend upon the
> meanings of the words (or other structural features) that compose
> them. Ask, for example, for the meaning of 'Theatetus flies'. A Fregean
> answer might go something like this: given the meaning of
> 'Theatetus' as argument, the meaning of 'flies' yields the meaning of
> 'Theatetus flies' as value. The vacuity of this argument is obvious. We
> wanted to know what the meaning of 'Theatetus flies' is; it is no pro-
> gress to be told that it is the meaning of 'Theatetus flies'. This much
> we new before any theory was in sight. In the bogus account just
> given, talk of the structure of the sentence and of the meanings of
> words was idle, for it played no role in producing the given descrip-
> tion of the meaning of the sentence (Davidson 1984b:20).

But the Fregean answer does *not* merely apply the logical law of identity to the meaning of 'Theatetus flies'—which would indeed be of no interest. Rather, it incorporates the principle of compositionality—a non-
trivial principle—by maintaining that the meaning of the result of applying
a function-expression to certain argument-expressions equals the result of
applying the meaning of the function to the meanings of its arguments. It is
therefore not at all true that our assumptions about the structure of a sentence, and about the meanings of its words, will play no role in our characterisation of the meaning of that sentence.

What *is* true is that we have not *identified* (in some peculiarly direct
sense) the meaning of 'Theatetus flies'. We have specified it merely via the
construction description 'the result of applying FLIES(x) to THEATETUS';
but we have not said what that result is, i.e. what the description describes.[6] However, a vital aspect of the deflationary attitude is to question
whether there is a need for any such deeper, more immediate characterisation
of that meaning. Consider, by analogy, the number we designate with the
term '15'—or, to spell out what this notation means, 'the sum of 10 and
5'. We would regard it as explanatorily otiose, indeed downright bizarre, to
insist on some more direct identification of the entity described in that way.
Arithmetic and its applications call for no more than the description. And

---

[6] For a sympathetic elaboration of Davidson's complaint that the deflationary approach fails
to specify directly what the meanings of complexes are, see James Higginbotham 1999.

the same goes in semantics for construction characterisations of the meanings of complex expressions.

It is also true, as a consequence, that we are not attempting to *explain* the phenomenon of compositionality. We are not associating specific, independently identifiable entities with the meanings of 'Theatetus', 'flies', and 'Theatetus flies', and then proceeding to show how the latter entity is determined by the former ones. The Fregean principle merely articulates the thesis of compositionality without explaining it. However, it was no part of the original problem to explain compositionality. Indeed one might well suppose that compositionality is explanatorily basic—simply not derivable from anything more fundamental. The original problem was to show how interpretations of words, together with assumptions about the structures of complex expressions, could yield interpretations of those complexes. And for this purpose we need merely assume that compositionality *does* hold. No explanation of *why* it holds is required.[7]

A little later in the same article, Davidson makes a further criticism of the deflationary approach:

> This is the place to scotch another hopeful thought. Suppose we have a satisfactory theory of syntax for our language, consisting of an effective method of telling, for an arbitrary expression, whether or not it is independently meaningful (i.e. a sentence), and assume as usual that this involves viewing each sentence as composed, in allowable ways, out of elements drawn from a fixed finite stock of atomic syntactic elements (roughly, words). The hopeful thought is that syntax, so conceived, will yield semantics when a dictionary giving the meaning of each syntactic atom is added. Hopes will be dashed, however, if semantics is to comprise a theory of meaning in our sense, for *knowledge of the structural characteristics that make for meaningfulness in a sentence, plus knowledge of the meanings of the ultimate parts, does not add up to knowledge of what a sentence means.* The point is easily illustrated by belief sentences. Their syntax is relatively unproblematic. Yet, adding a dictionary does not touch the standard semantic problem, which is that we cannot account for even as much as the truth conditions of such sentences on the basis of what we know of the meanings of the words in them (Davidson 1984b:21; my emphasis).

The central point here is that knowledge of the syntax of a sentence—for example, a belief attribution—plus knowledge of what its words mean, will not enable us to infer the sentence's truth condition. But I can find no construal of this claim in which it constitutes a good objection to deflationism.

---

[7] For further discussion and defense of the deflationary view of compositionality, see Horwich 1997. In that paper I suggest that the meaning-property of a complex expression is constituted by its being constructed in a certain way from words with certain meanings; and I offer this constitution thesis as a trivial 'explanation' of compositionality. But now it seems to me preferable to refrain from the constitution thesis and to take the principle of compositionality as explanatorily fundamental.

Does it mean that the imagined knowledge about a sentence, s, cannot yield any conclusion of the form 's is true if and only if p'? If so the claim is mistaken. Once we have determined, via the deflationary approach described and illustrated above, that a sentence means JOHN BELIEVES THAT DOGS BARK, we may straightaway conclude that it is true if and only if John believes that dogs bark. We may simply invoke the schema 's means P → (s is true ↔ p)'.

So, perhaps Davidson's claim is meant to be that the proposed account does not yield a *compositional* account of truth conditions—a deduction of them from premises about the referential properties of words. In that case, our response is that it is precisely the point of the deflationary approach to question the need for such an account. For we can interpret foreign speakers perfectly well without it, merely on the basis of the unexplained principle that meaning is compositional.[8]

Finally, Davidson's point might be that knowledge of the syntax of a sentence, plus knowledge of what its words mean, do not together suffice for us to be able us to say, for a variety of conditions, whether the sentence would be true in each of those conditions. And it is indeed clear that in order to decide if a sentence, 'A', would be true in specified circumstances, C, one must invoke relevant rules of inference to determine whether the sentence does or does not follow from how those circumstances are characterised: —i.e. to determine whether 'A' does or does not follow from 'C'. But, notice that the same would be true from within a Davidsonian framework. Even if we are given a truth-theoretic account of the meaning of 'A', there will be a need to consult logical rules in order to settle whether 'A' be true in circumstances C—i.e. whether it follows from 'C'. One might think that an advantage of the Davidsonian approach—stemming from the fact that it deals, in the first instance, with regimented or formalised sentences—is that the needed rules are well-established; they are the standard rules of predicate logic. Whereas it is relatively mysterious what rules of inference, applying to structurally-explicit *natural* language sentences, are available to be invoked by the deflationist. In fact, however, *both* approaches must confront this question. For remember that even the Davidsonian is compelled to recognise the existence of 'transformation principles' associating ordinary sentences with sentences in a regimented (formalised) part of the language; and such principles do not differ substantially from

---

[8] Note that the quoted passage appears before Davidson's presentation of his own solution to the problem of how interpretation is possible, in the context of critical discussions of various initial attempts to solve it. His arguments that these approaches are all evidently unsatisfactory are intended to give support to the truth-theoretic alternative which he goes on to articulate. But in that case these arguments cannot legitimately presuppose that we already accept that solution.

rules of deduction. Therefore, a commitment there being ordinary language inference rules is necessary on either strategy.[9]

I conclude that Davidson's resistance to the deflationary view of compositionality is unjustified. In order to interpret the expressions of a language it suffices to assume that meaning is compositional. There is no need to explain that fact by analysing sentence-meanings in terms of truth conditions. Indeed, there is no need to suppose that it *can* be explained.

Besides Davidson, two other philosophers who have drawn strong conclusions from the compositionality of meaning are Jerry Fodor and Ernie Lepore. In a series of papers, and in their book *Holism: A Shopper's Guide*, they argue that

> ...compositionality is the sovereign test for theories of lexical meaning. So hard is this test to pass, we think, that it filters out practically all of the theories of lexical meaning that are current in either philosophy or cognitive science. Among the casualties are, for example, the theory that lexical meanings are statistical structures (like stereotypes); the theory that the meaning of a word is its use; the theory that knowing the meaning of (at least some) words requires having a recognitional capacity for (at least some) of the things that it applies to; and the theory that knowing the meaning of a word requires knowing criteria for applying it (Fodor and Lepore 2001:1).[10]

Their strategy of argument is very simple. Suppose someone maintains that the meaning of a word (or the content of a mentalese term) is engendered by its inferential role (or associated stereotype, or recognitional capacity—or to put it schematically, by it's G-property). To refute any such claim, Fodor and Lepore deploy the following objection:— Meanings are

---

[9] Once we abandon the idea of explaining compositionality in truth-theoretic terms one influential reason for identifying semantic structures with expressions of 1st order predicate logic is undermined. Indeed, we might also begin to wonder about the need to draw any distinction at all between semantic and syntactic structures. Let me stress, however, that these further anti-Davidsonian speculations are not *integral* to deflationism about compositionality. Deflationism implies that we should take them seriously. But their correctness will hinge on whether the phenomena (including inferences and structural ambiguities) that are standardly explained by invoking predicate-logic semantic structures can be better explained without them. The above paragraph suggests that the prospects for finding such better explanations within a non-standard 'syntactic semantics' are by no means negligible. For we see that standard explanations (based merely on predicate logic) of inferences are often radically incomplete and that syntactically-oriented rules of logic are also needed. But an attempt to settle these issues would take us far beyond the scope of this paper. The central anti-Davidsonian claim here is quite independent of them. It is simply this: that however the semantic structure of a sentence is articulated—whether it be in terms of a predicate logic structure, a syntactic structure, or something else—the meaning of the sentence need not, and should not, be derived truth-theoretically; for it can be obtained, as illustrated above, merely on the basis of assumptions about its structure, the meanings of its words, and the principle of compositionality.

[10] See also Fodor 1998, Fodor and Lepore 1996, and Fodor and Lepore 1992.

compositional; G-properties are not (here they plug in one of the targeted theories, e.g. inferential roles, stereotypes, criteria, ...); therefore meanings aren't engendered by G-properties. Or, more explicitly:

(1) A complex's meaning what it does is determined by its structure and the meanings of its words.

(2) A complex's G-property is *not* determined by its structure and the G-properties of its words. (This is supported by examples: e.g. the stereotype associated with 'pet fish' is not determined by the stereotypical pet and the stereotypical fish).

(3) Therefore, the meaning of an expression is not engendered by its G property.

But there is a hole in this argument schema. No matter what is substituted for 'G', the argument is valid only in the presence of a further premise: the following 'Uniformity Assumption'.

If the meanings of words are engendered by their G-properties, then so are the meanings of complexes.

Without that assumption, the most one can conclude from (1) and (2) is that *either* the meanings of words aren't engendered by their G-properties, *or* the meanings of complexes aren't. Thus it would be perfectly coherent for someone to deny the uniformity assumption and maintain that whereas the meanings of *words* are engendered by their G-properties (e.g. inferential roles), the meanings of complexes are constituted in some other way.

For example, it might be supposed that,

The word 'pet' means what it does in virtue of the fact that $IR_1('pet')$

The word 'fish' means what it does in virtue of the fact that $IR_2('fish')$

The schema '$a\ n$' means what it does in virtue of the fact that $IR_3('a\ n')$

but that

The sentence 'pet fish' means what it does *not* in virtue of possessing some further inferential role, IR_4; but, rather, in virtue of the fact that it is the result of substituting words meaning what 'pet' and 'fish' do into a schema meaning what '$a\ n$' does.

This would be an instance of the deflationary view of compositionality—to take such facts about how the meanings of complex expressions are engendered to be explanatorily basic. From this perspective we should resist the impulse to begin by identifying the kind of fact in virtue of which (i) complexes and (ii) lexical items, mean what they do; to continue by proving that the former facts will indeed be determined by the latter; and to conclude that the compositionality of complex expressions has thereby been explained. This is the inflationary aspiration embodied in Davidson's truth-theoretic semantics; and the same mistake (in the form of their Uniformity Assumption) vitiates the strategy of argument deployed by Fodor and Lepore.

In defence of that assumption, and hence of their overall strategy, Fodor and Lepore cite what they aptly call 'the principle of reverse compositionality', according to which the fact that a complex means what it does determines the structure of that complex and the meanings of its constituents. This principle implies, for example, that an expression can mean PET FISH *only* if it is constructed from terms meaning PET and FISH. Their line of thought is then

(1)   that compositionality and reverse compositionality are both plausible;

(2)   that the conjunction of these facts is best explained by supposing that the meanings of words are *components* of (i.e. present in) the meanings of the complex expressions they form; and,

(3)   that this suggests that the Uniformity Assumption is indeed correct.

Now one might well accept their first step—at least with respect to our most fine-grained conception of meaning. And one might also accept the second step—at least if it is taken to say the the meaning of a complex 'contains' (in some suitable non-spatial sense) all and *only* the meanings of its component words. But surely (2) does not lead to (3). For one might naturally construe (2) as implying that the meanings of complexes are ordered *sets* whose members are the meanings of words. But then word meanings—which are presumably not sets—would be very different kinds of entity from the meanings of complexes. And in that case one would expect the kind of property in virtue of which a complex means what it does to be quite different from the kind of property in virtue of which a word means what it does. One might then very naturally agree with the deflationist that the property that is constitutive of a *complex's* meaning what it does *isn't* a use or inferential role, *isn't* a prototype, and *isn't* a recognitional capacity—but rather the property of being constructed in a certain way from words with certain uses (or associated prototypes, or recognitional capacities, …, or whatever other characteristic one takes to engender the meanings of words.[11]

---

[11] Although Fodor and Lepore believe that their Uniformity Assumption is correct and that it can be supported in the way just discussed, they maintain (in Fodor and Lepore 2001) that neither it, nor the argument of which it is it a part, are really needed in order to see that compositionality substantially constrains the nature of lexical meaning. For they think that there is a separate line of thought that yields this conclusion: viz.

Not that there is nothing to choose amongst these alternatives; but the need to accommodate the two compositionality principles won't be what decides the issue. The constraint we need in order to obtain a good theory of lexical meaning comes, not from the *compositionality* of meaning, but rather from the *use import* of meaning:—namely, that the overall use of a complex is explained by the meanings of its words and how they are combined. From this constraint we can infer that the property responsible for a word's having the meaning it does is the property that (in conjunction with other factors, including the meaning constituting factors of other words) can best account for the inferential character, and the circumstances of acceptance and rejection, of all the various sentences in which it appears. And this points us in the direction of a *use* theory of meaning. More specifically, we might well be led to conclude that the meaning of a word derives from the fact that the acceptance of certain specified sentences containing it (in certain specified conditions) is explanatorily basic.[12] But this is not to subscribe to a use theory of *sentence* meaning. Therefore there is no obligation to show how the uses of sentences are determined by the uses of words— and thereby to *explain* compositionality. Our only obligation—but this is a fairly onerous one—is to discover which particular basic acceptance properties of words will provide the best explanations of their overall uses (i.e. of the uses of all the sentences containing them). As for the *meanings* of those sentences, they derive from their construction out of words with certain uses. And nothing need be said about how and why.

Let me end with a word on understanding one's *own* language. In order that I understand for example the English sentence 'Mars rotates', it is conceptually (apriori) necessary and sufficient for me to *know* (in some sense)

---

1. Anyone who understands certain complex expressions (e.g. 'Flounders swim' and 'John snores') must also understand other expressions built from the same elements (e.g. 'Flounders snore'). ('systematicity')

2. Therefore, the meaning of a term does not depend on the complex expression in which it appears. ('context-independence')

3. But the stereotype associated with the word 'swim' in 'Flounders swim' is not the same as the stereotype associated with that word in 'John swims'

4. Therefore the meaning of 'swim' is not engendered by an associated stereotype.

But note (a) that any alert defender of the stereotype theory of meaning will simply deny premise 3 and will maintain that his theory, properly stated, is that the stereotype associated with the isolated word 'swim', whatever it may be, is the meaning of that word wherever it occurs; (b) that even if the above argument were persuasive it could tell against only the stereotype theory, but would have no bearing on any of the other accounts of lexical meaning (e.g. the use theory) that were alleged by Fodor and Lepore to be precluded by compositionality; and (c) the argument does not really hinge on compositionality, but rather on context-independence—so it cannot be presented as a justification of their claim that *compositionality* filters out virtually all theories of lexical meaning.

[12] For a sustained explanation and defence of this form of the use theory of meaning, see chapter 3 of Horwich 1998.

what it means—specifically, that it means MARS ROTATES. But it cannot be my *explicit* knowledge of this fact that constitutes my understanding of the sentence; for that would be too easy; I can explicitly infer it merely from the capitalising convention for naming meanings. Rather, the needed knowledge is *implicit*:[13]—it consists in the fact that what 'Mars rotates' means in my idiolect resembles its meaning in English. And that resemblance derives, in turn, from the fact that the basic uses of the words 'Mars' and '_rotates' (and their mode of combination) are similar in my idiolect and in the public language.[14] Consequently, if someone implicitly knows the meanings of the elements of a sentence of his language—whether it be a sentence-type or a sentence-token—and also knows how those elements are combined, he thereby satisfies the condition for understanding the whole. There is no need for any inference, or for any other sort of process, to take him from those antecedent items of knowledge to the state of understanding the sentence.

Contrary to Fodor and Lepore (2001) it is no objection to these theses that one may come across a sentence token (e.g. 'Dogs dogs dog dog dogs'), be informed about its structure (e.g. '[[Dogs [dogs dog]][dog dogs]]'), know what the words mean, and yet still not understand that sentence. For, the knowledge required for understanding a *word* does not amount to having some piece of *explicit* information about its meaning (e.g. that 'dog' means the same as 'chien') but is rather a matter of know-*how* (i.e. a mastery of its use). And similarly, the required knowledge of structure cannot take the form of theoretical characterisation of it, but must also be implicit and manifested in use (e.g. being disposed to infer 'Certain dogs dog dogs'). Once *this* sort of knowledge of word meanings and sentence structure is obtained, then understanding the sentence is guaranteed.

Nor is it reasonable to object that since understanding is a form of knowledge, and since knowledge yields further knowledge only by inference, our understanding of complex expressions *must* result from inference. This *conclusion* can't be right; because, regarding our understanding of the language of thought (whether it be ordinary language or universal mental-

---

[13] Fodor and Lepore stress the importance of distinguishing, on the one hand, the contrast between *occurrent* and *dispositional* mental states and, on the other hand, the contrast between *conscious* and *unconscious* states. And they think that my use of 'explicit' and 'implicit' oscillates confusingly between these alternatives. But in fact I am pointing to a *third* contrast by means of that terminology. Explicit commitments are articulated—i.e. spelled out in the 'belief box'—whereas implicit commitments are not. E.g. my implicit knowledge that 'Mars rotates' means, in my idiolect, MARS ROTATES, consists merely in the *fact* that it has that meaning. Therefore explicit commitments may be either conscious or unconscious, and either occurrent or dispositional; and the same may be said of implicit commitments.

[14] The emphasis on *resemblance* between idiolectal and public language meanings is intended to explain how understanding an expression is a matter of degree.

ese), there would be no language in which to conduct the alleged inferences. Moreover, the *argument* for that conclusion isn't right; because it is only for *articulated* (though perhaps unconscious) knowledge—i.e. spelled out in the language of thought—that transitions between states of knowledge are likely to be mediated by inference; but understanding is *implicit* knowledge.

Finally, it is not relevant to point out that if, as a matter of empirical fact, we think in a universal mentalese, then understanding a token of an ordinary sentence will require translating it into that mental language—a process which might conceivably involve explicit (yet unconscious) inferences. This is beside the point; for even if inferences are involved, they will enter merely into how we grasp the *structure* of the sentence token (and maybe into how we learned the meanings of its words). They will *not* be employed in the move from that grasp, and from our knowledge of word meanings, to our understanding of the token. For there is no such move. To see this once again, suppose that properly understanding a token of 'Mars rotates' is empirically constituted by unconsciously translating it into a specific sentence, 'm', of mentalese—a sentence consisting in a certain structure imposed on certain mentalese terms. Now imagine someone who happens to translate 'Mars rotates' into a *different* mentalese sentence 'm*'—i.e. his understanding is defective. Then it must be (as a matter of conceptual necessity) that either the *structure* of 'm' differs from the structure of 'm*', or that the *terms* making up these mentalese sentences are not all the same. In other words, either our subject hasn't on this occasion understood 'Mars' or '_rotates', or he hasn't grasped how those words have been combined. Thus once the meanings of the words in the token, and the way these words are combined, have been properly—i.e. implicitly—identified, there is nothing more to be done. The conditions for understanding have been met.[15]

References

Davidson, D. 1984. *Inquiries into Truth and Interpretation*. Oxford: Clarendon Press

Davidson, D. 1984a. Radical Interpretation. *Inquiries into Truth and Interpretation*, 125-40. Oxford: Clarendon Press.

Davidson, D. 1984b. Truth and Meaning. *Inquiries into Truth and Interpretation*, 17-36. Oxford: Clarendon Press. First published in *Synthese* 17:304-23.

---

[15] I would like to thank Jim Edwards, Jerry Fodor, Ernie Lepore, Stephen Neale, Paul Pietroski, Barry C. Smith and Mark Sainsbury for helpful discussions of the issues treated in this paper.

Fodor, J. 1998. There are no Recognitional Concepts; Not Even RED. *Philosophical Issues* 9, ed. E. Villanueva. Atascadero, Ca.: Ridgeview Publishing Company.

Fodor, J and Lepore, E. 1991. Why Meaning (Probably) Isn't Conceptual Role. *Mind & Language* 6:328-43.

Fodor, J and Lepore, E., 1992. *Holism. A Shopper's Guide.* Oxford: Blackwell.

Fodor, J and Lepore, E. 1996. The Pet Fish and the Red Herring: Why Concepts Aren't Prototypes. *Cognition* 58:243-76.

Fodor, J and Lepore, E. 2001. Why Compositionality Won't Go Away. Reflections on Horwich's 'Deflationary theory'. *Ratio* Volume XIV No. 4.

Higginbotham, J. 1999. A Perspective on Truth and Meaning. *The Philosophy of Donald Davidson*, ed. L. Hahn, 671-86. La Salle, Illinois: Open Court.

Horwich, P. 1997. The Composition of Meanings. *Philosophical Review* 106:503-31. Reprinted as chapter 7 of Horwich 1998.

Horwich, P. 1998. *Meaning.* Oxford: Oxford University Press.

Quine, W. V. 1960. Word and Object. Cambridge, Mass.: MIT Press.

7

What is Logical Form?

ERNEST LEPORE AND KIRK LUDWIG

> *Philosophy, as we use the word, is a fight against the*
> *fascination which forms of expression exert upon us.*
> Wittgenstein

1 Introduction

Bertrand Russell, in the second of his 1914 Lowell lectures, *Our Knowledge of the External World*, asserted famously that 'every philosophical problem, when it is subjected to the necessary analysis and purification, is found either to be not really philosophical at all, or else to be, in the sense in which we are using the word, logical' (Russell 1993:42). He went on to characterize that portion of logic that concerned the study of *forms* of propositions, or, as he called them, 'logical forms'. This portion of logic he called 'philosophical logic'. Russell asserted that

> ... some kind of knowledge of logical forms, though with most people it is not explicit, is involved in all understanding of discourse. It is the business of philosophical logic to extract this knowledge from its concrete integuments, and to render it explicit and pure (Russell 1993:53).

Perhaps no one still endorses quite this grand a view of the role of logic and the investigation of logical form in philosophy. But *talk* of logical form retains a central role in analytic philosophy. Given its widespread use in philosophy and linguistics, it is rather surprising that the concept of logical form has not received more attention by philosophers than it has.

The concern of this paper is to say something about what talk of logical form comes to, in a tradition that stretches back to (and arguably beyond) Russell's use of that expression. This will not be exactly Russell's conception. For we do not endorse Russell's view that propositions are the bearers of logical form, or that appeal to propositions adds anything to our understanding of what talk of logical form comes to. But we will be concerned to provide an account responsive to the interests expressed by Russell in the above quotations, though one clarified of extraneous elements, and expressed precisely. For this purpose, it is important to note that the concern expressed by Russell in the above passages, as the surrounding text makes clear, is a concern not just with logic conceived narrowly as the study of logical *terms*, but with propositional form more generally, which includes, e.g., such features as those that correspond to the number of argument places in a propositional function, and the categories of objects which propositional functions can take as arguments. This very general concern with form is expressed above in the claim that *all* understanding of discourse involves some knowledge of logical forms. It is logical form in this very general sense, which is connected with an interest in getting clear about the nature of reality through getting clear about the forms of our thoughts or talk about it, with which we will be concerned.[1]

---

[1] Russell expressed these views in numerous places. For example, in 'On Scientific Method in Philosophy', the Herbert Spencer lecture at Oxford in 1914, he says, 'Philosophy, if what has been said is correct, becomes indistinguishable from logic as that word has now come to be used' (Russell 1959, pp. 84-85). He distinguishes within logic two portions ('not very sharply distinguished' ibid.), one dealing with 'those general statements which can be made concerning everything without mentioning any one thing or predicate or relation'– roughly the topic neutral conception of logic – and one dealing with 'the analysis and enumeration of logical forms, i.e., with the kinds of propositions that may occur, with the various types of facts, and the classification of the constituents of facts' (ibid.). 'In this way,' Russell says, 'logic provides an inventory of possibilities, a repertory of abstractly tenable hypotheses' (ibid.). It is clear as well that Wittgenstein's concern with logical form in the *Tractatus Logico-Philosophicus*, a concern that grew out of his work with Russell from 1911 to the outbreak of the First World War, was a general concern for the form of representations, and in the case of natural languages, with the logical forms of expressions generally, not a concern more narrowly with a restricted set of terms to be called 'logical'. See, *e.g.*, 3.32-3.325 of the *Tractatus*, though it is clear throughout that Wittgenstein uses the notion of logical form very broadly for the form of a representation, including the forms of elementary propositions. These conceptions of the primary task of philosophy and the correlative role of the notion of logical form in articulating it have, needless to say, had an enormous, though somewhat inchoate, influence on the philosophical tradition in English speaking countries. Wittgenstein's greatest immediate influence was on the members of the Vienna Circle. Some sense of the impression created, and the importance attached to the general notion of logical form Wittgenstein worked with, can be gleaned from Moritz Schlick's 'The Turning Point in Philosophy' (the lead article in the first volume of *Erkenntnis*, Schlick 1959). The influence of the

The conception we will champion dispenses with talk of propositions, reified sentence meanings, as a useless excrescence, and treats logical form as a feature of sentences. Consonant with Russell's general interest in the form of propositions, we will treat talk about the logical form of a *sentence* in a language L to be essentially about *semantic* form as revealed in a *compositional meaning theory for L*. We do not, however, treat logical form itself as a sentence, or anything else. On our account, it is a mistake to think that logical forms are *entities*, or to think of logical form as revealed by what symbols occur in a sentence, either in its surface syntax, or in the syntax of its translation into an 'ideal' language. Rather, we will take the relation of *sameness of logical form* as basic. We will give a precise account of the notion of sameness of logical form between any two sentences in any two languages, first for declarative sentences, then for sentences in any sentential mood. Our account is inspired by remarks of Davidson, and we develop the account for declaratives in the context of a Davidsonian truth-theoretic semantics. We develop the account for non-declaratives in terms of a generalization of the notion of an interpretive truth theory, namely, that of an interpretive fulfillment theory.

We will also be concerned to say something about the relation of this characterization of logical form to logic more narrowly conceived, that is, a study of the semantics of logical terms or structures. We will urge that these are distinct, and, to some degree, independent concerns. We will also suggest a criterion (essentially due to Davidson) for picking out logical terms or structures that is particularly salient from the standpoint on logical form we advance, though we make no claim for its being the only way of extending in a principled way the use of the notion beyond where it is currently well-grounded. (This discussion will show, incidentally, that no good basis exists, contrary to what has been relatively recently alleged (Etchemendy 1983; Etchemendy 1988; Etchemendy 1990; Lycan 1989), for denying that a principled distinction between the logical and non-logical *terms* of a language can be drawn.)

The program of our paper is as follows. In section 2 we consider the origins of the notion of logical form in reflection on argument form, and criticize two traditional conceptions, one of which remains dominant. In section 3 we introduce the notion of logical form we wish to develop, logi-

---

Vienna Circle and its sympathizers in turn has had a central role in shaping contemporary philosophy. Of course, this broad notion of logical form did not arise first with Russell, but stretches back into the tradition. For example, it is clear that Kant's conception of the logical form of a judgment is in the same spirit as Russell's, a concern with very general common features of judgments which yield a basic taxonomy of their kinds, abstracting from their particular matter. And a concern with logical form in broadly Russell's sense, if not under that description, as Russell himself has said, is clearly something philosophers from ancient times have been concerned with in thinking about how our forms of speech and thought relate us to reality.

cal form as semantic form, and describe our conception of how to use a truth theory to give a compositional semantic theory for declarative sentences in a language as background for our development of this conception. In section 4 we give a precise characterization of sameness of logical form of sentences applicable across languages in terms of the notion of corresponding proofs of the T-sentences for them in *interpretive truth theories* for the languages. This allows us to clarify what could be meant by the expression '*x* is the logical form of *y*'. In section 5 we employ examples from natural language semantics in illustration of the usefulness of the present approach. In section 6 we show how the basic approach can be extended to non-declarative sentences. (This extension is based on some work by one of the authors (Ludwig) which the other (Lepore) has some reservations about, so it is put forward here as a *suggestion* about how this desirable extension might be effected.) In section 7 we discuss the relation of the conception of logical form we advance to the project of identifying logical terms or structures, and contrast it with an alternative conception articulated in terms of an invariance condition traceable back to Tarski 1986 and Lindström 1966. Section 8 is a brief summary and conclusion.

2

The origin of interest in logical form lies in the recognition that many intuitively valid natural language arguments can be classified together on the basis of common features, a form which guarantees their validity apart from their different content. We group together arguments which exemplify a pattern, and say that they share a form. Forms of arguments are represented by replacing (certain) of the expressions in their premises and conclusions with schematic letters – thereby abstracting away from what the arguments are about. This gives rise to a common characterization of the logical form of a sentence, namely, that structure of a sentence that determines from which sentences it can be validly deduced, and which sentences can be validly deduced from it and other premises, where these sentences are in turn characterized in terms of their logical structures.

This loose characterization is far from satisfactory because it leaves unexplicated how 'structure of a sentence' is being used. Logical form cannot be just any schema that results from replacing one or more expressions within a sentence. There are too many, and not every such schema will be taken to reveal logical form. In addition, for sentences with more than one reading, such as [1], we associate more than one logical form, but they will generate the same schemas.

[1]   Everyone loves someone.

Similarly, sentences we are intuitively inclined to assign distinct logical forms, such as the pairs [1]-[2], [3]-[4], and [5]-[6], yield the same schemas.

Likewise, sentences, as might be urged for the pair [6]-[7], to which we wish to assign the same logical form (in the same or different languages) may yield distinct schemas. Examples can be multiplied endlessly.

[2]   John loves Mary.

[3]   Dogs bark.

[4]   Unicorns exist.

[5]   The President is a scoundrel.

[6]   The whale is a mammal.

[7]   Everything which is a whale is a mammal.

Russell's response, of course, was to bypass sentences and to take logical form to be a property of the *propositions* that sentences express (as above). This renders intelligible talk of similar sentences having distinct logical forms, and of different sentences, in the same or different languages, having the same logical form. Sentences on this view can be said in a derivative sense to have logical form: sentences have the same logical form when they express propositions with the same logical form.

An alternative approach, more usual today, is to identify the logical form of a natural language sentence as the form of a sentence in a specially regimented, 'ideal', perhaps formal, language that translates it (or, in the case of an ambiguous sentence, the logical forms it can have are associated with the sentences that translate the various readings of it).[2] A regimented language must contain no ambiguities and syntactically encode all differences in the logical (or semantical) roles of terms. A common variant of this view, marking out a narrower conception of logical form, is to identify the logical form of the natural language sentence as the form determined by the pattern of logical constants in its regimented translation. Natural language sentences then can be said to share logical form if they translate into sentences the same in form in the regimented language of choice, and to have different logical forms if they translate into sentences different in form. (Cf. Frege in the *Begriffsschrift*, 'In my formalized language there is nothing that corresponds [to changes in word ordering that do not affect the inferential relations a sentence enters into]; only that part of judgments which affects the possible inferences is taken into consideration' (Black and Geach 1960:3).

---

[2] This can almost be called the official view. It has made its way into the *Cambridge Dictionary of Philosophy* as the canonical account: logical form is 'the form of a proposition in a logically perfect language, determined by the grammatical form of the ideal sentence expressing that proposition (or statement, in one use of the latter term).' (Note that this *mixes up* the two conceptions distinguished in the text.) The author goes on to characterize sameness of logical form as sameness of grammatical form in an ideal language, but in a way that resists characterization across languages of sameness of grammatical form or, hence, logical form.

Neither of these approaches is satisfactory. On the one hand, any grasp we have on talk of the structure of propositions derives from our grasp on sentence structure in a regimented language which aims to express more clearly than ordinary language the structure of the proposition. On the other, the trouble with identifying the logical form of a natural language sentence with a sentence structure expressible in a regimented language is that we wish to be able to speak informatively about the logical form of sentences in our regimented language as well. It is no more plausible that it is simply the *pattern* of expressions in the sentence in the regimented language than in natural language. There can be more than one ideal language a natural language can be translated into, whose translations into each other take sentences into sentences with different patterns of expressions. Appeal to the pattern of logical expressions is of no help. First, we have not said when a term (or structure) counts as logical. Second, the pattern alluded to cannot consist of the actual arrangement of the logical terms in the regimented language, for the same reason that appeal to patterns of expressions more generally is futile: there are clearly different regimentations possible which would be said to exhibit the same form but differ in syntax (Polish notation and standard logical notation, for example).

Some philosophers have concluded that all talk about *the* logical form of a sentence is confused. Quine has claimed that the purpose of providing a paraphrase in a regimented language of a sentence, which is treated as its logical form, is 'to put the sentence into a form that admits most efficiently of logical calculation, or shows its implications and conceptual affinities most perspicuously, obviating fallacy and paradox' (Quine 1971:452). He argues there will be different ways of doing this, and consequently there can be no demand for *the* logical form of a natural language sentence.[3] Davidson follows Quine in seeing logical form as relative to the logic of one's theory for a language (see 'Reply to Cargile,' in Davidson 1984b:140).[4] More recently, Lycan (1989) and Etchemendy (1988) have suggested that there can be no principled distinction between logical and non-logical terms, which, if correct, would undercut the possibility of an objective account of logical form by appeal to patterns relating to logical terms. These skeptical reactions are unwarranted, as the sequel will show.

---

[3] Quine also uses this argument to urge that the grammarian's deep structure need not be identified with what is usually taken by logicians to be logical form. He gives as an instance of two ways of regimenting the same sentences, for purposes of keeping track of their implication relations, a language which eliminates proper names in favor of predicates by treating the name 'a' as equivalent to '$x=a$', and introducing a predicate letter for it, and then regimenting 'Fa' as '$(\exists x)(Fx.x=a)$', and a language which retains individual constants.

[4] It is with some irony that we report this, since our own approach, which shows how to explicate the notion of sameness of logical form without relativizing to the logic of any particular theory, is, as we've said, based on the suggestion of Davidson's quoted below at the beginning of section 3.

3

The account of logical form we advocate generalizes and refines a view Davidson urged in some early papers. A clear statement of this conception occurs in 'On Saying That':

> What should we ask of an adequate account of the logical form of a sentence? Above all, I would say, such an account must lead us to see the semantic character of the sentence – its truth or falsity – as owed to how it is composed, by a finite number of applications of some of a finite number of devices that suffice for the language as a whole, out of elements drawn from a finite stock (the vocabulary) that suffices for the language as a whole. To see a sentence in this light is to see it in the light of a theory for its language. A way to provide such a theory is by recursively characterizing a truth predicate, along the lines suggested by Tarski. (Davidson 1968; Davidson 1984c:94)

His suggestion is not precise enough (or, as will emerge, general enough) for our purposes. Not every true Tarski-style truth theory for a language issues in an account of the semantic features of the language, only an *interpretive truth theory*. In order to explain this, we must first explain our conception of how a truth theory for a natural language L may be employed in giving a compositional meaning theory for L.

A compositional meaning theory for L should provide,

(R)   from a specification of the meanings of finitely many primitive expressions and rules, a specification of the meaning of an utterance of any of the infinitely many sentences of L.

Confining our attention to declaratives for the moment, a compositional meaning theory for a context *in*sensitive language L, i.e., a language without elements whose semantic contribution depends on context of use, would issue in theorems of the form,

(M) φ in L means that p,

where 'φ' is replaced by a structural description of a sentence of L and 'p' by a metalanguage sentence that translates it.

For context insensitive languages, the connection between a theory meeting Tarski's famous Convention T and a compositional meaning theory meeting (R) is straightforward: a truth theory meets that convention only if it entails every instance of (T),

(T) φ is true in L iff p,

in which a structural description of a sentence of L replaces 'φ', and a synonymous metalanguage sentence replaces 'p'. We shall call such instances of (T) *T-sentences*. The relation between a structural description that replaces 'φ' and a metalanguage sentence that replaces 'p' in a T-sentence is the same as that between suitable substitution pairs in (M). Therefore, every instance of (S) is true when what replaces 'p' translates the sentence denoted by what replaces 'φ'.

(S)   If φ is true in L iff p, then φ in L means that p.

Given a T-sentence for a sentence s, the appropriate instance of (S) enables us to specify its meaning. One advantage of a truth-theoretic approach (over trying to generate instances of (M) more directly) is its ability to provide recursions needed to generate meaning specifications for object language sentences from a finite base with no more ontological or logical resources than is required for a theory of reference. This turns out to be central also to its role in revealing something that deserves the label 'logical form'.

In natural languages, many (arguably all) sentences lack truth-values independently of use. 'I am tired' is true or false only as used. This requires discarding our simple accounts of the forms of theories of meaning and truth. In modifying a compositional meaning theory to accommodate context sensitivity, and a truth theory that serves as its recursive engine, a theorist must choose between two options. The first retains the basic form of the meaning specification, 'x means in language y that p', and correspondingly retains within the truth theory a two-place predicate relating a truth bearer and a language. This requires conditionalizing on utterances of sentences in specifying truth conditions. The second adds an argument place to each semantic predicate in the theory for every contextual parameter required to fix a context sensitive element's contribution when used. For concreteness, we will suppose that the fundamental contextual parameters are utterer and utterance time.[5] Either approach is acceptable. We adopt the second because it simplifies the form of the theories. This approach yields theorems of the forms (M2) and (T2).

(M2)   For any speaker s, time t, sentence φ of L, φ means$_{[s,t]}$ in L that p.

(T2)   For any speaker s, time t, sentence φ of L, φ is true$_{[s,t]}$ in L iff p.

As a first gloss, we might try to treat 'means$_{[s,t]}$ in L' and 'is true$_{[s,t]}$ in L' as equivalent to 'means as potentially spoken by s at t in L' and 'is true as potentially spoken by s at t in L'. However, as Evans (1985:359-60) points out, we cannot read these as, $\ulcorner$ if φ were used by s at t in L, then, as spoken by s at t, φ would be true iff/mean that$\urcorner$, since, aside from worries about how to evaluate counterfactuals, these interpretations would assign sentences such as 'I am silent' false T-theorems. What we need are the readings, $\ulcorner$ if φ were used by s at t in L, as things actually stand, φ would be

---

[5] Though we will not argue for it here, we believe these are the only contextual parameters we need in order to devise an adequate semantics. Throughout quantifiers over times will range over time intervals, and 'is a time' will be true of time intervals. We will include as a limiting case of a time interval temporal instants.

true iff/mean that⌝, or, alternatively, ⌜φ understood as if spoken by s at t in L is true iff/means that⌝; *mutatis mutandis* for other semantic predicates.

We replace adequacy criterion (R) with (R'):

(R')　A compositional meaning theory for a language L should entail, from a specification of the meanings of primitive expressions of L, all true sentences of form (M2).

The analog of Tarski's Convention T for recursive truth theories for natural languages we shall call *Davidson's Convention T*, given in (D).

(D)　An adequate truth theory for a language L must entail every instance of (T2) for which corresponding instances of (M2) are true.

A Tarski-style truth theory for L meeting (D) with axioms that *interpret* primitive expressions of L provides the resources to meet (R'). We will call any such theory an *interpretive truth theory*.

There are two parts of this requirement that deserve further comment. First, we have in mind a Tarski-style theory in the sense of a theory which employs a *satisfaction predicate* relating sequences or functions to expressions of the language and contextual parameters, supplemented by a similarly relativized reference function for assigning referents to singular terms. Second, the requirement that the axioms of the theory *interpret* primitive expressions of L is of great importance in understanding the present approach. We will therefore elaborate on this aspect of the requirement. For an axiom to be interpretive, it must treat the object language term for which it is an axiom as being of the right semantic category. Thus, predicates should receive satisfaction clauses that represent them as predicates, referring terms should receive reference axioms, recursive terms (or structures) should receive recursive axioms. For a context insensitive language, a base axiom interprets an object language expression just in case its satisfaction conditions (or referent) is given using a term in the metalanguage that translates it. Thus, for example, to give an axiom for 'x is red' in English, taking the metalanguage to be English as well, we would write (ignoring tense and suppressing relativization to language when dealing with English):

for all functions f, f satisfies 'x is red' iff $f('x')$ is red.

This is an interpretive axiom for 'x is red', for the predicate used to give the satisfaction conditions translates the object language predicate for which satisfaction conditions are given. In contrast,

for all functions f, f satisfies 'x is red' iff $f('x')$ is red and the earth moves,

is not interpretive since 'is red and the earth moves' does not translate 'is red'. A recursive term, such as 'and', will receive a recursive axiom. To be interpretive, the recursive structure used in the metalanguage must translate that of the object language sentence on which the recursion is run. Thus, for 'and' in English, using English as the metalanguage, we would give the following recursive axiom:

for all functions f, sentences φ, ψ, f satisfies $\varphi^\frown$ 'and' $^\frown \psi$ iff f satisfies φ and f satisfies ψ.

In contrast,

for all functions f, sentences φ, ψ, f satisfies $\varphi^\frown$ 'and' $^\frown \psi$ iff it is not the case that if f satisfies φ, then it is not the case that f satisfies ψ,

is not interpretive, because the recursive structure used to give satisfaction conditions does not translate that for which satisfaction conditions are given.[6] These remarks apply directly to context insensitive languages. For

---

[6] By way of another contrast, consider the approach to conjunction represented in PC' in Larson and Segal (1995:111-112). We need consider only the axioms for 'and', 'or', and sentences formed using them.

   (i)   Val($<z, z'>$, 'and') iff z=t and z'=t
   (ii)   Val($<z, z'>$, 'or') iff z=t or z'=t
   (iii) For any S, ConjP, Val(t, [$_s$S ConjP]) iff for some z, Val(z, S) and Val(z, ConjP)
   (iv) For any Conj, S, Val(z, [$_{conjP}$ Conj S]) iff for some z', Val($<z, z'>$, Conj) and Val(z', S)
   (v)   For all conjunctions α, Val($<z, z'>$, [$_{conj}$ α]) iff Val($<z, z'>$, α)
   (vi) For any elementary sentence ζ, Val(t, [$_s$ ζ]) iff Val(t, ζ)

'Val(x, y)' is read as 'x is a value of y'. '[$_s$S ConjP]' structurally describes a sentence formed from a sentence S and a conjunction ('and' or 'or') concatenated with a sentence P, the latter treated as a unit for purposes of decomposition. This is a device like the use of parentheses to disambiguate the order of evaluation of parts of complex sentences. Likewise '[$_{conjP}$ Conj S]' is a structural description of a conjunction concatenated with a sentence S. It should be obvious that this is not, in our usage, an interpretive truth theory (or a fragment thereof), for a number of reasons. First, as we have said, we have in mind a Tarski-style theory in the sense of a theory which uses a satisfaction predicate to relate sequences or functions to expressions of the language (and a reference function for singular referring terms). On our conception of an interpretive truth theory, no entities are assigned to any expressions in the language except referring terms; no terms (excepting referring terms) are said to have 'values' in the sense intended by Larson and Segal. The axioms above therefore fail to be axioms in an interpretive truth theory in our sense because they are not axioms in a Tarski-style theory in our sense. This point applies not just to PC', but to all of the theories Larson and Segal discuss. (The motives which prompt Larson and Segal to introduce 'semantic values' for all expressions of natural languages are not shared by us, and are not part of any project of giving compositional semantics for natural languages which concerns us.) This is not unconnected with another way in which the above theory fails to be interpretive in our sense. The appeal to the assignments of ordered pairs as values to conjunctions allows the formulation of axioms (iii) and (iv) above as part of the recursion to generate T-sentences. The result of this, however, has a quantified sentence (or quantified open sentence) representing the recursive structure of an object language sentence that is not quantified. An interpretive axiom for a sentence with a recursive structure must not introduce recursive structures not present in the target sentence. But, of course, the introduction of this quantifier is

context sensitive languages, when we have a verb which is context sensitive, e.g., tensed, we will have a metalanguage verb which has argument places expressing that relativization, which, because it is not itself context sensitive, will not be a strict translation of the object language verb. For example, consider the axiom for 'is red' when we take into account tense:

For all functions f, f satisfies$_{[s,t]}$ 'x is red' iff red(f('x'), t).

The metalanguage verb 'red(x, y)' is not tensed, but rather expresses a relation between an object and a time, the relation the object has to the time iff it is red at that time. What is it for such an axiom to be interpretive? Intuitively, the idea is clear: we want the metalanguage verb to express, relative to appropriate arguments, exactly the relation the object language verb expresses in use. We can make this precise as follows. Consider what we would say a predicate which is tensed *means* relative to use with respect to an object at a time. For example, we would say that a use of 'is red' relative to x and t means that red(x, t). Drawing on a generalization of this notion, we will say that an axiom for a predicate, with free variables 'x_1', 'x_2', ... 'x_n', denoted by 'Z($x_1, x_2, ... x_n$)', which is context sensitive relative to parameters, $p_1, p_2, ..., p_m$,

For all f, f satisfies$_{[p1, p2, ..., pm]}$ Z($x_1, x_2, ... x_n$) iff $\zeta(f('x_1'), ..., f('x_n'), p_1, p_2, ..., p_m)$,

is interpretive just in case the corresponding relativized meaning statement is true:

For all f, Z($x_1, x_2, ... x_n$) means$_{[f, p1, p2, ..., pm]}$ that $\zeta(f('x_1'), ..., f('x_n'), p_1, p_2, ..., p_m)$.

For a context sensitive referring term, the term must be assigned the right referent relative to the context of use by the rule giving its referent relative to contextual parameters.

With this conception of how a truth theory can serve as a component of a compositional meaning theory (at least for declarative sentences) in place, we can return to the question how such a truth theory helps to give content to the notion of logical form.

---

directly connected with the decision to assign entities to sentential connectives, which represents the most fundamental departure from the style of theory with which we are concerned. These points are relevant to the semantic categories of axioms in an interpretive truth theory which are relevant for our characterization of sameness of logical form through the notion of corresponding proofs, explained in section 4. Questions about the relation of our approach to that of Larson and Segal, which prompted this note, were raised by Peter Ludlow in his comment on an earlier version of this paper presented at a symposium on logical form at the 1998 Central Division Meetings of the American Philosophical Association.

4

An interest in the logical form of a sentence[7] is an interest in those semantic properties it may share with distinct sentences relevant to the conditions under which it is true, and the relations between the conditions under which it and other sentences are true. This interest is motivated by the traditional concern not to be misled by the surface form of sentences into assimilating one sort of claim to another quite different. The conception we are advocating is well-suited to meet this interest, since it identifies logical form with semantic form, insight into which is exactly what a compositional meaning theory provides. This can be made precise in terms of an interpretive truth theory for a language.

In addition to sentences, the notion of semantic form applies to significant subsentential expressions, complex and primitive. In this way, a notion of logical form associated with semantic form extends to include subsentential expressions, enabling us to talk of the logical form of a lexical item. The logical form of a sentence is determined by the logical forms of its lexical items and how their combination contributes to determining its interpretive truth conditions. The logical form of a lexical item is that semantic feature it shares (at least potentially) with other lexical items that determines how it interacts with other vocabulary items likewise characterized in terms of features shared with other expressions. For example, one-place predicates will interact systematically differently with quantifiers than will two-place predicates. This reveals itself in the base axioms of the truth theory, since all the axioms for one-place predicates will share a common form, and all the axioms for two-place predicates will share a different common form. The semantic type of a primitive term is given by the semantic type of the axiom it receives in the truth theory: its logical form is determined by its semantic type, i.e., sameness and difference of logical form for primitive terms is sameness and difference of semantic type.

There will be a variety of different levels of classification on the basis of semantic features that expressions have in common. Deictic elements can be classified together on the basis of their contributions to interpretive truth conditions being relativized to contextual parameters (speaker and time, if our assumptions are correct). Among deictic elements we may press a further semantic division based on whether contextual parameters alone determine the contribution of a deictic element to the interpretive truth conditions of an utterance of a sentence, or whether additional information is required, such as knowledge of a speaker's demonstrative intentions.

---

[7] We restrict our attention for the time being to declarative sentences.

In general, features of the axioms for primitive expressions in the language which capture the way the expression contributes to the truth conditions of sentences can be used to classify them by semantic type. The semantic theory for the language will contain all the information traditionally sought under the heading of logical form, but much more. In that sense this conception of logical form is a generalization as well as development of one strand in the traditional conception.

We said that the logical form of a sentence s is determined by the logical forms of the lexical items s contains and how they combine to determine the interpretive truth conditions of s. This needs to be made more precise. An interpretive truth theory for a language L can be cast as a formal theory. When it is, it must include enough logic to prove from its axioms every T-sentence. Its logic may be so circumscribed that it enables one to prove all *and only* T-sentences, or it may be more powerful. Intuitively, the contribution elements of a sentence s make to its interpretive truth conditions (or the contribution of the elements of s to the truth conditions of an utterance of s) will be revealed by a proof of its T-sentence which draws only upon the content of axioms. We shall call any such proof a *canonical* proof of the T-sentence (following Davidson). If the logic of the theory is so restricted that, for any object language sentence s, a T-sentence for s can be proved only by drawing solely upon the content of the axioms for terms in s, then every proof of a T-sentence will be canonical. If the logic is stronger, the characterization of a canonical proof will involve restrictions on the resources allowed in proofs and perhaps how these resources are deployed. (Of course, if one description of a proof procedure meets the intuitive condition for describing a canonical proof, many will.) Clearly, a canonical proof of a T-sentence for an object language sentence *shows* what its semantic structure is, for it *shows* how the semantic categories to which its constituent terms belong, determined by the type of axiom provided for each, contribute to determining its interpretive truth conditions. We can say that a canonical proof of a T-sentence for a sentence *reveals* its logical form. However, to identity logical form with canonical proof would be a mistake on the order of identifying logical form with a sentence in an ideal language.

A canonical proof is relative to a metalanguage and its accompanying logic, while logical form is not. The canonical proof, together with our understanding of the metalanguage, reveals logical form, i.e., semantic form. The logical form of a sentence s is determined by the *semantic category of each primitive in s* and *how these combine* to determine s's interpretive truth conditions and so meaning. Thus, the logical form of s is a property of s revealed by the structure of the proof and by the axioms for the primitives in s. This property is determined once we can characterize when two sentences, in the same or different languages, share logical form. That characterization should not depend on any particular formal theory with respect to which a canonical proof procedure is formulated. We want something which all canonical proofs of T-sentences for a sentence s in interpretive truth theories for its language share in common. Intuitively, we want to say that two sentences share logical form when the same canonical proof *can* be given for them, *adjusting* for differences due to *differences in the object language*, and *differences between the axioms employed which are not based on the semantic category to which a term belongs*. For then all the proofs for either will share in common what reveals their semantic structure articulated in terms of the categories of their semantic primitives and how they combine to determine interpretive truth conditions. With this intuitive characterization as a guide, we offer a more precise characterization. First, we define the notion of *corresponding proofs* in [8].

[8]   A proof P_1 of a T-sentence for s_1 in T_1 *corresponds* to a proof P_2 for a T-sentence for s_2 in T_2 iff$_{df}$

(a) P_1 and P_2 are sentence sequences identical in length;

(b) at each stage of each proof identical rules are used;

(c) the base axioms employed at each stage are of the same semantic type, and the recursive axioms employed at each stage interpret identically object language terms for which they specify satisfaction conditions (with respect to contributions to truth conditions).

Using [8], we define *sameness of logical form* as a four-place relation among sentences and languages as in [9].

[9]   For any sentences s_1, s_2, languages L_1, L_2, s_1 in L_1 has the same logical form as s_2 in L_2 iff$_{df}$ there are interpretive truth theories T_1 for L_1 and T_2 for L_2 such that

(a) they share the same logic;

(b) there is a canonical proof P_1 of the T-sentence for s_1 in T_1;

(c) there is a canonical proof P_2 of the T-sentence for s_2 in T_2, such that:

(d) P_1 *corresponds* to P_2.

[9] requires the contributions of the recursive elements and the way in which they combine with non-recursive elements in each sentence, relative to their languages, to be the same. Note that we have required sameness of interpretation up to contribution to truth conditions in [8](c). This qualification aims to exclude as irrelevant differences in meaning that make no difference to the way in which a recursive term determines how expressions it combines with contribute to fixing the conditions under which the sentence is true. For example, 'and' and 'but' arguably differ in meaning, but this

difference is irrelevant to how each determines the contribution of the sentences they conjoin to the truth of the sentences in which they occur.

The remaining free parameter is sameness of semantic type between base axioms in [8](c). There may be room for different classifications, but in general it looks as if we will wish to classify axioms together on the basis of features neutral with respect to the extensions of predicates, though not with respect to the structure of the extensions (i.e., we will treat the number of argument places as relevant for the purposes of classification). (This captures one feature of the idea that logical form is a topic neutral feature of a sentence.) Reference axioms we can treat as of the same type iff they provide the same rule for determining the referent of the referring expression (proper names are a limiting case in which no rule is employed and the referent is given directly). In general, we wish to identify semantic categories with those such that *that* a new base term falls into the category determines how it fits into the semantic pattern of sentences in the language independently of its extension or referent. (We do not suppose that any terms except predicates and non-quantificational noun phrases have extensions or referents, respectively.)

On our conception logical forms are not reified. The logical form of a sentence is not another sentence, a structure, or anything else. Talk of logical form is a *façon de parler*, proxy for talk of a complex feature of a sentence *s* of a language L determined by what all canonical proofs of T-sentences for *s* in various interpretive truth theories for L share. The relation *sameness of logical form* is conceptually basic. We want to urge that the expression '*x* is the logical form of *y*' should be retired from serious discussion. The basic expression is '*x* in L is the same in logical form as *y* in L''', where '... in ... is the same in logical form as ... in ...' is explicated as a unit as above. One can derivatively make sense of '*x* in L gives the logical form of *y* in L''. The practice of 'giving the logical form' of a sentence by exhibiting its paraphrase in a regimented language is a matter of replacing a sentence about whose semantic structure we are unclear with one whose semantic structure is clearer because it is formulated in a language for which the rules attaching to its various constituents and its structure have been clearly laid out. Thus, the relation expressed by '*x* in L gives the logical form of *y* in L''' is true of a 4-tuple <*x*, L, *y*, L'> just in case *x* in L is the same in logical form as *y* in L', and *x*'s syntax understood relative to L makes perspicuous the semantic structure of *y* in L'. A paraphrase of a natural language sentence in a regimented language may capture the semantic structure of the original more or less well, and it may be that the language does not contain resources needed to yield a sentence with the same logical form as the original. That this occurs when a formal language is chosen as the translation target accounts for our intuition that sometimes indeterminacy about the logical form of a natural language sentence arises when we are forced to try to represent its semantic form in the absence of a worked out semantic theory for the language. It is no wonder the fit is sometimes awkward when we attempt to lay the semantic form of a sentence into the Procrustean bed of familiar logics. We toss and turn, settling on one tentative translation and then another, but none leaves us feeling comfortable.

We have so far ignored awkward facts about natural languages for the purposes of keeping the discussion relatively uncluttered. No formal truth theory can be applied directly to a natural language to reveal logical form because of ambiguity. Structurally ambiguous natural language sentences lack unique logical forms. In these cases, we must first disambiguate the language before we apply a truth theory to it. This makes regimentation, at least whatever is required to remove such ambiguity, necessary for a useful discussion of logical form for natural languages. Additional regimentation, perhaps motivated by considerations about syntactic decomposition, may recommend applying additional transformations before applying a truth theory, but these should not be necessary, as long as some description of the sentence is possible which accommodates all the features required for applying axioms for primitive expressions to generate a T-sentence for it. In an account of the logical form of a sentence, of course, we would want to track syntactic transformations, but, in a sense, its semantic structure would be revealed by a canonical proof of the T-sentence for its spruced up cousin, plus the fact that it means the same.

5

Treating logical form as we have above can help free us from overly simple models of the logical form of natural language sentences.[8] Too often we reach for the tools of elementary logic when trying to understand how natural languages work. The idea that logical form is to be determined by the translation of a sentence into an ideal language encourages this practice. By thinking about how to integrate an expression or construction into an interpretive truth theory, we free ourselves from those constraints, and from misconceptions which may arise from trying to fit natural language constructions to a familiar pattern, in a well-understood, artificial language.

An example of the difficulty philosophers have been led into by thinking of translation into a formal language as the proper approach to exhibiting logical form is the traditional treatment of natural language quantifiers in philosophy. Until recently, it was common to translate quantified noun phrases in natural languages like English into a paraphrase suitable for rep-

---

[8] 'Language disguises thought. So much so, that from the outward form of the clothing it is impossible to infer the form of the thought beneath it, because the outward form of the clothing is not designed to reveal the form of the body, but for entirely different purposes.' (*Tractatus Logico-Philosophicus*, 4.002)

resentation in a simple first order logic (the practice is still common). 'All men are mortal' goes into 'For all x, if x is a man, then x is mortal'. 'The King of France is bald' goes into 'There is an x such that x is King of France and for all y, if y is King of France then $x = y$, and x is bald'. 'Some men run for office' goes into 'There is an x such that x is a man and x runs for office'. *Prima facie*, all these paraphrases are of different forms than the originals, even though necessarily equivalent. That these paraphrases do not capture the semantic form of the originals is shown when we consider quantifiers such as 'few men' and 'most philosophers', for which the kinds of paraphrases given above fail. While most philosophers are not rich, most x are such that if they are philosophers, they are rich – since most things are not philosophers. The solution in an interpretive truth theory is to employ a semantic structure in the metalanguage which functions in the same way as that for the object language sentence (indeed, this is required to meet the condition that the axioms be interpretive). Thus, the satisfaction clause for a restricted quantifier (regimenting the object language sentence to introduce explicit variables) would have the following form (when the metalanguage embeds the object language),

> For any function f, speaker s, time t, f satisfies$_{[s,t]}$ '[Qx: x is F](x are G)' iff Q 'x is F'/'x'-variants f' of f satisfy$_{[s,t]}$ 'x are G'.

We define 'φ/'x'-variant f' of f' in two stages as follows:

> Def. For any functions f, f', f' is a φ/'x'-variant of f iff f' is an 'x'-variant of f and f' satisfies$_{[s,t]}$ φ.

> Def. For any functions f, f', f' is an 'x'-variant of f iff f' differs from f at most in what it assigns to 'x'.

The virtues of this approach to logical form also emerge from its application to the puzzling case of complex demonstratives. Complex demonstratives are the concatenation of a demonstrative with a nominal, as in 'That man playing the piano is drunk'. What is the logical form of this sentence? Such constructions pull us in different directions. On the one hand, 'that' seems clearly to be a context sensitive singular term, and 'man playing the piano' appears to be modifying it. This suggests giving 'That man playing the piano' a recursive reference clause in the truth theory, and treating the sentence as of subject-predicate form. On the other hand, the nominal in a complex demonstrative appears to play the same role as the nominal in quantified noun phrases. 'That man playing the piano is drunk' implies 'Someone is drunk', 'Someone is playing the piano', 'That man is playing something' and 'That man playing something is drunk' (fixing contextual parameters). These implications require that the nominal be truth conditionally relevant, and the last in particular requires that we be able to quantify into the nominal, and thereby relativize it to a universe of discourse, and so relativize to a universe of discourse the contribution of complex demonstratives to truth conditions, which makes no sense if they are singular terms. Such considerations suggest complex demonstratives are quantified noun phrases. Yet 'that' is no quantifier word, since there can be vacuous uses of it in both simple and complex demonstratives.

The proper course is to write into the satisfaction conditions for such a sentence the requirements these facts reveal. 'That man playing a piano is drunk' will be true on an occasion of use provided that the object the speaker demonstrates (i.e., *that*), which is a man playing a piano, is drunk. That is, 'That man playing a piano is drunk' will have the same logical form as '[The x: x = that and x is playing a piano](x is drunk)'. This captures both features of the sentence noted above, the similarities in behavior between the complex demonstrative and quantified noun phrases, and the fact that 'that' functions as a genuine demonstrative. By refusing to look for a translation into a familiar idiom, but first asking how the parts contribute to the truth conditions of the whole, we are led to a novel suggestion for the logical form of complex demonstratives and sentences containing complex demonstratives which reconciles what appeared to be irreconcilable features of the construction (see Lepore and Ludwig 2000). With complex demonstratives, the concatenation of a demonstrative with a nominal must be treated as introducing a quantifier.[9] This illustrates how grammatical categories such as that of determiner (which subsumes 'this', 'that', 'these', 'those', 'all', 'some', 'the', 'few', 'most', etc.) can provide a poor guide to semantic role.

We find in complex noun phrases an interesting example of how surface grammatical form[10] (we drop the qualifier for brevity) and semantic (or

---

[9] It turns out that there is considerable leeway in which quantifier we use in our paraphrase: 'some', 'the', and 'all' would work equally well, since the predicate restriction requires the variable to take on a value identical to the referent of the demonstrative as used by the speaker on that occasion. Here, perhaps, is a case where we can say there is indeterminacy of logical form: each captures as well as any other the semantic behavior of complex demonstratives. This is generated by forcing the object language structure to be interpreted in a language which requires one or another of these quantifier words to be used. It would be possible, however, to introduce into the metalanguage a structure which mimics exactly that of the object language, for example: for all f, f satisfies$_{[s,t]}$ '[That x: x is F](x is G)' iff f' such that f' is a 'Fx and x = that'/'x'-variant of f is such that f' satisfies$_{[s,t]}$ 'x is G'.

[10] We use 'surface grammatical form' advisedly, since one can characterize grammatical form so that the form of a sentence is exhibited only in a notation in which every semantical feature of the sentence is syntactically represented. This would not be, however, something to be read off from the words and their order in the sentence we write down or speak, and so characterizing grammatical form makes any current grammatical categories we use, like that of 'determiner', hostage to a correct semantic theory. It is perhaps worth noting, to avoid any misunderstandings, that when we use 'sentence' we mean the string of symbols we write out or the sequence of symbols we utter in speech, not a string of symbols which represents its analyzed structure.

logical) form can come apart. Another example of this sort is provided by the contrast between attributive adjectives such as 'slow' and 'large', and those such as 'red' and 'bald'.[11] 'John is a bald man' and 'John is a large man' share grammatical form. But while the former will be treated by the truth theory as appealing to axioms for simple one-place predicates, 'is bald' and 'is a man', we propose that the latter appeal to a quantifier and a relational predicate 'is larger than' as well as to the monadic predicate 'is a man'. Satisfaction clauses are given for the respective predicates in [10]-[11].[12]

[10]   For all functions f, f satisfies$_{[s,t]}$ 'x is a bald man' iff f satisfies$_{[s,t]}$ 'x is bald' and f satisfies$_{[s,t]}$ 'x is a man'.

[11]   For all functions f, f satisfies$_{[s,t]}$ 'x is a large man' iff most 'y is a man'/'y'-variants f' of f satisfy$_{[s,t]}$ 'x is larger than y' and f satisfies$_{[s,t]}$ 'x is a man'.[13]

Once we consider how to provide recursive satisfaction conditions for our two intuitively different structures, vastly different logical forms are revealed – that is to say, we can see that the kinds of proofs of T-sentences for each and their starting points are different: they will appeal to different kinds of axioms, classified according to semantic type, and hence yield proofs with different structures, exhibiting the components which play a

---

[11] The treatment given below for attributives such as 'slow' and 'large' doesn't extend to all adjectives which do not interact purely extensionally with the nouns they modify. These form a semantically heterogeneous class since there is not a single mode of interaction. The treatment given here works well for attributive adjectives which have a related non-evaluative comparative, as 'slow' and 'large' do in 'slower' and 'larger'. The same treatment does not work, for example, for 'good', since to be a good knife or a good actor is not merely to be better than most knives or actors. Even a bad actor could be first among a very bad lot. In the case of evaluative attributives, it looks as if what is selected in the interaction for comparison is something like an ideal of the type modified. Likewise, other attributives can interact in distinct ways with nouns they modify. For example, adjectives which are formed from nouns for substances, such as 'iron', 'brass', or 'wooden', interact non-extensionally with some (though not all) nouns. While a brass railing is both brass and railing, a brass monkey is not both brass and a monkey, but monkey-shaped brass. This only helps to reinforce the point that surface grammatical form is a poor guide to semantic form.

[12] A general treatment will require a device for introducing variables not already present in a predicate. We elide this in [11] in the interest of keeping the presentation relatively perspicuous. A generalization is: For all functions f, f satisfies$_{[s,t]}$ 'x is a F G' iff most fresh('x is a F G')⌒'is a man'/fresh('x is a F G')-variants f' of f satisfy$_{[s,t]}$ 'x is larger than'⌒fresh('x is a F G') and f satisfies$_{[s,t]}$ 'x is a man'. The function fresh(φ) yields as value the first variable, in some standard ordering, not in φ.

[13] A caveat: often ambiguities will need to be resolved before an appropriate satisfaction clause can be assigned. 'Jean Paul is a subtle French philosopher' can be read either as 'Jean Paul is a subtle philosopher and Jean Paul is a French philosopher' or as 'Jean Paul is a subtle (French philosopher)'. Similarly, 'Paul Bunyan is a large quick man' may be read as conjunctive, or 'large' may be read as modifying 'quick man'. Once ambiguities are resolved, the recursive clause provided in the text will yield the right satisfaction conditions.

similar grammatical role as playing quite different semantic roles. The concatenation of an attributive adjective such as 'large' or 'slow' with a noun is revealed to be a kind of restricted quantification.[14] This case helps to make clear the importance for a semantic theory of sorting lexical items into categories on the basis of their semantical roles.[15] The adjectives 'red' and 'large' seem to share grammatical role, but play different semantic roles. No sorting of terms into grammatical categories by tests not sensitive to their semantic roles, such as the traditional test of invariance of judgements of grammaticality under substitution, will provide a grammatical classification of terms that we will have reason to think a certain guide to semantic structure. For the purposes of regimenting sentences for input into a formal semantic theory, it is the semantical roles of the words that should be our guide. Our aim will be to assign different syntactical categories where there are differences in semantic structure.

6

Non-declarative sentences, such as 'Open the door', and 'What time is it?', present an especially interesting challenge to any conception of logical form grounded in truth-theoretic semantics, since uses of them are neither true nor false. They have semantic form, and so, on a conception of logical form as semantic form, should have logical form. But how can it make sense to

---

[14] Gareth Evans (1975) tries to provide a satisfaction clause for attributive adjectives which makes no appeal to explicit quantifiers. Adapting it to our notation, his proposal for 'x is a large man' would be:

For any function f, f satisfies$_{[s,t]}$ $\ulcorner x$ is a large man$\urcorner$ iff $f('x')$ is an large satisfier$_{[s,t]}$ of 'x is a man'.

(Two different satisfaction relations are introduced on this account.) The attempt fails, however, because Evans's clauses are not recursive, but adjectival phrases can be of arbitrary complexity. Given that attributive adjectives can interact, as in 'x is a large slow man', so that we cannot represent this as 'x is a large man' and 'x is a slow man', on at least one of its readings, we must introduce a new axiom for each additional iteration. Since there is no end to the iterations, there will be no end to the axioms required, which would represent the language as unlearnable.

[15] The point is not novel. In 'The average man is no better than he ought to be' we do not suppose 'average' is contributing a predicate with a variable bound by the definite article, or that in 'I had a quick cup of coffee' the adjective 'quick' contributes a predicate or a comparative with places bound by a restricted quantifier whose restricting predicate is 'x is a cup'. In the first, 'average' modifies the sentence, and in the second 'quick' modifies the verb, despite their displacement. These cases may well count as idioms, however. Clearly the case involving attributive adjectives is not. Adjectives such as 'fake' and 'phony' present interesting cases. Such adjectives create an intensional context, which suggests they should receive a treatment as a part of a general account of opaque contexts. Such an account is presented in Ludwig & Ray, 1998. But it would take us too far afield to show how to apply that account to the present case.

talk about their logical form on the model we have been using up to this point, and to try to characterize it in terms of a truth theory?

A generalization of the truth-theoretic approach may show the way to an answer. To keep the discussion simple, we will concentrate here on imperatives, though we will indicate how the account might make room for interrogatives. Intuitively, uses of imperatives admit of a bivalent evaluation, though they are not truth-valued. Rather, they are complied with or not. To generalize the truth-theoretic approach, we might try introducing a notion of fulfillment conditions which subsumes both compliance conditions for imperatives and truth conditions for declaratives. Since it seems evident that our basic understanding of predicates and referring terms in imperatives should be provided by an interpretive truth theory, we might try to exhibit compliance conditions as recursively specifiable in terms of truth conditions. Imperative sentences would then be obtained from declaratives by a small number of transformations, from which the original declarative is easily recoverable. 'Open the door' might be obtained from 'You will open the door' by dropping its second person pronoun and modal auxiliary 'will'. Letting 'Core(ϕ)' represent the declarative core of an imperative sentence, Core('Tell me the time') = 'You will tell me the time'. The compliance conditions for imperatives will then be exhibited as given in terms of the truth conditions for their declarative cores. Intuitively, an utterance of an imperative is complied with iff the addressee(s) makes it the case that the declarative core of the imperative is true as a result of the intention to comply with the directive issued with the imperative. Introducing a satisfaction predicate relating functions to sentences and formulas in imperative mood, we can exhibit satisfaction conditions for 'Open the door' as in [12]:

[12]   For any function f, f satisfies$^i_{[s,t]}$ 'Open the door' iff ref$_{[s,t]}$('you') makes it the case that f satisfies$_{[s,t]}$ Core('Open the door') with the intention of obeying the directive s issues at t.[16]

The satisfaction relation employed on the right hand side of the quantified biconditional is that employed in the truth theory. So, the satisfaction, and so compliance conditions, for imperatives are characterized recursively by the satisfaction conditions of their declarative cores. Note also that the forward looking character of directives issued using imperatives is captured by the fact that the declarative core of an imperative is itself in future tense. A general satisfaction predicate, which we capitalize to distinguish it, can be defined in terms of the satisfaction predicates for imperatives and declaratives. For atomic sentences, we define 'Satisfies$_{[s,t]}$' as follows.

---

[16] A full treatment will introduce some additional complications, though none that affect the approach outlined here. Thus, for example, since more than one directive can be issued at a time, even using the same words (directed at different audiences), satisfaction and truth conditions ultimately need to be relativized to speech acts.

For any atomic sentence φ, function f, f Satisfies$_{[s,t]}$ φ iff

if φ is declarative, f satisfies$_{[s,t]}$ φ;

if φ is imperative, f satisfies$^1_{[s,t]}$ φ.

For molecular sentences, 'Satisfies$_{[s,t]}$' will be defined recursively in the usual way, with the caveat that for mixed mood sentences the recursion selects the satisfaction relation appropriate for the mood of the component sentences. Satisfaction of open sentences in the imperative mood or in mixed moods is a straightforward generalization of the above. (A similar approach can be employed with respect to interrogatives. See Ludwig 1997 for a fuller working out of this approach, and its extension to interrogatives, which present additional complexities.) The connection between a fulfillment theory for natural languages and a compositional meaning theory is given by a generalization of our earlier characterization. For an imperative (under which category we included molecular sentences which mix imperatives and declaratives), we wish a compositional meaning theory to entail all true instances of schema (I),

(I)   For all speakers s, times t, φ commands$_{[s,t]}$ that p,

where φ is replaced by a structural description of an object language sentence. For an interrogative (under which we include mixed interrogative and declarative mood molecular sentences), we wish a compositional meaning theory to entail all true instances of the schema (Q),

(Q)   For all speakers s, times t, φ requests$_{[s,t]}$ that p,

where φ is replaced by a structural description of an object language sentence. The condition on an interpretive fulfillment condition theory for a language L is that

if $\ulcorner$ φ is fulfilled$_{[s,t]}$ in L iff p $\urcorner$ is canonically provable from it,

then if φ is assertoric, then φ means$_{[s,t]}$ in L that p;

if φ is imperative, then φ commands$_{[s,t]}$ in L that p;

if φ is interrogative, then φ requests$_{[s,t]}$ in L that p.

This puts us in a position to extend the notion of logical form to nondeclaratives, and to generalize the notion of logical form as semantic form. Letting 'F-sentence' stand for an interpretive sentence of the form $\ulcorner$ φ is fulfilled$_{[s,t]}$ in L iff p $\urcorner$, we generalize the earlier characterization:

For sentences s_1, s_2, languages L_1, L_2, s_1 in L_1 has the same logical form as s_2 in L_2 iff there is an interpretive fulfillment condition theory F_1 for L_1 and an interpretive fulfillment condition theory F_2 for L_2 such that

(a) F_1 and F_2 share the same logic;

(b) there is a canonical proof P_1 of the F-sentence for s_1 in F_1;

(c) there is a canonical proof P_2 of the F-sentence for s_2 in F_2, such that:

(d) P_1 corresponds to P_2.

The notion of a corresponding proof similarly generalizes. Likewise, the notions of logical consequence, truth, etc., can be generalized in a straightforward way to include non-declaratives.

7

The above sections present our basic approach to explicating logical form. It will be useful, however, to consider the relation of this characterization to the notion of a logical constant, or a slight generalization of this notion, the topic of this section.

Logical constants are a subset of primitive terms of a language thought to be especially useful for identifying classes of arguments the same in form. The notion of a logical constant, however, conceived of as subsuming only terms, is too narrow to do the work needed for regimenting valid natural language arguments. The inference from [13] to [14] is intuitively valid in virtue of form.

[13]   Brutus is an honorable man.

[14]   Brutus is a man.

[13], however, has no logical constant. The term 'honorable' functions semantically to contribute a predicate to the sentence, as is shown by the fact that [13] also implies in virtue of its form 'Brutus is honorable' (that is, 'A is an F G $\supset$ A is F' is a valid schema).[17] The effect of modifying 'man' with 'honorable' is to add to the truth conditions the requirement that Brutus be honorable as well as a man. It is not the use of 'honorable' that signals this, but rather that it is an adjective modifying the noun from which the predicate 'is a man' is formed. Thus, we need to identify here the structure,

noun phrase + 'is a' + adjective + nominal,

as itself semantically significant to the semantic compositional structure of the sentence. Intuitively, modifying the nominal with an adjective does the same semantic work as adding a conjunct to the sentence – in the case of [13], of adding 'and Brutus is honorable'. These are different ways of 'encoding' the same semantic information. To recognize this is to recognize that we need to talk not just about logical terms, but logical structures. A logical structure will in general be characterized in terms of a pattern of

---

[17] Here we must place some restriction of course on the class of adjectives since the schema is not valid for all, e.g., for 'fake', and 'stone'.

types of terms in a grammatical expression. What are traditionally thought of as logical constants may or may not appear in the pattern of terms. When they do, they count as part of the pattern that constitutes the logical structure. Indeed, the idea that an argument is valid in virtue of its logical terms is a mistake. It is rather patterns which include the constants which render an argument valid. Logical constants are useful because they help form patterns which provide information about how to understand the contribution of component expressions in which they occur to a sentence's truth conditions. To express this notion of a logical structure, we will press into service the term 'logical syntax'.[18]

The aim of identifying logical syntax is to identify *syntactical* constants in sentences which help regiment natural language arguments into classes with shared forms that account for their validity. There will be in the nature of the case a variety of different levels of abstraction at which we can identify forms which help to regiment natural language arguments. We would like to find a way of isolating out for special consideration a class of structures salient from the point of view of a semantic theory for the language, and which seem to have something specially to do intuitively with the structures of the sentences of the language.

The notion of logical form we have articulated is neutral about what structures count as logical. Any of the competing criteria in the literature could simply be adjoined to our account. This points up an important fact about the relation between talk about logical form, if we are correct in holding that our explication tracks that use of the term back to interests expressed by Russell in the quotation at the beginning of this paper, and talk about logical syntax and the related notions of logical consequence and truth. The identification of *logical* syntax is not itself either central to or sufficient for understanding what talk of logical form comes to. Rather, it has been thought to be central because many of the kinds of terms identified as logical constants have been particularly important for understanding the semantic structure of sentences in which they appear. But identifying a particular class of terms as logical, for the purposes of identifying a class of logically valid sentences or argument forms, is not necessary to understand the semantic structure of such sentences. The interpretive truth theory contains all the information necessary whether or not we go on to select out a particular class of terms (or structures) for attention for more specialized interests. And, of course, the notion of the semantic structure of a sentence applies to sentences in which no logical constants as traditionally conceived appear.

---

[18] It should be clear that here syntax is not thought of as a purely orthographical feature of an expression, but includes information about the semantic category of terms or places in a sentence structure.

Despite this independence, there are differences among primitives terms (and primitive terms and structures which carry important semantic information) which are particularly salient from the standpoint of an interpretive truth theory, namely, that between terms which can receive base clauses and *terms or structures which require a recursive treatment*. It is natural to seize on this difference and to urge that 'the logical constants may be identified as those iterative features of the language that require a recursive clause in the characterization of truth or satisfaction' (Davidson 1984a:71).[19] We must generalize this a bit in the light of our discussion above. We will suggest that the recursive syntactical structures of the language be treated as its logical syntax. The recursive syntax of sentences gives them structure beyond that already expressed in the number of argument places in primitive predicates. It is natural to think of arguments made valid in virtue of the presence of recursive syntax in the premises and conclusion as valid in virtue of their *structure*. This gives one clear sense to the idea that in identifying the logical *terms* we identify those terms that we do not replace with schematic letters in identifying the structures or forms of sentences relevant to determining what other sentences similarly identified in terms of their structures they bear deductive relations to. The proposal rounds up many of the usual suspects, the so-called truth-functional connectives, and the quantifiers, as well as other iterative syntactical patterns that do similar work. As we have seen, truth-functionality is not always achieved lexically, as in 'Brutus is an honorable man'. Likewise, quantification need not be signaled

---

[19] See 'Truth and Meaning,' p. 33, 'In Defense of Convention T,' p. 71, 'On Saying That,' p. 94 in Davidson 1984. (Interestingly, Dummett gives a similar, if somewhat less precise, criterion in Dummett 1973, and includes, in a footnote, an anticipation of the generality conception we discuss below, in discussing the logical status of the identity sign, which is otherwise excluded.) The requirement that a term must receive a recursive clause to be a logical constant is important in this characterization, and rules out what would otherwise be counterexamples. Adjective modifiers can be given a recursive clause *if* we ignore the use of connectives in adjectives and focus only on extensional adjectives that don't interact with other adjectives, as in the following example.

For all functions f, speakers s, times t, and nouns φ, f satisfies$_{[s,t]}$ $\ulcorner x$ is a red $\varphi \urcorner$ iff f satisfies$_{[s,t]}$ $\ulcorner x$ is a $\varphi \urcorner$ and $f('x')$ is red.

However, clearly this is unnecessary. The only feature of such constructions which require recursive treatment is the concatenation of an adjective with a noun. The contribution of the adjective can, and in fact should, be cashed out in terms of the axiom for the corresponding predicate, as in the following.

For all functions f, speakers s, times t, and noun φ, f satisfies$_{[s,t]}$ $\ulcorner x$ is a red $\varphi \urcorner$ iff f satisfies$_{[s,t]}$ $\ulcorner x$ is a $\varphi \urcorner$ and f satisfies$_{[s,t]}$ 'x is red'.

We note also that the approach represented by the first clause requires an axiom for each adjective in addition to axioms for their occurrences in predicates formed using the copula, though it seems clear that our understanding of the use of adjectives is of a piece with our understanding of the predicates formed from them. We show in note 12, incidentally, that a similar recursive treatment of attributive adjectives such as 'large' and 'slow' is not viable.

by an explicit quantifier word, as in 'Whales are mammals'. Verb inflection for tense, too, is arguably best thought of as a quantificational device (Lepore and Ludwig 2002).

We have indicated that both terms and structures may be treated recursively. One cannot identify a recursive term or structure by a syntactic test of iterability. We may concatenate 'Time is short and' with any sentence, and concatenate it with the result, and so on indefinitely. This does not mean that 'Time is short and' is a logical constant or a recursive structure. For we need a recursive clause for the concatenation of a sentence with 'and' with another sentence. The rule attaches to that structure, not to particular instances of it. Similarly, though 'honorable' may be added any number of times before 'man' in 'Brutus is an honorable man', we do not suppose 'honorable' is a logical constant or itself receives a recursive clause. Again, the rule attaches to a pattern exemplified by the sentence, not to the particular terms instantiating that pattern.

These terms and structures by and large are intuitively topic neutral, as expected, since, with few exceptions, they determine only how the primitive predicates of the language contribute to the truth conditions of complex sentences. Exceptions in natural languages are primitive restricted quantifiers, such as 'someone' and 'anytime'. Artificial examples may be constructed as well. It seems appropriate to divide recursive terms into the logical and what we can call the *purely logical*. In the case of 'Someone is in hiding', the satisfaction clause would be:

> For all f, f satisfies$_{[s,t]}$ 'Someone is in hiding' iff some 'x is a person'/'x'-variant f' of f satisfies$_{[s,t]}$ 'x is in hiding'.

Alternatively:

> For all f, f satisfies$_{[s,t]}$ 'Someone is in hiding' iff some 'x'-variant f' of f such that $f'('x')$ is a person satisfies$_{[s,t]}$ 'x is in hiding'.

These suggest the following condition on a purely logical term or structure: a term or structure is purely logical iff its satisfaction clause does not (a) introduce terms requiring appeal to base clauses other than those required for the terms to which the logical term is applied, or (b) introduce nonlogical metalanguage terms not introduced by base clauses for the terms to which the logical term is applied.[20] If (a) or (b) is violated, the extra nonlogical material is contributed by the logical term or structure itself.

---

[20] Modal operators may be counterexamples as well if they must receive recursive clauses, for their contributions to determining the truth conditions of sentences in which they occur are not intuitively independent of features of objects picked out by the predicates in sentences to which they apply. The exclusion criterion just given would not exclude modal operators, so they would have to be excluded independently. If they are (implausibly) treated as

This conception of logical syntax does omit, however, terms often included, such as the identity sign. On this conception, the identity sign is treated as having the logical form of a two-place relational predicate, and, consequently, is not singled out for special attention. Likewise, the second-order relation 'is an element of', and such relational terms as 'is a subset of', 'is the union of', will not be counted as logical on this conception; and so on.[21] These sorts of terms would be counted on a conception introduced

---

quantifiers over possible worlds, then, as lexically primitive restricted quantifiers, the exclusion rule given in the text would exclude them as well.

[21] An alternative proposal by Peacocke 1976, which also draws on the resources of a Tarski-style truth theory, employs an epistemic criterion. Peacocke's proposal is that a term α is logical iff, with respect to a truth theory for a language containing α, from knowledge of (a) which sequences (or functions) satisfy formulas θ_1, θ_2, ...θ_n to which α can be applied and (b) knowledge of the satisfaction clause for α, one can infer *a priori* which sequences (or functions) satisfy $\alpha(\theta_1, \theta_2,...\theta_n)$. The main idea behind his proposal is that it identifies *as* logical those terms knowledge of whose contributions to satisfaction conditions requires no knowledge of the properties of, or relations into which, objects enter. This is a way of trying to cash out the idea that the logical terms are topic neutral. (We can extend the proposal to terms that apply not just to formulas but to variables and singular terms: α is a logical term just in case, with respect to a truth theory for a language containing α, from knowledge of (a) which sequences (or functions) satisfy formulas θ_1, θ_2, ... θ_n and which objects sequences assign to terms τ_1, τ_2, ..., τ_m to which α can be applied and (b) knowledge of the satisfaction clause for α, one can infer *a priori* which sequences (or functions) satisfy $\alpha(\theta_1, \theta_2, ...\theta_n, \tau_1, \tau_2, ..., \tau_m)$, or if it is a singular term, what object each sequence (or function) assigns to it.)

What terms count as logical constants on this view depends on what knowledge we suppose we have about the sequences (or functions) that satisfy formulas or apply to terms. For example, knowing that sequences σ_1, σ_2, satisfy 'x is F' is not in itself sufficient to know that every sequence satisfies 'x is F', even if these are all the sequences, unless we also know that they are all the sequences, which is an additional bit of knowledge. Likewise, application of the criterion to numerical quantifiers and terms like the identity sign depends on whether we are supposed to know facts about the numbers of sequences that satisfy a formula and facts about the identity and diversity of objects in sequences.

The same idea may be approached non-epistemically by appeal to entailment relations as follows: α is a logical term iff, with respect to a truth theory for a language containing α, which sequences (or functions) satisfy formulas θ_1, θ_2, ...θ_n and which objects sequences assign to terms τ_1, τ_2, ..., τ_m to which α can be applied and the proposition expressed by the satisfaction clause for α entail which sequences (or functions) satisfy $\alpha(\theta_1, \theta_2, ... \theta_n, \tau_1, \tau_2, ..., \tau_m)$, or if it is a singular term, what object each sequence (or function) assigns to it. Here too what terms are counted as logical will depend on what propositions about the sequences (or functions) that satisfy a formula we are including. For the universal quantifier to be a logical constant, we have to include propositions about all 'x'-variants of a given function or sequence.

Both these ways of spelling out the idea suffer from a obvious difficulty noted by McCarthy (1981), namely, there are *a priori* inferences (entailments) not obviously grounded in the meanings of what have been traditionally taken to be logical constants. To see the difficulty, consider an arbitrary formula Ω, and a operator on it Σ, with satisfaction conditions as given in,

For any function f, f satisfies $\Sigma^\frown\Omega$ iff f satisfies Ω or A,

independently by Tarski (1986) and Lindström (1966), and motivated by the idea that the 'logical notions' or terms have greatest generality (see Sher 1996 for a recent exposition of this line, though with differences from the way we develop it below). This is connected with the idea we have already invoked that logical syntax is topic neutral. But it is spelled out in a way that yields different results.

The basic idea is that terms express more general notions the more stable their extensions under transformations of the universe, and those terms that express the most general notions will be those whose extensions are invariant under all permutations of the universe, i.e., under all one-one mappings of the universe of discourse onto itself. For this to be applicable to all terms, of course, will require us to think of all terms as having extensions, and of truth conditions of sentences as being given in terms of their extensions. Thus, this approach is most natural on a Fregean conception of semantics on which sentential connectives like 'and' and 'or' are thought of as expressing functions, and the quantifiers as expressing second-order functions. It is not difficult to see the upshot of this approach. Terms associated with sets invariant under all permutations of the universe will be counted as logical terms.[22] Thus, e.g., proper names will not be logical terms because their referents (which we will treat as their extension) will not always be mapped onto themselves. Likewise, most n-place first-order relational terms

---

where 'A' is replaced by any *a priori* truth, e.g., '1 < 2'. Peacock's criterion will count Σ as a logical constant, though intuitively it is not. Similarly, as McCarthy points out, if *de re* knowledge of which objects sequences or functions assign to terms includes whether they are numbers, many function signs denoting functions that take numbers as arguments, such as 'the successor of ___', or '... + ___' will be treated as logical constants, though intuitively these are not topic neutral terms. Peacock intends to exclude from consideration number-theoretic terms, but this seems *ad hoc*, and in any case other *a priori* truths will do as well. An interesting example McCarthy mentions is the concatenation sign, '...⌢ ___'. Knowledge of what objects sequences assign to terms which can appear in the argument places for this functor and knowledge of the satisfaction clause for it suffices for knowledge of which objects sequences assign to the expression formed from those terms and the concatenation sign. Few will wish to treat '⌢' as a logical term, however. The feature that Peacock identifies seems at best a necessary condition on a term's being a logical term, but not a sufficient one.

McCarthy's own suggestion is a version of the invariance approach which we discuss in the text. McCarthy's proposal identifies a narrower class of terms than the invariance approach we consider below, and, in particular, fails to count cardinality quantifiers as logical terms. We will not discuss it further here. But it helps to illustrate the variety of notions of logical constants one can identity, and to suggest, as we will urge, that there is a family of related notions, to a greater or lesser extent topic neutral, which can be classified on the basis of a number of overlapping features, and that there is little point to insisting that one is the objectively correct way of extending the practice of using the term 'logical constant' beyond the territory in which it is currently well-grounded.

[22] We will be assuming that there are an infinite number of objects, e.g., all the real numbers, as well as spatio-temporal objects, so that concerns about the size of the universe need not affect this criterion.

will not be logical terms. Some will, however, for example, those one-place predicates whose extensions are the universal set ('exists' or 'is an object') and the empty set ('is nonexistent', 'is non-self-identical'), and those two-place predicates whose extensions are the set of ordered pairs consisting of an object and itself, and the set of ordered pairs of objects and some distinct object ('is identical with' and 'is nonidentical with'). There will be similar terms for any number of argument places. Likewise, there will be second-order relations (which take extensions of first-order relations as arguments) that will count as logical. If the universal quantifier has as its extension the set of the universal set, and the existential quantifier all subsets of the universal set except the empty set, these will count also as logical terms. 'Everything is F' will be true just in case ext('F') ∈ ext('everything'). Binary quantifiers can be treated as appropriate sets of ordered pairs of sets. 'All', for example, can be assigned as its extension the set of all ordered pairs of sets such that the first is a subset of the second. 'All A are B' will be true provided that <ext('A'), ext('B')> ∈ ext('All'). The result of systematically extending this idea is that all the so-called cardinality quantifiers will count as logical terms, as well as the standard set-theoretic relations. With contortions, truth-functional connectives can be treated as logical terms as well.[23] The approach could be extended straightforwardly to our broader notion of logical syntax.

We don't think there is an answer to the question which of these conceptions of logical syntax (or any of the others in the literature) is correct. Each is a projection from our intuitive starting point in thinking about argument form and what sorts of constant structures we can identify to help us classify together arguments which are valid (or invalid) in virtue of those structures. Against the invariance conception, it might be said that it counts some terms as logical which doesn't seem helpful to so regard, such as, e.g., 'is an object' and 'is nonexistent', and 'is nonidentical with'. Likewise, it might be said that if our aim is to identify intuitively topic neutral syntax, the set-theoretic relations should not count as logical terms. Likewise, one may object that in order to count many terms as logical on this approach we must resort to a representation of the semantics of expressions which seems both gratuitous and misguided. On the other hand, there is no point to denying that classifying terms together as logical in this way may for some purposes be useful. We are inclined to say then that there is no

---

[23] We need to assign the logical constants extensions invariant under all permutations of the universe. Frege treated them as functions from truth-values to truth-values. If we associate The True with the universal set and The False with the empty set, the invariance criterion will classify the usual truth functional connectives as logical terms. Rather than force truth-functional connectives to fit this criterion, Sher (1996) gives a separate criterion for them. This admits, however, that no one notion of generality applies to every term we deem as logical.

substantive, as opposed to terminological, issue here. It may well be that in the place of the term 'logical syntax' what we need is a number of different terms with overlapping extensions.[24] This fact in itself could not be a reason to conclude that no objective division is possible. Rather, it signifies that *many* objective divisions of 'logical' from 'non-logical' terms are possible, answering to different interests.

---

[24] Once we have a characterization of logical syntax, we can define in the usual way the notions of logical truth, logical consequence, and logical equivalence, with adjustments to accommodate for natural language sentences not being true or false independently of context. To do so, we relativize the notions to sets of contextual parameters. A sentence true under all interpretations of its nonlogical terms for a given set of values for contextual parameters C is a logical truth relative to C; a sentence φ is a logical consequence of a set of sentences $\{\psi_1, \psi_2 ... \psi_n\}$ relative to a given set of contextual parameters C iff there is no interpretation of nonlogical terms under which every sentence of $\{\psi_1, \psi_2 ... \psi_n\}$ is true relative to C and φ is false relative to C; sentences φ and ψ are logically equivalent relative to contextual parameters C iff each is a logical consequence of the other relative to C. (Stronger notions can be defined by universally quantifying over contextual parameters, though complications emerge for demonstratives.) Essentially, this picks out those consequences as logical (relative to contextual parameters) which are due to the meanings of the syntactical features of the language identified as logical.

We can also identify a notion of pragmatic consequence and necessity. φ is a pragmatic consequence of ψ iff φ is true in all contexts in which ψ is true; φ is pragmatically necessary iff true in all contexts. 'I am here now', e.g., is pragmatically necessary (well, almost–for one can use 'here' to designate a place one is not, e.g., by pointing to a map). But it is best to keep these notions distinct from those of logical consequence and necessity.

Evans 1976 has suggested distinguishing a notion of structural consequence from logical consequence. However, his proposal would identify structural consequences with a subset of what we are already committed to treating as logical consequences, on the basis of a feature of them which does not seem to mark them out as an interestingly distinct class. Evans treats logical consequences as hinging on the presence of logical *terms* in a sentence. Structural consequences hinge not on logical terms but on patterns in the construction of sentences. Thus, we recognize the validity of the argument from (i) to (ii) by recognizing forms (iii) and (iv):

    (i)   Brutus is an honorable man.
    (ii)   Brutus is honorable.
    (iii) noun phrase + 'is a' + adjective + noun
    (iv) noun phrase + 'is a' + noun

Understanding the semantic contribution of the adjective in a sentence of the first form is sufficient to know that the corresponding sentence of the second form is true if the first is. We have already, though, subsumed the sort of structure exhibited in (iii) under the heading 'logical'. It counts as logical because it, not the terms which instantiate it, receives a recursive treatment (the terms all get their own base clauses, or terms they are derived from do). Evans does not treat the entailment from (i) to (ii) as logical. But from our perspective, this is misguided. From the point of view of an interpretive truth theory, the difference between 'Brutus is an honorable man' and 'Brutus is honorable and Brutus is a man' is merely what syntactic features of a sentence are subserving a certain semantic role. Rather than distinguish a new notion of consequence, as Evans does, it is more reasonable to extend the notion of logicality from terms to structures.

8

In this paper, we have shown how to capture and generalize a notion of logical form used in the tradition in philosophy stretching back (at least) to Russell's enormously influential discussion of logical form in the first few decades of this century. To this end, we employed the notion of an interpretive truth theory for a natural language. The notion of logical form on this account is shown to be basically the notion of semantic form as it relates to the truth conditions of sentences. The basic notion is *not* the logical form of a sentence, but rather sameness of logical form as between sentences interpreted relative to languages. Derivatively, we can make sense of the notion of 'giving the logical form' of a sentence in terms of offering a translation in a language which marks more explicitly in syntax the semantic features of the original and for which we have a better worked out semantics. There is, however, strictly speaking, no such *thing* as the logical form of any sentence. We have characterized the notion of sameness of logical form in terms of T-sentences for sentences with corresponding proofs in interpretive truth theories for their languages. The proofs encode the semantic structure of the sentence, abstracting away from differences in base axioms irrelevant to understanding how they combine with other kinds of expressions, and from differences in recursive axioms that make no difference to truth conditions. Sameness of logical form of primitive terms is sameness of semantic type, characterized in terms of the way in which the terms systematically interact with other kinds of terms. The notion of logical form can be extended to non-declaratives, by way of a generalization of the truth-theoretic approach to giving a semantic theory for declaratives. The notion of sameness of logical form has been characterized independently of the notion of a logical constant or more broadly of logical syntax. The notion of logical form, i.e., semantic form, is more general. The interest in identifying logical syntax lies in its utility for classing together natural language arguments in terms of interesting broadly structural features they share which provide a common explanation for their validity. There is little reason to believe, so far as we can see, that the interest dictates a unique choice. However, we have urged a criterion for logical syntax particularly salient from the point of view of an interpretive truth theory, namely, logical syntax is that syntax which must be treated recursively in an interpretive truth theory. This provides one good reason for thinking of logical syntax as especially concerned with revealing the validity of arguments in virtue of the structures of the contained sentences, as well as respecting the requirement that logical syntax be topic neutral.[25]

---

[25] We wish to thank commentators on an earlier version of this paper presented at a symposium on logical form at the 1998 Central Division Meeting of the American Philosophical Association, Peter Ludlow, Robert May, and Robert Stainton, as well the audience at a de-

References

Black, M., and Geach, P. eds. 1960. *Translations from the Philosophical Writings of Gottlob Frege*. Oxford: Oxford University Press.

Davidson, D. 1968. On Saying That. *Synthese* 19:130-46.

Davidson, D. 1984a. In Defense of Convention T. In Davidson 1984b:65-75.

Davidson, D. 1984b. *Inquiries into Truth and Interpretation*. New York: Clarendon Press.

Davidson, D. 1984c. On Saying That. In Davidson 1984b:93-108.

Etchemendy, J. 1983. The Doctrine of Logic As Form. *Lingistics and Philosophy* 6:319-34.

Etchemendy, J. 1988. Tarski on Truth and Logical Consequence. *Journal of Symbolic Logic* 53:51-79.

Etchemendy, J. 1990. *The Concept of Logical Consequence*. Cambridge: Harvard University Press.

Evans, G. 1985. Does Tense Logic Rest on a Mistake? *Collected Papers*, 343-63. Oxford: Clarendon Press.

Larson, R. and Segal, G. 1995. *Knowledge of Meaning. An Introduction to Semantic Theory*. Cambridge, Mass:The MIT Press.

Lepore, E. and Ludwig, K. 2000. Semantics and Pragmatics Complex Demonstratives. *Mind* 109:199-240.

Lepore, E. and Ludwig, K. 2002. Outline of a Truth Conditional Semantics for Tense. *Tense, Time and Reference*, ed. Q. Smith. New York: Oxford.

Lindström, P. 1966. First Order Predicate Logic with Generalized Quantifiers. *Theoria* 32:186-95.

Ludwig, K. 1997. The Truth about Moods. *Protosociology* 10 *Cognitive Semantics I: Conceptions of Meaning*:19-66.

Ludwig, K., & Ray, G. 1998. Semantics for Opaque Contexts. *Philosophical Perspectives* 12:141-166.

Lycan, W. G. 1989. Logical Constants and the Glory of Truth-Conditional Semantics. *Notre Dame Journal of Formal Logic*:390-400.

Quine, W. V. O. 1971. Methodological Reflections on Current Linguistic Theory. *Semantics of Natural Language*, ed. D. Davidson and G. Harman, 442-54. Boston: D. Reidel Publishing Company.

Russell, Bertrand. 1993. *Our Knowledge of the External World: as a field for scientific method in philosophy*. New York: Routledge.

Sher, Gila. 1996. Semantics and Logic. *The Handbook of Contemporary Semantic Theory*, ed. S. Lappin, 511-37. Oxford: Blackwell.

Tarski, Alfred. 1986. What are Logical Notions? *History and Philosophy of Logic* 7:143-54.

partmental seminar at the University of Florida in February 1998. Particular thanks goes to Greg Ray.

8

Scheme-Content Dualism and Empiricism[1]

JOHN MCDOWELL

1

About the dualism of scheme and content, Donald Davidson says: 'To a large extent this picture of mind and its place in nature has defined the problems modern philosophy has thought it had to solve' (Davidson 1989:161). To rid ourselves of the dualism, then, would be to transform philosophy. We would no longer think we had those problems—which would not be the same as having solved them.

I think the dualism is important in just that way. But I want to suggest, with help from Davidson's own writings, that his diagnosis of the dualism's attractions does not go to the roots; and hence that his recipe for a transformation of philosophy is not quite the one we need.

---

[1] This is a shorter version of my paper of the same name in *The Philosophy of Donald Davidson*, ed. L.E. Hahn, 87-104. Library of Living Philosophers vol. 27. Chicago and La Salle: Open Court, 1999. The material is reused here by permission of Open Court Publishing Company.

2

What is the dualism of scheme and content?

Its parties are supposed to determine the significance of, say, bodies of belief or theories. The picture can be encapsulated in the Kantian tag: 'Thoughts without content are empty, intuitions without concepts are blind' (Kant 1929:A51/B75). So 'scheme' is 'conceptual scheme,' and 'content' is 'intuitions' or sensory intake. The idea is that beliefs or theories are significant, non-empty, because of an interaction between the conceptual and the sensory, dualistically conceived.

Thus in the dualism, concepts are supposed to be able to come into view in abstraction from any connection with the deliverances of the senses. So considered, employments of concepts are empty, as the Kantian tag says. We do not yet have in view anything we could recognize as the embracing of beliefs or theories, the adoption of determinate stands or commitments as to how things are in the world. That is supposed to be secured by adding the other half of the dualistic story.

If abstracting it from content leaves a scheme empty, what can be the point of identifying this side of the dualism as *the conceptual*?

In the dualism, the relation between scheme and content is evidently a case of the relation between form and matter. So we can put the question like this: why should it seem right to equate the formal with the conceptual, given that we are using the idea of form in such a way that form without matter is empty? We can find an answer to this question in two thoughts. First, that the linkages between concepts that constitute the shape, so to speak, of a conceptual scheme are linkages that pertain to what is a reason for what. Second, that if matter is supplied by the deliverances of the senses, then the structure of reason must lie on the other side of the matter-form contrast, and hence must be formal; reason is set over against the senses. If we can see how those two thoughts might be attractive, we can see how it might seem that the conceptual comes into view in a pure form only if we strip content away.

I think the first of those two thoughts, which connects the idea of a conceptual scheme with the idea of reason, need be no more than a determination of the relevant idea of the conceptual. The second thought, in which reason is kept pure of contamination by the mere matter yielded by the deliverances of the senses, is more problematic, and I shall return to it.[2]

---

[2] It would miss the point to protest that the connection of reason with form limits rational connections to those that would be exploited in inferences whose excellence is owed to their logical form. That is not the application of the concept of form that is in play here.

3

Why is this dualism of scheme and content a suitable case for deconstruction? I shall focus on one glaring problem.

Considered by themselves, employments of elements of a scheme—exercises of a conceptual repertoire—are empty; they are not yet recognizable as cases of adopting commitments concerning how things are in the world. If we take in only this side of the duality, we do not yet have in view any determinate answerability to how things are on the part of employments of concepts. We do not yet have the resources to see moves within a scheme as open to favorable assessment if things are a certain way and unfavorable assessment otherwise.

Now the other side of the duality is supposed to supply this missing requirement. A move within a scheme is answerable to the deliverances of the senses ('the tribunal of experience,' in W. V. Quine's phrase; Quine 1961:41). That is supposed to supply the missing requirement, because being answerable to the tribunal of experience is being answerable to the facts that impress themselves on the senses.

But the dualism reflects the idea that the linkages recognized by reason are the linkages that constitute the organization of schemes, and it places the deliverances of the senses outside schemes. And that makes it *incoherent* to suppose that sensory intake, on this conception, can mediate answerability to the world. If rational relations hold exclusively between elements of schemes, it cannot be the case that what it is for something within a scheme to be rationally in good shape is its being related in a certain way to something outside the scheme. 'Intuitions without concepts are blind,' Kant said. For present purposes, a more suggestive metaphor would be that intuitions without concepts are mute. They cannot intelligibly constitute a tribunal, something capable of passing favorable verdicts on some exercises of concepts and unfavorable verdicts on others.

4

Davidson has identified the dualism of scheme and content as 'the third dogma of empiricism,' and accordingly he has suggested that when we abandon the dualism, as we must, we are thereby discarding the last vestige of empiricism (Davidson 1984; the allusion is, of course, to Quine's 'Two Dogmas'). By 'empiricism' here, he means the thesis that the deliverances of the senses are epistemologically significant; they stand in relations of justification or warrant to world views or theories. He writes:

> Empiricism, like other isms, we can define pretty much as we please, but I take it to involve not only the pallid claim that all knowledge of the world comes through the agency of the senses, but also the conviction that this fact is of prime epistemological significance. The pallid

> idea merely recognizes the obvious causal role of the senses in mediat-
> ing between objects and events in the world and our thoughts and talk
> about them; empiricism locates the ultimate evidence for those
> thoughts at this intermediate step (Davidson 1990a).

This crediting of epistemological significance to sensory intake is exactly what I have represented the dualism as wanting but, by the way it
places intuitions outside the domain of rational linkages, making unavail-
able.

Now this unavailability marks a divergence between my account of why
the dualism must be rejected and Davidson's.

The trouble with the dualism as I have depicted it is that it is *incoherent*. The world's impacts on the senses are given the task of making it intelligible that moves within a conceptual scheme, taken to be such that considered in themselves they are empty, can nevertheless be adoptions of
stands as to how things are. There can be so much as an appearance that this
works only if we can see the world's impacts on the senses as a tribunal,
something capable of passing verdicts on moves within a scheme. But
when we distance content from scheme, in a way that reflects the idea that
rational interrelatedness is confined to elements in schemes, we ensure that
we cannot see experience as a tribunal. 'Intuitions without concepts' are
mute; they can pass no verdicts.

Contrast the problem Davidson finds in the dualism. When Davidson
finds the dualism in Quine, his complaint is not that Quine lapses into
incoherence, but rather that Quine makes himself vulnerable to standard
skepticism. He writes:

> Quine's naturalized epistemology, because it is based on the empiri-
> cist premise that what we mean and what we think is conceptually (and
> not merely causally) founded on the testimony of the senses, is open
> to standard skeptical attack (Davidson 1990b:136).

On my reading of the dualism, this is a curiously muted objection.
This objection would fit if an epistemology organized in the terms of the
dualism made it intelligible that the senses tell us *something*, with the
trouble being that it represents them as not telling us *enough* to warrant our
world view. On my reading, the trouble with the dualism is rather that the
very idea that the senses provide testimony becomes unintelligible. 'Intuitions without concepts' are mute. If one cannot see how anything but answerability to intuitions could ensure that thoughts are not empty, the upshot is more unnerving than any standard skepticism. Standard skepticism
takes for granted that we have a world view, and merely questions whether
we are entitled to it. The dualism, on my reading, generates a much more
radical anxiety about whether we are in touch with reality; within the dualism, it becomes unintelligible that we have a world view at all.

My claim that the dualism is incoherent depends on the thought that
the domain of rational interrelatedness is coextensive with the domain of

the conceptual. Suppose one wants to conceive the impacts of the world on us as 'intuitions without concepts,' but nevertheless wants those impacts to constitute a tribunal that world views must face. One will then be under pressure to avoid the threat of incoherence by denying that the domain of rational interrelatedness is coextensive with the domain of the conceptual.[3] But the thesis of coextensiveness is a way of putting a fundamental conviction of Davidson's. He is giving expression to it when he claims that 'nothing can be a reason for holding a belief except another belief' (Davidson 1986:310). The materials for the claim of incoherence come directly from Davidson himself, even though it is not the complaint he makes against the dualism.

5

If Davidson is right, as I believe, in claiming that the dualism has set much of the agenda for modern philosophy, something deep must account for its attraction. What might that be?

In at least one place, Davidson has offered an answer to this question. Summarizing a survey of the dualism, he writes: 'What matters, then, is ... that there should be an ultimate source of evidence whose character can be wholly specified without reference to what it is evidence for'. He goes on:

> It is easy to remember what prompts this view: it is thought necessary to insulate the ultimate sources of evidence from the outside world in order to guarantee the authority of evidence for the subject. Since we cannot be certain what the world outside the mind is like, the subjective can keep its virtue—its chastity, its certainty for us—only by being protected from contamination by the world. The familiar trouble is, of course, that the disconnection creates a gap no reasoning or construction can possibly bridge (Davidson 1989:162).

Now I would not dream of disputing that Davidson here captures a motivation that is familiar in modern philosophy. But do these remarks adequately account for the grip of scheme-content dualism?

This question becomes especially pressing when we note that the survey of scheme-content dualism to which these remarks are appended culminates in citing Quine as an adherent. I have mentioned this Davidsonian reading of Quine before. I do not want to question it; on the contrary, I think it is very perceptive. But surely Quine does not belong in the context of the temptation that these diagnostic remarks of Davidson's appeal to: the admittedly familiar temptation to 'interiorize,' or 'subjectivize,' the ultimate evidence for world views, so that whatever the fate of the world views, at

---

[3] Note that one is not already committed to the thesis of coextensiveness if one accepts the stipulation about how to understand the idea of the conceptual that I considered above. That involved no more than that conceptual linkages are included in rational connections, and left open the possibility that the inclusion is proper.

least the ultimate evidence is (supposedly) proof against skeptical challenge. A page further on, Davidson writes, summarizing the thought about trying to guarantee the authority of ultimate evidence:

> Instead of saying it is the scheme-content dichotomy that has dominated and defined the problems of modern philosophy, then, one could as well say it is how the dualism of the objective and the subjective has been conceived. For these dualisms have a common origin: a concept of the mind with its private states and objects.

Surely this concern with privacy does not fit Quine. Quine's concern, in espousing his version of scheme-content dualism, is to stress the freedom of play that our 'cues' leave us when we build or remodel a world view. What Quine wants to bring out is 'the extent of man's conceptual sovereignty' (Quine 1960:5). There is nothing in Quine's thinking that would lead him to hanker after a peculiarly solid authority for beliefs corresponding to the 'cues,' an authority supposedly achievable by insulating the subject matter of those beliefs from the external world. On the contrary, Quine is unmoved by the familiar epistemological anxiety to which that move is an intelligible, though, as Davidson rightly points out, unsuccessful response.

Davidson's suggested source for scheme-content dualism is bound to be unconvincing if one takes it, as I do, that the dualism is incoherent, in the way it tries to conceive experience as a tribunal while distancing it from the domain of rational interrelatedness. If we follow Davidson in supposing that the dualism responds to an anxiety about our *entitlement* to our world view, the sort of worry that might seem to be met by securing a solid authority for some supposedly basic evidence on which the world view is founded, then it becomes mysterious why that should lead to pushing the putative ultimate warrants for world views out of the domain of rational interrelatedness altogether, which in fact makes them incapable of intelligibly constituting warrants at all. This would be a much more radical case of a motivation's defeating itself than the one Davidson considers. In Davidson's case, the case of ordinary empiricism, we trade informational strength for immunity to skeptical challenge, and so secure the authority of the evidence only at the price of a vividly obvious gap between it and what it was supposed to be evidence for. The dualism undermines the capacity of the supposed evidence to be seen as evidence at all, weak or strong.

Of course if the dualism of scheme and content is incoherent, it will fail to satisfy any motivation that is operative in embracing it. I am not suggesting we should look for a motivation that the dualism would satisfy, as it does not satisfy the one that Davidson offers. The point is that a quest for epistemic security cannot explain why one might be led beyond the mere failure of *ordinary* empiricistic epistemologies into the incoherence of scheme-content dualism, in which the deliverances of the senses are simultaneously required to constitute a tribunal and rendered mute. To explain how this incoherence could stay hidden, and how the incoherent way of thinking could seem compulsory, we need something deeper than the motivation that Davidson considers.

6

I think we need to forget, for a while at least, that familiar anxiety about whether we are sufficiently entitled to our world view. If we allow ourselves to feel that anxiety, we presuppose that we have a world view. What underlies the dualism is something that lets that presupposition come into question. The dualism's felt need to conceive experience as a tribunal derives from an interest in the conditions of its being intelligible that we have a world view (or theories, or beliefs) at all. How is it that some moves we can make, moves we would like to think of as exploitings of concepts, are takings of stands as to how things are in the world? The thought is that this is intelligible only if we can see the moves as answerable, for their rational acceptability, ultimately to the facts themselves. And this required answerability to the world can be realized only as an answerability to the way the world puts its mark on us; that is, an answerability to the deliverances of our senses.

Once the question 'How is it possible that there are world views at all?' is in view, this thought is not easy to dismiss. Consider the thesis that responsiveness to reason is part of the content of the idea of exploiting conceptual capacities. I suggested that we can take that thesis simply to define a useful notion of conceptual capacities. Now it is a Kantian idea that responsiveness to reason is a kind of freedom. (The note of freedom sounds in Quine's talk of 'the extent of man's conceptual sovereignty.') We cannot gloss this freedom in terms of an unlimited absence of constraint; exactly not, since it consists in undertaking one's moves in allegiance to—if you like—restrictions, constituted by what is a reason for what. But if these restrictions are conceived as wholly formal, in that responsiveness to reason does not extend as far as answerability to impacts the world makes on us, then it becomes a live question how in exercising such a freedom we could be adopting commitments as to how things are in the world. If 'man's conceptual sovereignty' has no limits set by the facts themselves, it becomes unrecognizable as the power to make up our minds *about how things are.* And we do not put the right kind of limits in place if—like Davidson when he rejects empiricism—we say that impacts from the world exert a causal influence on how the sovereign power is exercised, but deny that they set rational constraints. If we say that, we deprive ourselves of a way to see exercises of this sovereignty as rationally answerable to the world itself, and then it becomes unintelligible how these exploitations of freedom can be otherwise than empty, just as 'thoughts without content' are in the Kantian tag.[4]

That is to say that empiricism, even in Davidson's interesting sense, is not easy to dismiss. Davidson is right that an ordinary empiricism, which 'interiorizes' the supposed warrants for world views in order to make the warrants safe from skeptical challenge, yields a quite unsatisfying picture of our entitlement to our beliefs. But empiricism is separable from that 'interiorizing' move, and the obsession with epistemic security that directly motivates it. We can concur with Davidson in rejecting that kind of epistemology, without threat to this thought: empiricism, in the interesting sense, captures a condition for it to be intelligible that thoughts are otherwise than empty.

I depicted scheme-content dualism as incoherent, because it combines the conviction that world views are rationally answerable to experience with a conception of experience that makes it incapable of passing verdicts. I have been suggesting that it is not easy to see how the first limb of that contradiction could be wrong. If it is not wrong, the diagnostic question that the dualism raises is this: 'Why is it difficult to see how the deliverances of the senses could constitute a tribunal that our world views face?' It is in answering that question that we shall understand the dualism's importance for modern philosophy.

Here is a quick sketch of an answer.

With the intellectual development that we can sum up as the rise of modern science, there became available a newly sharp conception of the proper goal of the natural sciences, as we can (significantly) call them: namely, an understanding of phenomena as interrelated perhaps causally, but certainly within a framework of laws of nature. This supersedes a premodern outlook, which did not sharply differentiate a natural-scientific mode of understanding from one that places its objects in rational relations with one another, and so works with categories like meaning. In this premodern outlook, it was sensible to look for meaning in phenomena like the movement of the planets—phenomena that we are equipped, with modernity's conception of a special mode of understanding, the natural-scientific, to see as appropriately brought within its scope, and so as exactly not something to look for meaning in. In step with the emergence into clarity of this idea of a special mode of understanding, to be radically contrasted with finding meaning in things, it is only to be expected that there was an

---

[4] It does not help to say that impacts from the world cause beliefs, which can then serve as a tribunal for world views to face. These beliefs would be just more items of the same kind as the items that make up world views. The question we are considering is how there can be anything of that kind (if not because some things of that kind are answerable to the tribunal of experience), and it is unresponsive to help ourselves to some things of that kind. The causal ancestry we cite for the ones we help ourselves to makes no difference to this.

increasing sense of how special—by comparison with the framework of natural law—are the patterns or structures within which things are placed when they are understood in the contrasting way; how special are the linkages that constitute the domain of rational interrelatedness.

Now the idea of the world making its impact on a sentient being is the idea of a causal transaction, an instance of a kind of thing that takes place in nature. And that differentiation of modes of understanding can easily make it seem that once we conceive a happening in those terms, we are already thereby conceiving it in a way that is distanced from placement in the domain of rational interrelatedness. Succumbing to that appearance, we might say something on these lines: 'The idea of the world's impacts on us is the idea of something natural. And we moderns now see clearly how the structure of rational linkages contrasts with the structure of the natural, the topic of natural-scientific understanding. Hence, given that the domain of the conceptual is the domain of rational interrelatedness, it must be that intuitions as such are without concepts'.

That suggests how a familiar feature of modern thinking might explain the idea that the sensory stands opposed to the conceptual, as it does for Davidson as well as in the dualism of scheme and content. And it is not that this line of thought uncovers a mistake in the idea that I have suggested underlies empiricism: the idea that thought can be intelligibly nonempty only by virtue of answerability to experience. What makes that plausible is independent, and the plausibility is undimmed by any conviction this line of thought confers on the idea that experience cannot be a tribunal. So if we can see how this line of thought might be gripping, that can explain how someone who is responsive to the question 'How is it possible that there are world views at all?' might be tempted into the incoherence of scheme-content dualism.

I have suggested that there is no clear way to avoid the idea that empiricism captures a condition for thought not to be empty. (Davidson does not even consider that recommendation for empiricism.) It cannot be obligatory to think incoherently. So if empiricism is compulsory, there must be a flaw in the line of thought that makes it look as if experience as such is 'without concepts.'

It is indeed an achievement of modernity to have brought into clear focus the contrast between two modes of understanding: one that involves placing phenomena in the framework of natural law, and one that involves placing things in the domain of rational interconnectedness. But to give proper credit to that achievement, we do not need to accept that when we see something as a happening in nature—as the world's making its mark on a sentient creature would indeed be—we are *eo ipso* placing it in the sort of frame that is characteristic of the natural sciences. If that were so, then, given the contrast, the fact that something is a happening in nature would be a ground for supposing that—at least in itself, viewed as the happening in nature it is—it is 'without concepts.' But it is not so. We need not accept what might seem to be implied by the label 'natural sciences,' that phenomena are conceived in terms of their place in nature only when they are conceived in terms of their place in the framework of natural law. If we reject that, we make room for supposing that the world's impacts on us, even considered in themselves as just that, the world's impacts on us, are not 'without concepts.' That would allow the tension within scheme-content dualism to be resolved in the direction of a coherent empiricism.[5]

7

What Davidson considers under the head of scheme-content dualism is an attempt to achieve security against skeptical challenge for evidence on which world views are putatively founded. This leads to a shrinkage in the informational content of the putative evidence, rather than, as in my reading of the dualism, a move that has the effect of disqualifying it from being evidence at all. I acknowledged that this quest for epistemic security is fundamental to modern epistemology. I also said that Davidson is right in placing scheme-content dualism at the root of what is unsatisfactory about modern philosophy. How can this hang together? How can what is in fact a disqualification of putative evidence from being evidence at all—with the upshot that, in the context of an empiricism that I suggested is hard to dismiss, our very possession of a world view becomes a mystery—be at the root of a philosophical tradition that is, as I acknowledge, driven by an obsession with the authority of our evidence for our world views, and takes it for granted that we have a world view and evidence for it?

The dualism is the outcome of a pair of intelligible temptations. It is intelligible that reflection should be shaped both by the genuine credentials of empiricism (which are not undermined by Davidson, since he does not even consider them), and by the conception of nature that underlies the idea that the world's impacts on us are 'intuitions without concepts'. Now someone who is susceptible to both those influences is thereby *en route*, as it were, to a frame of mind in which it is a mystery how thought bears on the world at all. But it is not to be expected that the destination would be obvious at all stages in the journey; especially not if the reflection is undertaken early in the evolution of the conception of nature whose finished product, in this context, is the idea that experiences are 'intuitions without concepts'. (That the destination is not obvious is surely a condition of continuing to let oneself be subject to both influences.) At a primitive stage in such reflection, a sense of where it is headed need not take any clearer shape

---

[5] I do not mean this lightning sketch to suggest that this resolution of the tension is easy. I discuss these issues slightly less breathlessly (to echo Davidson 1989:162) in McDowell 1994.

than something to this effect: thought's hold on the world is coming into question. And a disquiet that can be expressed like that is just what is responded to—ineptly given this account of its origin, but not at all surprisingly—by the sort of philosophy that is obsessed with the authority of our warrant for our world views.

8

I suggested that with the modern achievement of clarity about a distinctive sort of understanding—now available to be cited as the defining aim of a distinctive intellectual endeavor, the natural sciences—there comes an appreciation of how special, by comparison, is the sort of understanding that involves placing things in rational relations to one another. The sense of specialness is expressed in a genre of philosophical questions that we can sum up, exploiting the connection between reason and freedom, like this: how is freedom related to the natural world? This wording points to familiar questions about action and responsibility as paradigms of the sort of thing I mean. But the dualism of scheme and content belongs in this genre of philosophy too. Underlying the dualism of scheme and content is a dualism of freedom—the freedom of reason—and nature.

In 'Mental Events' and kindred writings, Davidson has undertaken to defuse philosophical anxieties about integrating freedom into the natural world. He endorses the sense of specialness; he puts forward on his own behalf a quasi-Kantian picture of, as we might say, the realm of freedom, according to which it is organized by a 'constitutive ideal of rationality,' wholly distinct from the organizing structure of the world as viewed by the natural sciences. But he aims to prevent this sense of specialness from generating metaphysical anxiety, by arguing that the distinction between freedom and nature reflects a duality of conceptual apparatuses and not a duality of ontological realms.[6]

Now I have cast the dualism of scheme and content as crystallizing a cognate philosophical anxiety; I have cast the question 'How are world views possible?' as a form of the question 'How is freedom possible?'. But here Davidson's way with other forms of the anxiety does not help. Davidson's invocation of a duality that is conceptual, and not ontological, does not undermine the thought that the world's impacts on us are 'intuitions without concepts'—that experience cannot be a tribunal. That is a thought

---

[6] Just because it involves endorsing the sense of specialness, this is a much more promising program for disarming the philosophical anxiety that the sense of specialness risks generating than that of Richard Rorty, at least in Rorty 1979. There Rorty pooh-poohed the sense of specialness, in debunking the idea of a philosophically significant contrast between the Naturwissenschaften and the Geisteswissenschaften.

that Davidson himself accepts. And it is a thought that, I have claimed, leaves the freedom of 'conceptual sovereignty' a mystery.

Davidson misses this, because he misidentifies the incipient philosophical anxiety that is crystallized in scheme-content dualism; he takes it that there is nothing there but the familiar concern about entitlement to world views, and he does not see that the familiar anxiety about freedom, applied in this context, takes shape fully only as a concern about how it is possible that exercises of 'conceptual sovereignty' are world views at all. This concern rests in part on a recommendation for empiricism that does not come into view in Davidson's thinking at all. To defuse the concern while respecting this quite different attraction for empiricism, we need to find a way to resist the idea that the impacts of the world on us are 'intuitions without concepts'. And for that we need a more radical counter to the underlying dualism of reason and nature than the one Davidson supplies. In the sources of what is unsatisfactory about modern philosophy, there is something that lies deeper than a misconception of subjectivity. A more fundamental source is a misconception of the intellectual obligations of naturalism.

References

Davidson, D. 1980. Mental Events. *Essays on Actions and Events*, 207-25. Oxford: Clarendon Press.

Davidson, D. 1984. On the Very Idea of a Conceptual Scheme. *Inquiries into Truth and Interpretation*, 183-98. Oxford: Clarendon Press.

Davidson, D. 1986. A Coherence Theory of Truth and Knowledge. *Truth and Interpretation: Perspectives on the Philosophy of Donald Davidson*, ed. E. LePore, 307-19. Oxford: Basil Blackwell.

Davidson, D. 1989. The Myth of the Subjective. *Relativism: Interpretation and Confrontation*, ed. M. Krausz, 159-72. Notre Dame: Notre Dame University Press.

Davidson, D. 1990a. Meaning, Truth and Evidence. *Perspectives on Quine*, eds. R.B. Barrett and R.F. Gibson, 68-79. Oxford: Basil Blackwell.

Davidson, D. 1990b. Afterthoughts, 1987 (a postscript to A Coherence Theory of Truth and Knowledge). *Reading Rorty*, ed. A. Malachowski, 134-7. Oxford: Basil Blackwell.

Kant, I. 1929. *Critique of Pure Reason*. Trans. Norman Kemp Smith. London: Macmillan.

McDowell, J. 1994. *Mind and World*. Cambridge, MA: Harvard University Press.

Quine, W. V. 1960. *Word and Object*. Cambridge, MA: MIT Press.

Quine, W. V. 1961. Two Dogmas of Empiricism. *From a Logical Point of View*, 20-46. Cambridge, MA: Harvard University Press.

Rorty, R. 1979. *Philosophy and the Mirror of Nature*. Princeton: Princeton University Press.

9

Meaning, Truth, Ontology

STEPHEN NEALE[1]

> *I believe in the ordinary notion of truth: there really are people, mountains, camels, and stars out there, just as we think there are, and those objects and events frequently have the characteristics we think we perceive them to have. Our concepts are ours, but that doesn't mean they don't truly, as well as usefully, describe an objective reality.*
>
> Donald Davidson 1999

1   Introduction

It is far from obvious that a systematic and comprehensive theory of meaning for a natural language must appeal to the idea that sentences have *references*. Our ordinary uses of 'refer', 'reference', and so on suggest it would be unnatural to view sentences (or even sentences-relative-to-contexts) as referring to things (except in the sense in which we might say, when exam-

[1] This paper is at once an expanded version of the paper I presented orally at Karlovy Vary and a compressed version of Chapter 2 of my forthcoming book *Facing Facts*. I thank Ernie Lepore, Peter Pagin, Gabriel Segal, and Bruce Vermazen for comments on various ancestors. I am especially indebted to Donald Davidson for detailed discussion over the past five or six years.

ining a text for example, that a particular sentence or verse refers to, say, the Melian massacre or man's despair). But the theoretical semanticist who appeals to the idea that sentences have references need not be entirely shackled by ordinary usage. Certainly we do well to begin with ordinary usage and depart from it grudgingly; but it is well attested that although (many of) our theoretical terms (in both the sciences and the humanities) derive from ordinary usage, as theorizing becomes more complex, such terms may start to diverge in meaning from their ordinary language counterparts, a normal pattern of linguistic development in any discipline that is not stagnant.

Is it possible to build a theory of meaning without taking sentences to stand for things? At what points in semantic theorizing do we encounter strong pressures to associate entities with *any* expressions? A full-blown entity-theoretic approach to meaning will proceed by assigning to each meaningful expression some entity, beginning with individual words (or perhaps morphemes) and working upwards in a compositional manner through phrases all the way to sentences. The theories of Frege and Russell do this. But there are other ways one might proceed: most notable is the truth-theoretic approach pioneered by Donald Davidson (1984, 1990, 2000). The starting point of a semantic theory is *truth*, which is not an entity but 'a concept ... intelligibly attributed to things like sentences, utterances, beliefs, and propositions, entities which have a propositional content' (Davidson 2000:65). Ontological issues arise only in so far as certain entities must be posited in the provision of such a theory. It is an interesting question, according to the truth-theorist, whether there are *any* expressions that must be seen as standing for entities, a question that can be answered only by attempting to construct theories of meaning.

Davidson (1980, 1984, 1990) contends (i) that we can go about constructing theories of meaning that do not assign entities to anything other than our standard referential devices (singular terms, including variables under assignment); (ii) that such theories will take *objects* and *events*, construed as particulars, to be the sorts of things to which singular terms refer; (iii) that as far as the theory of meaning is concerned, we can free ourselves from the idea that predicates refer to *properties* (or anything else) and the idea that individual sentences refer to, stand for, represent, correspond to, or are made true by particular *facts* (or by particular *states of affairs*, *situations*, or *circumstances* that obtain); (iv) that even if we wanted facts to serve as the references of true sentences, we could not have them because a slingshot argument demonstrates that such entities would collapse into one Great Fact; (v) that if there are no facts, then we cannot make sense of 'correspondence' theories of truth, for such theories are built upon the idea that a sentence is true if and only if there is some fact to which it corresponds; and (vi) that if there are no facts to which true sentences correspond, we cannot make sense of a distinction between 'conceptual scheme' and 'empirical content' and so must give up attempts to render intelligible talk of alternative conceptual schemes, representations of reality, relativism, and scepticism; traditional philosophical problems surrounding these notions simply evaporate for lack of genuine subject matter.

2   Meaning and Truth

Davidson's truth-theoretic approach to meaning forms the basis of a respected research programme in the semantics of natural language and is the best example, to date, of a systematic approach to semantics that seeks to do its job without appealing to universals, properties, functions or even classes as the semantic values of predicates, or to propositions, situations, states of affairs or facts as the semantic values of sentences. I want to present it in optimal light here, free of certain defects commentators have claimed to detect—the theory is frequently maligned through ignorance, which is not to say that it is without interesting problems.

Frequently it is said that a semantic theory for a language should specify what each of its sentences means. It is sometimes added that in order to achieve this a semantic theory must deliver *theorems*, one for each sentence, specifying what that sentence means. And this is often said to amount to the following (I think erroneously, but let that pass): putting to one side the complications raised by the existence of indexical and other context-sensitive expressions, a theory of meaning for a language L is a theory that delivers, for each sentence S of L, a theorem of the following form:

(M) S^* means (in L) that p

where instances of (M) are sentences in a metalanguage L^* rich enough to talk about sentences of the object-language L in which the expression replacing 'S^*' is an expression of L^* that uniquely describes S in terms of its structure—a so-called structural description of S—and the sentence replacing 'p' is a sentence of L^*.[2] On this definition, a theory of meaning for French (L), stated in English (L^*), must deliver (1)—or something very like (1)—as a theorem:

(1)   'La neige est blanche' means (in French) that snow is white.

The structural description functioning as the subject of 'means' in (1) is an expression of English created by putting quotation marks around a sentence of French. In a more precise statement, something like the following structural description might be used to describe the French sentence in question:

(2) $[_S[_{NP}[_D$ la$][_N$ neige$]][_{VP}[_V$ est$][_A$ blanche$]]]$.

---

[2] There are, I believe, serious worries about instances of (M); as they are not pertinent to my main theme I do not take them up here.

A definition of meaning in terms of theorems of form (M) is *not* Davidson's starting point. Nor is his point of departure one that overtly invokes the concept of *truth*. Davidson's main ideas can be set out as a series of six definitions and theses. The first of these is what he offers in place of the popular definition just given:

(i)   A theory of *meaning* for a language L is a theory with the following feature: knowing what the theory states would suffice for understanding (utterances of sentences of) L.

There is no overt talk here of theorems satisfying schema (M), indeed no overt talk of theorems at all. It is, of course, open to someone to say that the way to *construct* a theory of meaning in Davidson's sense is to construct a theory that issues in theorems satisfying schema (M). But this is not what Davidson does when he presents his positive proposals. He starts on a seemingly new topic: *truth*. Drawing inspiration from Tarski's (1956) celebrated definition of truth for well-behaved formal languages, Davidson offers us a second definition:

(ii)   Ignoring, for a moment, the complications raised by the existence of indexical and other context-sensitive expressions, a theory of *truth* for a language L is a theory that yields, for each sentence S of L, a theorem of the form

(T) S^* is true (in L) $\equiv p$

where instances of (T) are sentences in a metalanguage L^* used to talk about sentences of the object-language L, 'S^*' is a structural description (in L^*) of S, 'p' is a sentence of L^*, and '$\equiv$' (read 'if and only if') is the material biconditional. For example, if the object-language (L) is French and the metalanguage (L^*) is English, then the following would both be instances of schema (T):

(3)   'La neige est blanche' is true (in French) $\equiv$ snow is white

(4)   'La neige est rouge' is true (in French) $\equiv$ snow is red.

Instances of schema (T) Davidson calls *T-sentences* or *T-theorems*. Like any other theory, in the first instance a theory of truth will be judged by whether its theorems are true. In order for an instance of (T) to be true, it suffices that the sentences replacing 'S^* is true (in L)' and 'p' have the same truth-value (and hence, given our understanding of 'is true (in L)', that the sentence of L described by the structural description replacing 'S^*' have the same truth-value as the sentence replacing 'p'). No stronger connection is needed because '$\equiv$' is (only) the material biconditional.[3] Thus (3) and (4)

---

[3] Whereas Tarski takes the undefined semantic notion of *translation* (hence *meaning*) for granted and uses it to place constraints on what counts as an adequate definition of *truth* for a

are both true: in the former, '≡' stands between two true sentences; in the latter, it stands between two false ones.

Notice that no direct connection between a theory of *truth* and a theory of *meaning* is stated by (i) or (ii). However, (i) tells us what conditions a theory—*any* theory—must satisfy in order to be a theory of meaning, and since a theory of truth is a *theory*, we can infer (iii):

(iii)   A theory of truth (henceforth a *T-theory*) θ for a language L would be (qualify as, serve as, do duty as) a theory of meaning for L if knowledge of what θ stated sufficed for understanding L.

Davidson strikes out beyond definition with the following bold claim:

(iv)   For any natural language L there is at least one T-theory for L that qualifies as a theory of meaning for L.

And he goes further with the following claims:

(v)   As a matter of empirical fact, any T-theory for L qualifying as a theory of meaning for L has the following property: knowing what is stated by its *T-theorems alone* suffices for understanding L (knowledge of what its *axioms* state is not necessary);[4]

(vi)   The background logic used to derive T-theorems from the axioms of a T-theory is standard, extensional, first-order logic with identity.

There are a number of notoriously difficult issues involved in trying to establish whether the optimism expressed in (iv), (v), and (vi) is well-founded (see Davidson 1984, 1999c, Foster 1976, Segal 1999 and the references therein). My purpose here is not to settle the case one way or the other but to indicate clearly the character of certain perceived difficulties that bear on my main themes.

Let us say that a T-theory for L is *acceptable* if knowledge of what is stated by its T-theorems suffices for understanding L. The challenge for the Davidsonian is to explain how an acceptable T-theory can be constructed.

(a) It is usually agreed that not *every* T-theory is acceptable. Suppose there is a T-theory θ_1 for French that delivers the following T-theorem for the sentence 'La neige est blanche':

(5)   'La neige est blanche' is true (in French) ≡ JFK was assassinated.[5]

---

language, Davidson uses a primitive notion of *truth* in order to characterize what he takes to be the most plausible way of constructing a theory of meaning.

[4] This is something Davidson 1999c states explicitly in response to Segal 1999. Still more recently, he has argued in private that even knowledge of what is stated by the theorems may go beyond what is strictly necessary.

[5] If the background logic is unconstrained, extensional, first-order logic with identity, θ_1 will not deliver *just* (5) for 'la neige est blanche': it will deliver, for this sentence, a collection of T-sentences whose right-hand sides are logically equivalent to the right-hand side of (5). In

Since the left- and right-hand sides of this material biconditional are both true, it is a true instance of schema (T). But knowing what is stated by *this* T-theorem would not suffice for understanding 'la neige est blanche'. And from this definite fact, it might be inferred that knowing what is stated by *all of the* T-theorems of θ_1 would not suffice for understanding 'la neige est blanche' (or, quite probably, for understanding many other sentences of French, particularly those containing the words 'neige' or 'blanche'). The additional assumptions needed to draw the general conclusion are far from obvious—indeed the general conclusion may well be false—but let us suppose they are compelling: although delivering a true theorem of the form (T) for every sentence of French (including the sentence 'la neige est blanche'), θ_1 cannot do duty as a theory of meaning for French—it is impeccable as a theory of *truth* for French but inadequate as a theory of *meaning*. Something seems to be missing. Or so it might be argued.

(b) If θ_1 is not acceptable (i.e. if it does not qualify as a theory of meaning for French), then one task facing the Davidsonian semanticist is the specification of conditions a T-theory must satisfy to be acceptable, conditions that do not invoke the concept of understanding or related semantic concepts such as meaning, synonymy, or translation. It might be suggested that general considerations governing, or at least informing, the interpretation of empirical theories should be brought to bear: a theory of meaning for French is an empirical theory, so its theorems should be lawlike and support counterfactuals (see Davidson 1984:xiv,xviii;26,174). As proof of the failure of (5)—and thereby of θ_1—to support counterfactuals, the apparent falsity of (5') might be contrasted with the apparent truth of (3'):

(5') If JFK had not been assassinated, 'la neige est blanche' would not be true (in French)

(3') If snow were not white, 'la neige est blanche' would not be true (in French).

Hard questions must be faced by anyone wishing to pronounce on the utility of the apparent contrast. Are sentences to be individuated, in part, by their semantic features? Or will that threaten the whole project? Does the parenthetical appendage 'in French' occurring in the T-theorems we have been using signal a willingness to see the same structural description existing and meaning something in more than one language? Do (5') and (3') exhibit ambiguities of scope that may be interfering with judgments of truth and falsity, ambiguities attributable to the fact that the structural descriptions are Russellian definite descriptions? (For example, might not (2) above be read as 'the sentence formed by concatentating the noun phrase

principle, requiring the derivation of T-theorems to conform to the canons of a canonical proof procedure will pare down the collection. See below.

formed by concatenating . . .'?) What are the truth-conditions of counterfactuals in any case?

I shall not tackle these questions here. To keep things moving, I simply stipulate (without prejudice to the main discussion) (i) that structural descriptions are indeed Russellian descriptions (rather than names), (ii) that structural descriptions are language relative, and (iii) that (5') is false and (3') true whatever the scopes of the structural descriptions they contain. The first stipulation certainly has some independent plausibility; the second and third are controversial but will play no crucial role once we get past counterfactuals; they just simplify exposition. The second stipulation (which would probably be required to justify the third) allows us to drop the annoying appendage '(in French)' from T-theorems for French sentences, which henceforth can be read as exemplifying the form (T'):

(T')   the L sentence S^* is true $\equiv p$.

(Prefixes such as 'the French sentence' will be omitted where no confusion will arise.)

By the third stipulation, θ_1 can be discarded on the grounds that its theorems are not lawlike. But it might be argued that a T-theory θ_2 delivering (6) is not yet eliminated, witness the alleged truth of (6'):

(6)   'La neige est blanche' is true $\equiv$ snow is a form of frozen water.

(6')   If snow were not a form of frozen water, 'la neige est blanche' would not be true.[6]

If this is right, a criterion that goes beyond the nomological is required to deflect unacceptable T-theories.

(c) It might seem obvious *what* is missing from θ_1 and θ_2: the English (metalanguage) sentences 'JFK was assassinated' and 'snow is a form of frozen water' do not *mean* the same thing as the French (object-language) sentence 'la neige est blanche'. And so it might be supposed that a T-theory θ_3 for French with the following property will be acceptable: in every theorem of form (T), the metalanguage sentence replacing 'p' means the same as (or *translates*) the French sentence described by the expression replacing 'S^*'. To borrow a label from the literature, in order to be acceptable a theory of meaning θ_3 must be *interpretive*: a T-theory is interpretive just in case all of its T-theorems are interpretive; a T-theorem is interpretive just in case the metalanguage sentence replacing 'p' on the right-hand side of (T) means the same as (or translates) the object-language sentence described by the expression replacing 'S^*' on the left-hand side.

---

[6] A better pair might be the following, due to Segal 1999:

(i) 'Copper conducts heat' is true (in English) $\equiv$ copper conducts electricity.

(i') If copper did not conduct electricity, 'copper conducts heat' would not be true (in English).

An interpretive T-theory for *L* would be equivalent to what Tarski (1956) called a (materially adequate) *truth definition* for *L* (a definition of 'true-in-*L*'). Tarski could help himself freely to notions like synonymy or translation: his objective was to define (*i.e.* characterize) *truth* (in *L*), not meaning. But appeals to synonymy or translation are not available to Davidson, nor does he claim they are: the challenge, which Davidson and others have taken up, is to specify a set of conditions which hold only of interpretive T-theories but which do not invoke any threatening semantic concepts.[7]

(d) One way to avoid appealing to semantic notions would be to invoke only *formal* conditions. Some non-interpretive T-theories could be discarded by restricting attention to those producing their theorems in a *compositional* and *systematic* fashion, on the basis of the structurally significant parts of sentences. Any T-theory that delivers

---

[7] It is sometimes claimed—although not by Davidson—that in order to be acceptable, a T-theory must 'ultimately' yield theorems of the form (M):

(M) S^* means (in L) that p.

Someone insisting on this will then say that a T-theory is acceptable only if each of its T-theorems can be 'interpreted as', 'mapped onto', or 'converted into' the corresponding M-theorem. An M-theorem, it will be claimed, is 'more informative' than its corresponding T-theorem: the former (which is non-extensional) entails the latter (which is extensional), but not vice versa. Occasionally, Davidson (1984:60,175) allows statements of form (M) to pass unchallenged, but nowhere does he claim they form the backbone of a theory of meaning.

It is sometimes said that Davidson is proposing a 'truth-conditional' theory of meaning which identifies the meaning of a sentence with its truth-conditions—casual remarks in some of Davidson's articles have surely encouraged such claims—but they are confused on two counts. Firstly, a specification of the truth conditions of a sentence is a specification of the conditions necessary and sufficient for its truth. Since the connective '$\equiv$' in a T-theorem is the *material* biconditional, it is no part of what it is to be a T-theory that the sentence replacing 'p' in a true theorem of form (T) specify the truth conditions of the sentence described by the expression replacing 'S^*'. The connective would have to be at least as strong as the *strict* (modal) biconditional '$\Leftrightarrow$' to ensure a specification of truth conditions.

Secondly, the unadorned thesis that the meaning of a sentence is identical to its truth conditions is easily refuted: (a) to specify the truth conditions of a sentence is to specify conditions necessary and sufficient for its truth; (b) a necessary truth is true under all conditions; (c) so all necessary truths have the same truth conditions; (d) so (i) and (ii) have the same truth conditions:

(i)   snow is white
(ii)   snow is white and $2 + 2 = 4$;

(e) if the truth conditions of a sentence are identical to its meaning, then knowing its truth conditions is the same thing as knowing its meaning (this would seem to be the place to mount a challenge to the argument); (f) but knowing the meaning of (i) is not the same thing as knowing the meaning of (ii); (g) so the meaning of a sentence is not the same thing as it truth conditions. A further problem for the unadorned thesis is raised by expressions that give rise to what Frege calls *coloring* and Grice calls *conventional implicature*. Examples include 'but', 'although', 'yet', 'furthermore', and 'nonetheless', which seem to contribute to meaning without contributing to truth conditions. For discussion, see Neale 1999.

(7)   'Santorin est volcanique' is true ≡ Santorini is volcanic

via the following axioms for 'Santorin' and 'est volcanique' might be regarded as satisfying this requirement (at least as far as 'Santorin est volcanique' is concerned):

(Ax 1)   the referent of 'Santorin' = Santorini

(Ax 2) $(\forall \alpha)(\ulcorner \alpha$ est volcanique$\urcorner$ is true ≡ the referent of α is volcanic).

Notes: (i) 'α' ranges over proper names. (ii) There is no attempt to quantify into quotation in (Ax 2). The expression

(8) $\ulcorner \alpha$ est volcanique$\urcorner$

is just shorthand for the definite description

(9) $\alpha \frown$ 'is volcanic'

read as 'the expression produced by concatenating α and "est volcanique"'. (iii) For simplicity I have ignored the internal structure of the object language predicate.

Using extensional, first-order logic with identity, (7) can be derived (i.e. *proved*) from our axioms using the Principle of Universal Instantiation (UI) and the Principle of Substitutivity for Singular Terms (PSST).[8]

[1]   'Santorin est volcanique' is true ≡ the referent of 'Santorin' is volcanic

(from (Ax 2) using UI)

[2]   'Santorin est volcanique' is true ≡ Santorini is volcanic

(from [1] and (Ax 1) using PSST)

---

[8] I have made the simplification—harmless for immediate purposes—that (i) is a singular term:

(i)   the referent of 'Santorin'.

There are good reasons for thinking this is wrong, that (i) is really a quantified noun phrase by virtue of being a Russellian definite description. On such an account, the relevant rule of inference will not be PSST but Whitehead and Russell's *14.15, a derived rule of inference for extensional contexts. The issue assumes some importance when we are asked to consider T-theories intended to produce theorems for sentences in the object language containing modal operators and when we discuss certain types of counterfactual claims about reference. There is a reading of (ii) that is false,

(ii)   the referent of 'Santorin' might not have been Santorini

and this can be captured by reading the description as having large scope. To the extent that there is an additional true reading—some people want to dispute this—it is readily captured by reading the description as having smaller scope than the modal operator. Matters are further complicated by the fact that the description functioning as the subject noun phrase in (ii) contains a structural description as a part, giving it the same general form as (iii):

(iii)   the recipient of the development grant might not have been Santorini

which is several ways ambiguous.

The idea here, then, is to restrict attention to T-theories respecting the syntactic structure of sentences. Axioms for singular terms might look like (Ax 1), those for one-place predicates like (Ax 2), those for two-place predicates like (Ax 3), those for two-place connectives like (Ax 4), and so on:

(Ax 3) $(\forall\alpha)(\forall\beta)(\ulcorner\alpha$ aime $\beta\urcorner$ is true $\equiv$ the referent of α loves the referent of β)

(Ax 4) $(\forall\phi)(\forall\psi)(\ulcorner\phi$ et $\psi\urcorner$ is true $\equiv$ ϕ is true and ψ is true).[9]

(Here, 'α' and 'β' range over names and 'ϕ' and 'ψ' range over sentences.) Each axiom of a T-theory so constructed will have an impact on an infinite number of T-theorems, including those for sentences containing demonstrative and indexical elements, and this will have the effect of making it considerably harder for theories delivering non-interpretive T-theorems to produce only *true* T-theorems. In effect, then, the constraint of systematic compositionality narrows the class of T-theories towards convergence with the class of those that are interpretive. Or at least that is the idea.

But the question of potentially non-interpretive T-theories is still not behind us as we can see by examining the work done by reference axioms. The Greek island of Santorini has another name: 'Thera' (the Greek 'Théra' is 'more official' than 'Santoríni' and is the name typically (although not invariably) used in administrative or legal documents). The names 'Santorini' and 'Thera' (sometimes written 'Thira') are both used in English (i.e. by English speakers in sentences of English), and the names 'Santorin' and 'Thera' (sometimes written 'Thira') are both used in French (i.e. by French speakers in sentences of French). Now consider the T-theory obtained by replacing the reference axiom (Ax 1) for 'Santorin' by (Ax 1*):

(Ax 1*) the referent of 'Santorin' = Thera.

The resulting T-theory would deliver the following T-theorem in place of (7):

(10) 'Santorin est volcanique' is true $\equiv$ Thera is volcanic.

(10) is just as true (and as lawlike) as (7); but is it interpretive? One's answer to this question is almost certainly going to be tied to one's views about what happens when 'Santorin est volcanique' and other sentences are embedded in constructions that have triggered talk of 'opacity' (the failure of PSST), for example sentences containing verbs of propositional attitude such as 'croire' ('believe'). The nature of appropriate axioms for such verbs

[9] As it stands, (Ax 3) does not actually respect syntactic structure. Syntactic theory tells us that 'Pierre aime Claire' has more or less the following syntactic structure [s [np Pierre] [vp aime [np Claire]]]. For T-theories that respect syntactic structure, see Larson and Segal 1995. In order to produce axioms of the required form, Larson and Segal assign entities as semantic values of verbs and verb phrases, which involves an interesting departure from Davidson's austere line.

and the way in which T-theories should produce T-theorems for such sentences are matters of debate; but presumably when all is said and done, a T-theory containing (Ax 1) for 'Santorin' would deliver (11), whereas one containing (Ax 1*) would deliver (12):

(11)   'Pierre croit que Santorin est volcanique' is true ≡ Pierre believes that Santorini is volcanic

(12)   'Pierre croit que Santorin est volcanique' is true ≡ Pierre believes that Thera is volcanic.

Following Frege, it is widely held that the right-hand sides of (11) and (12) are not synonymous, that there are circumstances in which they can differ in truth-value. Given the definite connections between (i) the English 'Santorini' and French 'Santorin', and (ii) the English 'Thera' and French 'Thera', it might plausibly be argued that (12) is not interpretive and that, in consequence, any T-theory producing it, although systematic and compositional, is not acceptable.[10]

(e) Axioms for predicates also leave room for non-interpretive T-theories. If the background logic is unconstrained, standard first-order logic with identity, then it is possible to produce T-theories that are non-interpretive by virtue of delivering T-theorems such as (13):

(13)   'Santorin est volcanique' is true ≡ Santorini is volcanic and everything physical is physical.

Some of these T-theories could be cut out by requiring the procedure by which T-theorems are derived to conform to the canons of some narrowly circumscribed proof procedure (see Davidson 1984:61,138). One would have to be careful, however, not to constrain the proof procedure so tightly as to deprive oneself of the resources needed to produce T-theorems that are still interpretive—for example, one would not want to leave any syntactic, logical, or set-theoretic junk on the right-hand side of T-theorems derived for French sentences containing quantified noun phrases ('chaque homme', 'quelques hommes'), adverbs of quantification ('toujours', 'jamais', etc.), indexicals ('je', 'ici', 'maintenant', 'cet homme'), verbs of propositional attitude ('croire', 'savoir'), or verbs that register quantification over events

---

[10] Similar issues arise in connection with sentence connectives such as 'et' ('and') and 'mais' ('but'). (Ax i) is interpretive; but what about (Ax i*)?

(Ax i) $(\forall\sigma)(\forall\tau)$ ($\ulcorner\sigma$ mais $\tau\urcorner$ is true ≡ σ is true but τ is true)

(Ax i*) $(\forall\sigma)(\forall\tau)$ ($\ulcorner\sigma$ mais $\tau\urcorner$ is true ≡ σ is true and τ is true).

For a card-carrying Fregean, there is an important difference between, on the one hand, 'Santorin' and 'Thera', and, on the other, 'et' and 'mais': the former differ from one another in *sense*; the latter have the same sense and differ from one another only in *coloring*. So even if sense can be invoked to decide between (Ax 1) and (Ax 1*) above, it will not help in distinguishing (Ax i) from (Ax i*) as these axioms express the same *thought* for Frege. For discussion, Neale 1999.

('sortir', 'se tomber'). But requiring a T-theory for French to produce its T-theorems in conformity to a canonical proof procedure will not eliminate *all* systematic and compositional theories that deliver (13). Replacing axiom (Ax 2) above by (Ax 2*) seems to pre-load the requisite trouble before the canonical proof procedure ever gets into action:

(Ax 2*) $(\forall\alpha)$ ($\ulcorner \alpha$ est volcanique$\urcorner$ is true $\equiv$ the referent of α is volcanic and everything physical is physical).

——(f) At this point, it is tempting to appeal to further considerations governing, or at least informing, the construction and testing of empirical theories: economy and simplicity.[11] It might be pointed out in connection with the case at hand that in comparing the T-theorems flowing from a T-theory θ_1 containing (Ax 2) with those flowing from a T-theory θ_2 that differs only in containing (Ax 2*) in its place, the right-hand sides of certain T-theorems of θ_2 entail the right-hand sides of the corresponding T-theorems of θ_1 (and not *vice versa*), and that this is reason enough to cast θ_2 aside.

——(g) If there remain further non-interpretive T-theories for French that have not been ruled out by any of the aforementioned constraints, it might be suggested that since a theory of meaning for French is meant to be (or form part of) an empirical theory about the utterances of members of our species, the theorist can dismiss any T-theory whose theorems do not possess some property *P* (to be elucidated) answering to general constraints governing the way we make sense of what other members of the species are doing (see Davidson 1984:ch. 9). To this it might be countered that once the appropriate conditions of dismissal are made sufficiently clear they will be seen to invoke semantic concepts that render the larger enterprise viciously circular.

—— (h) Even if the class of interpretive T-theories for French is satisfactorily delimited, it is not obvious that an interpretive T-theory is *ipso facto* acceptable. For it might be argued that in addition to knowing what is stated by the T-theorems of an interpretive T-theory θ for French, in order to *understand* French one would need to know (or believe) something that is not deducible from θ's theorems, viz. *that the theorems themselves are interpretive* (or at least that one would need to know (or at least believe) that the theorems satisfy a set of constraints that, as a matter of fact, render them interpretive (or at least nomic)) (see Davidson 1984:xviii,172–4; Foster 1976). The problem here is not that possessing this additional knowledge would require the possession of certain theoretical concepts not involved in knowing what is stated by θ's T-theorems—for this is unclear until more is said about what is involved in knowing what is stated by a T-theorem.

---

[11] This idea is taken very seriously by Larson and Segal 1995 and Segal 1999, and for good reason: they aim to construct a T-theory that might form (at least the basis of) a theory of semantic competence.

Rather, the objection is that *no* T-theory will be acceptable because its T-theorems will never state enough information for understanding. To this it might be countered that the perceived need for such additional knowledge is symptomatic of reading too much into the notion of understanding. Knowledge of what θ's theorems state does, in fact, suffice for understanding French, but it does not, in addition, furnish anyone possessing that knowledge with direct grounds for knowing (or even thinking) that it does; and this is as it should be because that was never part of the original bargain.

Self-reflexive paradoxes are apt to drift into and out of focus at various junctures in thinking through these matters. Suffice to say the matter of whether a suitably constrained T-theory can serve as a theory of meaning has not been resolved to everyone's satisfaction.

3 Reference and Ontology

We might think of the ontology of a sentence as those things that must exist for the sentence to be true; and we might think of the things in 'our ontology' as the ontology of all the sentences we hold true. To specify what the ontology of a sentence is we need to invoke a semantic theory, and in this connexion Davidson's approach to the construction of such a theory yields interesting ontological results.

There is a *double asymmetry* between sentences and singular terms within Davidson's theory. Thus far, no appeal to the notion of *reference* (or *predication*) has surfaced in the discussion of what an acceptable T-theory must do. A theory's deliverances with respect to *whole sentences* are all that matter: it is irrelevant how the internal workings of the theory treat the parts as long as things come out right for the wholes: '... how a theory of truth maps non-sentential expressions on to objects is a matter of indifference ... nothing can reveal how a speaker's words have been mapped onto objects' (Davidson 1984:xix).

> Since T-sentences say nothing whatever about reference, satisfaction, or expressions that are not sentences, the test of the correctness of the theory is independent of intuitions concerning these concepts. Once we have the theory, though, we can explain the truth of sentences on the basis of their structure and the semantic properties of the parts. The analogy with theories in science is complete: in order to organise and explain what we directly observe, we posit unobserved or indirectly observed objects and forces: the theory is tested by what is directly observed. ... what is open to observation is the use of sentences in context, and truth is the semantic concept we understand best. Reference and related notions like satisfaction are, by comparison, theoretical concepts (as are the notions of singular term, predicate, sentential connective, and the rest). There can be no question about the correctness of these theoretical concepts beyond the question whether they yield a satisfactory account of the use of sentences. ... There is no rea-

son to look for a prior, or independent, account of some referential relation (Davidson 1990:300).

In principle, then, it might be possible to construct an acceptable T-theory
that does not utilize a notion of, say, reference at all. Only attempts to
build a theory will reveal what appears to be needed.

According to Davidson, an acceptable T-theory will, in fact, utilise a
lean, formal notion of reference, by virtue of containing axioms capable of
handling quantification, and this fact is ontologically significant. If we were
dealing with an infinite extensional language L containing only (a finite
number of) names, predicates, and sentence connectives, but no quantifiers,
in fact it would not be necessary to invoke a concept like reference: a finite
theory consisting of one axiom for each atomic sentence and one recursive
axiom for each sentence connective would suffice because L would contain
only finitely many *atomic* sentences. So it is not the existence of singular
terms *per se* that foists a referential notion upon us: it is *quantification* that
does that, because it is quantification that forces us to abandon the construction of straightforward theories whose axioms take the form

(14)   _ _ _ is true ≡ . . .

in favor of T-theories that take a detour through *satisfaction*—'a generalized
form of reference' (Davidson 1990:296)—a T-theory whose predicate and
quantifier axioms take the form

(15) $(\forall s)(s$ satisfies _ _ _ ≡ . . . s . . .)

where '*s*' ranges over (infinite) sequences of objects. The 'logical form' of a
sentence S belonging to a language L is, for Davidson, the structure imposed upon S in the course of providing an acceptable T-theory for L as a
whole. Work on the syntax and semantics of natural language suggests we
will not get very far in our attempts to construct acceptable T-theories for
French, English and so on unless we view the logical forms of certain sentences as encoding something very like the quantifier-variable structures
familiar from formal languages such as the first-order predicate calculus.
Following (e.g.) Field 1972, one formally useful way of pulling together
names and variables (and other singular terms, if there are any) within a T-
theory—a notational variant of many other ways, and perfectly consonant
with Davidson's approach—is to use the notion of *reference-relative-to-a-
sequence*, which we can abbreviate as *Ref*. On this account, the axiom for
the name 'Santorin' is given not by a simple reference axiom such as (Ax 1)
but by (Ax 1')

(Ax 1)   the referent of 'Santorin' = Santorini

(Ax 1') $(\forall s)(Ref('Santorin', s) = $ Santorini)

where '*s*' ranges over sequences. The purpose of this relativization will
emerge shortly. (Ax 1') is just as much a 'reference' axiom as (Ax 1): it

connects a piece of language with some entity or other, some piece of the world. (For ease of exposition, let us put aside names that allegedly fail to refer, if there are such expressions.) Reference, for Davidson, is no more than such a pairing—any pairing that works as far as grinding out T-theorems is concerned; there is no need, on Davidson's account, to provide an *analysis* of the reference relationship.

Axioms for verbs, adjectival expressions, and ordinary common nouns might treat such expressions as predicates as in the following:

(Ax 2') $(\forall s)(\forall \alpha)(s$ satisfies $\ulcorner\alpha$ est volcanique$\urcorner \equiv Ref(\alpha, s)$ is volcanique)

(Ax 3') $(\forall s)(\forall \alpha)(\forall \beta)(s$ satisfies $\ulcorner\alpha$ aime $\beta\urcorner \equiv Ref(\alpha, s)$ loves $Ref(\beta, s))$

where 'α' and 'β' range over singular terms (for ease of exposition, let us put aside so-called 'intensional' predicates like 'faux').[12] Axioms for (truth-functional) sentence connectives will also be straightforward ('ϕ' and 'ψ' range over sentences):

(Ax 4') $(\forall s)(\forall \phi)(\forall \psi)(s$ satisfies $\ulcorner\phi$ et $\psi\urcorner \equiv s$ satisfies ϕ and s satisfies ψ).

Axioms for individual variables can be read off the axiom schema:

(Ax 5') $(\forall s)(\forall k)(Ref(\ulcorner x_k\urcorner, s) = s_k)$

where 'k' ranges over the natural numbers and s_k is the kth element of s. The difference between a name and a variable, then, is that the *Ref* of a name is constant from sequence to sequence—see (Ax 1') above—whereas the *Ref* of a variable depends upon the sequence in question.[13] The utility of the axioms flowing from the axiom schema (Ax 5') lies in their interaction with axioms for quantifiers. If quantification in French turns out to be unrestricted and completely analysable in terms of the first-order quantifiers $\forall$ and $\exists$—a more realistic proposal will be considered in due course—a T-theory for French can get by with an axiom based on (Ax 6') or its universal counterpart:

(Ax 6') $(\forall s)(\forall k)(\forall \phi)(s$ satisfies $\ulcorner(\exists x_k)\phi\urcorner \equiv$ there is at least one sequence differing from s at most in the kth place that satisfies ϕ).

A sentence is true if and only if it is satisfied by every sequence. Assuming an adequate background logic (e.g., extensional, first-order logic with identity), we could then prove T-theorems such as the following:

(16) 'Santorini est volcanique' is true $\equiv$ Santorini is volcanic

---

[12] There are notorious difficulties involved in providing a uniform predicational analysis of these categories. For present purposes, the differences between these categories can be ignored as they do not raise problems that bear directly on my main theme.

[13] The constant-variable distinction should not be confused with Kripke's rigid–nonrigid distinction: variables (with respect to sequences) are just as rigid as names.

(17) 'Pierre mange quelque chose' is true ≡ Pierre is eating something.[14]

If it turns out that an acceptable T-theory cannot be constructed without making use of a 'generalised form of reference' such as satisfaction—or a notational variant tailored to singular terms such as *Ref* above—i.e. without axioms that connect pieces of language with other entities, let us say that such a notion is *theoretically ineliminable*.

According to Davidson, accepting that reference (in some form or other) is theoretically ineliminable does not mean accepting that *any particular set of reference axioms* is ineliminable. Indeed, it is Davidson's position that any acceptable set of T-theoretic axioms *X* can be transposed into another acceptable set *Y* that contains, as a subset, a set of reference axioms quite different from those contained in *X*. The predicate axioms would also differ, of course; but the axioms for the logical constants would remain fixed (indeed, they *must* remain fixed on Davidson's account in order to preserve first-order inferential relations).[15] The reason that reference and predication axioms can be transposed into others is because a particular axiomatization is tested only by its T-theorems, i.e., by its deliverances at the level of whole sentences. So the notion of reference employed by Davidson is philosophically lean in two senses: (i) no particular set of reference axioms is privileged; (ii) to say that 'Santorin' refers to Santorini is just to say that there is a successful axiomatization containing as one of its axioms (Ax 1')—or some notational variant that hooks up 'Santorin' and Santorini.

Two points need to be made in this regard. First, as Davidson stresses repeatedly, the fact that an acceptable T-theory might make an 'unnatural' assignment of objects to individual words does not affect the overall ontology to which the language is committed. (Of course, no *successful* assignment is really 'unnatural' on Davidson's account.) Second, no appeal to modes of presentations, causal chains, informational packages, or intentionality is needed in order to characterise the theoretical notion of reference that Davidson employs. As Rorty observes, for Davidson 'any "theory of truth"

---

[14] More precisely, we could prove such theorems if (i) we had a modicum of translational machinery for purging talk of sequences from the right-hand sides of T-theorems for quantified sentences and (ii) we treated '*Ref*('Santorin', *s*)' either (a) as a Russellian definite description ('the referent of 'Santorin' with respect to *s*') and hence as a first-order definable device of quantification, or (b) as a complex singular term formed from a singular term and a functional expression. If method (a) is selected, proofs will make use of Whitehead and Russell's derived rule of inference for extensional contexts (*14.15) rather than straightforward applications of PSST (see Neale forthcoming). If method (b) is selected, a version of first-order logic with functors must be selected. There are, I believe, reasons for preferring method (a).

[15] Can acceptable T-theories for languages containing Russellian descriptions together with words like 'necessarily' and 'possibly' allow of the sorts of straightforward reference permutations Davidson has in mind?

which analyses a relation between bits of language and bits of non-language is already on the wrong track' (Rorty 1986:333).

The referential and predicational axioms in a successful T-theory differ from one another in a crucial way. The former assign particular entities (individuals) as the semantic values (references/satisfiers) of expressions; the latter do no such thing (although they can still *have* satisfiers). This is important. On Davidson's account, since reference axioms are theoretically ineliminable, we must accept the entities that these axioms specify as satisfying our singular terms, even though we do not have to regard any particular satisfaction function as privileged. Predicate axioms invoke no new entities: the only semantically and ontologically significant notion they use is satisfaction, and satisfiers are just sequences of objects. By hypothesis, a successful axiomatization construes singular terms as *standing for* (or *satisfied by*) objects and construes sentences as satisfied by sequences of objects. Thus, Davidson's 'realism' about 'the familiar objects whose antics make our sentences and opinions true or false' (Davidson 1984:198). (On the word 'realism', see below.)

Davidson reads an ontology of objects directly off an acceptable T-theory given the (standard and natural) way he views the axioms for singular terms and predicates; an adequate truth theory will require not just satisfaction axioms but satisfaction axioms that relate bits of language to *objects*. In his view, Tarski's work

> ... make[s] it evident ... that, for a language with anything like the expressive power of a natural language, the class of true sentences cannot be characterized without introducing a relation like satisfaction, which connects words (singular terms, predicates) with objects (Davidson 1990:296).

> ... there is no way to give a [truth] theory without employing a concept like reference or satisfaction which relates expressions to objects in the world (Davidson 1990:302).[16]

Events—which Davidson construes as unrepeatable particulars—will get into the picture along with objects because a successful axiomatization will

---

[16] There is room for substantial disagreement here. Colin McGinn, for example, has argued (in a seminar we taught together) that, without compromising the acceptability of a T-theory, the referential relations involved in term and predicate axioms can be inverted so that predicates have axioms that treat them as referring to *properties* while singular terms receive axioms structurally more akin to those commonly used for predicates. McGinn is certainly correct that the possibility of such an inversion, if systematic, would undermine Davidson's idea of unambiguously reading ontology off semantics. However, it is not clear to me that a systematic and acceptable inversion can be effected once two-place predicates, quantifiers, adverbs, and attitude verbs are introduced. Considerable ingenuity is going to be required to pull it off (if it can be pulled off), and the degree of ingenuity itself may provide a reason for Davidson to doubt the utility of such an axiomatization given other features of his philosophy, particularly his ideas about radical interpretation.

have to deal with sentences which involve quantification over events, for example (18) and (19):

(18)   There was a fire and there was a short-circuit
$\exists x$(fire x • $\exists y$(short-circuit y))

(19)   There was a fire because there was a short-circuit
$\exists x$(fire x • $\exists y$(short-circuit y • y caused x)).

Sentences containing action verbs and adverbs ('John left quickly') and those containing bare infinitives ('John saw Mary leave') also appear to require quantification over events (see Davidson 1980 and Higginbotham 1983). In addition to claiming that we will need to pair bits of language with *objects* and *events* in order to construct an acceptable T-theory, Davidson suggests that if the need to posit a particular ontological category does not arise in the construction of such a theory, then the need cannot arise at all. (Of course, linguistic categories and set-theoretic entities like sequences are posited by the metalanguage.) The thought behind this suggestion appears to be (roughly) the following (although I have not actually found it stated quite this way anywhere in Davidson's work): An acceptable T-theory for L delivers a true theorem of the requisite form for *every* sentence of L: so there is nothing one can say in L that outstrips the ontology revealed by such a theory; so there is no sense to be made of ontological categories not forced upon us by the construction of a viable semantics.[17] (It might be objected that in doing semantics we can appeal only to entities that we think exist, so a semantic theory offers us no more by way of ontological insight than ordinary reflection upon our thought and talk. But this misses the fact that an adequate semantics is *systematic* in ways that ordinary reflection is not.)

One interesting question left open concerns competing T-theories with different ontologies. If θ_1 posits As, Bs, and Cs while θ_2 posits only As and Bs, then if both are acceptable T-theories for L we have reason to posit only As and Bs. In this case our ontology is given by the intersection of the things posited by the competing theories. But what if θ_2 posited only Bs and Cs? Perhaps it is unlikely that we will find ourselves in such a situation (we are unlikely to find even *one* T-theory that covers all the data), but the question is still of philosophical interest if we take seriously the idea that ontology flows from semantics in the way Davidson suggests. Presumably Davidson will prefer a theory that posits objects and events over one that posits (e.g.) events and properties on the grounds that (i) identity conditions for objects and events are clearer than they are for properties, and

---

[17] Rovane 1986 argues that ontological commitments seem to be made *prior to* the construction of a theory of meaning—at least if such a theory is characterized in the way Davidson envisions—because articulating the conditions a theory must satisfy in order to qualify as a theory of meaning (see above) will itself involve such commitments.

(ii) our best accounts of nature and our most cogent statements of traditional philosophical problems concerning (e.g.) causation, time, change, human action, and the mind-body problem appear to presuppose the existence of objects and events. For present purposes, there is no need to pursue this matter.

4   Complicating Features of Natural Language

Forms of semantic complexity we have hitherto ignored could, in principle, have a bearing on the ontology and final shape of an acceptable T-theory. Davidson sees a tidy ontology of objects and events flowing from such a theory: there are no facts, no situations, no states of affairs, no propositions, and no properties because (so far) we have seen no need to posit them. Davidson does not claim to have a *proof* that we need only objects and events; he is, in effect, throwing down the gauntlet: 'Show me sentences that appear to require more than objects and events and I think I can show you that objects and events suffice'. Various features of natural language might suggest Davidson needs more, and it is worth indicating some of the moves available to the Davidsonian semanticist in dealing with features of natural language that seem to engender complexity.

T-theoretic Axioms for 'I', 'we', 'you', 'he', 'she', 'they', 'this', 'that', 'these', 'those', 'yesterday', 'today', 'tomorrow', 'here', 'there', 'local', 'distant', 'now', 'then', 'earlier', 'later', 'recent', 'hitherto', 'henceforth', 'present', 'current', 'former', 'longstanding', 'contemporary', 'previous', 'prior', 'next', 'subsequent', and no doubt many other words must take into account contextual features of one sort or another. In view of this, the Davidsonian will naturally treat truth as a property not of sentences but of utterances, or of sentences relativized to utterances or contexts. The hope is that nothing of ontological consequence will arise because an utterance can be construed as an event (or an event-object pair); and a context can be construed as some sort of *n*-tuple of objects or events. For example, if truth is taken as a property of utterances, then, simplifying somewhat, sample axioms might be rewritten as follows with metalanguage semantic predicates taking on a parameter for an utterance event e, giving us (e.g.) (25) for 'Santorini' and (26) for 'I' (henceforth, I shall take the object language to be English rather than French)

(20) $\forall s \forall e (Ref(\text{'Santorini'}, s, e) = \text{Santorini})$

(21) $\forall s \forall e (Ref(\text{'I'}, s, e) = e_u)$

where e_u is the utterer, the person producing the utterance (e.g. the speaker or writer; for more sophisticated treatments of indexicals, see, e.g., Larson and Segal 1995). It might be claimed that Davidson will need more than objects and events to implement this idea, but I am not aware of any good argument to this effect.

One matter that needs to be taken up at some point is the precise resources needed to derive T-theorems for indexical sentences. Another concerns the extent to which the T-theorems for such sentences are *interpretive* in the sense discussed earlier. Dealing with these matters will mean resuscitating questions about the delimitation of those T-theories that can do duty as theories of meaning, particularly if the idea of a canonical proof procedure is to play a role.

A sentence like (22) might be thought to present Davidson with an interesting challenge as it appears to involve quantification over colours, construed as *properties*:

(22)   This is the same color as that.

However, as Davidson has stressed, we need to distinguish two claims: (i) that the role of predicates in a theory of meaning consists in their standing for properties; (ii) that an interpretive T-theory will, at some point, require an ontology of properties (Davidson 1999b:88-9). Davidson rejects (i), which he associates with Russell and others. But rejecting (i) need not involve rejecting (ii).[18] If there turns out to be no other way to account for the place of (22) within a language without positing properties, so be it, says Davidson, as long as properties are regarded as abstracta. In the meantime, he is perfectly justified in exploring whether (22) and related sentences might by-pass appeals to properties once their logical forms are properly revealed.

An acceptable T-theory for English must be able to handle sentences that contain modal expressions such as 'necessarily', and 'possibly'. Will this require an ontology of 'possible worlds'? Or the use of non-extensional connectives that are sensitive to what sentences stand for, entities of finer grain than truth-values? If the axioms of a truth theory are modalised, a richer background logic (a suitable modal logic) can be used to derive T-theorems of the requisite form while treating modal adverbs as non-extensional sentence connectives. But Davidson himself has little time for such talk and, following Quine, he has argued that a slingshot argument can be used to demonstrate the impossibility of usefully non-extensional connectives. If, on the other hand, the axioms of a T-theory are left as is, it seems it will be necessary to allow the quantifiers to range over something

---

[18] The importance of the general form of this distinction in Davidson's thinking about the relationship between meaning and ontology seems to have been spotted early on by Rovane (1986) who notes that when it comes to drawing ontology out of the theory of meaning '[t]he presumption is that the *large and constant* [my emphasis, SRAN] features of language that would emerge in any theory of meaning either correspond to, or reflect, or in some way gauge, certain large features of reality' (Rovane 1986: 417).

like worlds. A question that then arises is whether, as some have suggested, the best way to make sense of worlds involves viewing them as very big facts, situations, or states of affairs, or as sets of propositions. There are, I believe, good reasons for thinking that all of the work can be done using models alone; if this is correct, there is considerably less of a threat to Davidson's project in modal talk than many have thought.

It is well-known that *natural* language quantification is more complex than it is in standard first-order languages. However, work in generative linguistics and mathematical logic has revealed elegant methods for extending Tarski's insights so that T-theories can be provided for quantified fragments of natural languages while making precise the relationship between the superficial grammatical form of a sentence and its logical form. Many of the details need not concern us here. Suffice to say that noun phrases such as 'some man', 'no farmers', 'the king', 'most tall soldiers', etc. can be viewed as restricted quantifiers composed of quantificational determiners ('some', 'no', 'the', 'most', etc.) combined with simple or complex nouns ('man', 'tall man', etc.). Axioms such as the following make things run very smoothly:

(23) $(\forall s)(\forall k)(\forall \phi)(\forall \psi)$ (s satisfies $\ulcorner [some\ x_k \colon \phi]\ \psi \urcorner$ ≡ some sequence satisfying ϕ and differing from s at most in the kth place also satisfies ψ)

(24) $(\forall s)(\forall k)(\forall \phi)(\forall \psi)$ (s satisfies $\ulcorner [most\ x_k \colon \phi]\ \psi \urcorner$ ≡ most sequences satisfying ϕ and differing from s at most in the kth place also satisfy ψ).

It is not necessary to pack any additional set theory or overtly higher-order machinery into the right-hand sides of (23) and (24): they have the same form as axioms for the traditional unrestricted quantifiers *modulo* the relevant restriction concerning the satisfaction of ϕ.

A further complicating feature of natural language is the existence of anaphoric relations between expressions which cannot be handled in terms of either co-reference or standard variable-binding (e.g. those in 'If a man own a donkey he vaccinates it', 'several men who own donkeys feed them hay', or 'Every pilot who shot at it hit the MiG that was chasing him'). I have argued at length elsewhere that the semantic facts are much simpler than is commonly supposed once a proper syntactic theory is in play and that the truth-conditions of sentences involving such links drop out systematically once it is recognized that some pronouns are referential whilst others are quantificational—as is the case with non-pronominal noun phrases—and that no new entities are quantified over (See *Descriptions*, Chapters 5 and 6). If this is correct, just as there is nothing of semantical significance in anaphora, so there is nothing of ontological significance in the notion.

Finally, of course, propositional attitude ascriptions ('Pierre believes that Santorini is volcanic', 'Marie doubts Cicero is Tully'). Notoriously, Davidson (1984) has proposed a paratactic account that is meant to avoid talk of propositions by focussing again on acts of utterance. I feel no need to comment on the proposal here, except to say that it is widely held to be beset with difficulties (just like every other theory of propositional attitude ascriptions) (see, e.g., Burge 1986 and Schiffer 1987).

5   Correspondence and Facts

If variables had to range over, say, *facts* or *situations* in order to provide a theory of meaning, then on Davidson's account, facts or situations would also be part of our ontology. But Davidson suggests (i) that the need will not arise, and (ii) that entities like facts and situations (under their most common construals) are ruled out independently, as can be demonstrated by a slingshot argument.

_____ (i) The sorts of sentences that might tempt one to posit facts include the following:

(25)   The fact that there was a short-circuit caused it to be the case that there was a fire

(26)   There was a fire because there was a short-circuit.

The thought here is that (25) and (26) express causal relations between two facts. But Davidson argues that these sentences do no more than express a relation between events, that (27) gives the logical form of both:

(27) $\exists x(\text{fire } x \cdot \exists y(\text{short-circuit } y \cdot y \text{ caused } x)).$[19]

_____ (ii) Davidson (1984, 1990, 1996) has argued that we cannot have facts of any significance because of slingshot arguments:

> ...facts or states of affairs have never been shown to play a useful role in semantics....This is not surprising since there is a persuasive argument, usually traced to Frege (in one form) or Kurt Gödel (in another), to the effect that there can be at most one fact (Davidson 1996:266).

One of the things I demonstrate in *Facing Facts* is that the various forms of slingshot argument do not actually *rule out* facts although they do impose very definite constraints on what theories of facts must look like, constraints that many theories do not satisfy.

---

[19] A more difficult case for Davidson might be the following

(i)   The fact that Mary left Bill's party did not upset him; but the fact that she left so suddenly did.

Davidson is surely correct that events, just like objects, can be described in a myriad of ways. But if Mary's leaving was Mary's sudden leaving, then how is it that (i) can be true if only an event upset Bill?

Let us call any theory according to which true sentences stand for, or correspond to facts—construed as non-linguistic entities—a 'sentential-correspondence' theory. And let us call any sentential-correspondence theory that takes the *constituents* of true sentences to correspond to the *components* of facts—e.g., objects, properties, and relations—a 'structural-correspondence' theory.

Russell (1918) presents a theory of facts that involves structural correspondence. By contrast, Austin (1950, 1954) defends the intelligibility of a correspondence theory that does not presuppose structural correspondence. On Austin's account, there is, as he puts it, '... no need whatsoever for the words used in making a true statement to "mirror" in any way, however indirect, any feature whatsoever of the situation or event' (Austin 1950:125). In English, there are, in fact, words that stand for certain things in the world; but this is not, says Austin, a necessary feature of languages that can be used to make true statements. Austin's theory—which I shall examine later—is not, then, a structural-correspondence theory because the structure of a true statement does not reflect the structure of a fact to which it corresponds.

From his earliest work on truth and meaning in the 1960s to his most recent articles, Davidson has consistently opposed the idea of sentential correspondence. In 'True to the Facts', he did, however, call a Tarski-style T-theory a correspondence theory; but at the same time he argued against facts by providing a slingshot argument deemed to show that all facts, if there are any, collapse into a single Great Fact. This might seem odd: if there are no facts, to what do true sentences correspond? The tension is only verbal and completely resolved in later work.

In his 1984 preface to *Inquiries into Truth and Interpretation,* Davidson points out that T-theories are correspondence theories only in the unassuming sense that their internal workings 'require that a relation between entities and expressions be characterised ("satisfaction")' (Davidson 1984:xv), and not in the sense that they presuppose any entities (facts) to which true sentences correspond. A T-theory was called a correspondence theory in 1969 because of the roles played by (sequences of) *objects* and *events*: we find correspondence lurking in the axioms, through reference and satisfaction, but not in the T-theorems (by recourse to which the theory is evaluated).

In his 1990 article 'The Structure and Content of Truth', Davidson is blunt: it was a (verbal) mistake to call T-theories correspondence theories, a source of regret (Davidson 1990:302-4). All that was meant was that '... there is no way to give such a theory without employing a concept like reference or satisfaction which relates expressions to objects in the world' (Davidson 1990:302). Only in what Davidson now sees as a 'contrived' sense is this correspondence:

> [t]ruth is defined on the basis of satisfaction: a sentence of the object language is true if and only if it is satisfied by every sequence of the objects over which the variables of the object language range. Take 'corresponds to' as 'satisfies' and you have defined truth as correspondence. The oddity of the idea is evident from the counterintuitive and contrived nature of the entities to which sentences 'correspond' and from the fact that all true sentences would correspond to the same entities (1990:302; also see Davidson 1984:48,70).

Still more recently:

> The sequences that satisfy sentences are nothing like the 'facts' or 'states of affairs' of the [sentential] correspondence theorists since if one of Tarski's sequences satisfies a closed sentence, thus making it true, then that same sequence also satisfies every other true sentence, and thus also makes it true, and if any sequence satisfies a closed sentence, every sequence does (Davidson 1996:268).

The implication here is that if there is any remote sense to the idea that sequences function as 'truth-makers', since every true sentence is satisfied by every sequence, sequences are less like facts than they are like the world (the Great Fact).

We must be careful, then, to distinguish the 'unassuming' or 'contrived' sense of 'correspondence' (associated with talk of satisfaction of formulae by sequences of objects) from the sense used in characterizing theories that appeal to entities (e.g. facts, situations, states of affairs, or propositions) to which *sentences* correspond. Following Davidson's lead, then, let us reserve the label 'correspondence theory' for sentential correspondence theories. The hallmark of a correspondence theory of truth is the idea that a sentence (or statement) is true if there is some particular fact (state-of-affairs, situation, or other non-linguistic entity) to which the sentence, if true, corresponds. (Some correspondence theories—such as Russell's—will also involve structural correspondence between constituents of sentences and components of facts; but this is not an essential feature of correspondence theories.)

One does not need to have Davidson's perspective on semantics in order to see little point in positing facts as truth-makers. Strawson 1950, Quine 1960, and Geach 1972 see philosophers' appeals to facts as parasitic upon noun phrases of the form 'the fact that φ', and in places they have heaped scorn on such entities. And along lines suggested by Frege (1919), Brandom 1994 and Hornsby 1996 have argued that the only useful application of the words 'fact' and 'factual' is to thoughts (or claims) that are true.

Geach sees the postulation of facts as a relatively recent development and offers the following explanation:

> Facts came to be counted among the entities in the philosopher's world only after the construction whereby 'the fact,' or its synonym in another language, is put in opposition with an indirect-statement clause had spread like the pox from one European language to another,

largely by way of journalism. This happened at the turn of the last century; only then did philosophers come to postulate facts as individual entities, answering to the phrases so formed. Once stated, the philosophy of facts flourished mightily, especially in Cambridge (Geach 1972:21).[20]

In a discussion of *entia non grata*, Quine suggests that use of the noun 'fact' no more requires entities to which it applies than do the nouns 'sake' and 'mile' (Quine 1960:246-8). Moreover, says Quine, unreflective consideration of the way 'fact' is used seems to confer a spurious air of intelligibility on the distinction between analytic and synthetic: a sentence is analytic if and only if it is true and lacks factual content. Quine also offers arguments against facts being concrete objects and against explaining truth via the idea that facts are what make true sentences true. If true, the sentences 'Fifth Avenue is six miles long' and 'Fifth Avenue is a hundred feet wide' state distinct facts, 'yet the only concrete or at least physical object involved is Fifth Avenue' (Quine 1960:247). And the two sentences are true 'because of Fifth Avenue, because it is a hundred feet wide and six miles long, ... because of the way we use our words'. The word 'fact', says Quine, in all of its uses can be paraphrased away or dealt with in some other way that avoids positing entities to which it applies.

In responding to Austin's paper 'Truth' (Austin 1950), Strawson says that although certain parts of a statement may refer or correspond to parts of the world,

> [I]t is evident that there is nothing else in the world for the statement itself to be related to....And it is evident that the demand that there should be such a relatum is logically absurd.... But the demand for something in the world *which makes the statement true* (Mr Austin's phrase), or *to which the statement corresponds when it is true*, is just this demand (Strawson 1950:194-5).

Davidson cites this passage approvingly; furthermore, he endorses Strawson's claim that, 'while we certainly say that a statement corresponds to (fits, is borne out by, agrees with) the facts', this is merely 'a variant of saying it is true' (Davidson 1990:304).[21] 'There is nothing interesting or instructive to which true sentences might correspond' (Davidson 1990:303).

---

[20] Olson 1987 suggests this cannot be quite right because Mill, Bradley, and Peirce talk about facts before the atomistic Russell and Wittgenstein, before Moore and Ramsey, and before the expression-type 'the fact that φ' took a firm hold. According to Olson, a deeper explanation for the emergence of facts must be sought, and he claims that Mill, Bradley, and Peirce took facts to be indispensable for making sense of *relations*; hence Russell's talk of relations when motivating facts. I suspect Olson is wrong about Bradley, but he is certainly correct to claim that Russell and Wittgenstein were moved by reflections on relations.

[21] Strawson's precise position on facts seems less clear than these remarks, taken alone, might suggest. He says that facts are not entities in the world and also that they are 'pseudo-material'. Some of the difficulties involved in piecing together Strawson's overall position and what it entails about facts are discussed fruitfully in Searle 1998.

If Davidson's 'nothing interesting or instructive' is read as 'nothing potentially explanatory of truth', then Brandom 1994 and Hornsby 1996 concur when they endorse Frege's position that facts are just thoughts (or claims) that are true. (Brandom sees this position as supported by the fact that it is customary to say that facts are *about* objects rather than that they *contain* or *consist of* them (Brandom 1994:622), an observation that should impress both Austin and Strawson; the same observation is made in Aune 1985.)

Davidson does more than simply nod in agreement with Strawson on this matter: he presents a logico-semantic collapsing argument aimed at showing that there is at most one fact to which true sentences correspond: '... if we try to provide a serious semantics for reference to facts, we discover that they melt into one; there is no telling them apart' (Davidson 2000:66). The argument is discussed in detail in *Facing Facts* (Neale forthcoming). Right now, I want to look at the role of its conclusion in Davidson's thinking.

6   The Dualism of Scheme and Content

Davidson (1984, 1989) argues that no good sense can be made of (a) 'conceptual relativism'—the idea that different people, communities, cultures, or periods view, conceptualise, or make the world (or their worlds) in different ways—or (b) a distinction between 'scheme' and 'content', *i.e.* a distinction between conceptual scheme (representational system) and empirical content ('something neutral and common that lies outside all schemes' (Davidson 1984:190).

The main argument against relativism is intertwined in subtle ways with one of two arguments deployed against scheme-content dualism, a dualism which relativism is meant to presuppose. For concreteness, Davidson associates conceptual schemes with sets of intertranslatable languages (some find this problematic, but for my purposes here it is not). The first argument against scheme-content dualism proceeds by way of undermining the notion of a scheme; the second by way of undermining the (relevant) notion of content. The former involves an appeal to the conditions something must satisfy in order to qualify as a conceptual scheme (conditions that some have found too stringent). I shall not discuss it here. Rather, I want to examine the anti-content argument and explain why its ultimate success depends upon the rejection of facts. I can then explain the relevance of this for talk of 'anti-representationalism'.

Davidson detects two contenders for the role of 'content' in writings advocating forms of relativism: (1) *reality*, (*the world, the universe, nature*) and (2) *uninterpreted experience*. And since we find talk of conceptual schemes (languages/systems of representation) either (a) *organizing* (*systematizing, dividing up*) or (b) *fitting* (*describing/matching/corresponding to*) reality or experience, there are four distinct ways of characterizing the relationship between scheme and content: schemes organize reality, organize experience, fit reality, of fit experience.

None of the four possibilities is meant to be viable. For present concerns, it is the argument against *schemes fitting reality* that is important as it connects directly with talk of an ontology of facts. But a few brief remarks about schemes organizing will help forestall potential confusion.

A good ordinary language point gets the ball rolling. No clear meaning can be attached to the notion of organizing a single object (the world, nature, etc.) unless the object in question is understood to contain (or consist in) other objects. As Davidson observes, someone who sets out to organise a closet or a desk arranges the things in or on it. A man who is told to organize not the shoes and shirts in a closet, but the closet itself would be bewildered (Davidson 1984:192).

He continues:

> A language may contain simple predicates whose extensions are matched by no simple predicates, or even by any predicates at all, in some other language. What enables us to make this point in particular cases is an ontology common to the two languages, with concepts that individuate the same objects (ibid.).

Davidson is not here making the mistake of claiming that if we are to render intelligible the idea that there is 'something neutral and common that lies outside all schemes' organized by two purportedly distinct schemes, then the schemes must have the same *concepts*; rather, he is making the point that they must have the same *ontology*. The closet analogy is useful again. If we are to make sense of the idea of different ways of organizing the same closet, we must make sense of the idea of different ways of organizing the things that are in it. And we can do this only by thinking of the entities in the closet as fixed across ways of organizing them, whether we separate things into shirts, trousers and shoes, or into black things, white things, and things that are neither black nor white, or into woollens, cottons, and leathers.

Notice that this line of thought does not *directly* undermine the scheme-organizing-reality form of scheme-content dualism: rather, it undermines the idea that this particular form of scheme-content dualism can be used to make sense of radically different conceptual schemes. Within the context provided by Davidson's objectives, however, this is not a severe limitation. For if the intelligibility of the idea that there are radically different conceptual schemes presupposes a scheme-content distinction, and if there are just four ways of making the distinction viable—the four ways that Davidson mentions—then even if he manages to demonstrate only that each of the four ways *either* fails to be intelligible or else entails that alternative schemes are not radically different, then he will have shown that the idea of radically different schemes is unintelligible. And surely this will be enough for Davidson to have shown, in addition, that the scheme-content distinction itself is unintelligible: he will have shown that there is at most one conceptual scheme; and we cannot make sense of the idea of *one* conceptual scheme unless we can make sense of more than one; and this we cannot do if we have shown that there is *at most* one; so there are none. That is the idea.

I want no quarrel with Davidson on the matter of schemes organizing. I see him as presenting a more serious challenge: to show how the idea of schemes *fitting* experience or reality is intelligible and at the same time allows for the possibility of distinct schemes. According to Davidson,

> When we turn from talk of organization to talk of fitting, we turn our attention from the referential apparatus of language—predicates, quantifiers, variables, and singular terms—to whole sentences. It is sentences that predict (or are used to predict), sentences that cope or deal with things, that can be compared or confronted with the evidence. It is sentences also that face the tribunal of experience, though of course they must face it together (Davidson 1984:193).

A sentence or a theory (*i.e.* a set of sentences) 'successfully faces the tribunal of experience ... provided that it is borne out by the evidence', by which Davidson means 'the totality of possible sensory evidence past, present, and future' (ibid.). And for a set of sentences to fit the totality of possible evidence is for each of the sentences in the set to be true. If the sentences involve reference to, or quantification over, say, material objects and events, numbers, sets, or whatever, then what those sentences say about these entities is true provided the set of sentences as a whole 'fits the sensory evidence' (ibid.) Davidson then adds that

> [o]ne can see how, from this point of view, such entities might be called posits. It is reasonable to call something a posit if it can be contrasted with something that is not. Here the something that is not is sensory experience—at least that is the idea (ibid.).

The allusion to the theory of meaning is clear. A set of sentences involves reference to, or quantification over, material objects, events or whatever, only if an acceptable T-theory for the language as a whole must appeal to such entities in delivering T-theorems for the sentences in the set in question. And the entities are part of our ontology: they are the posits of our 'scheme' and can be contrasted with (sensory) experience, *i.e.* 'uninterpreted content'.

But now Davidson makes what I take to be an important move, a move against schemes fitting either experience or reality. There is no alternative to quoting the relevant passage in close to its entirety:

> The trouble is that the notion of fitting the totality of experience, like the notion of fitting the facts, or of being true to the facts, adds nothing intelligible to the simple concept of being true. To speak of sen-

sory experience rather than the evidence, or just the facts, expresses a view about the source or nature of evidence, but *it does not add a new entity* [my italics] to the universe against which to test conceptual schemes. ... [A]ll the evidence there is is just what it takes to make our sentences or theories true. Nothing, however, no *thing*, makes sentences or theories true: not experience, not surface irritations, not the world, can make a sentence true. *That* experience takes a certain course, that our skin is warmed or punctured, that the universe is finite, these facts, if we like to talk that way, make sentences and theories true. But this point is put better without mention of facts. The sentence 'my skin is warm' [as uttered by me, here, now] is true if and only if my skin is warm [here and now]. Here there is no reference to a fact, a world, an experience, or piece of evidence. *Footnote:* See Essay 3 [*i.e.* 'True to the Facts', SRAN] (Davidson 1984:193-4).

Here there is allusion both to the theory of meaning and to a collapsing argument against the viability of *facts*. The theory of meaning doesn't need them, and the collapsing argument (slingshot) is meant to show that we can't have them anyway.

On Davidson's conception of a scheme—which I shall not contest here—if the *schemes-fitting-reality* story is to succeed, there must be something extralinguistic for true sentences or beliefs to fit, match up to, or correspond to. He sees just two plausible candidates: the world itself or individual facts.[22] But neither will work, he claims, because each trades on the

---

[22] The idea that the objects true beliefs and sentences are *about* will suffice is not canvassed. On Davidson's view, 'The question what objects a particular sentence is about, like the questions what object a term refers to, or what objects a predicate is true of, has no answer'' (Davidson 1984:xix); 'nothing can reveal how a speaker's words have been mapped onto objects' (ibid.).

If the (true) belief that Brutus stabbed Caesar is about Brutus and Caesar, isn't the (true) English sentence that expresses that belief, viz.

(i)   Brutus stabbed Caesar

also about them? And if so, do Brutus and Caesar themselves constitute enough for the sentence and belief to match up to? Russell 1918 thought not. The sentence

(ii)   Brutus knew Caesar

is also true. If the things a sentence (or belief) matches up to are restricted to the objects it is about, then (i) and (ii) match up to the same things. It is here that Russell invokes *relations* and ends up with *facts*, composed of objects and relations, as the things that true sentences stand for. Composition is not a matter of simply lumping together particulars and universals, witness the truth of (ii) and falsity of (iii):

(iii)   Caesar stabbed Brutus.

'The failure of correspondence theories of truth based on the notion of fact' says Davidson, traces back to a common source: the desire to include in the entity to which a true sentence corresponds not only the objects the sentence is 'about' (another idea full of trouble) but also whatever it is the sentence says about them' (Davidson 1984:49). 'A theory of truth based on satisfaction is instructive partly because it is less ambitious about what it packs into the entities to which sentences correspond: in such a theory these entities are no more than arbitrary

idea that the entity in question 'makes the sentence true'. Why, exactly, does Davidson think that no legitimate appeal can be made to the idea of an extralinguistic entity that 'makes the sentence true'? He thinks individual true sentences are not made true by individual facts because he has confidence in his collapsing argument, which is meant to show there is at most one fact; this is surely part of what is suggested by his back-reference to 'True to the Facts' (first published in 1969) in the footnote quoted above. So if this attack on the scheme-content distinction is to succeed, an argument against facts is required in order to thwart the schemes-fitting-reality option.

But what of the alternative position, that individual true sentences are made true not by facts but by *the world*? Why does Davidson say explicitly, in the passage quoted above, that not even *the world* will do? In the course of rejecting the idea of schemes *organizing* the world, he points out that such a story presupposes distinct entities in the world to be organized. Distinct entities are called for by the meaning and use of the word 'organize' (you cannot organize a closet without organizing the things in it). But they do not appear to be called for by the meaning and use of the word 'fit'. And, interestingly, in later works Davidson seems to suggest that the world—or at least how it is arranged—is, in fact, one of two things that does make a (true) sentence true, as in the following passage:

> What Convention T, and the trite sentences it declares true, like '"Grass is green" spoken by an English speaker, is true if and only if grass is green' reveal is that the truth of an utterance depends on just two things: what the words as spoken mean, and how the world is arranged. There is no further relativism to a conceptual scheme, a way of viewing things, a perspective. Two interpreters, as unlike in culture, language, and point of view as you please, can disagree over whether an utterance is true, but only if they differ on how things are in the world they share, or what the utterance means (Davidson 1990:304).

If the sentence 'Smith is in London' is true, it is true because of 'how the world is arranged': one of the entities in the world, Smith, is in London. Indeed, this much is given by a T-theory (and no appeal to an alternative set of axioms will alter this fact). So the world makes the sentence true in at least this sense: if the world had been arranged differently—i.e., if the *things* in the world had been arranged differently (for a world to be arranged, the things in it must be arranged)—if Smith were, say, in Paris, the sentence 'Smith is in London' would not be true. To deny this would be to drain all content from the concept of objective truth (see below).

There might seem to be no barrier, then, to making the scheme-content distinction viable by thinking of schemes fitting reality (the world), for it is

what the words mean and how it world is arranged

---

pairings of the objects over which the variables of the language range with those variables' (ibid.).

still open to pursue the idea that a true sentence fits, or is made true by, the world without endorsing the (possibly hopeless) idea that it fits, or is made true by, a particular fact. Davidson recognizes how harmless this way of talking really is:

> ... can't we say that true sentences represent, or better correspond to, or are made true by the world, as Neale suggests? As long as this way of talking isn't thought to explain anything about the concept of truth, it is harmless and may even make those happy who want to be sure that the truth of empirical sentences depends on something more than words and speakers (Davidson 1999e:668).

There is nothing to console the sentence-fact correspondence theorist here. It is no more illuminating to be told that a sentence is true if and only if it corresponds to the world than it is to be told that a sentence is true if and only if it is true, states a truth, says the world is as the world is, or fits the facts. For the last of these phrases, perfectly ordinary as it is—unlike the philosopher's invention 'corresponds to a fact'—seems to be an idiomatic form of 'is true'. Indeed it is sometimes hard to resist the points that all talk of 'facts' is idiomatic and that the logical forms of sentences do not involve quantification over facts ('it is a fact that p' = 'it is true that p'; 'that's a fact' = 'that's true'; 'the fact that p caused it to be the case that q' = a sentence involving quantification over events).[23]

Davidson goes on to suggest that ultimately there is nothing here to console the conceptual relativist either:

> Meanwhile there is the question raised by Neale: why isn't the fact that the world can be said to make our sentences true or false enough to justify the scheme-content distinction and conceptual relativism? Why, he asks, did I say in 'The Very Idea of a Conceptual Scheme' that 'Nothing, ... no *thing*, makes our sentences makes our sentences and theories true: not experience, not surface irritations, not the world, can make a sentence true'? That was a mistake. I was right about experience and surface irritations, but I gave no argument against saying the world makes some sentences true. After all, this is exactly as harmless as saying that a sentence is true because it corresponds to the One Great Fact, and just as empty. ... Maybe we can't locate a part of the world that makes an individual sentence true, but the world itself makes the true sentences true ... . those three little words ('not the world') were seriously misleading (Davidson 1999e:668-9).

A separate argument is needed, Davidson recognizes, to show that if the world is what makes true sentences true, then the resulting conceptual relativism is of only 'a mild sort that I have always accepted' (Davidson 1999e:668), an argument that focuses on the fact that the notion of a scheme falls apart if the basic conceptual resources of two divergent

---

[23] See Strawson 1950 and Davidson 1984. Related to this point is the observation in Brandom 1995 that the word 'fact' has clear application only to thoughts (or claims), facts being those thoughts (or claims) that are true.

schemes differ in any non-trivial way. I have no need to discuss that argument here as my work on the scheme-content distinction is done. My main conclusion is this: In order to demolish the scheme-content distinction, Davidson needs (i) an argument against facts, and (ii) an argument showing that interestingly divergent schemes are not forthcoming on the view that true sentences are made true not by facts but by the world.

7 Realism and Objectivity

Some philosophers see in Davidson's recent work a denial of 'realism' or an inconsistency or unclarity in his positions on the external world, objectivity and truth. Claiming that someone is (or is not) in the extension of 'realist' is a risky business because the word has been applied so widely in philosophy, often in ways that are quite at odds with one another. Once certain anachronisms and terminological issues are ironed out, however, Davidson's position seems rather robust. Firstly, he is explicit that rejecting the scheme-content distinction 'does not mean that we must give up the idea of an objective world independent of our knowledge of it' (Davidson 1984:xviii) or give up '... an objective public world which is not of our own making' (Davidson 1986:310):

> In giving up the dependence on the concept of an uninterpreted reality, something outside all schemes and science, we do not relinquish the idea of objective truth—quite the contrary. Given the dogma of a dualism of scheme and reality, we get conceptual relativity, and truth relative to a scheme. Without the dogma, this kind of relativity goes by the board. Of course the truth of sentences remains relative to a language, but that is as objective as can be. In giving up the dualism of scheme and world, we do not give up the world, but re-establish unmediated touch with the familiar objects whose antics make our sentences and opinions true or false (Davidson 1984:198).

Secondly, there is Davidson's original response to epistemological skepticism and its relation to the idea that an ontology flows naturally from an acceptable T-theory:

> What stands in the way of global skepticism of the senses is, in my view, the fact that we must, in the plainest and methodologically most basic cases, take the objects of a belief to be the causes of that belief. And what we, as interpreters, must take them to be is what they in fact are. Communication begins where causes converge: your utterance means what mine does if belief in its truth is systematically caused by the same events and objects (Davidson 1986:317-8).

> ...the general outlines of our view of the world are correct; we individually and communally may go plenty wrong, but only on condition that in most large respects we are right. It follows that when we study what our language—any language—requires in the way of overall ontology, we are not just making a tour of our own picture of

things: what we take there to be is pretty much what there is (Davidson 1984:xviii-xix).

Davidson seems to be responding to the skeptic as follows. Creatures to whom it makes sense to ascribe beliefs at all must be substantially right in what they believe. More precisely, the act of ascribing erroneous beliefs to an agent makes sense only in so far as the person making such an ascription is willing to see the agent in question as possessing a much more substantial set of *true* beliefs—a set of beliefs can be more *substantial* than another in other than a numerical way.[24] And in the most basic cases—but certainly not in all cases—ascribing true beliefs to an agent makes sense only in so far as we are willing to see the objects of beliefs as their causes.[25]

The passages just quoted sit well with Davidson's general ontological outlook: ontologies of objects and events flow straightforwardly from acceptable T-theories (unlike ontologies of, say, facts and properties). Giving up the scheme-content distinction does not mean abandoning the view that objects and events are (or were)'out there' or 'happening' in an objective world (largely) not of our own making. That Davidson is not averse to talk of an objective world is reinforced in two recent passages:

> ... I believe in the ordinary notion of truth: there really are people, mountains, camels, and stars out there, just as we think there are, and those objects and events frequently have the characteristics we think we perceive them to have. Our concepts are ours, but that doesn't mean they don't truly, as well as usefully, describe an objective reality (Davidson 1999a:19).

> I certainly don't reject realism, at least not until I know what it is I am rejecting. I decided not to call myself a realist because I found that for a large number of philosophers being a realist meant accepting a correspondence theory of truth which held that one could *explain* the concept of truth as correspondence with the facts. I have always been clear that I was not an antirealist about any theoretical entities over which a theory I held true quantified. Quantification (in Quine's ontic sense) is the key to the significant connections between language and belief and the world, since there is no way to give an account of the truth of

---

[24] Following Lepore (1986), I am reluctant to couch what Davidson really has in mind in terms of the sheer *number* of beliefs.

[25] According to Rorty (1986, 1991), rejecting the scheme-content distinction provides a much shorter way with the skeptic: without representations and facts, the sceptical problematic cannot even be stated: '... once we give up tertia, we give up (or trivialize) the notions of representation and correspondence, and thereby give up the possibility of formulating epistemological scepticism' (Rorty 1986:139). On this view, the debate between 'skeptics' and 'antiskeptics' evaporates with representations and facts. There is an alarming simplicity to this train of thought; whatever its merits, it presupposes the rejection of the scheme–content distinction, which in turn presupposes that there are no facts. By contrast, Davidson's original argument against skepticism can be deployed even by those who have eked out for themselves theories of facts in the narrow gully which provides limited cover from Gödel's slingshot.

sentences in a language with general quantification except by relating parts of sentences to entities. Tarski's device of satisfaction expresses such a relation: it is, of course, a fancy form of reference (1999d:123).

This is not the place for a full-scale examination of the way the word 'realism' has been used in philosophy; but once we distinguish several distinct uses Davidson's positions on particular issues that might be stated using the word 'realism' can be located with some precision and seen to cohere rather well with what he says elsewhere about T-theories, reference, correspondence, facts, representation, and the scheme-content distinction.[26]

———— (i) In older (particularly mediaeval) literature, a realist is sometimes said to be someone who claims that, outside the mind and in addition to particulars, there exist universals (or properties, or qualities, or attributes, or Platonic Forms, or at any rate things that particulars can share, partake of, instantiate, exemplify, or participate in). The opponent of realism in this sense is usually said to be a nominalist. Such a realism is likely to be held in conjunction with the semantic view that predicates typically stand for universals (or whatever), although certain nouns (e.g., 'wisdom', 'courage') might stand for them too (or things very like them). Davidson certainly does not hold the semantic view: the semantic role of a predicate, on his account, is exhausted by its contribution to the T-theorems flowing from an acceptable T-theory for the language to which the predicate belongs. And since Davidson holds that an acceptable T-theory can probably be assembled without positing entities other than particular objects and events, he is not endorsing realism in this narrow sense.

———— (ii) A realist in the sense just adumbrated might be said to be a realist in another, broader sense. Someone who believes that there exist X's, where 'X' is label for a basic ontological category, is sometimes said to be a realist about Xs.[27] Thus a realist in the sense of (i) above would be a realist about universals (or whatever). But it is perfectly possible to deny realism about universals whilst affirming realism about some other ontological category, for example objects or events. Davidson is a realist (in this sense) about objects and events (construed as particulars), but he is not a realist

---

[26] I am concerned here only with the word 'realism' as it might be used to label certain doctrines in metaphysics. Some metaphysical doctrines are also irrelevant (e.g. modal realism) as well as certain semantic doctrines: Davidson might be said to be a non-realist about reference if this means only that he sees no particular set of reference axioms as more faithful to the truth than any other set forming part of an acceptable T-theory.

[27] This is to be distinguished from realism about X where 'X' picks out a region of discourse, e.g. ethics, aesthetics, or psychology (to avoid potential confusion I shall use 'realism with respect to X' for this): the realist with respect to X claims that statements in X are apt for truth or falsity. Someone who denies this is often called a non-factualist with respect to X.

about universals or facts.[28] (Is there an important connection between realism about universals and realism about facts? Russell seemed to think so: universals were components of facts on his account, and this was no arbitrary decision. For discussion, see *Facing Facts*).

(iii) Perhaps the most common use of the term 'realism' today is in application to various elaborations of the following meager claim: at least some portion of reality ('what there is') exists independently of our minds (or anything else's mind).[29] (The opponent of realism in this sense might be called an idealist.) This very non-committal 'realism' can be elaborated in a dizzying array of non-equivalent ways, which may overlap in some places and conflict in others. Some elaborations invoke the concepts of truth or correspondence and, as such, may seem to presage a change of subject matter; indeed it is in this connection that some of the contemporary battles over the word 'realism' have been (and perhaps still are being) fought. My aim here is not to pass judgment on competing uses or to come down on any particular side. I seek only to understand the evolution of Davidson's own position with respect to various elaborations of the meager thesis and its connection to his avowed 'realism' (in sense (ii) above) about the entities flowing from an acceptable T-theory and his consequent 'non-realism' (in sense (ii) above) about facts and rejection of the scheme-content distinction. Some of the attempted elaborations I shall outline give rise to commitments involving truth, correspondence, facts, and uniquely privileged descriptions. As the last of the passages just quoted reveals, it is precisely the threat of such commitments that makes Davidson reluctant, at times, to call himself a realist.[30]

A first, weak, elaboration might be the following: (a) Material objects exist (and material events occur) objectively, i.e. they exist (and occur) independently of our thoughts, languages, or perspectives; they are 'out there' to be discovered (in principle) rather than constituted or brought about by our thoughts, languages, or perspectives. As a way of trying to say a little more, some philosophers have added epistemic or linguistic coloring: (b) The objects (and events) we perceive, think about and talk about—or at least a good number of them—are among the objective existents (and occurrents); and so are many objects (and events) whose existence (or occurrence) we infer in one way or another, and many objects (and events) we never

---

[28] Orthogonally, it is possible to ask whether someone is a realist about *mental* entities, e.g. mental events. Davidson's (1980) position is that any mental event that enters into causal relations with material events can be redescribed in a material vocabulary.

[29] The qualification is meant to allow the 'realist' to deny that mental or social facts (amongst other things) are mind-independent.

[30] I should mention that I find *all* of the following elaborations problematic where they are not vague; certainly a great deal of work would be required to spell them out in ways that would make any of them simultaneously precise and interesting.

perceive, think or talk about. Certain philosophers have sensed a need to invoke the notion of *truth* in order to fill out the idea, a move others have seen as instantly self-defeating: (c) Many beliefs and statements about objective existents and occurrents are objectively *true* or *false*, i.e. true or false independently of our thoughts, languages, or perspectives. An appeal to 'correspondence' sometimes follows close behind: (d) Beliefs and statements that are objectively true correspond to an objective reality (and those that are false do not). The idea of correspondence is sometimes fleshed out by appeal to individual facts: (e) In order for a belief or statement to correspond to an objective reality, there must be an objective fact to which it corresponds (where an objective fact is another objective existent). Talk of an objective reality, facts, and truth has encouraged some philosophers to fill out the meager thesis with talk of a uniquely privileged description of reality: (f) In order for a true statement to correspond to an objective reality (or to a fact within it) the statement must form part of a unique description of that reality (or of the objective facts which it comprises), a description of 'Reality As It Is In Itself'.

Davidson accepts elaborations (a) and (b); but what of the others? He rejects (f) outright: '... no sensible defender of the objectivity of attributions of truth to particular utterances or beliefs is stuck with this idea' (Davidson 2000:66). (If Rorty thinks otherwise, he is mistaken.) And he certainly rejects (e), which entails 'realism' about facts in the sense of 'realism' given in (ii) above. With (d) matters are more complicated, but the work has already been done. If 'correspondence' is understood as expressing a relation between sentences and facts, then Davidson rejects (d) because it amounts to (e). But if, on the other hand, 'correspondence' is understood as invoking only a relation between singular terms and particular objects and events, then Davidson accepts (d).

This leaves us with (c), which goes beyond (b) in bringing in truth: 'Many beliefs and statements about objective existents and occurrents are objectively true or false, i.e. true or false independently of our thoughts, languages, or perspectives'. Seen one way, this might seem an obviously false, paradoxical, or self-defeating elaboration; but seen another, it might seem just an overly cognitive or linguistic way of restating (b). A recent paper by Davidson (2000) brings together what is needed to see where he stands. The key notion is *objectivity*—at least once this is detached from any problematic notion of sentential correspondence. There is no good reason, says Davidson, to depart from the 'traditional' view that truth is objective (Davidson 2000:67,72) where 'Truth is objective if the truth of a belief or sentence is independent of whether it is justified by all our evidence, believed by our neighbors, or good to steer by' (Davidson 2000:67). At the same time, he explicitly rejects the idea that objective truth requires truth to be an object (Davidson 2000:65): truth, he maintains, is 'a concept ... intelligibly attributed to things like sentences, utterances, beliefs, and propositions, entities which have a propositional content' (ibid.). Furthermore—and this is the key—truth 'depends upon how the world is' (Davidson 2000:73):

> It is possible to have a belief only if one knows that beliefs may be true or false. I can believe it is now raining, but this is because I know that whether or not it is raining does not depend on whether I believe it, or everyone believes it, or it is useful to believe it; *it is up to nature* [my italics, SRAN], not me or my society or the entire history of the human race (Davidson 2000:72).

Whether my belief that it is raining is true is 'up to' nature, the world, reality; and there is no harm in stating this as follows: my belief that it is raining is, if true, *made true* by the world. There is neither harm nor explanatory value in saying that a true belief, sentence, or statement is made true by the world as long as this is not taken to mean that individual facts in the world are truth-makers. Davidson is embracing a notion of objective truth without the trappings of what he once called the 'realist' conception of truth, with its seeming commitment to facts.[31] In short: Davidson accepts elaboration (c) as long as it can be further and fruitfully elaborated without commitment to facts.[32]

It is now easy to say everything that needs to be said about Rorty in connection with 'realism'. Davidson is an 'antirepresentationalist', says Rorty, because he rejects the 'reciprocal relations' of 'making true' and 'representing'; and the antirepresentationalist eschews discussion of 'realism' by denying that the notion of 'representation' or that of 'fact of the matter' has any useful role in philosophy (Rorty 1991:2). When the smoke has cleared, all Rorty's Davidson is doing is rejecting 'realism' in the sense of elaboration (e)—scarcely news. That Rorty himself has only elaboration (e) in mind seems to be supported by his claim that Davidson is an antirepresentationalist because he is committed to the thesis that 'there is no point to debates between realism and antirealism, for such debates presuppose the empty and misleading idea of beliefs "being made true"' (Davidson 1986:128). By undermining the scheme–content distinction, he says, Da-

---

31. As he once put it, 'The realist view of truth, if it has any content, must be based on the idea of correspondence, correspondence as applied to sentences or beliefs or utterances—entities that are propositional in character, and such correspondence cannot be made intelligible' (Davidson 1990:304). It cannot be made intelligible because it would require individual facts to which true sentences or beliefs or utterances correspond.

32. Davidson also insists that without a grasp of the concept of objective truth, language and thought are impossible: no sentence can be understood and no belief entertained by someone lacking the concept of objective truth (Davidson 2000:72). For discussion of this paper, especially of the idea that Davidson's notion of objectivity amounts to the thesis that we can never tell which of our beliefs are true, see Bilgrami 2000.

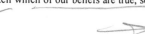

vidson has made it impossible to get the realist–antirealist debate off the ground:

> If one gives up thinking that there are representations, then one will have little interest in the relation between mind and the world or language and the world. So one will lack interest in either the old disputes between realists and idealists or the contemporary quarrels within analytic philosophy about 'realism' and 'antirealism'. For the latter quarrels presuppose that bits of the world 'make sentences true', and that these sentences in turn represent those bits. Without these presuppositions, we would not be interested in trying to distinguish between those true sentences which correspond to 'facts of the matter' and those which do not (the distinction around which the realist-vs.-antirealist controversies revolve) (Rorty 1992:372).

If Rorty had meant to be claiming that Davidson denies elaborations (a) or (b), or 'realism' about objects and events in the sense of (ii) above, then he would have been wrong. Charity dictates that we see Rorty as trying to say something true but uncontroversial about Davidson and 'realism': Davidson rejects elaboration (e).

8   Representation

According to Davidson, if we are able to demonstrate that there are no facts, the consequences for 'correspondence' and 'representation' are clear:

> The correct objection to correspondence theories [of truth] is ... that such theories fail to provide entities to which truth vehicles (whether we take these to be statements, sentences, or utterances) can be said to correspond. If this is right, and I am convinced it is, we ought also to question the popular assumption that sentences, or their spoken tokens, or sentence-like entities or configurations in our brains, can properly be called 'representations', since there is nothing for them to represent. If we give up facts as entities that make sentences true, we ought to give up representations at the same time, for the legitimacy of each depends on the legitimacy of the other (Davidson 1990:304).

If there are no individual facts, then we cannot say with any felicity that a true sentence (or belief) corresponds to, or represents a fact. When Davidson says that neither 'sentences, [n]or their spoken tokens, [n]or sentence-like entities [n]or configurations in our brains can properly be called 'representations', since there is nothing for them to represent', he is proposing an injunction against certain statements of the forms (R) and (C)

(R)   X represents Y

(C)   X corresponds to Y

where 'represents' and 'corresponds to' are transitive verbs and 'X' and 'Y' are replaced by noun phrases. Firstly, instances of (R) and (C) are not true if the noun phrase replacing 'X' describes a sentence (statement or utterance)—one minor concession, noted earlier: if 'X' is replaced by a description of a true sentence S and 'Y' is replaced by 'the world' (or, in a Fregean vein, 'the True'), the resulting sentence will be true but no more informative than the statement that S is true.[33] Secondly, instances of (R) and (C) are not true if the noun phrase replacing 'Y' is meant to describe (or refer to) a *fact (situation, state of affairs, circumstance)*. So no sentence, statement, utterance, gesture, mental state, computer state, sculpture, painting, or photograph can be said to represent a fact.

It is important to see that Davidson is not claiming that there *cannot be* useful representatives of *objects* or *events*. Without any charge of inconsistency, Davidson can accept the truth of many instances of (R) where the noun phrase replacing 'X' describes or refers to (e.g.) a painting or a sculpture and the noun phrase replacing 'Y' describes or refers to (e.g.) a person, a place, or an event (e.g., a battle). He can say that a map of London represents London, that various marks on the map represent its streets, parks, churches and so on. Similarly for remarks one might make about wind-tunnel or computer-generated models of objects (e.g., aircraft and automobiles) or events (e.g., hurricanes and earthquakes). So anyone seeking an explicit argument against the existence of representations of objects and events had better look elsewhere; no such argument can be extracted from the rejection of facts or the rejection of the scheme-content distinction. I mention this because it appears Rorty wants to draw more from these rejections, for example when he says that 'antirepresentationalism'—to which he sees Davidson as subscribing—is 'the claim that *no* linguistic items represent *any* non-linguistic items' (Rorty 1986). If we are meant to take this at face value—the italics are Rorty's—then Rorty is drawing a conclusion that Davidson is not from the rejection of facts and scheme-content dualism. Schematically, Rorty is ascribing to Davidson the view that there are no true sentences of form (R) where the noun phrase replacing 'X' describes or refers to a linguistic item and the noun phrase replacing 'Y' describes or refers to a non-linguistic item. But Davidson's position is that there are no true sentences of this form where the noun phrase replacing 'X' describes or refers to *anything whatsoever* and the noun phrase replacing 'Y' describes or refers to a *fact (situation, state-of-affairs, circumstance)*; and this entails only that no linguistic items represent *facts* (etc.), not that no linguistic items represent *any* non-linguistic items. Davidson holds there are no true instances of (R) where the noun phrase replacing 'Y' is of the form 'the fact that so-and-so' (or some similar form designed to describe a fact) because he believes he can show (by way of a slingshot) that there are no facts. It's as simple as this: nothing can be said to represent a fact since there are no facts

---

[33] Of course certain philosophically irrelevant instances are acceptable. We might adopt a convention according to which sentences of French are used to represent the temperature or chess moves.

to be represented. There is no reason to see a stronger injunction flowing from Davidson's reasoning.

It is possible that Rorty wants to draw the stronger conclusion about linguistic representations because the only viable linguistic contenders for being described by noun phrases replacing 'X' are sentences and singular terms (including variables under assignments), and the only viable non-linguistic contenders for being described by noun phrases replacing 'Y' are objects, events, and facts. If sentences and singular terms cannot represent facts (because there aren't any) then the only way for linguistic entities to represent non-linguistic entities is for sentences or singular terms to represent objects or events.

Davidson's slingshot is meant to show that any two true sentences will represent the same entity (by whatever name); so there is no merit to the idea that sentences are representations. We are left, then, with the task of making sense of singular terms representing (i.e. referring to) objects or events. But the thesis that no singular term can represent an object or event certainly does not follow from the rejection of facts or scheme-content dualism. However, there is another thread of Davidson's work that Rorty might pick up here: no particular set of reference (i.e. satisfaction) axioms for singular terms is privileged on Davidson's account since no complete set of truth-theoretic axioms (of which a set of reference axioms will form a proper subset) is privileged; so the reference relation cannot be considered usefully representational in any sense that will satisfy a 'realist' about reference or representation. Perhaps it is this feature that encourages Rorty to say that no linguistic item represents any non-linguistic item for Davidson. But the theoretical ineliminability of reference (i.e. satisfaction) within such a theory threatens to take the sting out of this. For while it is true that no particular set of working reference axioms is privileged, and while it is true that no philosophical account of the reference relation is invoked beyond the idea of a theory-internal pairing of singular terms and objects (and events)—Davidson does not have to see reference as determined by (e.g.) description, baptism, or causal or informational chains—reference is theoretically ineliminable (he says) in the sense that any adequate axiomatization for a natural language will treat names and variables (relative to sequences, and via axioms of satisfaction) as 'standing for' particular objects and events. The theory of meaning reveals an ontology of objects and events. We should not, I think, infer from Davidson's faith in the existence of alternative axiomatizations (containing different singular term axioms) that he means to be claiming that there is no useful sense in which a singular term can be said to stand for, or represent an object or event: relative to a particular axiomatization (and assignment) that is precisely what such an expression is doing.

References

Aune, B. 1985. *Metaphysics. The Elements.* Minneapolis: University of Minnesota Press.

Austin, J. L. 1950. Truth. *Proceedings of the Aristotelian Society,* suppl. vol. 24:111-28. Reprinted in *Philosophical Papers*, eds. O. Urmson and G. J. Warnock, 1961, 85-101. Oxford: Oxford University Press.

Austin, J. L. 1954. Unfair to Facts. *Philosophical Papers*, eds. O. Urmson and G. J. Warnock, 1961, 101-22. Oxford: Oxford University Press.

Bilgrami, A. 2000. Is Truth a Goal of Inquiry? Rorty and Davidson on Truth. *Rorty and his Critics*, ed. R. Brandom, 242-62. Oxford: Blackwell.

Brandom, R. 1994. *Making It Explicit. Reasoning, Representing, and Discursive Commitment.* Cambridge, Mass.: Harvard University Press.

Burge, T. 1974. Truth and Singular Terms. *Noûs* 8:309-25.

Burhe, T. 1986. On Davidson's 'Saying That'. *Truth and Interpretation*, ed. E. Lepore, 190-208. Oxford: Blackwell.

Church, A. 1943. Review of Carnap's *Introduction to Semantics*. *Philosophical Review* 52:298-304.

Church, A. 1956. *Introduction to Mathematical Logic*. Princeton: Princeton University Press.

Davidson, D. 1969. True to the Facts. *Journal of Philosophy* 66:748-64.

Davidson, D. 1974. On the Very Idea of a Conceptual Scheme. *Proceedings and Addresses of the American Philosophical Association* 47:5-20. Reprinted in Davidson 1984:183-98.

Davidson, D. 1980. *Essays on Actions and Events.* Oxford: Clarendon Press.

Davidson, D. 1984. *Inquiries into Truth and Interpretation.* Oxford: Clarendon Press.

Davidson, D. 1989. The Myth of the Subjective. *Relativism: Interpretation and Confrontation*, ed. M. Krausz, 159-72. Notre Dame: University of Notre Dame Press.

Davidson, D. 1990. The Structure and Content of Truth. *Journal of Philosophy* 87:279-328.

Davidson, D. 1993. Method and Metaphysics. *Deucalion* 11:239-48.

Davidson, D. 1996. The Folly of Trying to Define Truth. *Journal of Philosophy* 93:263-78.

Davidson, D. 1999a. Is Truth a Goal of Inquiry? *Donald Davidson: Truth, Meaning and Knowledge* ed. U. Zeglen, 17-9. London: Routledge.

Davidson, D. 1999b. Reply to Stephen Neale. *Donald Davidson: Truth, Meaning and Knowledge*, ed. U. Zeglen, 87-9. London: Routledge.

Davidson, D. 1999c. Reply to Gabriel Segal. *Donald Davidson: Truth, Meaning and Knowledge*, ed. U. Zeglen, 57-8. London: Routledge

Davidson, D. 199d. Reply to J.J.C. Smart. *The Philosophy of Donald Davidson*, ed L.E. Hahn, 123-5. Chicago and La Salle, Ill.: Open Court.

Davidson, D. 1999e. Reply to Stephen Neale. *The Philosophy of Donald Davidson*, ed L.E. Hahn, 667-9. Chicago and La Salle, Ill.: Open Court.

Davidson, D. 2000. Truth Rehabilitated. In *Rorty and his Critics*. R. Brandom, ed. Oxford: Blackwell:65–74.

Field, H. 1972. Tarski's Theory of Truth. *Journal of Philosophy* 69:347-75.

Foster, J. 1976. Meaning and Truth Theory. *Truth and Meaning: Essays in Semantics,* eds. G. Evans and J. McDowell, 1-32. Oxford: Clarendon Press.

Frege, G. 1919. Der Gedanke. Eine logische Untersuchung. *Beiträge zur Philosophie des deutschen Idealismus,* vol. I. (Translated as 'The Thought: A Logical Inquiry', by A. M. and M. Quinton, *Mind* 65:289–311. Reprinted in *Philosophical Logic*, ed. P. F. Strawson, 17-38. Oxford: Oxford University Press, 1967.

Geach, P. T. 1972. *Logic Matters*. Berkeley: University of California Press.

Gödel, K. 1944. Russell's Mathematical Logic. *The Philosophy of Bertrand Russell*, ed. P. A. Schilpp, 125-53. Evanston and Chicago: Northwestern University Press.

Higginbotham, J. 1983. The Logic of Perceptual Reports: An Extensional Alternative to Situation Semantics. *Journal of Philosophy* 80:100–27.

Higginbotham, J. 1988. Contexts, Models, and Meanings: A Note on the Data of Semantics. *Mental Representations: The Interface between Language and Reality*, ed. R. M. Kempston, 29-48. Cambridge: Cambridge University Press.

Hornsby, J. 1996. The Identity Theory of Truth. Presidential Address, *Proceedings of the Aristotelian Society* 97:1–24.

Kripke, S. A. 1980. *Naming and Necessity*. Cambridge, Mass.: Harvard University Press.

Larson, R. K. and Segal, G. 1995. *Knowledge of Meaning: An Introduction to Semantic Theory*. Cambridge, Mass.: MIT Press.

Lepore, E. 1986. Truth in Meaning. *Truth and Interpretation*, ed. E Lepore, 3-26. Oxford: Blackwell.

Loar, B. 1976. Two Theories of Meaning. *Truth and Meaning: Essays in Semantics*, eds. G. Evans and J. McDowell, 138-61. Oxford: Clarendon Press.

Neale, S.R.A. 1990. *Descriptions*. Cambridge, Mass.: MIT Press.

Neale, S. R. A. 1995. The Philosophical Significance of Gödel's Slinsghot. *Mind* 104:761-825.

Neale, S. R. A. 1999. Coloring and Composition. *Philosophy and Linguistic,* ed. R. Stainton, 35-82. Cambridge, Mass.:MIT Press.

Neale, S. R. A. forthcoming. *Facing Facts*. Oxford: Oxford University Press.

Olson, K. 1987. *An Essay on Facts*. Stanford: CSLI Publications.

Quine W. V. 1960. *Word and Object*. Cambridge, Mass.: MIT Press.

Rorty, R. 1979. *Philosophy and the Mirror of Nature*. Princeton: Princeton University Press.

Rorty, R. 1986. Pragmatism, Davidson and Truth. *Truth and Interpretation: Perspectives on the Philosophy of Donald Davidson*, ed. E. Lepore, 333-53. Oxford: Blackwell.

Rorty, R. 1991. *Objectivity, Relativism, and Truth: Philosophical Papers.* Vol. 1. New York: Cambridge University Press.

Rorty, R. 1992. Twenty-Five Years After. *The Linguistic Turn,* 2nd ed, ed. R. Rorty, 371-4. London: Hackett.

Rovane, C. 1984. The Metaphysics of Interpretation. *Truth and Interpretation: Perspectives on the Philosophy of Donald Davidson*, ed. E. Lepore, 417-29. Oxford: Blackwell.

Russell, B. 1918. The Philosophy of Logical Atomism. *Logic and Knowledge*, ed. R. C. Marsh, 1956, 177-281. London: George Allen and Unwin.

Searle, J. 1998. Truth: A Reconsideration of Strawson's Views. *The Philosophy of P.F. Strawson,* ed. L. E. Hahn, 385-401. Chicago: Open-Court.

Segal, G. 1999. A Theory of Truth as a Theory of Meaning. *Donald Davidson: Truth, Meaning and Knowledg,* ed. U. Zeglen, 48-56. London: Routledge.

Soames, S. 1992. Truth, Meaning, and Understanding. *Philosophical Studies* 65:17–36.

Soames, S. 1994. Introduction. (To section on Meaning and Truth). *Basic Topics in the Philosophy of Language,* ed. M. Harnish, 493-516. Englewood Cliffs: Prentice Hall.

Strawson, P. F. 1950. Truth. *Proceedings of the Aristotelian Society*, suppl. vol. 24:129–56.

Tarski, A. 1956. *Logic, Semantics, Metamathematics.* Oxford: Clarendon Press.

Taylor, B. 1976. States of Affairs. *Truth and Meaning: Essays in Semantics,* eds. G. Evans and J. McDowell, 263-84. Oxford: Clarendon Press.

Taylor, B. 1980. Truth-Theory for Indexical Languages. *Reference, Truth and Reality*, ed. M. Platts, 182-98. London: Routledge and Kegan Paul.

Taylor, B. 1985. *Modes of Occurrence: Verbs, Adverbs, and Events.* Oxford: Blackwell.

Weinstein, S. 1974. Truth and Demonstratives. *Noûs* 8:179–84.

Whitehead, A. N. and Russell, B. 1925. *Principia Mathematica*, vol. I, 2nd ed. Cambridge: Cambridge University Press.

Wittgenstein, L. 1921. Logisch-Philosophische Abhandlung. *Annalen der Naturphilosophie.* Translated by D. F. Pears and B. F. McGuinness, *Tractatus Logico-Philosophicus.* 1961. London: Routledge and Kegan Paul.

10

Semantic Triangulation

PETER PAGIN

1 The Metaphor and General Idea

Suppose you are stranded on an island and you want to get over to the nearby mainland.[1] Your only option is to swim. But is the other shore close enough? If you embark and it isn't, you drown. So you prefer to know before taking off. Happily, you are well equipped. You have not only a yardstick, but also a theodolite for measuring angles, and a good knowledge of trigonometry. You then determine the distance to the other shore by means of *triangulation*. You fix two points, A and B, on your own shore, and identify a third point, C, in sight on the opposite shore. You then measure the distance between A and B with your yardstick, and the two angles ABC and CAB with your theodolite. With this information you can calculate the distances AC and BC to the other shore.

---

[1] The first version of this text was presented at the Davidson conference in Karlovy Vary in September 1996. A revised version was completed in November that year. This was before the publication of other texts on triangulation, such as Talmage 1997, Verheggen 1997 and Glüer 1999. I also had not taken Davidson 2001, presented at the conference, into account. The present revisions are, in general, prompted by the availability of those texts. For helpful comments I am indebted to Donald Davidson and Kathrin Glüer.

Most of the work on this paper was made in 1996 while I was fellow at SCASSS, the Swedish Collegium for Advanced Study in the Social Sciences, Uppsala, Sweden.

In this case you have started out by identifying three points, and from there you measure one distance and two angles. But you can imagine a different epistemic situation. Suppose you know two points only, A and B, but for some reason you also know the two angles ABX and XAB to some as yet not identified point X. These angles determine the directions of the lines AX and BX. The point X is then located at the intersection of these two lines.

This can be called triangulation, too. In this case you have started out by knowing two points and two angles. Angles can be regarded as three place relations: 90° is a relation that holds between three points in a right angled triangle. Then, in general, triangulation, in this second sense, can be described as a way of determining a third point from two given points and a complex three place relation holding between the three points. And described in this way, the notion of triangulation lends itself as a metaphor.

This metaphor was introduced, ingeniously, into the philosophy of language by Donald Davidson (Davidson 1982:327). Davidson considers a 'triangle' of two speakers and some third point, and relations of *semantic* import, which together help to determine the third point, also of *semantic* import. Here is how Davidson depicts it in one passage:

> We may think of it as a form of triangulation: each of two people is reacting differentially to sensory stimuli streaming in from a certain direction. If we project the incoming lines outward, their intersection is the common cause. If the two people note each others' reactions (in the case of language, verbal reactions), each can correlate these observed reactions with his or her stimuli from the world. The common cause can now determine the contents of an utterance and a thought. The triangle which gives content to thought and speech is complete. But it takes two to triangulate. Two, or, of course, more (Davidson 1991a:159).

From Davidson's suggestion, let's settle for the term 'semantic triangulation'. What does this term stand for? I shall try to put my understanding of it in very general terms, since this will prove important later on.

I shall take *semantic triangulation* to be a kind of determination of semantic content, a determination of what a term, or a concept, or a thought, is *about*. In semantic triangulation, this is the third point X, the entity to be determined. The two others are speakers/interpreters, A and B. These two speakers/interpreters communicate with each other. When they communicate, they communicate *about* something. We then have the three place relation: A's communicating with B about X. Because of the conditions for the possibility of communication, this relation determines what X must be.

That is the general idea of semantic triangulation. I think it is an idea of greatest philosophical importance. However, as stated so far, it is rather vague and difficult to get a good understanding of. Moreover, the *picture* of

SEMANTIC TRIANGULATION / 201

semantic triangulation can be employed in different ways, depending on what is accepted at the outset.

One way of using it is as telling us something about what linguistic meaning, or thought content, must be like. You then start out with a realistic picture of, say, the physical world, with its objects and events, and state general conditions on thought, or meaning, in terms of relations between objects and pairs of thinkers.

But you can use the same picture in the other direction. You start out with thoughts, and frame conditions of objectivity, or objecthood, in terms of shared availability. To be an object, it can be said, is to be epistemically available to several subjects, given that these subjects also can know about the cognitive sharing itself. In this case you start out with a kind of interpersonal idealism, and take the physical world to be, in some sense, constituted.

In fact, I favor neither of these two ways of employing the triangulation picture, but a third way. I shall return to that towards the end. First I want to get a clearer view of Davidson's way of using it. My version will emerge out of a criticism of what I take to be Davidson's view.

As I see it, there are two different kinds of semantic triangulation in the passages Davidson devotes to the idea. One is more Quinean in nature, and is presented from a third person perspective. The second is more Wittgensteinean, and is presented from a first person perspective.

2   Davidson's First Triangulation

Sometimes, when Davidson writes on the triangulation theme, it seems clear that triangulation is a way of determining relevant *stimuli*. In the first place, the presence of the second person is a *necessary condition* of there being a unique stimulus at all:

> If we consider a single creature by itself, its responses, no matter how complex, cannot show that it is reacting to, or thinking about, events a certain distance away rather than, say, on its skin (Davidson 1992:263).

Anything that is a cause of behaviour of a creature is a candidate stimulus, i.e. possible to regard as what that behaviour is a reaction to. Davidson claims that without the presence of a second creature there is nothing further to determine any one of those causes as the relevant stimulus. There is no answer to the question (Davidson 1991a:159).

In the second place, the relation to the second person provides a way of *determining* what the relevant stimulus is.

> It's a form of triangulation: one line goes from us in the direction of the table, one line goes from the child in the direction of the table, and the third line goes from us to the child. Where the lines from child to

table and from us to table converge 'the' stimulus is located (Davidson 1992:263).

The lines in question are causal lines:

Communication begins where causes converge (Davidson 1986:317).

The first part of the answer, then, is that *the* relevant stimulus is *a* common cause of reactions of two persons. Here, two questions to Davidson naturally arise.

First, there is a question about convergence. If an event c is a common cause of two other events, a and b, then any further event d which is a cause of c is also a common cause of a and b. So there is no such thing as *the* common cause. There can, however, be a unique *closest* common cause. There doesn't have to be, but in case there is one, this is most plausibly what the talk of *the* intersection of causal lines comes down to. Anyway, I shall presently just assume that the idea of converging causal lines is clear and precise enough.

Secondly, there is a question about necessary and sufficient conditions of being the relevant stimulus. Clearly, being the common cause of two persons' reactions cannot be a sufficient condition for being the relevant stimulus of those reactions. Counterexamples are too easy to come by. What more is needed, then?

At this point the third line of triangle, that directly connecting the two persons, is introduced into the account. As far as I can make out, there are two different ideas involved here, i.e. ideas about what further relation there shall be between the two persons, beside the existence of a common cause of their reactions.

The first idea seems to be that what an individual reacts to, i.e. what the relevant stimulus is in some particular situation, is something that cannot be determined by any single reaction in that situation. We need to find the common denominator of a number of situations in which that individual gives the same response. Take your response of shouting 'cow' as a reaction to certain stimulations of your retina. The most salient common denominator, common type of cause of these reactions, is the presence of a cow visible to you. It is also the smallest common denominator, in the sense of being the farthest common type of cause: any other cause of your reaction of shouting 'cow', that is of a type common to those situations in which you do, is in turn caused by the presence of a cow. We then say that the cow, or the presence of a cow, is what you are properly reacting to. That is the relevant stimulus, although this could not be determined from one single reaction alone. I think this idea is to be found in several of Davidson's passages, but not in pure form, because it is constantly intertwined with the other ingredients.

If this idea of a common type of cause of one person's reactions is correct, then it may seem that there is no need for a second person to provide an answer to the question of what the first person is reacting to. According to Davidson, however, a second person is needed, because without her, there is no fact of the matter as to which of the first person's responses are similar!

> The criterion on the basis of which a creature can be said to be treating stimuli as similar, as belonging to a class, is the similarity of the creatures responses to those stimuli; but what is the criterion of the similarity of the responses? This criterion cannot be derived from the creature's responses; it can come only from the responses of an observer to the responses of the creature. And it is only when an observer consciously correlates the responses of another creature with objects and events in the observer's world that there is any basis for saying the creature is responding to those objects and events (rather than any other source of the creature's stimuli) (Davidson 1991a:159).

Responses of the first person are the same or similar in virtue of being treated as such by an observer. Sometimes that observer is 'we':

> [...] we group together the causes of someone's responses, verbal or otherwise, because we find the responses similar. What makes these the relevant similarities? The answer again is obvious; it is we, because of the way we are constructed (evolution had something to do with this), that find these responses natural and easy to class together. If we did not, we would have no reason to claim that others were responding to the same objects and events (i.e. causes) that we are (Davidson 1991b:200).

So the second person is needed for providing a standard of similarity of the first person's responses. And, I suppose that, despite the occasional first person plural, the relation is symmetrical. The two persons must therefore be mutually aware of each other as reacting to shared causes:

> The only way of knowing that the second apex of the triangle—the second creature or person—is reacting to the same object as oneself is to know that the other person has the same object in mind. But then the second person must also know that the first person constitutes an apex of the same triangle, another apex of which the second person occupies (Davidson 1992:264).

To sum up: mutual awareness of each other and the shared cause of reactions is needed for providing standards of similarity of responses, and those standards are needed for finding the common denominator of situations giving rise to similar responses. These common denominators are the relevant stimuli, and therefore also objects of any thoughts which are caused by those stimuli.

This is how I understand Davidson's first kind of triangulation. I must confess that I find it puzzling.

There is one feature in this picture that I find questionable, but which I shall touch on only briefly. It is the rather anti-realistic view that there is no such thing as similarity of responses save as from the perspective of an observer. Davidson moves in one sentence from asking for the criterion for saying that a creature treats stimuli as similar to asking for a criterion of similarity of responses, i.e. (normally) behavior. To me the difference between these two questions is enormous.[2]

Be that as it may. What is more puzzling to me is that I cannot even see what kind of account this is supposed to be. My overriding impression of these passages about triangulation is that they present what makes the difference between being *a* cause of someone's reaction and being *the* relevant stimulus of that reaction. If the reaction happens to be that of having a thought, then the relevant stimulus is what the thought is about. The account then introduces the second person and converging causal lines, and so far so good. The next step, however, is to introduce such requirements as that the observer 'consciously correlates the responses of another creature with objects and events in the observer's world', and as *knowledge of the triangular situation itself.* And now it looks as if part of the difference between just reacting and reacting to specific objects or events is having knowledge not only of those objects and events but also of other persons and their knowledge of the same objects or events and of oneself. On the surface, this is a clear case of invoking, in the account itself, those categories and capacities that were supposed to be accounted for. We are not much helped by being told that the difference between reacting to a particular object and just reacting consists in part in being aware of that object, even as an object of shared attention.

Of course, this is *not* what Davidson is telling us. He cannot reasonably be seen as attempting to tell us what the difference in question *consists* in. If that could be achieved in a non-circular manner, we would have an ac-

---

[2] In (2001:8) Davidson criticizes Kripke and Burge for just helping themselves to the idea of relevantly similar responses and, respectively, stimuli. According to Davidson it is circular to appeal to similarity in an account of conceptualization, because it is to explain what is natural for us by appeal to what is natural for us. This suggests two different interpretations. According to the first, there is, on Davidson's view, no such thing as e.g. the similarity of two responses beyond being treated as similar by us. This is an utterly problematic view, implying e.g. that we could not be wrong about similarities.

According to the second, Davidson holds only that the relevant respect of comparison of responses (or stimuli or other entities) is not determined independently of us, or of our concepts (whereas, given some respect of comparison, it is an objective fact whether or not two entities are similar in that respect). On the one hand this could mean that our concepts of response, etc, hang together with what we select as the relevant respect of comparison. This, however, is truistic, and does not add anything of substance. On the other hand it could mean that without "us" there is no relevant respect of comparison at all. But this appears almost as problematic as the first interpretation. Would the similarities of tigers in terms of mating behavior not be relevant to anything unless we endorsed it as such?

On p 12 Davidson (2001) dispenses with the first person plural, and speaks of "seeing the relevant similarity of one animal's responses through the eyes of another animal". But now a vicious regress threatens, for appeal to the eyes of the other animal apparently is an appeal to perceptual similarity, for which similarity of response is supposed to be the criterion.

count of psychological notions in terms of non-psychological notions, i.e. a *reductive* account, and Davidson does not believe in the possibility of a successful reductive account:

> So far I have left out of explicit account the concepts of belief and intention, which are clearly essential to speaking a language. I have no thought of trying to introduce these concepts in terms of the simple conditioning situations I have been describing; the concept of thought is not reducible to these simple concepts. All I have tried to show so far is that interaction among similar creatures is a necessary condition for speaking a language. (Davidson 1992:264; cf Davidson 2001:9).

In this passage Davidson is explicit about not attempting to reduce the full-blown psychological notions of belief and intention to notions concerning conditioning. He does not, here or elsewhere, to my knowledge, speak explicitly of a reduction of the half-psychological notion of *reacting to something* to concepts of causality. But the sketches he provides indicate that he does not believe in this either.

On the other hand Davidson clearly affirms, in the quotation above and elsewhere, that the triangular situation is a *necessary condition*, both of having thoughts and of reacting to particular objects or events. Now we can present *part* of the necessary condition—that a second creature is present—in a non-question-begging way, even if we cannot give both necessary and sufficient conditions, i.e. not an entire account, without conceptual circularity.

However, I don't think this is right either. Why should we believe that the presence of a second creature really *is* a necessary condition of thought, or of intentional reactions? Well, one reason to believe this would be that we have a convincing account of how the presence of the second creature helps *determining* what the relevant stimulus, or the intended object, is. For instance, if we were convinced that the intersection of causal lines by itself determined the relevant stimulus, we could reason to the conclusion that this point of intersection could not be located *without* the presence of the second creature. This presence would then be necessary.

But, as things actually stand in Davidson's account, we cannot understand *why* the second creature or person would be needed *except* by attributing thoughts, awareness and knowledge to the two creatures to begin with. Of course, in a sense this is obviously and trivially right: you cannot have thoughts without having thoughts, but this does not serve as much of a reason for believing that you cannot have thoughts, or cannot react to particular events, all alone. And of course it is right to say that when we do talk about an object or an event which we both observe, this object or event is located at the intersection, or an intersection, of causal lines, but this does not begin to indicate that the intersecting itself is *needed* for providing an answer to the question what it is that either of us is observing (cf. Talmage 1997, Verheggen 1997, and Glüer 1999:69-79).

Because of this I find Davidson's triangulation picture difficult to understand also when considered as an account of *why* it is a necessary condition that a second creature be present. Neither do I know of any other good way of understanding it, and so I am indeed puzzled. I am pretty certain, however, that Davidson intends to make a *conceptual* point: our concepts of intentionality, of reacting *to* something, of believing and desiring, are not *applicable* to isolated individuals. As is clear from the above, I haven't been able to find a good reason for this view in Davidson's first version of semantic triangulation.

I think, in effect, like Davidson, that there is a need for the second person, but I don't think it is a condition for the application of intentional concepts. I shall return to this after considering Davidson's second kind of triangulation.

3 Davidson's Second Triangulation

There is second theme involved in Davidson's remarks about triangulation and the need of the second person. This time it is a question, not of locating what a person is thinking about, or reacting to, but of securing the objectivity of thought. It is concerned more with truth than with reference, and it appears to have an inspiration in Wittgenstein:

> Someone who has a belief about the world—or anything else—must grasp the concept of objective truth, of what is the case independently of what he or she thinks. We must ask, therefore, after the source of the concept of truth. [...] I believe Wittgenstein put us on the track of the only possible answer to this question. The source of the concept of truth is interpersonal communication. Thought depends on communication. This follows at once if we suppose that language is essential to thought, and we agree with Wittgenstein that there cannot be a private language. The central argument against private languages is that unless a language is shared there is no way to distinguish between using the language correctly and using it incorrectly; only communication with another can supply an objective check. If only communication with another can provide a check on the correct use of words, only communication can supply a standard of objectivity in other domains, as we shall see. We have no grounds for crediting a creature with the distinction between what is thought to be the case and what is the case unless the creature has the standard provided by a shared language; and without this distinction there is nothing that can clearly be called thought (Davidson 1991a:156).

Several ideas are involved here. The first concerns the need of grasping the concept of objective truth, of facts obtaining independently of our own thoughts. Davidson claims, if I understand him, that a person cannot have a belief about the world without also believing, or at least understanding the very idea, that the world is as believed to be independently of the belief, and that is to have the idea of objective truth.

I am skeptical about that claim, since it seems to require a speaker to have beliefs about beliefs in order to have beliefs about stones and tables.[3] This seems to me implausible, but it is not a point I shall dwell on.[4]

The next step in this line of reasoning is the claim that *grasping the concept of truth requires communication with others*. As far as I can see, Davidson tries to support this claim in two ways. According to the one there is something special about coming to have the idea of truth, which requires communication, and according to the other, thinking in general requires language, which in turn requires communication.

I begin with the first way of supporting it. In one passage Davidson writes

> If you and I can each correlate the other's responses with the occurrence of a shared stimulus, however, an entirely new element is introduced. Once the correlation is established it provides each of us with a ground for distinguishing the cases in which it fails. Failed natural inductions can now be taken as revealing a difference between getting it right and getting it wrong, going on as before, or deviating, having a grasp of the concepts of truth and falsity. A grasp of the concept of truth, of the distinction between thinking something is so and its being so, depends on the norm that can be provided only by interpersonal communication, and, indeed, the possession of any propositional attitude, depends on a grasp of the concept of objective truth (Davidson 1994:15).

This passage indicates that Davidson's view is this: if you are by yourself, the idea of objective truth just wouldn't *occur* to you. It does take interaction with another creature for planting that idea in your mind.

It does not seem that Davidson here is arguing for the more conceptual point that whatever goes on in a person's mind, while isolated, it could not count as, or be truly characterized as, thinking a thought that involved the notion of objective truth. Rather, the point seems to be that it takes some particular causal history for this particular thing to go on in your mind. But, so far as I can see, this is sheer empirical speculation.[5] Even if the claim is empirically true[6], this is of no direct philosophical significance. Maybe the brain doesn't develop properly unless the child receives impulses

---

[3] This point is apparently first made in Davidson 1984:170.

[4] In Glüer and Pagin (typescript) it is argued in detail that some persons with autism should be considered as language users (and as having beliefs) and also as *not* having the *concept* of belief.

[5] Virtually the same point is made in Glüer 1999:78. Glüer stresses that the issue *is* an empirical one.

[6] I recall having read that the little experience we have of so called *wild children* (having spent their first years with animals) reveals that, after the age of eight, if a child hasn't by then mastered language, it will remain an impossible task for it.

from interaction with adults. This would not show that grasp of the concept of truth in any philosophically interesting sense depends on social interaction, because that sense would be no different from the sense in which grasp of the concept of truth depends on the presence of oxygen.

I now turn to Davidson's second way of supporting the claim. In a passage quoted above Davidson gives an indirect argument for this, via the intersubjective nature of language. But this in effect makes the appeal to grasping the concept of truth superfluous in the context. Davidson believes that thought depends on language, and that language is by its nature intersubjective. These beliefs, of course, are sufficient for concluding that having thoughts requires interaction with others. The appeal to grasp of the concept of objective truth provides no additional support.

I shall therefore turn to the reason for the intersubjectivity of language that Davidson presents. As Davidson says, this argument is essentially Wittgenstein's, or at least it conforms roughly to one kind of interpretation of Wittgenstein's private language argument. On this kind of interpretation, sometimes called the community view, or the majority view, the private language argument fits well into the triangulation model. The idea is, roughly, that one creature by itself cannot use language either correctly or incorrectly, since there is no independent standard of evaluation, and therefore no basis, for one single agent, for distinguishing between applying an expression correctly and applying it incorrectly. But if you bring in several speakers—maybe two, or perhaps three, is enough—then the required independent standard is provided. The practice of the community forms the basis of evaluation. Each speaker can compare himself or herself with the community, to see if the individual use matches the community use.

Therefore, if two or more speakers are similar enough in their applications of a term, intending to use it the same way, then a standard of evaluation of use of the term, and hence a meaning, is established. It is established, so to speak, at the intersection of individual usages. The triangulation is then completed.

I doubt that this is exactly how Davidson views the matter, but clearly Davidson claims that the presence of the second speaker is, again, a *necessary* condition for having thoughts. But again, I think this account suffers from exactly the same kind of problem as the first kind of triangulation.

We cannot really view this sketch of how the community provides a semantic standard as an account of the difference between speaking meaningfully and not speaking meaningfully. The reason is that the members are supposed to *compare* their respective applications, and therefore asked to perform mental operations of the kind that was supposed to be explained. In effect, Wittgenstein hints at this when criticizing the idea that going in accord with a rule should be explained in terms of agreement:

It is no use, for example, to go back to the concept of agreement, for it is no more certain that one proceeding is in agreement with another, than that it has happened in accordance with a rule (Wittgenstein 1978:392; VII-26).

Going by a rule, or applying a concept, involves grasping a criterion of sameness in respect of that rule, or that concept. Agreement between persons is a concept of sameness in judgement, and using agreement as a standard of evaluation therefore involves grasping both this very concept of agreement and also specific criteria of sameness of judgement in particular cases. Therefore, in explaining the grasp of concepts, or the grasp of the correct use of a term, in terms of agreement, we already appeal to the grasp of the general concept of agreement, and of the specific criteria. Without a grasp of these criteria, the noise making creatures would not know in what respect to compare their respective noises.

So we cannot really regard this community view as an account of the difference between uttering meaningfully and just uttering. And, as before, this sketch of an account cannot serve either as an argument that the community, or the standards of a shared language, is a *necessary condition* of speaking meaningfully, for if the interesting difference between being on one's own and being in a community cannot be stated without presupposing that the community members have the capacities that were considered problematic to begin with, we haven't even been given a reason for disbelieving that isolated individuals can have them, too. Therefore, this second, Wittgensteinean, kind of triangulation argument fails as well.

4 Explanatory Triangulation

In both of the varieties of triangulation considered so far, there is an attempt at explaining why certain intentional concepts, like belief, thought, grasping concepts, using terms rightly or wrongly, or reacting to particular objects or events, cannot be applied—either applied meaningfully, or applied truly—to isolated individuals. I think such attempts are bound to fail in precisely the way that these two have failed: we cannot explain why these concepts don't apply to isolated individuals, because in doing so we would have to provide something of a *reductive* account of these intentional concepts. We would have to explain, without appeal to these very notions, the relevant difference between the isolated individual and the group, and this would, indeed, constitute a reductive account. I believe such an account to be impossible. I think that Davidson does, too.

In effect, I think this opposition to reductionism is part of the motivation behind the very idea of triangulation. The picture is the following. We imagine an isolated individual, and we inquire into the basis for applying intentional concepts to him. It seems that what is available to us, as the basis for applying those concepts, are just physical facts. If we were to state conditions for applying intentional concepts to an individual, just in terms of physical facts, we would have to provide a reductive account. This cannot be provided. The conclusion, then, is that these concepts cannot be applied.

I think there is something right about this. I also think the conclusion is mistaken. What is right about it is that the intentional notions really are at home in an interpersonal setting. Whatever account we can give of these notions, or of some of them in terms of others, we can give only by considering interaction and interpersonal relations. On this score I am in full agreement with Davidson.

However, this means only that our *explication* of such concepts must make reference to interpersonal relations, and to situations of interaction. It does not mean, in my view, that our *application* of these concepts is restricted to such situations. This is the shortest way of stating what I believe is the difference between Davidson and myself in this respect. Semantic triangulation is needed for the *explic*ation of semantic concepts, but not for their *appl*ication.

There is, I believe, a tacit assumption, which leads from the correct view that triangular situations are required for explication, to the incorrect view that they are also needed for application. This is the view that if an intentional or semantic concept is applicable to an individual in isolation, it must be possible to identify those non-intentional properties in virtue of which that concept is applicable to her, given only facts about her considered as isolated. I am not attributing this view to Davidson, of course, since that would be pure speculation.

I do hold that this view is mistaken. The most obvious alternative is that in which you are allowed to appeal to *dispositions,* or counterfactuals. We might say e.g. that a creature has beliefs, even when isolated, provided it has such and such *dispositions* to interaction, or again provided it *would*, or *could*, act in such and such a way in a triangular situation. We need not know what kind of physical, or non-intentional, properties the creature has, in isolation, in virtue of which such counterfactuals are true of it. Talk about dispositions is one way of extending the application of a concept—solubility, say—from situations with respect to which it can be explained, to situation with respect to which it cannot. We can explain what solubility is by appealing to situations in which something dissolves; we cannot explain it by appealing only to situations where nothing dissolves. I am not claiming that disposition talk is the only way to effect such extending, or the best way. It is just a well known way.

So far, however, I have not given any positive reasons for the claim that intentional concepts really are applicable to isolated individuals. Let me conclude by giving one. My basic assumption is that intentional concepts, and semantic concepts in particular, are introduced in *explanations* of behavior. In our attempts at giving a systematic account of such concepts we introduce them for explaining certain phenomena.

I think semantic triangulation, much as Davidson presents it, belongs in this picture. Thus, suppose we have two persons, A and B. We have reason to think that they are co-ordinating their behavior, and on this basis that they have beliefs and intentions which they manage to communicate to each other. We assume that they have beliefs and intentions as a way of explaining this co-ordination.

Do we have any principles for finding out what beliefs and intentions they do have and communicate? Yes, we do. One such principle, in my view the overarching principle, is that of selecting the *best explanation* of the success of communication.

So, what is the best explanation of the assumed fact that creatures manage to identify the contents of each others' thoughts? Well, part of the explanation is that they succeed because they often communicate about easily identifiable objects or events. We shall therefore have reason to believe that in many situations they communicate about something they both observe and also believe they both observe. What they both observe is a common cause, or perhaps the closest common cause, of their beliefs. Therefore, the fact that an event is the closest common cause of two creatures' thoughts, can be, and often is, part of the best explanation of the (assumed) fact that they manage to communicate thoughts about that event.

Here we do have the triangular situation that Davidson pictures. What the respective thoughts of the two creatures are about gets identified as the third point of a triangle of causal lines. What the creatures communicate about is that object or event X which enters into the best explanation of success of communication, and the fact that it is located in the intersection of causal lines qualifies it precisely as being part of the best explanation. Clearly, then, I think Davidson, with the idea of triangulation, has brought something of great importance into the philosophy of language.

But now, precisely because it is a question of *explanation*, we must assume that what we appeal to in the explanation has an independent existence. We have assumed that A *has* a thought, with a determinate content, irrespective of what B thinks, and that B *has* a thought, with a determinate content, irrespective of what A thinks, and that they also manage to identify each other's thoughts. It is not part of *this* picture that X is constituted, or metaphysically determined, as the object of thought *because* of the triangular situation.

What is it, then, that does get determined? Answer: what does get determined, or partly determined, in this triangulatory fashion, is our *concept* of thought and reference, or aboutness. It is, I suggest, part of our concept of the *aboutness* of thoughts, or perhaps of the best systematic reconstruction of that concept, that the *aboutness relation* between thoughts and objects is that relation which, in triangular situations, best explains how creatures manage to identify what other creatures are thinking about.

In this way we don't explain the creation, or instantiation, of the aboutness relation as holding between a particular speaker's thought and a particular object or event. We explain why an already existing relation between the thought and the object qualifies as instantiating the aboutness relation. And in this social psychology, semantic triangulation, as part of the best explanation of the success of communication, plays a decisive role.

References

Davidson, D. 1982. Rational Animals. *Dialectica* 36:317-27.

Davidson, D. 1984. Thought and Talk. *Inquiries into Truth and Interpretation*. Oxford: Clarendon Press.

Davidson, D. 1986. A Coherence Theory of Truth and Knowledge. *Truth and Interpretation: Perspectives on the Philosophy of Donald Davidson*, ed. Lepore., 307-19. Oxford: Basil Blackwell.

Davidson, D. 1991a. Three Varieties of Knowledge. *A. J. Ayer: Memorial Essays*, ed. P. Griffiths, 153-66. Royal Institute of Philosophy, Suppl. 30.

Davidson, D. 1991b. Epistemology Externalized. *Dialectica* 45:191-202.

Davidson, D. 1992. The Second Person. *The Wittgenstein Legacy, Midwest Studies in Philosophy* XVII, eds. P.A. French, T.E. Uehling, and H. Wettstein, 255-67. Notre Dame, IN: University of Notre Dame Press.

Davidson, D. 1994. The Social Aspect of Language. *The Philosophy of Michael Dummett*, eds. B. McGuinness and G. Oliveri, 1-16. Dordrecht: Kluwer.

Davidson, D. 2001. Externalisms. This volume.

Glüer, K. 1999. *Sprache und Regeln: Zur Normativität von Bedeutung*. Berlin: Akademie Verlag.

Glüer, K and Pagin, P, typescript. Meaning Theory and Autistic Speakers.

Talmage, C.J.L. 1997. Meaning and Triangulation. *Linguistics and Philosophy* 20:139-45.

Verheggen, C. 1997. Davidson's Second Person. *The Philosophical Quarterly* 47:361-69.

Wittgenstein, L. 1978. *Remarks on the Foundations of Mathematics*, 3rd edition. Oxford: Basil Blackwell.

11

What Davidson Said to the Skeptic *or*: Anti-Representationalism, Triangulation, and the Naturalization of the Subjective

BJØRN RAMBERG

1 Introduction

Davidson believes that 'it is good to be rid of representations'—good, we may presume, for the purposes of giving a philosophical account of the relations between thinking, language-using creatures—agents—and the world they think and talk about (Davidson 1989a).[1] He also thinks that we have good reason to reject the hypothesis that our beliefs about the world are largely mistaken (Davidson 1980a, 1986c, 1989a, 1991). The second

---

[1] A first attempt to grapple with this material was presented to the Philosophy of Language Group at McGill University in the spring of 1994. A draft much closer to the present paper was my contribution to the 1996 Karlovy Vary symposium on the work of Donald Davidson. A third presentation of the ideas was given to the Philosophy Department at the University of Victoria, in October 1996. On all three occasions I benefited from comments that affected my understanding of the issue and hence the content of the paper as it now appears. I am grateful to the participants at all three venues. I would like in particular to thank Davidson for his comments in Karlovy Vary. Many thanks go also to the organizers of that happy occasion.

contention has received a great deal more attention than the first (Brueckner 1986a and 1986b; Craig 1990; Dalmiya 1990; Kemp 1992; Klein 1986; Ludwig 1992; McGinn 1986; Manning 1995; Rorty 1991; Vermazen 1983; Williams 1991). Nevertheless, these two claims are so closely related that they may be seen as manifestations of a single line of thought, which we might call Davidson's anti-representationalism. In this paper I try to understand that line of thought. To that end, I will address the following questions. Firstly, what does Davidson mean to reject when he rejects representations? Secondly, exactly how are the considerations Davidson musters against the idea that thoughts are representations related to his arguments against skepticism? Finally, what is the force of Davidson's anti-skeptical considerations?

We can think of the last of the three as asking about the nature of the beliefs and commitments to which Davidson's considerations must appeal for their persuasive power. Once the question of argumentative force is posed in this way, the answer I offer will be thoroughly unsurprising; my daring diagnosis will be that while Davidson has no knock-down argument against the skeptical hypothesis, he is not merely telling its hosts to get lost, either. However, I comfort myself, even this tepid conclusion may be worth securing, if only because friends and foes alike often write as if Davidson must either be refuting the skeptical hypothesis or else be begging the question against it. This is a very unfortunate way of slicing the options, one that is deeply at odds with the naturalistic view of thought in general and philosophical theorizing in particular that I should like to attribute to Davidson.

A contrast that will be important for my diagnostic purposes is the following. The papers in philosophy of language that set off the so-called Davidsonic Boom are notably modest, when measured along a particular axis—the account offered of what it is to speak some language, or understand some language, assumes, by its appeal to the radical interpreter, a being already equipped with language and states of mind. They do not (with the important exception of 'Thought and Talk') claim to say anything about how we in general might characterize the difference between mere noise-makers and language-users. With papers such as Rational Animals, 'The Conditions of Thought', 'Three Varieties of Knowledge', and 'The Second Person', the ante is upped quite considerably. We now have a description of the nature of intentional vocabulary—our indispensable tool-kit for the ascription of thought and the description of action, which I will refer to as the vocabulary of agency—which concerns exactly this point; Davidson here proposes that our vocables are expressions of thought, and our behavior action, by virtue of the existence of a certain kind of pattern of causal interactions. In this latter group of papers, Davidson ascends from the idea of the field linguist, employed to elucidate linguistic competence, to the much more abstract metaphor of triangulation, which is intended to illuminate the conditions under which our vocabulary of agency has grip. A burden of my remarks will be to show that it is only with this ascent that the anti-skeptical consequences of Davidson's view become fully expressed in his thinking. This move, moreover, points to the kind of naturalism for the sake of which Rorty seeks to appropriate Davidson.[2] To resist the move is to refuse to see the field linguist itself as a device subject to the conditions embodied in the metaphor of triangulation. One is then free, even while endorsing the radical-interpretation model of linguistic competence, to view interpretability as the critical correlate of thought, and thus, as I shall claim, to retain the representationalist view of the relation between the subjective and the objective that Davidson is intent on undermining.[3] Let us call this position that of the Conservative Davidsonian. Davidson himself, however, is a Radical Davidsonian; his suggestion is that we require actual, dialogical interpretation for there to be thought (though not, it should be clear, as an antecedent condition!). This is what distinguishes the position embodied in the triangulation-metaphor from the presuppositions of the model of the field linguist, and it is what lends the arguments against representations their motivation and those against the skeptic their force. Davidson's anti-representationalism, and hence his form of naturalism, comes to expression exactly in his view that interpretative interaction, and not merely interpretability, is required for a creature to be an agent.

2 Against Representations

Davidson's account of linguistic competence enshrines the rational constitution of belief and the public nature of meaning by making central the third-person perspective of the radical interpreter. Davidson frequently refers to this view as a species of externalism. It is a view that purports to secure the objectivity of thought by making the causal relations through which persons are involved with the rest of the world constitutive of the meaning of the concepts that compose the contents of their intentional psychological

---

[2] If I am right about this, then it appears that the value of Davidson for Rortyans is increased with the expansion of the scope of Davidson's announced philosophical ambitions. This is perhaps a little ironic, at least for those who think Rorty's stance is fundamentally anti-philosophical.

[3] Davidson is quite explicit on this, for instance in Davidson 1989a: 'Instead of saying it is the scheme-content dichotomy that has dominated and defined the problems of modern philosophy then, one could as well say it is how the dualism of the objective and the subjective has been conceived. For these dualisms have a common origin; a concept of the mind with its private states and objects...What we are about to see is the emergence of a radically revised view of the relation of mind and world'.

states. Here I have expressed the bare externalist claim.[4] But, as I will emphasize, the interesting issues turn on the way in which one conceives of the constituting that these causal relations do. For Davidson, as we know, that constitution happens through the ascriptions made by the radical interpreter. The radical interpreter looks for connections between speaker and environment, in order to formulate Tarski-style truth-characterizations that specify the set of languages to which that agent's utterances belong. To secure the empirical constraints that make this possible, the radical interpreter must adhere to principles of charity. Among other things, this means, as Davidson tells us in 'A Coherence Theory of Truth and Knowledge', that the interpreter must 'in the plainest and methodologically most basic cases, take the objects of a belief to be the causes of that belief' (Davidson 1986c:317-8). As he puts it in 'Empirical Content', 'the causal relations between our beliefs and speech also supply the interpretation of our language and of our beliefs' (Davidson 1986b:332). The 'basic cases', the entry points for radical interpretation, will typically be spatio-temporally indexed assertions, the kinds of assertions we make by uttering Quinean occasion sentences. However, as Bilgrami emphasizes, when the radical interpreter ascribes belief and assigns meaning in such basic cases, the attitudes and concepts thus assigned are necessarily constrained by the other attitudes and concepts which the interpreter fixes for the interpretee (Bilgrami 1992). The causal relation between assertoric utterance of an occasion sentence and distal stimulus settles meaning and belief only as mediated by the other elements in a projected total theory of meaning and belief.

Letting the general plausibility of this view go unchallenged, let us ask whether anything I have so far said militates against the view that intentional states—what Davidson calls thoughts—are representations. Why can we not accept the third-person view of content, appreciate that patterns of causal relations between persons and objects in the world are what the radical interpreter must look to for evidence, accept that thoughts are individuated with reference to the mind's environment, and still think of the thoughts thus specified as representations in the mind? This is precisely the issue between the Conservative and the Radical Davidsonian. As we will see, the difference between them shows up in their diverging attitudes toward the skeptical hypothesis.

---

[4] This characterization is not intended to provide a smallest common denominator of all those views that announce themselves, or have been labelled as, forms of externalism. I doubt that such a lowest common denominator exists, at least one that is at all interesting. So for example, the bare characterization I offer is at odds with externalist doctrines that lead to a bifurcation of content into a semantic component and an action-explanatory psychological component. See Bilgrami 1992 for the case against such bifurcation. It also fails to capture the Burgean anti-individualistic view that the meaning of a speaker's concepts depends on the norms governing the use of those concepts in relevant speech communities.

To sort this issue out, however, we must first try to hone in on what it is Davidson takes himself to be getting rid of when he rejects the idea of representation. That is the task for the remainder of the first section of the paper.

One important clue is Davidson's sustained attack on empiricist epistemological projects, which 'attempt to ground belief in one way or another on the testimony of the senses' (Davidson 1986c:310). What Davidson rejects here is the idea of representation as epistemic intermediary (Davidson 1986c:312). Davidson's expression 'epistemic intermediary' is intended to capture the generic idea behind various notions of the evidential content of the given; the epistemic pay-load delivered by the world to the subject, on the basis of the internally observed, noted, or somehow registered presence of which would-be knowers either arrive at views about the properties of the source of the delivery, or, alternatively in the face of the notorious difficulties of such derivation construct a systematic account of the interrelations between the deliverances themselves. That knowledge-acquisition is to be described according to some version of this rough model is what Davidson dubs the third dogma of empiricism.[5] If we relinquish the dogma, we thereby deprive the nature of our sensory interfaces with the world of any particular significance in an account of what justifies a belief.[6] This deprivation appears catastrophic—indeed, incoherent—on an internalist view of the mental, which posits it as a fundamental task of epistemology to explain how the mind can be in touch with what is beyond itself. For Davidson, however, the application-conditions of our vocabulary of agency ensure that thinking is inevitably in touch with the world; from his perspective, the explanatory concern with the nature of the causal connections between believers and the objects of their beliefs are just irrelevant to the epistemological concern with the justification of belief.[7]

---

[5] This appellation may suggest that an attachment to the dualism of mind's scheme and world's given is specifically a feature of empiricism. It is at least as plausible, I think, to see this dualism as a defining commitment of a rather more catholic philosophical perspective, one which entrenches a metaphysical chasm between operations of mind and events and objects in the world. Certainly, both classical and logical empiricism operate within this perspective. What distinguishes empiricists, however, is not the attachment to the dualism, but the attempt to resolve the epistemological tensions resident in the catholic perspective in a particular direction.

[6] Davidson suggests that Quine remains an internalist—a 'Cartesian'—precisely in so far as he remains committed to a proximal theory of meaning and of evidence. See Davidson 1990b. Already in 1972, Richard Rorty (Rorty 1972) draws attention to the difficulty that Davidson elaborates. What, Rorty wonders, in the context of Quine's empiricism, could possibly license the transition from talk of 'stimulation' to talk of 'information'?

[7] Clearly I am not trying to defend this line of reasoning here. It is certainly possible to doubt that a coherentist view of justification is the inevitable outcome of abandoning the third dogma of empiricism. So for example John McDowell offers precisely an attempt to construct an epistemology which is liberated from the presuppositions that lead to the dichotomy

Evidently, the epistemic-intermediary concept of representation, tied as it is to an empiricist notion of justification founded on a notion of sensory content, is not the only way to generate or sustain a philosophical view of thoughts as representations. In 'The Myth of The Subjective', Davidson connects the idea of representations to the correspondence theory of truth, and to relativism:

> Beliefs are true or false, but they represent nothing. It is good to be rid of representations, and with them the correspondence theory of truth, for it is thinking that there are representations that engenders thoughts of relativism (Davidson 1989a:165-6).

What enables Davidson to connect his attack on the third dogma of empiricism with an attack on the correspondence theory of truth and on relativism, is the rejection of private, subjective 'objects of the mind'. Depriving sense-perception of theoretical epistemic import, Davidsonian externalism leaves us without any 'basic need', epistemologically speaking, for intensional objects. And without such objects, there is 'nothing left with respect to which the problem of representation can be raised', nor is there any clear sense to the idea that states of mind individually might be said to stand in a correspondence-relation with reality.

Davidson is here suggesting that the notion of representation can be dropped from epistemology. However, one might reply, while we may not need representations as foundations in an empiricist theory of knowledge, we nevertheless do want to talk about representational states of subjects as that by virtue of which they stand, when they do, in a truth-relation to the world. If we want to be correspondence theorists of truth, the considerations that Davidson offers in 'A Coherence Theory of Truth and Knowledge', and in 'The Myth of the Subjective', do little to persuade us that we should give up the idea that thoughts are representations of reality. We might think that skeptical problems are a price worth paying for, e.g., the explanatory force and the regulative function that the idea of truth as correspondence with reality appears to offer.

This response to Davidson conceives of representational accounts of content as tied to the idea that indicative thoughts stand individually related to worldly truth-makers. To remind ourselves that this strand of representationalism is quite distinct from the notion of representations as sensorily-delivered epistemic intermediaries, it is enough to observe that one can conceive of thoughts ascribed to a person as differentially made true by some structured realm without being committed to the idea that some of those thoughts represent an epistemic foundation for others. The idea that mind represents world by virtue of entertaining thoughts which may correspond

---

of scheme and given, yet which preserves the idea that the world 'rationally constrains' our empirical judgements. See McDowell 1994. By contrast, Rorty, and probably also Davidson, do not see how there could be any point to the idea once the liberation is achieved.

differentially with the world's objective features is distinct from, and a great deal more general than, a commitment to a view of representations as justificatory foundations derived from the world's impingements on our extra-mental receptors.

Davidson's criticism of this more general notion goes by way of an attack on the correspondence theory of truth. The basic argument against correspondence theories as explications of truth has been around for some time; Davidson uses it first in 'True to the Facts' (in Davidson 1984a) Here he refers to the Frege-Church argument, which is alleged to demonstrate that the individuation of facts as ontological correlates of truth-vehicles collapses. Davidson revisits the argument in 'The Structure and Content of Truth', where he attacks representationalism precisely by casting doubt directly on the idea that we can rely on a correspondence relation with truth-makers to sustain the notion of representation. He says:

> The correct objection to correspondence theories is not, then, that they make truth something to which humans can never legitimately aspire [for this, Davidson holds, would be question-begging against the realist or objectivist]; the real objection is rather that such theories fail to provide entities to which truth vehicles (whether we take these to be statements, sentences, or utterances) can be said to correspond. If this is right, and I am convinced it is, we ought also to question the popular assumption that sentences, or their spoken tokens, or sentence-like entities or configurations in our brains, can properly be called 'representations', since there is nothing for them to represent. If we give up facts as entities that make sentences true, we ought to give up representations at the same time, for the legitimacy of each depends on the legitimacy of the other (Davidson 1990a:304).

We saw that when Davidson attacks the epistemic-intermediary notion of representation, he seeks to undermine our faith in the correspondence theory of truth by relieving us of the sense that we need representations to account for the way in which the senses support our beliefs. In 'The Structure and Content of Truth', Davidson comes to the issue from the other side. He argues here that unless we can make sense of the idea of objective and differentially effective truth-makers, we cannot make sense of representations. For without truth-makers we stand without objective relata reference to which might give point to the notion of an individual item of representation as a subjective correlate.

The relation between this argument and Davidson's externalist view of content is less direct than in the case of the anti-empiricist argument. In that case, the externalist element is what allows us to abandon the idea that sensory surfaces are a distinctively significant focal point of epistemological theory (Davidson 1990b). In the present case, the attack on truth as correspondence trades on the externalist conception of content in this way: if such a conception of content were not available, the rejection of correspondence would amount to the assertion of an idealist (or, in Davidson's terms, 'epistemic' or 'subjectivist') view of truth. Externalism, Davidson believes, gives us the freedom to reject correspondence-theories of truth without reverting to idealism. But here it is important to pay attention to the nature of the externalism Davidson invokes. For if one conceives of the externalist point simply as the claim that content-states are individuated with reference to the mind's environment, it is not at all clear how externalism permits us to reject correspondence while saving us from idealism. The reason is that one might accept this point about individuation without rejecting the view of thought as epistemically mediating the subject's access to reality, that is, of thought as representation. An externalist metaphysics of content, that is to say, is not in itself an immediate threat to representationalism, if one remains committed to a first-person epistemology of mind. In fact it is to this latter view that Davidson opposes his brand of externalism. It is not to be construed simply as the bare doctrine that identification of content requires reference to causes in the world beyond the thinker. Though Davidson endorses this claim, by itself it does little work in his argument. Indeed, it falls out of two prior claims; firstly, that the epistemology of interpretation is public; secondly, that the predicates which serve in the vocabulary of agency are anchored in this epistemology, in the sense that they take their point from the roles they have in it. The resulting constraint on content, that it is constituted by radical interpretation, is what does the work against idealism, for this is what puts the subject's states of mind directly in touch with objective world.

The externalist claim that thoughts have their identities by virtue of what the interpreter takes to be their causes might appear to invoke the threat that a subjective mind might lose touch with its own states. This appearance is exploited in a further, third strand in Davidson's attack on representations, developed in his papers on first person authority (Davidson 1984b, 1986a). For those externalists who remain unpersuaded by the slingshot argument against the prospect of correspondence-theories of truth, and who therefore see their way clear to endorsing representations as truth-vehicles, the notion of first person authority creates, Davidson argues, a difficulty: if the contents of our thoughts are individuated with reference to external relations of which the subject may well be unaware, then what reason do we have to believe that people for the most part know what they think? Davidson claims that the only way out for an externalist who wants to preserve our intuitions about first person authority, is to abandon the idea that thoughts are to be construed in terms of a subject's relation to some intensional object, or content. Once we posit such objects of the mind, then, unless the essence of the object, the content, lies in being perceived by the self-observing mind, our epistemic relation to them becomes questionable. And since the bare externalist view of content denies precisely that the *esse* of an intensional object of a thought is its first-person *percipi*, it follows that we must be skeptical of the contents of our own minds. The choice Davidson leaves us with here is either to revert to an internalism of content that restores the phenomenal transparency of mental states, allowing that, at the very least, we do know the contents of our own mind, or to give up entirely on the idea that minds stand, except in the parasitic and derivative case, in any sort of epistemic relation at all to their own contents.

We find, then, that there are three strands in Davidson's attack on representations. First, there is the attack on empiricist sensory-based epistemology; secondly, there is the attack on the idea of correspondence as explication of truth; and finally we have a direct attack on the very idea of intensional objects of the mind. The view of thought as constitutively identified from the perspective of the radical interpreter serves as a premise of all three arguments. In the first case, it deprives the particular point of the causal routes between world and mind constituted by the interface between world and sense organ of any special relevance for semantic and epistemic purposes. In the second case, it poses a conception of our connection with objective reality that does not depend on a correspondence-relation, and thirdly, it ensures first person authority by rendering non-epistemic the relation of thinkers to the contents of their thoughts.

There is a basic feature common to the cluster of views Davidson seeks to dislodge by dispelling the representation-metaphor from philosophical thinking about mind. This basic feature is a commitment to an image of the mind as primarily a self-knowing thing; as something regarding which we must wonder what its mode of epistemic access is to the rest of the world. If this is right, the core notion of representation that Davidson rejects—what the three strands in Davidson's case against representationalism work together to undermine—is the idea of a kind of entity such that by knowing it, the mind knows its own content, thereby coming to know, perhaps, and in a mediated fashion, also what is not itself. Now, it can appear meaningful to wonder about the nature of the access the mind enjoys to the world only in so far as we are able to convince ourselves that we can give, at least in a rough and preliminary way, reasonably clear and reasonably independent answers to questions about the nature or identity of each of the two relata whose relation we are thus attempting to determine. The belief that we can use the notion of representations to illuminate what thoughts are, and thus what mind is, is critical to our efforts to sustain this conviction; the appeal to representation as explication of thought is exactly what gives us a feeling of knowing what mind is, as something quite apart from the external world which, if things go well, it depicts for its possessor. When the claim is stated thus baldly, it may perhaps seem that I am attributing to Davidson a rather worn and tired target. However, this image of mind still haunts not only theorizing but also many of those easy habits of speech which make up our common notion of the mental. I hope to persuade you that it is precisely the effort to think about agency in a manner that consistently eschews this conception of mind that takes Davidson to his anti-skeptical conclusions, and to the controversial claim that intentional concepts have application only in so far as there is an interaction of interpreters.[8] If that is indeed so, the resistance with which these conclusions have been met might suggest that the horse Davidson is flogging is not yet quite dead.

Before we turn explicitly to Davidson's way with the skeptic, a few qualifying points should be made with regard to the exegetical conclusions so far drawn. Firstly, nothing in Davidson's position suggests that we ought not to think of persons as representing the world as being this way or that. The point, as I take it, is that we make a mistake if we think we explain such locutions by attributing representations; we are mistaken if we think that someone represents the world a certain way—that is, believes certain things of it—in virtue of tokening, in some suitable module, certain states with particular representational contents. Similarly with regard to the correspondence locution: true beliefs do correspond to reality—true beliefs are true because the world is the way it is. What we cannot say, if we are with Davidson, is that this adds anything to the claim that a belief is true; we must resist the idea that the nature of true beliefs can be illuminated by appeal to some relation which obtains differentially between truth vehicles and particular ontological structures. It is correspondence as explanatory of truth—and the associated idea that truth is the sort of substantive relation that will explain the virtues of true belief—that Davidson denies, not the intuition that truth is objective and independent of our epistemic efforts. This view has remained constant with Davidson.

Secondly, while Davidson does believe that the fallout of these considerations for the theory of knowledge is (or ought to be) nothing less than revolutionary, it is not obvious that he takes his attack on the idea of thought as representation to entail the demise of the epistemological project conceived as the attempt to give normative accounts of human knowledge

---

[8] This image is deeply ingrained in our habits of thought. Manning summarizes (without endorsement) the alleged tension between externalism and first person authority thus:

> If the factors that fix content are external to the mind, they are presumably outside the epistemic ken of the agent, and it is hard to see how an agent can discriminate among his thoughts without having access to what gives them the content they have and thus makes them distinct or the same (Manning 1995:359).

Here 'presumably' points to the intuition that drives the conclusion. The metaphor of inner space with its access-problematic relations to the outside world are taken for granted, delivering the assumption that the mind is primarily a self-knowing thing. But the very idea of 'having access' to our own thoughts is altogether misguided. We do not know our own thoughts, except in parasitic and derivative cases. Predominantly and paradigmatically we *have* thoughts, and to have thoughts is to stand related in various complex and interrelated ways to the rest of the world.

(Davidson 1989a). Epistemology may be altered when it ceases to be oriented by representationalism, but it does not, for Davidson, disappear. His revisionistic description of the mental 'leaves almost untouched the task of specifying the conditions of knowledge' (Davidson 1986c:319). Making his case for the veridical nature of belief, Davidson says he has

> not been concerned with the canons of evidential support...but to show that all that counts as evidence or justification for a belief must come from the same totality of belief to which it belongs (ibid.).

This might seem to leave epistemologists of a recognizably traditional kind with their hands full. We might note, though, the bracketed remark suppressed by the ellipses in the quotation; '(if such there be)'. I suspect—and hope—Davidson here flags a doubt that there are such things as canons of evidential support which are both perfectly general and in possession of content that might serve regulative purposes. Even if he does, though, he may also doubt that the very idea of epistemology depends on the assumption that there are.

Thirdly, and importantly, I cannot see that any of Davidson's considerations cast aspersions on the prospect of sciences of human behavior that invoke the concept of representations. What Davidson cannot allow, is a reduction of thought (as Davidson understands this term) in the different manners proposed, by, e.g., Dretske, Fodor, or Millikan (or an elimination of it in the manner hinted at by the Churchlands and by earlier incarnations of Stich). For Davidson, the naturalization of thought, as the paradigmatic act of subjectivity, cannot go by way of a reductive naturalization of a representation relation, either in information-theoretic or evolutionary terms. Still, as far as I can see, this does not prevent us from employing the notion of representation (regarded as a functionally or physiologically described constellation which is the bearer of a certain information content) in a science of behavior—or, more cautiously, a science of the mechanisms involved in behavior. What Davidson denies is that such a science might tell us what knowledge is, or specify in what linguistic competence or having thoughts consists. This is because he believes the application of these concepts ineliminably depends on our appreciation of norms, which will be lost from view when we are engaged in the project of articulating the empirical laws that govern some domain. It is not to say, however, that a science invoking representations could not enlighten us about what goes on in us when we exercise the capacities involved in our thinking and acting, capacities that we rely on the vocabulary of agency to characterize.

3 Against Skepticism.

All three strands in Davidson's case against representation involve versions of the claim that the picture of the mind as self-knower leads to skepticism.

In the case of the epistemic intermediary, the skeptical result is the familiar Humean predicament; we have no way of certifying those amongst the multifarious internal traces or indicators that the mind observes in itself that are truthful representatives of a world beyond it. In the second case, a commitment to representations as truth-vehicles combines with the collapse of the individuation of objective truth-makers to produce what Davidson calls epistemic or subjectivist views of truth (see Davidson 1990a; 1991). Such 'theories are skeptical in the way idealism or phenomenalism is skeptical; they are skeptical not because they make reality unknowable, but because they reduce reality to so much less than we believe there is' (Davidson 1990a:298). Finally, the arguments from first person authority reveals that bare externalism, when combined with the notion that to have a thought about the world is to entertain a semantic representation of it, leads to skepticism about the contents of our own minds.

The strategy Davidson pursues against the philosophical utility of the idea of representation is to create a tight, multi-strand link between skeptical positions and various routes to a conception of thought as representation. This yields a conditional conclusion, Davidson's anti-representational conditional: if we want to avoid skepticism, we must give up representations. But of course, one may just not be moved by the antecedent. One may be a Willing Skeptic. As Willing Skeptics, we might grant that Davidson's anti-skeptical conditional derives from a correct diagnosis of a consequence of our views. And certainly, we concede, the skeptical hypothesis may be an unsettling thought. However, until we properly refute it, the right response to this fact is just to toughen up a little; philosophy, after all, is not for the squeamish or faint of heart, and the skeptical hypothesis, we shouldn't forget, has kept us many of us in business.

Even if we are not Willing Skeptics, however, even if we were to agree with Davidson that a skepticism-inducing account of thought is a sign of something gone wrong, we might not find that Davidson's conditional tells against the representationalist understanding of what it is to be a thinker and an agent. For it can do this only if there is an attractive, alternative conception of thought and agency on the table that is not representational in structure, and which thereby successfully avoids the skeptical predicament. And we may well doubt that Davidson offers such an alternative. If we find that Davidson's own conception of thought and agency fails to avoid the skeptical predicament, then we might feel the force of the conditional Davidson poses, without being motivated to embrace his anti-representationlist account. We would be Unhappy Skeptics, and we would press against Davidson what we may think of as an internal question. The issue, for the Unhappy Skeptic, is whether Davidson's view, on its own terms, disarms the skeptical challenge. If it does, then, indeed, an Unhappy Skeptic has a reason for accepting Davidson's account. Now I am about to argue that the internal question goes in Davidson's favor; in the context of Davidson's account of agency, to show that a view has skeptical consequences is to provide a *reductio ad absurdum* argument. What transforms a diagnosis of skepticism into a *reductio* is the fact that it is supported by a conception of thought and agency in terms of which the skeptical hypothesis cannot be coherently explicated.

We can still hold out for the Willing Skeptic's response to Davidson's line of thought about representation and skepticism. But we should note that when we in that case raise an external question, and ask why anyone would want to give up skepticism by being a Davidsonian anti-representationalist, the burden of argument shifts. A Willing Skeptic cannot now simply rest with the claim that one can preserve the coherence of skepticism by refusing to endorse Davidson's account of agency. Of course this is possible. To motivate this refusal, however, it is no longer enough simply to appeal to skepticism-inducing intuitions (perhaps about the phenomenology of envatted brains and other esoterica), with no constraint on what is a possible belief other than what can be imagined by the philosopher (Manning 1995 makes this point). Once it is granted that the internal question goes Davidson's way, the Willing Skeptic assumes an obligation to motivate his preference by providing a skepticism-friendly general conception of thought and agency.

Indeed, that the skeptic of all entities might be forced to assume an internally inconsistent description of itself and thus cease to be, seems a remarkably implausible notion. Anti-skeptical arguments worth considering are not intended to induce such self-annihilation. They do not claim that the skeptic can be forced, through the judicious application of metaphysics, to give up skepticism. Davidson's position with regard to skepticism is that the basic features of his account of the vocabulary of agency makes the thought of minded creatures dependent on the world in such a way that the creatures cannot be largely and generally mistaken in their thoughts about the world. Davidson cannot claim to have arguments that force one to adopt this account, irrespective of one's philosophical interests. The claim is that if one does adopt it, one no longer maintains conceptual space for the hypothesis that common-sense accounts of what there is and scientific theories alike suffer from such crippling ontological inadequacy that our beliefs about the way the world is are largely false. As we evaluate this claim—i.e., as we try to settle the Unhappy Skeptic's internal question to Davidson—the challenge will be to locate as precisely as possible those elements of Davidson's conception of thought and agency that block skepticism. If Davidson's anti-skeptical claim is to be sustained, we must find that we can preserve skepticism only by abandoning the distinctive features of that conception.

I will approach the internal question posed by the Unhappy Skeptic somewhat indirectly, by way of two commentators who are not skeptics at all, but are nevertheless critical of Davidson's case against skepticism. Williams and Rorty both diagnose, in different ways, troublesome relations between the following three elements: firstly, Davidson's description of what he is up to in his argument against skepticism; secondly, the burden such an argument should assume; and thirdly, what Davidson's argument actually shows.

'Davidson's announced intention', Williams says, commenting on Davidson's argument in 'A Coherence Theory of Truth and Knowledge', 'was to argue that "coherence yields correspondence". This is the form that a direct answer to the skeptic must take' (Williams 1991:313, quoting from Davidson 1986c). However, he argues, this creates a problem for Davidson, because

> if we concede the legitimacy of calling in question all our beliefs about the world, and all at once, then, the most we can suppose ourselves to have in the way of a basis on which to construct our answer to the skeptic is knowledge of the relations between our beliefs, coherence. This is why, if truth is not defined in terms of coherence, it is hard to see why our beliefs should have the slightest tendency to be true (ibid.).

Davidson's response, Williams claims, is to subtly but crucially change his strategy:

> Under pressure from this difficulty, Davidson shifts to an argument that derives both coherence and correspondence from charity. But the appeal to charity turns out to involve the idea of unproblematic access to certain causal relations between speakers and objects in the world. If, in the context of the skeptic's question, we grant ourselves this access, the game is over before it begins (ibid.).

Thus, according to Williams, Davidson begs the question against the skeptic.

Rorty, too, doubts that Davidson's announced intention describes what he is doing: 'If there is to be a problem here', Rorty says,

> it must be because the skeptic has been allowed to construe 'objective' in such a way that the connection between coherence and objectivity has become unperspicuous. What sense of 'correspondence' will both preserve this lack of perspicuity and yet be such that Davidson can argue that coherence will yield it (Rorty 1991:137)?

Rorty agrees with Williams that Davidson may be pretending to answer the skeptic's challenge, but is really begging the question at issue. Once Davidson has reduced 'correspondence to reality' to a stylistic variant of 'true', Rorty claims,

> then his argument against the skeptic comes down to: you are only a skeptic because you have these intensionalistic notions floating

around in your head, inserting imaginary barriers between you and the world ...(Rorty 1991:138).

Davidson should have been clear, Rorty insists, that 'he was going to offer the skeptic a way of speaking that would prevent him from asking his question', and not that 'he was going to answer that question' (ibid.)

In 'Afterthoughts, 1987', which appears as an appendix to 'A Coherence Theory of Truth and Knowledge', reprinted in a volume of essays on Rorty, Davidson agrees that his announcement of the argument was misleading, and also that he 'did not set out to "refute" the skeptic' (Davidson 1986c). And surely to dismiss the skeptic without a refutation is tantamount to begging the question that the skeptic intends to place at issue. The concession Davidson is making here, however, amounts to no more than an acknowledgement that he has no argument that forces the skeptic to abandon skepticism. Since the very idea of such an argument is illusory, the concession does not amount to very much. It recognizes simply that any argument against the skeptic must involve theoretical desiderata the value of which it is always possible for the skeptic to question. So in a sense Rorty is right that Davidson is simply offering the skeptic a new way of talking. But this offer is also a kind of answer, in so far as the anti-skeptical consequences are derived from an account of the vocabulary of agency, an account the attractions of which may be assessed at other points. To see how that answer goes, let us return to Williams's critique.

The issue now is whether Davidson's description of this vocabulary is in fact, on its own terms, skeptic-proof in the way he claims. This, we remind ourselves, is crucial also to the persuasiveness of his anti-representationalist case. Now the seriousness of Williams's charge that Davidson begs the question can be brought out in this way: it points to the possibility that Davidson blocks skepticism only by building its impossibility into his account of thought and agency in an ad hoc manner. The issue on which Davidson's anti-skeptical claim turns is the question of the intra-theoretical rationale for the move that keeps the skeptical question from being sustainable. The rather blunt charge of question-begging is really the charge that this rationale is not very deep, that peripheral modifications and minor surgery could reinvigorate the skeptical challenge, in recognizably Davidsonian terms. If this is possible, then Davidson's move against the skeptic would appear as question-begging from the perspective of his own account. If this charge of 'internal question-begging' sticks, then Davidson is no better off than the Unhappy Skeptic, and his anti-representational conditional stands without the support it needs if it is to tell against a representational conception of thought. Let us look more closely at Williams's charge.

The relevant contention of Williams's is that 'the appeal to charity turns out to involve the idea of unproblematic access to certain causal relations between speakers and objects in the world', and that this assumption simply disqualifies the skeptic. It is undeniable that the principle of charity has deep roots in Davidson's account of thought, and so it might appear that Williams here simply concedes that what I called the internal question is settled in Davidson's favor. The critical issue, however, concerns the content of the notion of charity. The question pressing behind Williams's remark is whether the notion of charity to which Davidson is indeed entitled, the sense of 'charity' in which it is a requirement for radical interpretation, is a notion of charity rich enough to foreclose the possibility raised by the skeptical hypothesis. The suspicion that this is not the case, might be fleshed out as follows: successful radical interpretation does not depend, one might argue, upon the correct identification of causes of assent to occasion sentences. To get determinate ascriptions, what the interpreter needs are correlations—but correlations could be derived, so this line of thought goes, not only when causes are correctly identified, but also if causes were to be systematically misidentified. In this case you would have holistic individuation of thoughts, by virtue of an interpreter's correlation of speaker-events and other world-events, but those thoughts would still be systematically false of the world because the interpretations assigning content to occasion sentences would, ex hypothesi, be out of whack with their actual, real, causes. If this is a genuine possibility, one Davidson blocks out simply by stipulating that radical interpretation gets causal connections right, then Williams's sort of objection will be sustained. In this case, Davidson's claim to have a sound argument against the representational picture, the picture of the mind as primarily and fundamentally a self-knowing entity, would be seriously compromised. This is because, we recall, if the internal case against skepticism is not tight, then to diagnose skeptical consequences of representationalism is not a reason for abandoning it in favor of Davidson's story. If Williams's worry is on the right track, then it may turn out, within the terms set by the radical-interpretation model of linguistic interpretation, that appearance is fundamentally other than the reality to which we would like to be able to treat it as a guide.

The point I now want to make is that Davidson is in a position to offer a rebuttal to the criticism we extracted from Williams just in so far as he moves beyond the framework of the early papers on radical interpretation and endorses a strongly naturalistic position concerning the constitution of thought per se. This strong position is what I earlier dubbed Radical Davidsonianism; it makes the presence of thought contingent not on the presence of in-principle interpretable patterns of events, but on actual interpretation. It also precludes the possibility, just broached, that the radical interpreter could exercise a content-identifying function through systematic misinterpretation. The position emerges when we transpose the radical-interpretation model of linguistic competence into the more ambitious project of offering

an account of the causal dynamics that we capture by employing the vocabulary of agency.

To appreciate the significance of the transition from the idealized field
linguist to the triangulation-model, we must be quite clear about how the
sorts of doubts that Williams raises about the anti-skeptical implications of
charity are sustained. We can bring out the relevant feature of
this—Conservative Davidsonian—understanding of the radical-
interpretation model as follows. When we specify content in terms of a
radical interpreter's attributions, it appears that the presence of intentionality
is already secure—assumed with the idea of the radical interpreter. This
appearance is responsible for our sense that it is legitimate to speak of the
possibility of a systematic misidentification of causal connections on the
part of the radical interpreter. This apparent possibility, in turn, is precisely
what makes it seem as if we get the veridicality of the thoughts of the subject of interpretation only by begging the question against the skeptic at the
level of the specifying device, the radical interpreter.

Davidson is himself aware of this impression, and gives expression to
it by asking, 'why couldn't it happen that speaker and interpreter understand
one another on the basis of shared but erroneous beliefs' Davidson
1986c:317)? Davidson answers by invoking the notion of 'an interpreter
who is omniscient about the world, and about what does and would cause a
speaker to assent to any sentence in his (potentially unlimited) repertoire
(ibid.) But the so-called omniscient-interpreter argument will not help the
Conservative Davidsonian. Indeed, the very notion of an omniscient interpreter reinforces the impression that intentionality is assumed, functioning
as a primitive notion which falls outside the explanatory scope of the radical-interpretation model. And from a perspective on radical interpretation
informed by this impression, the natural response to Davidson's omniscient
interpreter is that all the work is done by assuming that an omniscient interpreter actually is capable of getting us right, in the right circumstances.[9]
However, that we seem to think that we have thoughts and utter sentences,
that we appear to be radically interpretable by someone more or less like
ourselves, just does not guarantee that we are in fact interpretable by an
omniscient being—the omniscient being could find, what would in that
case be correct, that we really are not interpretable. There may, for all we
know, be no point in describing as sentences the complicated patterns of
noises that we under certain conditions, known to the omniscient one, are
disposed to make. This train of what we thought was thought then triggers

---

[9] Ludwig points out that it is question-begging to assume that an omniscient interpreter will
get us fallible ones right in *every possible* environment (Ludwig 1992:337). A speaker must
perhaps have mostly true beliefs in *some* environment, for example the one in which those
beliefs were first acquired, but what warrants the thought that that environment remains the
actual one?

the highly unstable conclusion that among our many illusions was the idea that our noises and inscriptions sometimes are expressions of thought.

It seems, then, when we confine our attention to the idea of radical interpretation, particularly with Quine's explicitly methodological construal of charity ringing in the back of our heads, that Davidson is indeed making just the question-begging move that Williams (and others) finds. When Davidson poses the idea of a radical interpreter who is omniscient about the world and who interprets us according to charity, he appears to take for granted that a being constrained by truth would indeed find just those kinds of patterns in our behavior that make the vocabulary of agency applicable. However, that we, fallible believers, appear to find such a pattern, cannot warrant this assumption.

Let us contrast with this the view of thought that Davidson expresses by elaborating the metaphor of triangulation. A main feature of this account is that nothing is in the picture prior to the intersection of causal lines between persons and worldly objects that has the sort of robustness which error requires. In triangulation, natural saliencies fix content all round; with respect to their status as agents, two triangulators are on a par and interdependent. Not only the attitude which expresses itself as assent to some sentence prompted by an event in the world, as spotted by a radical interpreter, but also the interpreter's thought that expresses itself as assent to some sentence caused, in turn, by that causal connection, is fixed by common saliencies. We can perhaps think of triangulation as symmetrical radical interpretation, where each is both interpreter and interpreted, and each has the very beliefs she has about the causal relations that obtain between the world and the other because the world causes her to have them.

The triangulation metaphor brings to the fore the fact that the constituting activity of interpretation is dialogical, and constitutive of intentionality all round. Causal dispositions become describable in norm-governed terms—thus allowing the possibility of error, or of failure, the hallmark of agency—only when environmental saliencies converge, and only when the responses to these common saliencies themselves are mutually salient to the creatures involved. Thus, not only the thoughts of a speaker, but the intentional nature of those causal states that emerge, in this context, as interpretations of another, are dependent on triangulation.

What this means is that misidentification of the causal connections which give point to talk of thought becomes conceivable only once enough intersections are occurring that a pattern of reason is beginning to form. Only a quite developed pattern would provide sufficiently strong constraints on an emerging interpreter to motivate attributions of the kinds of divergences from goodness and truth that the concepts of belief and desire are designed to accommodate. Such attributions require strong rational linkages between the thoughts attributed as well as the dependence of the preservation of this pattern on the semantic values assigned to predicates already fixed. Even so, the misfirings that any such pattern will lead an interpreter to diagnose in a living subject, in the form of attributions of error or failure of one kind or another, will remain dependent on and determined by the pattern of interacting causal dispositions that gives the ideas of thought and agency their application. Conceiving of triangulation as the causal interaction of interpreters with each other and the world, and as constitutive of the thoughts of either, regarded both as interpreter and interpreted, we have to conclude that we can no longer make sense of the idea of a radically mistaken radical interpreter.

To accept this description of thought is to preclude the possibility that the radical interpreter could predominantly misidentify the causal patterns constitutive of content. And if this possibility is illusory, we can dismiss the suggestion that the radical interpreter's ability correctly to identify causes of assent to occasion sentences is an ad hoc assumption, a gratuitous addition to Davidson's account of thought. Davidson's case against skepticism is deeply rooted in his conception of what it is to be an agent. Hence, also, by the anti-representationalist conditional, does he have an argument against the notion of mind as self-knowing representor, and the Unhappy Skeptic can be rid of the cause of her unhappiness—provided we are Radical Davidsonians. The proviso is crucial; Conservative Davidsonians, demanding of thought only interpretability, retain a picture of thought as something that is conceptually prior to communicative interaction. For Conservatives, the radical interpreter enters as a specifying device, ensuring that thought and meaning are in an important sense accessible, but without implying that an agent's being an agent hinges on there being a community of interactive agents. Conservatives thus conceive of the pattern that interpretation traces in a way that is fundamentally different from the conception of a pattern of causal interaction embodied in the triangulation metaphor. The pattern captured in attributions of thought and ascriptions of meaning performed by the radical interpreter is something the interpreter discovers. There is thought and meaning if the pattern, specifiable by appeal to the radical interpreter, is there.

The Radical position claims that there is such a pattern of thought and meaning for an interpreter to discover only when the causal interactions of a creature with its environment is responded to, and engaged with, in a certain way, by another creature. Only then do we get the patterns that we capture with the vocabulary of agency. The Radical position implies that without others, I am just another complicated thing in the world, with no more inner space than an anthill or a colony of viruses. Subjectivity, as a perspective on the world expressed by my thoughts about it, arises only once certain dispositions to respond to the activities of conspecifics (in the typical case) are activated. On this view, ascriptions of thought, the very idea of perspectives on the world, have a primarily comparative point; we rely on them partly to register and partly to accommodate or even to ignore in a systematic way certain kinds of similarities and differences between the causal dispositions that each of us manifests in his or her behavior.

Holding out for a richer notion of subjectivity, for a conception of thought as having an aspect which is inherently subjective, for some vestige of an inside view of the mind, is the project which joins the Conservative Davidsonian and the Skeptic. The account of agency that Davidson offers gives up entirely on this project. We might say that he undermines skepticism by emasculating the notion of subjectivity.

An effect of conservative resistance to this emasculation is that the intentionality of the radical interpreter is itself left primitive—perhaps we might say, 'unnaturalized'. As a consequence, the Conservative Davidsonian is vulnerable to the pro-skeptical point that a field linguist under certain systematic misperceptions of the causal relations between a speaker and the world, could charitably, and correctly, interpret someone whose thoughts were largely and in related ways in error about the world. For a Conservative Davidsonian, however—say a fan of the 'Programme' in philosophy of language who also has a weak spot for the notion that thoughts have an intrinsically subjective aspect—such vulnerability is hardly lamentable; on the contrary, for anyone with a penchant for the traditional problems of epistemology, it is something to cherish and treasure.[10] Indeed, the wish to preserve it may be the very motivation for resisting the description of thought and agency that Davidson's metaphor of triangulation points toward.

This brings us right back round to face the Willing Skeptic. Conceding the anti-skeptical consequences of Davidson's account of the vocabulary of agency, the Willing Skeptic, perhaps in the form of a Conservative Davidsonian, presses the external question; why should I want to be a Radical Davidsonian about thought and agency? I will conclude with some bald assertions in response to this question.

The attractions of representationalist models of the psyche, the oddly masochistic relish in the distress induced by the skeptical hypothesis, the perceived legitimating significance of reductive endeavours, these are all more than vestigial attachments to a vocabulary of self-understanding originally shaped by an interest in preserving the idea of a perspective on the world that is not itself of the world—at least not of a piece with that part of the world on which it is a perspective. Reductivist efforts in the philosophy of mind, for example, seem important to exert only once we have swal-

---

[10] McGinn, for whom mysteries appear to hold a certain appeal, illustrates the attitude: 'In fact, I had the idea of using the anti-skeptical consequences of the principle of charity as a *reductio* before I learned that Davidson regards this as a *virtue* of his account of interpretation' (McGinn 1986:359,6n)

lowed the idea that the vocabulary of thought and agency leaves us not quite in touch with the sort of things that really make up the world. The result of this ingestion is an almost oxymoronic attempt to validate, from within the presuppositions of this anti-naturalistic metaphysical perspective on the vocabulary of agency, the idea that we really are natural creatures after all. This paradoxical position finds paradigmatic expression in Fodor's fear of letting down Granny; the worry that a team of philosophers and scientists might discover that we are not entitled to be thinking of ourselves as deliberating agents with thoughts and attitudes.

In the face of this picture, Davidson is issuing an invitation to assume a philosophical stance that lets us see thinking and acting as manifestations of natural capacities in a natural world, as deriving their particular nature from the particular interests they serve. It is a stance that preserves a genuine distinctiveness for the kinds of descriptions we deploy in order to depict ourselves as creatures engaged in deliberate pursuit of deliberated ends. This preservation, moreover, does not reduce the essential terms of such descriptions to second-class concepts, nor does it impose on us the cost of placing the denotata of these terms outside the order of nature. Davidson has a naturalistic conception of philosophy, but he does not share Quine's thought that philosophical problems ought to be seen as genuine problems, i.e., solvable problems, only in so far as they are connected to and brought under the purview of natural science. In fact, a determined resistance to this scientistic attitude strikes me as a prominent feature of Davidson's stance. Nevertheless, Davidson's anti-representationalism is informed by Quine's dictum that 'knowledge, mind and meaning are part of the world they are of', and evinces thoughts as states of natural beings, beings of the very sort that evolutionary biologists concern themselves with. One way that this naturalism comes to the surface in Davidson's philosophy is in the form a commitment to the ubiquity of causation. The center in Davidson's philosophical universe is the concept of causation itself ; he is an extensionalist about causality and takes the concept as primitive. The states of mind countenanced by Davidson's theory are all causal states, whatever else they may be, and to that extent on a par with the states of any old thing in the world. What makes states intentional for Davidson is that the causal relations in which they are embedded can be construed as patterns susceptible to descriptions of a particular kind.

Davidson's naturalism culminates in the proposal that we should regard our various modes of description as distinctive ways of characterizing patterns of causal relations, and these distinctive ways themselves—that is to say, our vocabularies—as the artifices of the bio-evolutionary and, eventually, cultural history of natural creatures with aims befitting their natures. This kind of naturalism is very different from Quine's stringent behaviorism, and from the reductive physicalism of Quine's more scientistic prog-

eny. Though as intolerant of ontological dualisms as any, Davidson's naturalism is anti-reductionist, and not happily regarded as a version of physicalism, with its distinctive ontological bias, at all. Causal relations are not
physical, though the vocabulary of physics has as its constitutive interest
the aim of describing the causal structure of the world as a closed system of
laws. The vocabulary of agency also describes causal relations, but in terms
that reveal a different kind of pattern. What I have argued in this paper, is
that the ascent from field linguistics to triangulation makes explicit the
suggestion that the bahavior we describe as communicative interaction is
itself a critical part of that pattern. Without interaction so describable, the
causal pattern that gives thought-attributions their point are simply not
there. This is what makes the Davidsonian account of agency radical, for
this is what drives the conclusion that whatever is worth retaining of our
notion of the subjective is interactively constituted.

If we stick with the field linguist but refuse triangulation, we forego the
Davidsonian account of agency. Willing Skeptics who wish, like Conservative Davidsonians, to preserve a notion of the subjective which accommodates the skeptical hypothesis, are faced with the challenge of convincing us
that they are in possession of something more than 'intuitions'. To be taken
seriously, they must produce an alternative account of the vocabulary that
enables us to describe some creatures as agents, because this is the very
vocabulary that the skeptic helps himself to in order to express the intuitions that support the skeptical hypothesis in the first place.

It seems clear that when we try to adjudicate between accounts at this
level of abstraction, we are led inexorably to considerations of the tasks that
we, at this point, look to a philosophical description of ourselves to perform. I have suggested that Davidson's case against representationalist
thinking is responsive to a certain conception of what naturalism demands.
An assessment of this conception would take us even further into what
some like to label meta-philosophy. At this point in the paper, you will be
relieved to hear, I will content myself with making the point that this is so.

References

Bilgrami, A. 1992. *Belief and Meaning: The Unity and Locality of Mental Content*. Oxford: Blackwell Publishers.

Brueckner, A. 1986a. Brains in Vats. *Journal of Philosophy* 83:148-167.

Brueckner, A. 1986b. Charity and Skepticism. *Pacific Philosophical Quarterly*
67: 264-268.

Craig, E. 1990. Davidson and the Skeptic: The Thumbnail Version. *Analysis*
50:213-4.

Dalmiya, V. 1990. Coherence, Truth, and the 'Omniscient Interpreter'. *Philosophical Quarterly* 40 (158):86-94.

Davidson, D. 1980a. The Second Person. *Midwest Studies in Philosophy: The Wittgenstein Legacy.* Series XVII.

Davidson, D. 1980b. *Essays on Actions and Events.* Oxford: Clarendon Press.

Davidson, D. 1982. Rational Animals. *Dialectica,* 36.

Davidson, D. 1984a. *Inquiries into Truth and Interpretation.* Oxford: Clarendon Press.

Davidson, D. 1984b. First Person Authority. *Dialectica* 38.

Davidson, D. 1986a. Knowing One's Own Mind. APA (Western Div.) Presidential Address. *Proceedings and Addresses of the American Philosophical Association.*

Davidson, D. 1986b. Empirical Content. *Truth and Interpretation,* ed. E. LePore, Oxford: Blackwell Publishers, 320-32.

Davidson, D. 1986c. A Coherence Theory of Truth and Knowledge. . *Truth and Interpretation,* ed. E. LePore, Oxford: Blackwell Publishers, 307-19.

Davidson, D. 1989a. The Myth of the Subjective. In *Relativism: Interpretation and Confrontation,* ed. M. Krauz. University of Notre Dame Press.

Davidson, D. 1989b. What is Present to the Mind? *The Mind of Donald Davidson,* eds. J. Brandl and W. Gombocz. *Grazer Philosophische Studien* 36, Amsterdam: Editions Rodopi,

Davidson, D. 1989c. The Conditions of Thought. *The Mind of Donald Davidson,* eds. J. Brandl and W. Gombocz. *Grazer Philosophische Studien* 36, Amsterdam: Editions Rodopi,

Davidson, D. 1990a. The Structure and Content of Truth. *Journal of Philosophy* 87:279-328.

Davidson, D. 1990b. Meaning, Truth, and Evidence. In *Perspectives on Quine,* eds. R. Barrett and R. Gibson. Oxford: Blackwell, 68-79.

Davidson, D. 1990c. Afterthoughts, 1987 (a postscript to 'A Coherence Theory of Truth and Knowledge'). *Reading Rorty,* ed. A. Malachowski, 134-7. Oxford: Basil Blackwell.

Davidson, D. 1991. Three Varieties of Knowledge. In *A.J. Ayer Memorial Essays,* ed. A. P. Griffiths. Cambridge: Cambridge University Press, 153-66.

Kemp, G. 1992. Davidson, Quine, and our Knowledge of the External World. *Pacific Philosophical Quarterly* 73:44-62.

Klein, P. Radical Interpretation and Global Skepticism, *Truth and Interpretation,* ed. E. LePore, Oxford: Blackwell, 369-86.

Ludwig, K. 1992. Scepticism and Interpretation. *Philosophy and Phenomenological Research* 52:317-39.

McDowell, J. 1994. *Mind and World.* Cambridge, MA: Harvard University Press.

McGinn, C. 1986. Radical Interpretation and Epistemology. . *Truth and Interpretation,* ed. E. LePore, Oxford: Blackwell Publishers, 356-68.

Malachowski, A. 1990. *Reading Rorty.* Oxford: Blackwell Publishers.

Manning, R. 1995. Interpreting Davidson's Omniscient Interpreter. *Canadian Journal of Philosophy* 25:335-74.

Rorty, R. 1972. Indeterminacy of Translation and of Truth. *Synthese* 23:443-62.

Rorty, R. 1991. *Objectivity, Relativism, and Truth.* Cambridge: Cambridge University Press, 1991.

Rorty, R. 1995. Is Truth a Goal of Inquiry? Davidson vs. Wright. *Philosophical Quarterly* 45:281-300.

Vermazen, B. 1983. The Intelligibility of Massive Error. *Philosophical Quarterly* 33:69-74.

Williams, M. 1991. *Unnatural Doubts: Epistemological Realism and the Basis of Scepticism.* Oxford: Blackwell Publishers.

12

Davidson's Measurement Theoretic Reduction of the Mind

PIERS RAWLING

1 Introduction

Donald Davidson has made seminal contributions in many areas of philosophy.[1] I hope to fulfill two goals here. On the one hand, I shall give an
account of Davidson's views on various issues, including his novel account
of the mental. On the other, I shall explore how a central claim in his philosophy of language—the indeterminacy of interpretation—coheres with
others of his views in the philosophy of mind and action. This exploration
reveals, I think, a schism: Davidson cannot hold fast both to his account of
indeterminacy and certain of his other views (such as, for instance, his
justly famous defense of the claim that reasons cause actions).

Davidson poses the transcendental question: what makes interpretation
possible? His answer, which I shall adumbrate in section 2, invokes the

---

[1] I have had much help with the topics treated here from Donald Davidson, Lawrence H.
Davis, John Heil, Siggi Kristinsson, Kirk Ludwig, Bob Maydole, Al Mele, Thad Metz, Greg
Ray and Paul Roth, and from audiences at: the 1996 V. Karlovy Vary Symposium on Analytic
Philosophy: *Interpreting Davidson* (Czech Republic), Davidson College, Keele University
(England), and the University of St. Andrews (Scotland). Of course, those from whom I have
learned do not necessarily agree with me. Financial support was provided by the University
of Missouri Research Board and the University of Missouri-St. Louis.

structural restrictions built into the very nature of the interpretative enterprise. These structural restrictions are, however, insufficient to determine interpretations uniquely. According to Quine, 'translation is found to be involved in a certain systematic indeterminacy' (Quine 1960:ix). For Davidson, this is perhaps better phrased as an indeterminacy of interpretation. In section 3, I address Davidson's attempt to render this indeterminacy benign. His leading idea is that there is an analogy between the way sentences function in the attribution of propositional attitudes, and the way numbers function in measurement theory: the fact that there are different ways of interpreting our fellows is no more alarming than the fact that, say, length, can be represented by different 'schemes of measurement', such as feet and meters. Insofar as I go beyond the Davidsonian corpus, it will be to raise a difficulty that arises if we press this analogy: it follows from the analogy that there are no such states of mind as belief states[2] (even externally construed), nor indeed any states corresponding one-to-one with any of the 'propositional attitudes'. In section 4, I explore some of the ramifications of this result.

Davidson has argued that 'there is no such thing as a language' (Davidson 1986:446), but he does not mean by this that we must abandon speech. Rather, he means to prompt the rejection of a certain linguistic picture. The position that emerges here, whilst largely independent of this latter argument, can be interpreted as sharing with it the aim of shifting a perspective. Davidson has drawn a new map of the mental; my goal here is to give some sense of this map in its entirety, and bring certain of its features to the fore. In the end, however, the extent to which all of these features sit comfortably one with another is, I think, unclear.

2

As Davidson acknowledges, two of his progenitors are Ramsey and Quine. I begin with Ramsey's classic 'Truth and Probability', in which one of his (Ramsey's) main concerns is the notion of degree of belief, and how to measure it on a numerical scale (Ramsey 1931; see also Jeffrey 1983:ch. 3). He sees two possible ways of going about this. We might 'suppose that the degree of a belief is something perceptible by its owner; for instance that beliefs differ in the intensity of a feeling by which they are accompanied, which might be called a belief-feeling or feeling of conviction, and that by

---

[2] Some have worried that Davidson's 'anomalous monism' (see Davidson 1980b:214-25) has 'epiphenomalist tendencies' (see e.g. Kim 1993). My worry is more radical: I claim that Davidson's views on indeterminacy yield the result that there are no propositional attitude states. Davidson attempts to render indeterminacy benign by analogizing the attribution of mental states to standard measurement theory. But, I hope to show, this analogy, ironically, makes vivid the case against propositional attitudes.

the degree of a belief we mean the intensity of this feeling' (Ramsey 1931:169). Ramsey rejects this account: 'it seems to [him] observably false, for the beliefs which we hold most strongly are often accompanied by practically no feeling at all; no one feels strongly about things he takes for granted' (ibid.). His favored account is that 'the degree of a belief is a causal property of it, which we can express vaguely as the extent to which we are prepared to act on it' (ibid.). This he cashes out in terms of preferences amongst gambles. There are, however, two determinants of such preferences: in addition to the degrees of belief in the propositions on which the outcomes of the gambles hinge, the degree to which those outcomes are desired is clearly also crucial. Here Ramsey invokes his ingenious technique (independently rediscovered by Davidson) for getting both utilities and degrees of belief from information merely about preferences amongst gambles.

Ramsey's method, roughly speaking, begins as follows. Call a possible event, E, 'ethically neutral' (Ramsey 1931:177) for an agent if, for all outcomes α, the agent is indifferent between [α & E] and [α & $\neg$E]. We must find an ethically neutral possible event E and two outcomes, α and β, such that our agent, Anne, is indifferent between the two gambles:

G α if E; β if $\neg$E

H β if E; α if $\neg$E

yet strictly prefers α to β. Now we suppose that if any other outcomes (compatible with both E and $\neg$E) are substituted for α and β in G and H, Anne is indifferent between the resulting gambles; and we define Anne's degree of belief (p) in E to be one half. This comports with the notion of expected utility (EU). We have:

$$EU(G) = utility(\alpha)p(E) + utility(\beta)p(\neg E)$$

$$EU(H) = utility(\beta)p(E) + utility(\alpha)p(\neg E)$$

Since $p(\neg E) = 1-p(E)$, and utility(α) $\neq$ utility(β), equating EU(H) and EU(G) entails that $p(E) = 1/2$.

From here, Ramsey goes on to show how to measure utilities and degrees of belief generally—on the proviso that the agent's preferences satisfy certain axioms. Ramsey proves a representation theorem: if an agent satisfies these axioms, then, given any proposition p, we can attribute to her a unique numerical degree of belief in p (and measure it); and her degrees of belief across the multiplicity of propositions are coherent (i.e., obey Kolmogorov's axioms (see de Finetti 1972:67-9. Axiom VI can be ignored for present purposes)). The numerical measure of (expected) utility represents the agent's preference ranking on an interval scale.

For present purposes, the following of Ramsey's insights are key. We have the notion that degrees of belief necessarily fit a rational pattern—we need not insist that they be perfectly coherent in order for her to qualify as having degrees of belief, but a degree of coherence is surely required lest we be tracking the wrong feature of the agent. Furthermore, this rational pattern ensures that degrees of belief are accessible from without: we can determine them from observable behavior—they cannot transcend the actual and potential behavioral evidence. And we see the possibility of rejecting their introspectibility. These insights provide a window on Davidson's account of the mind: he applies them to mental states across the board.

Davidson poses a transcendental question: what makes interpretation possible? Ramsey, in his account of how we might access another's degrees of belief, invokes structural rationality constraints built into the very notions of preference and degree of belief. Davidson, in his account of how we might access another's mind more generally, invokes structural restrictions built into the very nature of mental states, which in turn constitute restrictions upon what is to count as interpretation. The restrictions on mental states are what make interpretation possible, but they are famously claimed to be insufficient to determine interpretations uniquely—and being the only restrictions, they leave interpretation to a certain extent indeterminate.

Davidson focuses primarily on the propositional attitudes. (He says little about pains, for example.) But amongst the propositional attitudes he includes the attitude of 'meaning that'. (Davidson (1986) speaks of the 'first meaning' of an utterance: it is first meaning to which 'means that' here corresponds.) Admittedly, this attitude has an added component in the form of utterances: an agent means that *p* by uttering S. However, the interdependence of meaning with the other attitudes suffices for its classification with them.

But what of Davidson's project of employing a theory of truth as a theory of meaning: why does Davidson countenance an attitude of 'meaning that' when he is apparently trying to do away with meaning? The answer lies in noting that Davidson is not an eliminativist about meaning when it is construed qua propositional attitude. In applying Tarski's work on truth, Davidson's goal is to replace schemata of the form:

S means in L that p

where 'S' is to be replaced by the name of a sentence of L, and 'that p' is to be replaced by the name of a proposition, with schemata of the form:

S is true in L if and only if p

where 'p' is now to be replaced by a sentence of English. Should the project prove successful, we shall have learned much about meaning and truth. And we shall have a way of recursively stating a theory of meaning for a language, thus satisfying, in principle, a crucial condition for the possibility of interpretation: that interpretations be graspable by finite minds. But in seeing how meaning rests upon truth, we shall not have eliminated the former notion. Just as Tarski explicitly invokes a prior understanding of the concept of truth in formulating his criterion of 'material adequacy' (Tarski 1943-44) for his definition of truth in a language (the prior understanding enables us to see the correctness of this criterion), so Davidson presupposes a prior understanding of 'means that' in his attempt to use a theory of truth as a theory of meaning.

The success of the latter project is to be measured in terms of the degree of conformity between the output of the theory of truth concerning the sentences in its domain, and our understanding of what the relevant speakers mean by those sentences. The presupposed understanding of 'means that' emerges clearly in the following well-worn problem case:

'Es regnet' is true in German if and only if: it is raining and 2+2=4

Yet 'Es regnet' does not mean in German that it is raining and 2+2=4. From the perspective of a theory of meaning, we might say that the equivalence has arisen via a 'deviant' derivation within the truth theory. If a theory of truth is to serve as a theory of meaning, we have to ensure that:

S is true in L if and only if p

holds because, and only because, S means in L that p. We can, perhaps, ensure this by placing restrictions on permissible derivations within the truth theory. The details of such restrictions are not my concern here. Rather, I merely want to emphasize that their selection is driven by our prior understanding of 'meaning that'.

With meaning in place, it is time to position Davidson with respect to Quine. Central to my theme is Quine's opening to *Word and Object*:

Language is a social art. In acquiring it we have to depend entirely on intersubjectively available cues as to what to say and when. Hence there is no justification for collating linguistic meanings, unless in terms of men's dispositions to respond overtly to socially observable stimulations. An effect of recognizing this limitation is that the enterprise of translation is found to be involved in a certain systematic indeterminacy (Quine 1960:ix).

Davidson, with a pair of provisos, agrees. The first proviso is that Davidson takes a distal view of stimulation, in contrast to Quine's proximal view. (Davidson's distal view makes him an externalist when it comes to propositional attitude attribution.) The second proviso is addressed in section 2 below: Davidson puts a new spin on indeterminacy by drawing an analogy with measurement theory. Davidson agrees with Quine on two crucial counts: first, there can be nothing more to meaning (and the propositional attitudes more generally) than what can be gleaned from observation (propositional attitudes are evidence dependent in this sense); and second, observation will never determine these attitudes uniquely.

What makes interpretation possible, according to Davidson, 'is the structure the normative character of thought, desire, speech, and action imposes on correct attributions of attitudes to others, and hence on interpretations of their speech and explanations of their actions' (Davidson 1990a:325). Davidson's purpose is to show how it is possible to attribute meanings and other propositional attitudes when observable behavior is our only evidence (and is, furthermore, constitutive evidence). He gives us a sketch of how an idealized interpretation might proceed. Neither the procedure nor the implicit procedural sequence in the sketch is, however, to be taken literally. The sequence in which interpreters gather evidence and formulate hypotheses is a matter of skill and serendipity, and interpreters do not, for example, assign precise degrees of belief and utilities to the interpretee's sentences. Rather, the function of the sketch is to illustrate the structural restrictions on interpretation: interpretation is possible because the interpreter is forced to interpret the behavior of interpretees as conforming to patterns dictated by the 'principle of charity'—i.e., it is constitutive of the propositional attitudes that they be largely rational, where rationality encompasses, amongst others, norms of evidence, preference, desirability, and action (the term was coined by Wilson (1959)). This is not to say that there is no room for irrationality; but it cannot be too pervasive.

Interpretation begins with observable behavior, where this is restricted to bodily movements, non-intentionally described, and their attendant circumstances. Various hypotheses are then mooted—concerning such matters as which behaviors are actions, which of those are utterances of sentences, and what certain of the agent's attitudes toward those sentences are. Two key sentential attitudes for Davidson are those of holding true a sentence, and preferring one sentence true above another. But even access to these attitudes does not eliminate indeterminacy.

Suppose we have worked out that an agent holds true one of her sentences, S, under certain circumstances, but holds it false under others. How are we to work out what she means by it? We confront the following difficulty: her holding S true is dependent both upon what she means by it, and upon what she believes the circumstances to be. Meaning and belief must be accessed simultaneously. As Davidson notes, there is a striking parallel here to Ramsey's problem of moving from preference to both utilities and degrees of belief (see, e.g., Davidson 1990a:318-19). In general, the problem is even more challenging: in interpreting patterns of bodily movement, we must invoke a host of propositional attitudes. Within the bounds of the constraints imposed by charity, there are arbitrarily many ways of attributing the attitudes so as to explain bodily movements. And indeterminacy would remain even if, *per impossible*, we could determine the totality of an agent's behavioral dispositions. As Quine puts it for the case of vocalization: 'translation [is] indeterminate in principle relative to the totality of speech dispositions' (Quine 1960:221).

Decision theory is a crucial part of the normative structure imposed by interpretation. Davidson (1985) employs a modification of Jeffrey's *Logic of Decision* to impose normative constraints (such as, e.g., transitivity) on preferences for the truth of (initially uninterpreted) sentences. Jeffrey employs a uniform ontology of propositions, and sees preference as a matter of preferring some propositions true above others. It can be proven (the proof of the representation theorem is due to Bolker 1967; cf. Jeffrey 1983) that, provided an agent's preferences over propositions meet certain qualitative conditions (such as transitivity), there are (for a given scale) two mappings of the set of propositions to the real numbers: one yielding degrees of belief, the other yielding conditional expectations of utility. The degrees of belief are coherent and the conditional expectations of utility represent preference.

Davidson modifies Jeffrey's ontology to quantify over (initially) uninterpreted sentences of a language, rather than propositions, because access to the propositions that sentences express (insofar as they do) is, of course, a goal, not a starting point, of interpretation.[3] Davidson supposes that we have formulated hypotheses as to the agent's preferences across uninterpreted sentences, and that we have identified a sentential connective with certain properties as a truth-functional connective. He then shows that, provided the agent's preferences conform to the Bolker–Jeffrey preference axioms as applied to sentences, the agent's sentential connectives are structurally fixed relative to our hypotheses concerning the agent's sentential preferences (Davidson 1985, and Davidson 1990a:326-28).

Given that the agent's preferences for the truth of her sentences conform (roughly) to the Bolker-Jeffrey axioms, the representation theorem ensures that (to a rough extent) the sentences carry coherent degrees of belief and (conditional expected) utilities. Hence we have part of the initial infrastructure upon which to build a complete interpretation. (Notice that if we have access to degrees of belief, it seems we can determine which sentences the agent holds true—those which are assigned degree of belief one. But perhaps holding true should be taken less strictly: degree of belief one is 'infinitely stringent' in the sense that if $p(A)=1$, the ratio $p(A)/p(\neg A)$ is infinite.)

To say that interpretation must follow the dictates of the principle of charity is to say, amongst other things, that interpretation must make out the interpretee as rational. Decision theory and traditional logic give, in combination, an account of what it is to be rational in the 'thin' sense of

---

[3] There are technical difficulties here that Davidson does not go into—for example, Bolker's representation theorem requires that the domain of preference be a complete atomless Boolean algebra. I shall ignore such difficulties for present purposes.

being coherent and consistent in one's preferences and beliefs. A more mundane illustration of charity is furnished by the interactions between quantifiers and sentential connectives. For example, the existential quantifier has a very different relation with disjunction than does the universal ('someone's a prince or a pauper' is equivalent to 'someone's a prince or someone's a pauper;' 'everyone's a prince or a pauper' is not equivalent to 'everyone's a prince or everyone's a pauper'). These relations between quantifier and connective place constraints on interpretation. But no sequence of interpretative discovery is thereby dictated. Interpretation is a matter of formulating, testing, and revising hypotheses in light of the behavioral evidence. What makes it possible is the normative structure imposed by the principle of charity.

Charity goes beyond mere requirements of consistency and coherence—for example, 'it cannot happen', according to Davidson, 'that most of our plainest beliefs about what exists in the world are false' (Davidson 1990b). The strictures of charity notwithstanding, however, complete interpretations are far from unique: even in the face of all the relevant evidence (were we able to acquire it) the principle of charity leaves many interpretations open: '... the evidence on which all these matters depend gives us no way of separating out the contributions of thought, action, desire, and meaning one by one. Total theories are what we must construct, and many theories will do equally well' (Davidson 1984d:241).

Interpretation is only possible if the attitudes we attribute are publicly available; yet all we wear on our sleeves, as it were, is our behavior, nonintentionally described. From this behavior, the interpreter constructs a theory—and, on pain of violating publicity, any construction that saves the behavioral phenomena and satisfies charity is as good as any other. Hence, given the view that there can be nothing more to the propositional attitudes than the phenomena provide, myriad interpretations must be true of any agent. It is in making sense of this 'myriad interpretations' picture that Davidson employs measurement theory analogically.

3

Davidson attempts to render this indeterminacy benign by invoking an analogy between the way sentences function in the attribution of propositional attitudes, and the way numbers function in measurement theory: the fact that there are different ways of interpreting our fellows is no more alarming than the fact that, say, length can be represented by different 'schemes of measurement' such as feet and meters. If we press this analogy, however, it emerges that the indeterminacy is more alarming than Davidson concedes: on his view it transpires that there are no such states of mind as belief states (even externally construed), nor indeed any states corresponding one-to-one with any of the propositional attitudes.

The notion of a representation theorem was introduced above. Here is a simple case. Consider the measurement of length. The notion 'is at least as long as' conforms to certain qualitative criteria, such as transitivity and connectedness—any concept that fails to conform to these criteria is not the concept of length (see e.g. Davidson 1980b). If certain structural conditions are added to the essential qualitative criteria, then the relevant representation theorem can be proven: there is a mapping of the entities to be measured (the possessors of 'lengths') to the non-negative reals that represents the relation 'is at least as long as.' And, since in the case of length there is a natural zero, we have a ratio scale: the mapping is unique up to multiplication by a positive real. Note the ingredients: we have the entities to be measured, a qualitative relation on those entities, and a mapping (unique up to some transformation) from the entities to the measuring domain (the non-negative reals in the case of length) that preserves relevant structure (so that, in the case of length, the longer the object, the greater the associated real).

The basic idea of Davidson's analogical strategy is clear enough (see e.g. Davidson 1989). We use sentences to track the propositional attitudes of an agent; we use the reals to track the lengths of objects. The sentences in the former attribution play the role of the real numbers in the latter. We might maintain that there is an 'indeterminacy of length': there are infinitely many serviceable schemes for attributing lengths. Similarly, there are various (Davidson (1984d) would argue infinitely many) serviceable schemes for attributing meanings and the other attitudes to a given interpretee. And the latter indeterminacy is as benign as the former. But the details of the analogy need spelling out.

Davidson does not deny that there are many disanalogies between the two cases. There is, for example, an algorithm for moving from one scale of length measurement to another (multiply by the relevant positive constant); there is no such algorithm in the case of interpretations. However, we do need at least the following. In the measurement theoretic case, we map to numbers from an underlying framework that is invariant between scales. Thus, in the case of using sentences to attribute attitudes, we need to identify an underlying framework that is invariant across the various schemes of interpretation. The invariant framework must consist of relata and relations between them. In the case of the measurement of length, we have physical objects standing in the relation 'is at least as long as'. Infinitely many different mappings of the objects to the reals will serve to track the relation, but the objects and the relation do not vary across the mappings.

In the case of attitude attributions, I shall concern myself only with the relevant relata. It might initially appear that the relata are the propositional attitudes of the interpretee. However, this cannot be. The relata cannot comprise the propositional attitudes themselves, since we identify propositional attitudes by the sentences we use to track them. And it is precisely the assignment of these sentences that varies between schemes of interpretation. On Davidson's picture, indeterminacy is simply the fact that we can use different locutions to locate the same node in some pattern. But what are the invariant nodes? They cannot be propositional attitudes: the belief that p, say, under one scheme, will be the belief that q under another—two different propositional attitudes (both attributions are couched in the one idiolect of the interpreter).

One might respond here by wondering whether there is not some 'neutral' way of identifying propositional attitudes—so that, despite appearances to the contrary, the belief that p and the belief that q are in fact the same belief. This notion, however, runs counter to the Davidsonian picture. For example, propositional attitudes in one scheme need not map one to one onto propositional attitudes in another. Consider the following possibility: on one interpretation, a piece of behavior, B, is interpreted as a signal; on another interpretation (that also saves all the relevant phenomena), B is interpreted as a simple scratch.[4] Thus, on the first interpretation, B is explained by a complex of propositional attitude states that is simply larger than that invoked in the second.

There are alternative approaches to the application of measurement theory to the propositional attitudes. Matthews' account is a case in point (Matthews 1994). In the case of length, as we have seen, the 'empirical relational system' to be represented comprises objects and the qualitative relation: 'is at least as long as.' And the 'representation space' (the space that is to represent the empirical relational system, to which that empirical system is mapped) comprises the real number system. In the case of propositional attitudes Matthews supposes that there is a substrate of propositional attitudes to be 'measured' (these are the invariant relata), although he (sensibly) leaves open the issue of exactly which relations among the attitudes are to be represented. (He rightly notes that care must be taken in 'reading back' relations that hold between entities in the representation space into the empirical system being measured: consider the use of the reals to measure temperature on the Celsius and Fahrenheit scales where ratios have no empirical relevance.) He argues that the appropriate representation space for representing the propositional attitudes comprises a set of 'ordered pairs $<a_i,<s_j,r_k>>$, consisting [of] an attitude-type a_i and what [he calls] a designated proposition $<s_j,r_k>$, where r_k is a Russellian proposition and s_j a sentence-type, a token of which in a particular (unspecified) context serves to designate (express) that Russellian proposition' (Matthews 1994:136).

---

[4] This example is similar to one suggested to me by Kirk Ludwig.

What is it for there to be two different scales of propositional attitude measurement on Matthews' account (comparable to the imperial and metric scales of length measurement)? Matthews furnishes an example of a variety familiar from discussions of *de re* and *de dicto* attributions:

> Suppose that Smith describes the man that he knows only by the name 'Tully' as being destitute by saying, 'Tully is destitute'. I might explain Smith's remark to someone who knows Tully only as 'Cicero' by saying, 'Smith believes that the wealthy Cicero is destitute', thereby conveying not simply that Smith is mistaken in his belief, but also who his belief is about, namely, the man that my interlocutor knows only as 'Cicero'. In the context, the representations associated with sentence types *Tully is destitute* and *the wealthy Cicero is destitute*, both of which share the same attitude-type and Russellian proposition, represent one and the same belief. In a different explanatory context, e.g., one in which Smith's actual words were important, these same representations might represent different beliefs (Matthews 1994:143).

As Matthews correctly notes, the context dependence here marks a difference between his account of propositional attitude 'measurement' and the measurement of length. Nevertheless, suppose we concede that in the first explanatory context in the cited passage we have one belief mapped to two different elements of the representation space. This is the analogue of an object being mapped to two different reals in measurement of its length. In the latter case, we have two different scales (feet and meters, say) at work; so perhaps this is so in the former (with propositional attitudes being the measured entities that are invariant across the scales).

Matthews picture is in marked contrast to my construal of Davidson's account, however. Suppose Davidson were to interpret Matthews as ascribing one and the same belief to Smith with his (Matthews') utterances of 'Smith believes that the wealthy Cicero is destitute', and 'Smith believes that Tully is destitute'. That would be because, in saving the relevant phenomena in his interpretation of Matthews, Davidson had to interpret these two utterances as attributions by Matthews to Smith of only one belief. Thus Matthews is not proposing two distinct interpretations of Smith. On this Davidsonian account, then, we do not have an analogue of two different scales of measurement.

What, then, are the invariants across interpretations on Davidson's account? As we have seen, Quine has us tracking 'men's dispositions to respond overtly to socially observable stimulations' (Quine 1960:ix). And according to Davidson, ' ... a satisfactory theory is one that yields an acceptable explanation of verbal behaviour and dispositions' (Davidson 1984d:237). Behavioral dispositions are key; and they are apparently the invariant nodes across different schemes of interpretation—they are what propositional attitude attributions 'measure'. Just as we attribute numbers in the form of lengths to track the relation 'is at least as long as,' and numbers in the form of degrees of belief and expected utilities to track preference, so we attribute propositional attitudes to track behavioral dispositions.

The invariants, then, have the following form: a disposition to B under circumstance C, where B is a bodily movement non-intentionally described, and C is specified without reference to propositional attitudes of the agent. A full interpretation of an agent—something unattainable by mere mortals—would account for the totality of the agent's behavioral dispositions. And all adequate interpretations must agree on these dispositions; but that is all they must agree on. Propositional attitude states are mere posits; they vary from interpretation to interpretation. That we cannot re-identify a belief across interpretative schemes is a consequence of the fact that there is no such state to re-identify.[5]

An instrumentalist in the philosophy of science holds something akin to the following. The constraints on a theory are that it save the phenomena, and that it meet some criteria of coherence and simplicity (and elegance, perhaps). Theories will (usually) posit entities that underlie the appearances; but, according to the instrumentalist, these are only posits—constructions designed to save the phenomena. If two theories were to save the phenomena, score equally well in other respects, but disagree as to posits, the instrumentalist would have no difficulty in countenancing both: the posits, being merely that, would not compete.

Davidson's view of the mind, then, appears to be instrumentalist. The relevant criteria of coherence are provided by the principle of charity; the posits comprise, amongst other things, propositional attitudes. About some of the other posits Davidson is quite explicit: 'words, meanings of words, reference, and satisfaction are posits we need to implement a theory of truth. They serve this purpose without needing independent confirmation or empirical basis ... [Satisfaction and reference are] notions we must treat as theoretical constructs whose function is exhausted in stating the truth conditions for sentences' (Davidson 1980c:222-3). And: 'degree of belief is a construction based on more elementary attitudes' (Davidson 1990a:322). When it comes to the propositional attitudes he seems, however, more wary.

Davidson does say:

---

[5] I note in passing that this argument to the effect that propositional attitude states are mere posits is independent, in large part, of Davidson's argument that 'there is no such thing as a language' (Davidson 1986:446). That argument is concerned with the vagaries of usage that prompt revisions in an ongoing single sequence of interpretations. One way of differentiating the current claim is to note that it is concerned, rather, with the notion that there will be myriad distinct, but equally good, ways of accommodating any single vagary; hence there will be myriad distinct ongoing sequences of interpretations.

> In thinking and talking of the weights of physical objects we do not
> need to suppose there are such things as weights for objects to have.
> Similarly in thinking and talking about the beliefs of people we
> needn't suppose there are such entities as beliefs (Davidson 1989).

But in the same paper, he speaks of beliefs as mental states with identity
conditions. However, if there is genuine indeterminacy, then even if the use
of sentences to track propositional attitudes is analogous to the use of numbers to track weights or lengths, there will in general be no trans-scheme
identity of propositional attitudes, and hence no propositional attitudes.
Drawing an analogy with measurement theory fails to render indeterminacy
anodyne. On the contrary, it makes even plainer a consequence of combining the claim that interpretation is indeterminate with the view that the interpretee's propositional attitudes cannot transcend the interpreter's evidence: this pair of tenets alone is sufficient to imply that there are no propositional attitude states. Analogy or not, trans-scheme identity of propositional attitudes fails, and the propositional attitudes are lost.

Before turning to the ramifications of this consequence, it should be
noted that Davidson's holism is not the issue here: holism is quite consistent with the existence of propositional attitude states, complaints to the
contrary notwithstanding. Holism is the view that propositional attitudes
must be attributed in interdependent blocs. And various authors worry that,
for example, if all attitudes are interdependent, then an agent cannot move
from believing that *p* to believing that *not p*, because interdependence entails that the proposition that *p* can be no part of the content of the new
belief. I cannot, for example, move from believing that today is Tuesday to
believing that today is Wednesday, because my concept of 'today' will not
remain invariant across the two beliefs.

This, however, is to misconstrue the nature of the interdependence (I am
not the first person to note this: Priest (1981:78), for example, makes the
point). There are dependences in which changes in one factor can leave other
factors stable. Consider Ohm's law: voltage (in certain ideal circuits, at
least) is the product of resistance and current (V=RI). Here we have three
mutually interdependent quantities, and certainly a change in one of them
must result in a change in *one* of the others; but the third can remain fixed
(e.g., by increasing the voltage in a circuit of fixed resistance, we increase
the current). In the case of the contents of propositional attitudes and utterances, of course, we have a vast number of variables—but the same point
applies: changes cause disruptions, but their scope will typically affect only
a very small portion of the web of propositional attitudes and meanings.
And I can share part of your web without sharing all of it (we can have two
circuits at three volts, with differing currents and resistances). The number
of connections can be as large as you like; it is the nature of the dependence
that is crucial. Holism per se, then, is no threat to the propositional atti-

tudes. Their demise is a consequence of indeterminacy and evidence dependence.

4

What are the ramifications of the demise of the propositional attitudes? Davidson (1989) emphasizes the anti-Cartesian aspect of his view. In the *Meditations*, we find a view of the mental on which it makes sense to ask whether 'the ideas which are in me are similar ... to the things which are outside me' (Descartes 1955: vol. I:160). Although Descartes rejects the view that our 'ideas' are similar to their causes, it is common to attribute to him a view on which the mind contains ideas that somehow correspond to external objects.[6] There are many well-known and varied objections to this sort of picture. On Davidson's novel alternative, such Cartesian 'ideas' are simply rejected—and this is consistent with the present reading of Davidson, which has him advocating a measurement theoretic reduction of the propositional attitudes to mere posits. (Note that Davidson only culls the Cartesian population: there remain pains and their like—these are not mere posits.)

Furthermore, on Davidson's account perhaps we can maintain our ordinary ways of talking about our fellows. Indeed, at the very heart of his account lies the notion that the so-called 'folk psychological' locutions track the dispositions of our neighbors—instrumentalism and realism agree that the phenomena must be saved. Besides dispositions to behave, there are, however, other features of the mental to be saved here.

There is a catalogue of difficulties with a view that abandons propositional attitudes, most of which I shall not detail. For example, epistemology (and much else, of course) is apparently undercut, since there is no such state as knowing that p.[7] Also, in his monistic metaphysics, Davidson quantifies over mental events. Davidson's 'anomalous monism' is the view that all mental events are also physical, but the mental and the physical are linked by no strict laws (Davidson 1980b:214-25). Coming to have a certain propositional attitude is an event on this view, but if there are no propositional attitudes there are no such events. There is no occupant for the mental side of the monistic equation.

---

[6] He says the following in the *Meditations*:

> ... although in approaching fire I feel heat, and in approaching it a little too near I even feel pain, there is at the same time no reason in this which could persuade me that there is in the fire something resembling this heat any more than there is in it something resembling the pain; all that I have any reason to believe from this is, that there is something in it, whatever it may be, which excites in me these sensations of heat or of pain. (*Meditations on First Philosophy*, vol. I:193-4).

[7] My thanks to Eve Garrard for this point.

Thirdly, propositional attitudes are also intrinsic to Davidson's causal account of action. Davidson famously argues that propositional attitude states of the agent cause actions (Davidson 1980a). And he challenges those who would deny this to furnish an account of the distinction between merely rationalizing reasons for a particular act, and those rationalizing reasons for which the agent acted. A politician presses for environmental legislation. She believes that pressing the legislation will garner votes in the impending election. She also abhors the destruction of the environment. She claims that she acted only for the latter reason. On Davidson's account, her claim is tantamount to claiming that the latter, but not the former, propositional attitude was part of the cause of her pressing of the legislation. What becomes of Davidson's account if there are no propositional attitude states? Of course, there are still behavioral dispositions, but these dispositions can do no rationalizing—they have no propositional content (and there is the standard worry that dispositions can perhaps do no explanatory work). Furthermore, if actions are bodily movements caused by propositional attitude states then, absent the latter, there no actions.[8]

Realists standardly ask of instrumentalists, concerning a predictively successful theory: if the theory's constructions are fictional, how do we explain its predictive success? In the case of an instrumentalist account of decision theory, the question can be answered: degrees of belief and expected utilities are merely 'measuring' preference, and preferences are real enough. Similarly, instrumentalism concerning the propositional attitudes might be defended by noting that we attribute propositional attitudes to track 'real' behavioral dispositions. However, there are strong arguments for realism, one of which is the fruitfulness of the essays collected in Davidson's *Essays on Actions and Events*.

Some aspect of Davidson's view has to give way. I shall argue that we should not abandon our attitudes.

The conclusion that there are no propositional attitudes results from the combination of indeterminacy and evidence dependence with respect to them. But, concerning the latter, recall Davidson's remark that, when it comes to interpretation, ' ... a satisfactory theory is one that yields an acceptable explanation of verbal behaviour and dispositions' (Davidson 1984d:237). With this remark he seems already to have endorsed evidence transcendence: dispositions can be present without ever being made manifest. Why suppose that propositional attitudes are any different? Why insist that propositional attitudes be evidence dependent, when evidence transcendent dispositions are countenanced?

---

[8] For Davidson's defense of the view that actions are bodily movements caused (in nondeviant fashion) by propositional attitude states, see Davidson 1980a (I ignore here the distinction between states and events). Akeel Bilgrami makes, in a different context, the point that there are no actions in the absence of propositional attitude states.

There appear to be two notions of evidence transcendence at work. Davidson is willing to countenance 'potential' evidence; so although dispositions are evidence transcendent in the sense that they can be present without ever being made manifest, perhaps there must be potentially available evidence for their presence (Davidson 1984d:230). However, this line continues, the indeterminacy of propositional attitude attribution outruns even the totality of potential evidence. (Recall Quine: 'translation [is] indeterminate in principle relative to the totality of speech dispositions' (Quine 1960:221).) What distinguishes propositional attitude attribution from disposition attribution, then, is that, unlike the latter, the former outruns all potential evidence—hence the non-existence of propositional attitude states.

However, such a line will lead to a form of anti-realism with respect to many dispositions. Many current dispositions will evaporate without ever being made manifest or even leaving a trace for future generations. They are currently real because they do not now outrun all potential evidence. Yet their claim to have existed will eventually outrun all potential evidence, and thereby come to languish in the no-man's-land between truth and falsity. To reject this anti-realist line is to acknowledge the truth and falsity of dispositional claims that outrun even all potential evidence. And then there would seem to be no barrier to the ontological admission of the attitudes. Davidson countenances behavioral dispositions, thus he should do the same for propositional attitudes, and see indeterminacy as simple underdetermination of theory by observation.

We have arrived at realism concerning the propositional attitudes by dropping evidence dependence, which has the result of altering the significance of indeterminacy: given evidence transcendence, indeterminacy is simply underdetermination. However, another way to save the attitudes would be to establish that there is no indeterminacy—this would render evidence dependence harmless. I think it is clear that there is indeterminacy; but what is its extent? I shall not address this general question here. Rather, I shall confine myself to one of Davidson's arguments to indeterminacy.

One major apparent source of indeterminacy is the inscrutability of reference: if matters are as Davidson portrays them, inscrutability generates an infinitude of empirically equivalent interpretations, since there are infinitely many permutations of the universe. [9] However, these interpretations are all equally satisfactory only if all that counts is the preservation of the truth conditions of the interpretee's sentences. Consider one of Davidson's examples. He supposes we have two interpretations of an utterance of 'Wilt is tall'; on theory one, it is interpreted as meaning that Wilt is tall; on theory two, it is interpreted as meaning that the shadow of Wilt is the shadow of a

---

[9] See Davidson 1984d. My discussion focuses upon 229-30. Kirk Ludwig prompted me to take a closer look at inscrutability. I suspect that what follows is a version of his worry about it.

tall thing. According to Davidson, theory one is satisfactory if and only if theory two is satisfactory, since Wilt is tall if and only if the shadow of Wilt is the shadow of a tall thing. But this is tantamount to letting derivations run rampant within theories of truth that are supposedly serving as theories of meaning. In section 2, it was noted that, in the absence of derivational restraint, our theory of meaning for German might yield the unfortunate conclusion: 'Es regnet' means that it is raining and 2+2=4. The truth conditions for 'Es regnet' and 'it is raining and 2+2=4' are the same. Thus, if truth conditions were all that mattered to meaning, our conclusion would not be unfortunate after all—and neither would the conclusion: 'Wilt is tall' in English means that the shadow of Wilt is the shadow of a tall thing.

Inscrutability of reference is only a source of indeterminacy of meaning if meaning is a matter only of truth conditions. But then, why bother with derivational restraint within the truth theory? Evidence transcendence is implicated here. On the one hand, it is supposed that we can obtain evidence only about truth conditions, and hence, absent evidence transcendence, there can be no more to meaning than truth conditions. And then we can let derivations within the truth theory run rampant. But on the other hand, a prior understanding of 'meaning that' is invoked in order to place derivational constraints on the truth theory.

A partial resolution here might emerge from considering whether it is possible to obtain evidence that distinguishes between theories of truth, which, though equivalent qua theories of *truth*, are not equivalent qua theories of *meaning*. If, for example, we admit the relevant pointing behavior as evidence that 'Wilt' refers to Wilt, then only, '"Wilt is tall' is true if and only if Wilt is tall,' will serve as a meaning clause in the theory of truth that provides us our theory of meaning, even though it remains the case that: 'Wilt is tall' is true if and only if the shadow of Wilt is the shadow of a tall thing. Such evidential considerations might decrease markedly the putative indeterminacy of meaning, whilst in no way compromising the use of theories of truth (with derivational constraints) as theories of meaning.

Indeterminacy can, however, never be eliminated. In some cases the evidence might take us further than Davidson supposes, but in others perhaps the propositional attitudes outrun even all potential evidence. I began with Ramsey's two-for-one deal: two theoretical constructs (degrees of belief and utilities) for one piece of behavioral evidence (preferences amongst gambles). The interpretative task is Ramsey's writ large: a host of theoretical constructions to save all the behavioral evidence. We have seen that, Davidson's measurement theoretic analogy notwithstanding, if we are to be realists about these constructions, we must acknowledge that they are evidence transcendent.

References

Bolker, E. A. 1967. Simultaneous Axiomatization of Utility and Subjective Probability. *Philosophy of Science* 34:333-40.

Brandl, J. and W. Gombocz, eds. 1989. *The Mind of Donald Davidson*. Editions Rodopi (*Grazer Philosophische Studien Band 36*).

Davidson, D. 1980a. *Essays on Actions and Events*. Oxford: Clarendon Press.

Davidson, D. 1980b. Mental Events. *Essays on Actions and Events*, 207-25. Oxford: Clarendon Press.

Davidson, D. 1984a. *Inquiries into Truth and Interpretation*. Oxford: Clarendon Press.

Davidson, D. 1984b. On the Very Idea of a Conceptual Scheme. *Inquiries into Truth and Interpretation*, 183-198. Oxford: Clarendon Press.

Davidson, D. 1984c. Reality Without Reference. *Inquiries into Truth and Interpretation*, 215-25. Oxford: Clarendon Press.

Davidson, D. 1984d. The Inscrutability of Reference. *Inquiries into Truth and Interpretation*, 227-41. Oxford: Clarendon Press.

Davidson, D. 1985. A New Basis For Decision Theory. *Theory and Decision* 18:87-98.

Davidson, D. 1986. A Nice Derangement of Epitaphs. *Truth and Interpretation. Perspectives on the Philosophy of Donald Davidson*, ed E. Lepore, 433-446. Oxford: Basil Blackwell. Also in *Philosophical Grounds of Rationality*, eds. Grandy and Warner, 156-74. Oxford: Oxford University Press.

Davidson, D. 1989. What is Present to the Mind? *The Mind of Donald Davidson*, eds. Brandl and Gombocz; *Grazer Philosophische Studien* 36:3-18.

Davidson, D. 1990a. The Structure and Content of Truth. *Journal of Philosophy* 87(6):279-328.

Davidson, D. 1990b. Epistemology Externalized. *Dialectica* 45:191-202. Also in *Análisis Filosófico* 10. (In Spanish; E. Rabossi, trans.)

de Finetti, B. 1972. *Probability, Induction and Statistics: The Art of Guessing*. London: John Wiley & Sons.

Descartes, R. *Meditations on First Philosophy*. Vol. I. *The Philosophical Works of Descartes*. Haldane and Ross, trans. New York: Dover.

Jeffrey, R. 1983. *The Logic of Decision*. 2nd ed. Chicago, Ill: University of Chicago Press.

Kim, J. 1993. Can Supervenience and 'Non-Strict Laws' Save Anomalous Monism? *Mental Causation*, eds. J. Heil and A. Mele, 19-26. Oxford: Clarendon Press.

Matthews, R. J. The Measure of Mind. *Mind* 103:131-46.

Priest, G. 1981. Review of D. Papineau's *Theory and Meaning*. *The Philosophical Quarterly* 31:77-9.

Quine, W. V. O. 1960. *Word and Object.* Cambridge, Massachusetts: MIT Press.

Ramsey, F. P. 1931. Truth and Probability. *The Foundations of Mathematics and other Logical Essays*, ed R. B. Braithwaite, 156-98. London: Routledge and Kegan Paul.

Tarski, A. 1943-44. The Semantic Conception of Truth and the Foundations of Semantics. *Philosophy and Phenomenological Research* IV:341-76.

Wilson, N. 1959. Substances Without Substrata. *Review of Metaphysics* XII:521-39.

13

The Vacant Mind

FREDRIK STJERNBERG

1 Introduction

The title of this paper refers to the way in which Davidson proposes that we should handle the possible conflict between externalism and first person authority. If externalism means that the contents of our beliefs in part are determined by factors external to the subject, and first person authority means that we normally know what we mean and believe, it seems that a conflict could arise: how can I be presumed to know what I believe, if what I believe is often partly determined by factors lying outside me? Since both externalism and first person authority are accepted by Davidson— the present author also accepts both—there better not be any conflict between the two. Showing that the two are compatible also has the advantage that it takes us a long way towards presenting a case against scepticism. And, according to Davidson, there is no conflict, once we give up certain preconceptions. Give up the idea that there are objects of thought, and the threatening conflict disappears. It is in this fairly specific sense that I shall be speaking of a *vacant mind*—a mind without objects of thought.

In this paper, I will examine Davidson's diagnosis of the threatening conflict, and see how Davidson's general claims about first person authority should be understood. I will accept some version of externalism, and the

257

first questions to be dealt with concern first person authority. What is it, and why do we have it?

2 The Presumption Argument

In Davidson's paper 'First Person Authority', first person authority is characterised in terms of the presumption that when a speaker sincerely asserts that he has a belief, then he is not mistaken. There are lots of cases where such a presumption has to be given up, but they are exceptions, and have to be; the presumption is, and has to be, that the speaker is generally correct about his own beliefs. In that paper, Davidson first examines and rejects accounts found in the literature, then presents his own, new, argument for first person authority.

I will call this argument the *presumption argument,* since it sets out to establish precisely that—that a presumption of first person authority is indispensable for the radical interpreter, and hence that the subject can justifiably be credited with first person authority. Therefore, in the overwhelming majority of cases, the subject knows what he believes. We should in any case not hold out for anything stronger—there can be cases where we were not aware of an intentional state of ours. In a simple setting with a radical interpreter and an interpretee, it makes no sense to suppose that the speaker is wrong about the meaning of his words: 'the idea of the speaker misusing his language has no application' (Davidson 1984:111). The interpreter can wonder if he is getting the speaker's words right, but the speaker 'cannot wonder whether he generally means what he says' (Davidson 1984:110). This accounts for both first person *asymmetry* and authority. The former is the claim that we know in some different way what *we* mean, compared with how we know what someone else means. The latter is the claim that we have authority over what we believe. The special character of our knowledge of our own beliefs is also stated in terms of truth-conditions: *I* couldn't improve on 'My utterance of "Wagner died happy" is true iff Wagner died happy,' whereas the interpreter cannot assume that that would be *his* best way of stating the truth-conditions of my utterance of 'Wagner died happy' (Davidson 1984:111). This latter point has some affinities with Quine's talk of 'acquiescing in one's mother tongue' (Quine 1968). There, we put an end to the threatening regress of new background languages in which to explain how we take our words to refer by acquiescing in one's mother tongue, and taking our words *at face value.* Wittgenstein's view of first-personal avowals is at times similar: 'My own relation to my words is wholly different from other people's. ... If I listen to the words of my mouth, I might say that someone else was speaking out of my mouth' (Wittgenstein 1953:192e). When I am the speaker, I do not treat my words in the same way as I treat the words of other speakers.

Davidson's presumption argument, as presented in 'First Person Authority', relies on the use of Davidsonian principles for interpretation, especially the Principle of Charity—speakers should be interpreted in such a manner as to make them as right as possible. The presumption argument does not invoke special faculties, kinds of acquaintance or objects. I will accept the argument as presented, but there are a few things that should be looked at more closely.

One—minor—thing is that the argument as stated is not applied to our silent thoughts; it is an argument about a speaker's utterances. There is nothing in this argument as stated above to show that a speaker has first person authority concerning what he thinks silently. If this really were a problem, realizing this, and accepting the presumption argument, might turn everyone into a compulsive speaker. But being a compulsive speaker wouldn't really help. If I only knew that I had first person authority concerning my spoken words, I could still be unsure about my silent thoughts, even if I put them into words—I would need some further assurance that there is the right kind of fit between my words and my thoughts. And, if I have such an assurance, there is no need for compulsive chattering. The Davidsonian intimate connection between thought and talk, together with the stress on interpretability, takes care of this problem. There is thus for Davidson no real need to formulate the argument in a way that deals explicitly with silent thought.

The presumption argument functions in a way similar to the appeal to charity when it comes to ordinary scepticism about our senses. There, the argument shows that speakers cannot be massively wrong about their surroundings; there is still room for the occasional mistake, however. Something similar holds for the result of the presumption argument—as already quoted, the speaker 'cannot wonder whether he *generally* means what he says' (italics added). This would still leave room for some instances of misuse. It seems that I can't wonder whether I'm generally mistaken about what my words mean, but I could wonder what I meant when I said 'water'.

A further issue is that a really determined sceptic might try to tough it out by holding that one actually *could* wonder whether one is interpretable, whether one in general means what one says, and so on. This is not very convincing, but there appears to be *some* room for such a move. Remember Swampman, from Davidson's 'Knowing One's Own Mind'. At first, Swampman had very little cognitive activity. There was some thinking (perhaps it should just be called mental activity), but no meaning or thoughts. Perhaps there could be mental activity going on in Swampman, activity which was tantamount to 'Do I have any thoughts?'[1] Or take what

---

[1] Burge 1996:92 brings up the possibility to doubt that one has thoughts, but dismisses it as pathological: 'I do not claim that judgements like (1) [I am thinking that there are physical entities] are indubitable. The scope for human perversity is very wide. One could be so far

would happen, if both I and my Swamp replica survived. For some time, only one of us (me) would be making sense, be interpretable, but there's no real telling which one (unless someone actually had seen the creation of Swampman). Perhaps the determined sceptic could say something like this, but it seems to me that this line of reasoning is not very interesting. As I see it, the interesting versions of scepticism try to show that even if we do the best we can, even if we gather all the justification that can be had for something, we might go wrong, or not know that we had gotten things right. The kind of scepticism sketched here says roughly that we maybe are not doing so well, maybe we are completely crazy or without minds. Perhaps this is a tenable view, but it appears to be less interesting.

Another issue is that the presumption argument has one small loophole, one which appears to be straightforward to fix, but should be fixed. The argument, as stated, only requires that the interpretee has first person authority. At first, it is silent about the interpreter's own first person authority, and first person authority has only been demonstrated for interpretees. Right now, there is thus a problem. Either the interpreter has first person authority, or he doesn't. If he hasn't, then the presumption argument has not accomplished all that much; and if he has first person authority, then his first person authority would have to be explained (otherwise first person authority is simply assumed). Just repeating the argument, introducing another interpreter to guarantee the original interpreter's first person authority, would start us off on a regress, so that doesn't help much. I think there are two, not necessarily incompatible, main ways to fix this loophole.

The first is slightly more centred on the individual, and holds that beliefs should be weighted, and that nothing could manage to interpret others while being self-blind, as it were—(almost) completely without first person authority. A reason for weighting beliefs in precisely this manner is that the ability to revise your own beliefs in the light of new evidence is so important for rationality, so that a being unable to monitor his own beliefs could make no claim to being rational. Without first person authority, the revision of beliefs could not proceed in an orderly manner, so important for critical reasoning (cf. Burge 1986 and Burge 1996).

The other way is to say that the existence of the above loophole actually shows why we have to bring in other speakers—the second person—from the outset. To be an interpreter is to be interpretable, to be in contact with a

---

gone as to think to oneself: 'I do not know whether I am now thinking or not; maybe I am dead or unconscious; my mantra may have finally made me blissfully free of thought'. Such mistaken doubt would evince cognitive pathology, but I think it possible. It is an error, however, that most people would avoid without swerving.' The relevant kind of case discussed in the text above does not deal in this kind of pathology; the issue is rather whether the mental activity I am having amounts to *thinking* in the full, semantically loaded, as it were, sense of the word. This kind of worry is not as clearly pathological as Burge's cases.

second speaker. On this construal, what the original presumption argument showed was at most that we had something that could be called conditional first person authority, that we have first person authority only if there are other speakers that have first person authority in their turn (and that the same, *mutatis mutandis*, holds for them).

This other way is thus more openly externalist, and actually sets out to show something stronger than what some of Davidson's original arguments about externalism indicated. Those other arguments, as for instance that in 'The Second Person', set out to show that other speakers were needed for the objectivity of thought; this one shows that first person authority rests directly on other speakers and their first person authority. I need other speakers, not just to have beliefs at all, but to know that I know what I believe or mean.[2] A brief statement of this position is the following: 'Neither knowledge of one's own mind nor knowledge of the "outside" world is possible except in a social setting; "impersonal" thoughts, like other thoughts, depend on interpersonal connections' (Davidson 1988:665).

I think these two lines of reasoning are compatible, possibly true, and in some sense Davidsonian. There is a lesson from this tightening of the loophole—that, on this account, externalism is what *ensures* first person authority, so if there is a conflict between first person authority and externalism, we are in deep trouble. How deep, more exactly? That is not entirely clear. If we accept a presumption of first person authority, and hold that our other beliefs are normally right, then the room for scepticism about one's attitudes cannot be that big. Still, the scepticism about our own attitudes that looms here is disquieting enough for us to be concerned, and first person asymmetry seems to be left out of the picture. But, of course, Davidson has made a case for their compatibility.

3 Compatibility

In 'Knowing One's Own Mind' and subsequent writings, Davidson pursues two lines of reasoning in support of the compatibility of externalism and first person authority. One is more defensive, the other more diagnostic or constructive. The argument I call defensive is the argument which is intended to show that externalism is compatible with token physicalism or anomalous monism. This argument is to show how it is at least possible that mental states, despite being identified by reference to things outside the

---

[2] Some problems remain with this suggested development. How is it to be understood more exactly? Is the idea that I have first person authority because I am in contact with someone who has first person authority because I have first person authority? How could I know what other speakers mean, unless I know what I think they mean?

subject's body, still could be identical with events in the body (Davidson 1989a; Davidson 1986).[3] I will not discuss that argument in this paper.

The argument for the compatibility of externalism and first person authority which I have called constructive or diagnostic is that which purports to solve the threatening problem by showing that it is only apparent. Why, and what solves the problem? Here it should be remembered that the presumption argument was made without invoking any special objects, faculties, or modes of acquaintance; and it is held that reliance on *objects of thought* is that which creates the apparent conflict between first person authority and externalism:

> If we rid ourselves of preconceptions, I think it is easy to see where we have gone wrong. It does not follow, from the facts that a thinker knows what he thinks and that what he thinks can be fixed by relating him to a certain object, that the thinker is acquainted with, or indeed knows anything at all about the object. It does not even follow that the thinker knows about any *object* at all (Davidson 1989b:12).

If we give up the idea that there are objects of thought, we will in one fell swoop ensure first person authority *and* its peaceful co-existence with externalism:

> [Loss of first person authority] would follow if the object used to identify my thought were something I had to be able to discriminate in order to know what I think. But this is the assumption we have abandoned. ... The possibility of error, or of failure to distinguish one's own state of mind due solely to the external elements that help determine the state of mind, is intelligible only on the supposition that having a thought requires a special psychological relation to the object used to identify the state of mind (ibid.).

4   Objects of thought

Several readers have wondered at how this diagnosis came about, and how it solved the original problem (e.g. Berneker 1996 and Bilgrami 1992). But before I tackle that problem, I will try to sort out what these objects of thought might be. In essence, objects of thought have the following properties.

They are before the theatre of the mind, they are within the ken of the believer, they are perceived by the mind's eye, grasped by the mind, or the mind is in some other suitable sense acquainted with them. It is impossible to misidentify them; in Hume's words, they are what they seem, and seem

---

[3] This argument, also known as the 'sunburn argument' will only provide one part of a defence of the compatibility of externalism and first person authority—it will, if accepted, show that externalism could be reconciled with identifying thoughts by recourse to what is going on locally in the subject. Added arguments are needed to show how first person authority works in general.

what they are—their *esse* is *percipi*. In many versions of this idea, they are thought of as intermediaries of some sort, going between the epistemically potentially hostile world and the epistemically safer theatre of the mind. Russell's conception of objects of acquaintance, known with complete accuracy by the subject, would be one version of the idea of objects of thought; Fregean senses, on most interpretations, would be another example.

Davidson's main attack on objects of thought in the above sense can be seen as a dilemma. Take Hume's conception of such objects: 'They are what they seem, and seem what they are'. Should objects of thought have such properties? If the answer is *no*, i.e., if we introduce a set of objects of thought for which a distinction between appearance and reality holds, then we would be no closer to giving an account of first person authority. If such objects had unnoticed or unknown properties, appeal to such objects couldn't guarantee first person authority, since I might be unable to tell object A from object B, despite their being different objects, as long as the *noticed* properties were the same. 'For unless one knows *everything* about the object, there will always be senses in which one does not know what object it is' (Davidson 1986:455). This point is well-taken, unless one is prepared to adopt one of the following lines of defence in support of these objects. One option is to say that no one else is in any better position to know what object I have before the mind, so even if I might be wrong about which object I am entertaining before the mind's eye, no one could do any better; hence, first person authority would remain. Another option would be to say that all the *important* properties are authoritatively known by the subject, whereas there may be some other for which complete authoritative knowledge is not to be had. Davidson in fact discusses something similar to this last suggestion in a footnote to 'What is Present to the Mind?', and finds it unacceptable, due to difficulties in spelling out how to distinguish the two kinds of properties (Davidson 1989b:4n). Perhaps one of these suggestions could be made to work, but I will not discuss them here. They do not seem very promising as viable alternatives.

So what if we said that the answer was *yes*, that there are objects of thought whose *esse* is *percipi*, objects that cannot be misidentified by the subject? For one thing, no one has been able to present a clear theory of such objects, and there is no widely accepted account of our relations with them. Whatever objects of thought may turn out to be, they cannot be combined with externalism about the determination of thought contents. How could connections to the outside world be essential aspects of the contents of the subjects' beliefs, if the subject already by having the belief knows all there is to know about the content of that belief? There is also a more specifically Davidsonian reason for denying such objects: if there had been such objects, they would have been there all the time, so there would have been no real need for the second or third person in communication.

I think that these points are well-taken, though the real villain of this piece is the *perceptual* or *observational* view of first person knowledge—the Cartesian theatre of the subjective is under attack, rather than the very idea of objects of thought. If there are no objects, there would be no point in having a quasi-perceptual view of first person knowledge, but it need not be the case that giving up the quasi-perceptual view makes you give up the object view.[4]

The result of Davidson's arguments concerning objects of thought is that these should be abolished. If we follow this advice, we now have what I call a *vacant mind*, a mind without objects of thought. Perhaps it would be better to say, echoing Wittgenstein, that we have a mind with things that are not somethings, but not nothings either.

As a result of this, the conflict between externalism and first person authority is to have been solved. But how was this accomplished? As the above quotation from 'What is Present to the Mind?' indicated, the claim here is quite strong—belief in objects of thought is necessary for holding that there is a potential conflict between first person authority and externalism: 'The possibility of error, or of failure to distinguish one's own state of mind due solely to the external elements that help determine the state of mind, is intelligible *only* on the supposition that having a thought requires a special psychological relation to the object used to identify the state of mind' (Davidson 1989b:12, italics added). As far as I have made out, the main line of reasoning is as follows. Without the pernicious objects of thought, one's beliefs are in direct contact with one's environment, and knowing one's own mind doesn't require that we search through the contents of the world. Why not? Because our second-order thoughts automatically inherit their content from the contents of our ordinary first-order thoughts. This kind of inherited content is what is encapsulated in the account of first person authority. The very same external factors contribute to determining both the first- and second-order thoughts, so nothing comes apart there. In general, in the second-order thought 'I believe that I believe that water quenches thirst,' the content of the first-order, contained, belief carries over, since the very same cognitive act—*and not any object of thought*—is part of the second-order thought (cf. Burge 1986:660). After presenting an argument to that effect, Davidson concludes (again) that there is no reason for saying that 'thinkers don't generally know what they think' (Davidson 1989b:13). This may well be true, since we have already accepted the presumption argument, at least with some provisos. But if that

---

[4] Compare this with different conceptions of mathematical knowledge. Someone could insist that there are mathematical objects, while resisting the idea that mathematical knowledge has a perceptual or quasi-perceptual character (Frege would be an example of this). On the other hand, it seems that a person who held on to the idea that mathematical knowledge was perceptual or quasi-perceptual would have to postulate mathematical objects.

really is true, then perhaps the detour via a criticism of objects of thought wasn't really needed. If we already have a guarantee for the presumption that speakers generally are right about what they believe, then no further specific moves would be needed to ensure first person authority. This latter complaint is a rather small worry about the strategic role of the argument against objects of thought in Davidson's thinking. A more substantial issue is that some worries seem to remain concerning the diagnosis. *Is* the alleged incompatibility really refuted by getting rid of objects of thought? Couldn't there be cases of faulty self-knowledge, due to external switching or twin situations, even if one doesn't conceive of belief in terms of relations to objects of thought? It appears that the banished objects of thought are simply *irrelevant* here. If aspects of the contents of my mind are (partly) fixed by external factors, isn't it still the case that I wouldn't know the contents of my mind without finding out about empirical facts? Even if the presumption argument is accepted, it seems that first person authority is still in some danger of being diminished as a result of the externalist account of thought contents. This situation is still problematic, it seems to me, but I will turn to a final problem.

What is belief like for the vacant mind? How do we on this account know what we mean and believe? There are no objects of thought or belief present to the mind. *Believes* relates the believer or thinker to an object which we don't have to think of as being within the ken of the believer; that was the point of getting rid of objects of thought. On the new account presented, there is not really all that much to say about what belief is like: having removed the obstacles, there is little left to say about how we know what we think. In the interesting, and originally puzzling cases, there *is* no *way* we know—for there is no evidence to be sought, no inner object to be scrutinised, no competing hypothesis to be weighed (Davidson 1989b:17).

But even if there is 'no *way* we know', something remains to be said—or else, we are just postulating *that* we know, and this would not be very helpful. There is an account. A person who has a thought generally knows it in ways others cannot, and 'this is all there is to the subjective'(Davidson 1989a:171). The difference resides in the asymmetry; we have to interpret others, but we don't have to interpret ourselves.

But I sense a problem here. In cases of first person knowledge, the attribut*er* of beliefs is also the attribut*ee*. The ersatz object of thought ('believes that' is still relational) is the content of an utterance of the attributer/interpreter which he believes, or takes to, have the same truth-conditions as the identified belief, the interpretee's/attributee's belief. And what happens if the interpreter is the interpretee? Tentatively, it appears that there are two main options, neither of which is very appealing.

One alternative is that such self-attributions work as the statements concerning what the vacant mind says. Here this appears to mean that they are simply *attributive*, or prehaps expressions of the first person authority of the subject. Why? Because in such cases, the subject, as a brute fact, treats himself as authoritative. But this cannot be the whole story—if first person authority in the final account simply is a matter of *treating* oneself as authoritative, what is ensured is not knowledge of one's mental states, but just the brute fact that we treat our own states in that manner. This is in effect not too far from the Rorty/Sellars view of first person authority, which Davidson discussed and rejected in his 'First Person Authority' (Sellars 1956; Rorty 1970; Davidson 1984:106).

This may also be Wittgenstein's considered opinion on the subject. In *Last Writings*, Wittgenstein writes: 'The language-game simply is the way it is' (Wittgenstein 1992:35e). Taken out of context, these words could mean just about anything, but in this context (Wittgenstein 1992:34-7), a discussion of avowals, confessions, and reports about what is the case with me, in distinction from what is the case about someone else, an interpretation that lies close at hand is that the passage indicates the way in which we, deep down, just actually treat ourselves as authoritative with respect to our own beliefs.

The other alternative works by in effect reinstating some kind of object of thought, which in this case actually has to be within the ken of the believer (since the attributer is identical with the attributee in this case), and in virtue of which the attribution holds. But it seems that this cannot be right, either, not as an interpretation of Davidson, and not right in general—the Davidsonian attacks on objects of thought were accepted earlier.

This seems to be a genuine dilemma, and I'm afraid that I don't really know the way out of it. It seems that first person authority still in many ways is a mystery, and that much remains to be said about the relations between first person authority and externalism. Perhaps a certain pessimism is called upon here. It may be that the root of these problems is that we are, misguidedly, looking for explanations where there simply is no explanation—at least not of the right kind—to be found. First person authority is simply a very basic fact to be reckoned with in our understanding of ourselves and others. But perhaps it is time to step back here. That first person authority can be made to *seem* mysterious from a certain point of view doesn't show it to *be* mysterious. This is, however, a subject for another paper.

References

Berneker, S. 1996. Davidson on First-Person Authority and Externalism. *Inquiry* 39:121-39.

Bilgrami, A. 1992. Can Externalism be Reconciled with Self-Knowledge? *Philosophical Topics* 20:233-67.

Burge, T. 1988. Individualism and Self-Knowledge. *Journal of Philosophy* 85:649-63.

Burge, T. 1996. Our Entitlement to Self-Knowledge. *Proceedings of the Aristotelian Society* 96:91-116.

Davidson, D. 1984. First Person Authority. *Dialectica* 38:101-11.

Davidson, D. 1986. Knowing One's Own Mind. *Proceedings of the APA* 60:441-458.

Davidson, D. 1988. Reply to Burge. *Journal of Philosophy* 85:664-65.

Davidson, D. 1989a. The Myth of the Subjective. *Relativism: Interpretation and Confrontation,* ed. M. Krausz, 159-172. Notre Dame, Ind: University of Notre Dame Press.

Davidson, D. 1989b. What is Present to the Mind? *Grazer Philosophische Studien* 36:3-18.

Quine, W.V. 1968. Ontological Relativity *Journal of Philosophy* 65:185-212.

Rorty, R. 1970. Incorrigibility as the Mark of the Mental. *Journal of Philosophy* 67:399-424.

Sellars, W. 1956. Empiricism and the Philosophy of Mind. *Science, Perception, and Reality*, 127-196. London: Routledge 1963.

Wittgenstein, L. 1953. *Philosophical Investigations*, tr. by E. Anscombe. Oxford: Blackwell.

Wittgenstein, L. 1992. *Last Writings on the Philosophy of Psychology*, vol. II. Oxford: Blackwell.

14

Davidson and Quine's Empiricism

FOLKE TERSMAN

1 Introduction

Donald Davidson rejects empiricism. That is, he does not deny that 'all knowledge stems from the senses', if this simply means that the senses have a crucial *causal* role in our acquisition of knowledge. Rather, the target of his criticism is a specific semantical view. This is the view that meaning is essentially tied to sensory impressions or some similar form of subjective evidence; a view he thinks has remained central in Quine's modern version of empiricism, due to the role it assigns to stimulation of sensory receptors. Davidson suggests that this view is questionable, since it allows for a radical kind of skepticism.

However, Davidson is not only skeptical towards the view that sensory stimulation provides the basis for *meaning*. He has also raised some doubts about the idea that such phenomena provide the basis for *knowledge*. For example, he rejects the idea that the acceptance of an observation sentence could somehow be justified by the stimulations that normally cause it. This in turn leads him to doubt the thesis that observation sentences have a privileged epistemological status; a thesis that is central to all forms of empiricism, Quine's included. [1]

---

[1] Davidson develops this criticism in several papers, but see especially Davidson 1986, and Davidson 1990a.

The purpose of this paper is to examine and comment upon Davidson's criticism. I shall defend Davidson's claim that the view that ties meaning to some private form of evidence yields skepticism, and try to explain why Davidson's own view is not open to a similar challenge. I shall also discuss whether Davidson has provided any reasons for being skeptical about the thesis that observation sentences have a privileged epistemological role. I shall argue that a moderate version of this thesis survives Davidson's attack, and indeed obtains support from his views on meaning and interpretation. In particular, I shall argue that Quine's version of the thesis that observation sentences have a privileged role is untouched by Davidson's criticism.

2 The Proximal View and Skepticism

The semantical view that provides the target of Davidson's criticism is, of course, 'the proximal view'; a doctrine that is contrasted with his own—'distal'—view. Davidson has urged that both these views could be discerned in Quine's writings, but that the proximal view has been predominant, at least in Quine's earlier writings (Davidson 1990a; Davidson 1994). That claim may perhaps be doubted. However, since the significance of Davidson's criticism goes beyond this exegetical issue, I shall not pursue it. [2]

The proximal and the distal views differ as to which role is assigned to sensory stimulation. According to the proximal view, the meanings of a speaker's sentences are *determined* by such stimulation (in a sense to be indicated below). However, notice that sensory stimulation is supposed to *directly* determine only the meanings of observation sentences. [3] The meanings of further sentences are rather determined by how they are conditioned on observation sentences (Davidson 1986:313). Notice also that Davidson does not take the proximal view to imply that observation sentences are in some sense 'about' stimulation or sensory receptors.

---

[2] In fact, Quine has recently indicated that he accepts Davidson's distal view: '[M]y position in semantics is as distal as his' (Quine 1993:114). But this might merely mean that he thinks that observation sentences 'treat of' the distal world, rather than of stimulations or sense data, which is, of course, a point on which he has insisted for a long time (see, e.g., Quine 1973:38).

[3] How the notion of an observation sentence is to be defined more precisely has little bearing on the argument in this and the next section. It suffices to say that a speaker's observation sentences are such that he is prompted to accept them when confronted with some patterns of sensory stimulation, and prompted to reject them when confronted with others. Typical examples are 'That's red', 'It's raining', and so forth. Quine's views on the notion of observationality, and their relation to the view that observation sentences have a privileged epistemological role will be considered in section 4.

In order to bring out how the proximal view yields skepticism, David-son takes the perspective of an interpreter. Let us say, with Quine, that the *stimulation* a speaker undergoes on a given occasion is the (temporally or-dered) set of all those of his sensory receptors that are triggered on that oc-casion (Quine 1992:17), and that the *stimulus meaning* of a given observa-tion sentence for a given speaker is the ordered pair of the set of all stimula-tions that would prompt him to accept the sentence and the set of all stimu-lations that would rather prompt dissent (Quine 1960:32; Quine 1992:3). Now, Quine has suggested that a field linguist should translate observation sentences 'by significant approximation of stimulus meanings', and that he assembles evidence for translating the native's sentence 'Gavagai' with his own sentence 'Rabbit' by seeing 'that the native will assent to "Gavagai" under just those stimulations under which we, if asked, would assent to "Rabbit"' (Quine 1960:30;40). In accordance with these suggestions, Da-vidson takes the proximal view to imply that an interpreter, in trying to uncover the meanings of a speaker's observation sentences, should settle for a translation manual such that, for each of the speaker's observation sen-tences, the manual assigns a sentence of his own with (approximately) the same stimulus meaning.

Now, the point Davidson argues is that this strategy allows the linguist to attribute massive error. For it implies that he can correctly interpret a speaker's observation sentences (and thus also the speaker's further sen-tences) by assigning meanings to them such that they are, in many cases, *false* when the speaker accepts them (by the linguist's lights). This suffices, in Davidson's view, to show that skepticism looms, since it may legiti-mately prompt the linguist to doubt his *own* beliefs. The reason is that 'once he notices how globally mistaken others are, and why, it is hard to think why he would not wonder whether *he* had it right'. (Davidson 1990a:74). This is the sense in which the proximal view yields skepticism.

But *why* is the proximal view supposed to allow an interpreter to at-tribute massive error? The point of departure of Davidson's argument for this claim is the assumption that external objects and events may trigger different patterns of receptors in different persons. This allows us to imag-ine the following scenario. Suppose (1) that a speaker is prompted to accept his sentence 'Gavagai' by the same patterns of stimulation as those that prompt an interpreter to accept his sentence 'Rabbit'. Suppose also (2) that the speaker accepts 'Gavagai' in the presence of warthogs, while the inter-preter accepts 'Rabbit' in the presence of rabbits. Given (1), the proximal view implies that the interpreter should translate 'Gavagai' with 'Rabbit'. However, given (2), this means, in effect, that an interpreter could correctly translate a speaker's observation sentence with a sentence of his own such that the speaker is regularly disposed to *reject* his sentence on the occasions on which the speaker *accepts* his sentence. In other words, the proximal view seems to imply that an interpreter could correctly interpret a speaker's observation sentence by assigning a meaning to this sentence such that the speaker systematically accepts it on occasions on which it is false (by the interpreter's lights).

Now, this argument raises several worries. One obvious worry is how to make sense of (1)—that a speaker is prompted to accept his sentence 'Gavagai' by *the same* patterns of stimulation as those that prompt an interpreter to accept his sentence 'Rabbit'. In view of the obvious fact that people do not share receptors, this might be difficult. Of course, we might try to account for (1) by assuming an approximate *homology* of receptors, as Quine indeed did at one point (Quine 1973:23). But in more recent writings, Quine does not wish to rely on that assumption. Indeed, Quine has recently said that it is doubtful if such homologies really exist, and cites Darwin in support of this skepticism (see Quine 1999). Accordingly, as for intersubjective likeness of stimulation, he has said that 'we can simply do without it'. (Quine 1992:42) Hence, in so far as the proximal view relies on such a notion, it cannot be attributed to Quine.

Does this mean that Davidson has been flogging a dead horse? It does not. For Davidson's point could be made also if we look away from the problematic intersubjective case, and focus instead on an *intra*subjective one.

As I indicated above, the proximal view implies that the meaning of a speaker's observation sentence is determined by its stimulus meaning. Thus, the proximal view might plausibly be taken to imply that if the stimulus meaning of a speaker's observation sentence is unchanged over a period of time, so is its meaning. Now, suppose that an interpreter notices that (1*) a speaker's observation sentence S had the same stimulus meaning before and after a time t, although (2*) the speaker before t was disposed to reject S in the kind of circumstances in which he, after t, is disposed to accept S, and vice versa. For instance, we may imagine that he has undergone some eye disease, so that light reflected by certain (say, red) objects after t trigger the same of his receptors that used to be triggered by other (say, green) objects, or, more speculatively, that he was placed in a vat at t by some playful scientists. This is not a *likely* case, of course, but it does not seem impossible in a relevant sense.

In any case, given (1*), the proximal view implies that if S was correctly translated by one of the interpreter's sentences before t, this sentence represents the meaning of S also after t. However, given (2*), for any of the sentences that the interpreter before t might have been disposed to translate S with, the following seems to hold: Either the interpreter is disposed to reject this sentence in the kind of circumstances in which the speaker *after* t accepts S. Or the interpreter is disposed to reject this sentence in the kind of circumstances in which the speaker *did, before t*, accept S. Thus, on the assumption that any of these sentences correctly translated S before *t*, the interpreter is led to conclude *either* that the speaker *was* (before *t*) disposed to accept S when it was false, or that the speaker *is* (after *t*) disposed to accept S when it is false. So he is led to conclude that it is possible for a speaker to systematically accept one of his observation sentences on occasions on which the sentence is false.[4]

Notice that the point of this reasoning is not that it is in itself implausible to hold that the speaker in the above example systematically is in error about the sentence after *t*. Maybe that conclusion is justified by the assumption that the speaker has undergone an eye disease (a fact that would provide an explanation of the errors). The aim is rather to illustrate how the proximal view may allow an interpreter to attribute massive error at the observational level, independently of whether we can make sense of talk of intersubjective likeness of stimulation.

Notice also that the crucial assumption in this argument is the undoubtedly correct claim that the same stimulations could be produced by different external circumstances. Or as Davidson puts it: '[C]learly a person's sensory stimulations could be just as they are and yet the world outside very different' (Davidson 1986:313). This is why the stimulus meaning of a sentence could remain the same even if the speaker becomes disposed to accept it in different external circumstances. Moreover, since the same holds for *any* kind of sensory evidence, *any* view that assigns a similar semantic role to such evidence, or indeed to *any* kind of epistemic intermediary between our beliefs and the world, could be shown to yield skepticism by a similar argument.

I will briefly consider two objections to Davidson's argument, and recapitulate Davidson's responses to them. The first objection appeals to Quine's *naturalism*. Davidson thinks that the proximal view yields the result that we may have legitimate doubts about the truth of our observational beliefs, and thus also about the *theoretical* beliefs that we may be disposed to infer from them, even if our theory squares perfectly well with our observational beliefs. This might seem to make him committed to some kind of 'first philosophy', that is, to the view that there is a higher tribunal than science for determining truth and falsity.

In my view, this objection is not convincing. Davidson's point is that, on the proximal view, we could, in some cases, correctly translate a speaker's observation sentences with sentences of our own even if we systematically reject those sentences when the speaker accepts his sentences.

---

[4] This and other implications of the view that if the stimulus meaning of a speaker's observation sentence is unchanged over a period of time, so is its meaning, as well as some problematic implications of the converse claim (the claim that the meaning of an observation sentence is changed whenever its stimulus meaning changes), are examined in Tersman 1998a.

Obviously, since not *both* the beliefs we thus attribute to the speaker *and* those of our own beliefs that conflict with these, can be true, either we or the speaker holds mostly false observational beliefs. This is the simple insight that may shake our confidence in our own beliefs, at least, I presume, if we have no independent reason for thinking that the speaker's cognitive equipment is somehow inferior to ours. However, none of the considerations to which Davidson appeals in support of the claim that the proximal view could have this implication seems to *conflict* with any scientific result. Thus, he seems not committed to the notion of a supra-scientific tribunal.

Another response is to appeal to Quine's claim that truth is 'immanent', where this (partly) is supposed to mean that the only way in which our theory of the world may be wrong is that it will turn out to conflict with our (future) observational beliefs (Quine 1986). However, even if this suggestion might save the proximal view from skepticism, it invites, as Davidson argues, a further charge of relativism.

The reason is that even if we accept this view, the proximal view does still not rule out our correctly attributing observational beliefs to a speaker, and therefore also theoretical beliefs, that we think are false.[5] Thus, we may end up with the implausible consequence that while a sentence of the speaker is true for *him*, since it squares with all his observations, an interpreter may correctly translate this sentence with a sentence of his own that is false for *him*, since the belief that it is false squares equally well with his observations. As Davidson has put it: 'This is relativity of truth not of the familiar [...] kind that relativizes the truth of sentences to a language, but a further and independent relativization to *individuals*' (Davidson 1990a:75). And such a relativism is surely not a more plausible implication than skepticism, especially since it emerges not only at the theoretical level, but also at the *observational* level.

3   The Distal View and the Problem of Error

The view of meaning that Davidson offers as a superior alternative to the proximal view is the distal view. Davidson characterizes this view as follows:

> As a radical interpreter I correlate verbal responses of a speaker with changes in the environment. Inferring a causal relation, I then translate those verbal responses with a sentence of my own that the same changes in the environment cause me to accept or reject. This is the distal theory at its simplest [...] (Davidson 1990a:73).

---

[5] I assume, with Davidson, that to ascribe a meaning to a sentence held true by a speaker is to attribute a belief to this speaker.

Similar views are expressed by Davidson in many other places. For instance, he insists that an interpreter should interpret 'sentences held true [...]according to the events and objects in the outside world that cause the sentence to be held true', (Davidson 1986:317) and moreover that

> when the interpreter finds a sentence of the speaker the speaker assents to regularly under conditions he recognizes, he takes those conditions to be the truth conditions of the speaker's sentence (Davidson 1986:316).

So, as any reader of Davidson's writings notices, the distal view is nothing but an application of Davidson's well known Principle of Charity. Indeed, the Principle of Charity and the distal view do not represent different strands in Davidson's philosophy. They are both manifestations of the same fundamentally externalist view on meaning.

In formulating the distal view, Davidson speaks of the situations, 'external circumstances', conditions, and so forth, that cause us to hold sentences true (Davidson 1990b and Davidson 1996:275). This leaves him open to the criticism that it is difficult to see how such entities can be individuated. However, for present purposes, we may simply formulate the relevant implication of the distal view in terms of *occasions*, where an occasion is simply a time and a place. Thus, the distal view implies that we interpret someone's observation sentences correctly only if we assign meanings to his observation sentences such that they are, generally, true (by our lights) on the occasions on which he accepts them. This is the central implication of the distal view in the present context.

Notice that Davidson does not, of course, fail to recognize the crucial *causal* role of sensory stimulation. On the distal view, the meaning of a speaker's observation sentence is determined by the occasions on which he is disposed to accept and reject it. However, since the speaker undergoes certain stimulations on some occasions and other stimulations on other occasions, the stimulus meaning of a sentence for a given speaker causally determines on which occasions he accepts it and on which he rejects it. Thus, on the distal view, its stimulus meaning causally determines its meaning for the speaker.

But it does not conceptually determine the meaning of the sentence. For assume that a change in its stimulus meaning would *not* prompt the speaker to accept/reject the sentence on other occasions. Then its meaning could still remain the same, on the distal view. However, it would *not* remain the same if the speaker *were* to accept and reject the sentence on other occasions, even if its stimulus meaning were unchanged (at least unless the changes are insignificant and could be explained in terms of some cognitive shortcoming on the part of the speaker). This is why the fact that our stimulations could be 'what they are and the world very different', given the distal view, simply is irrelevant to the question of whether our *beliefs* could be what they are 'and the world very different'. Simplifying somewhat, on the distal view, if the world were different, so would the contents of our beliefs.

Some writers have argued that Davidson at best has shown that an interpreter must attribute beliefs that he *thinks* are true, not that they *are* in fact true, and that he, therefore, has not provided a response to skepticism. In my view, this objection misses the point. The point is that, on the distal view, we could never, no matter how much our epistemic perspective were to improve, expect to discover that a speaker holds beliefs most of which are false. Thus, if we insist that the speaker's beliefs may still *be* false, we seem committed to the assumption that a speaker's beliefs can be generally false even if this could never, even in principle, be discovered. In my view, this assumption is not plausible. In *this* context, the charge of a commitment to a 'first philosophy' seems more appropriate.

However, I will not pursue this discussion. Instead, I shall consider another objection to Davidson's distal view, namely the objection that his argument, if sound, proves too much, namely that a speaker's observation sentences are *always* true on the occasions on which he accepts them. The reason is that the distal view might seem to imply that it could *never* be reasonable for an interpreter to attribute observational beliefs to the speaker that he thinks are false. This may in turn seem objectionable, since observational mistakes are surely possible.[6]

It seems to me that this objection fails to acknowledge the *holistic* element in Davidson's view on interpretation. According to Davidson, knowledge of the meanings of a speaker's sentences can be captured by a theory of interpretation for that person. This is a finitely axiomatized theory that specifies truth conditions for each of the sentences of the speaker's language. In view of the complexity of human behavior, no simple theory is likely to assign truth conditions to the speaker's observation sentences such that they are *never* false (by the interpreter's lights) when the speaker accepts them. Thus, since some degree of simplicity is necessary in order for a theory to be viable, an interpreter must attribute error. This is how Davidson's views admits of, or indeed *explains*, the possibility of observational mistakes.[7]

---

[6] For this objection, see, e.g., Fodor and LePore 1992, and Bergström's contribution in this volume.

[7] Thus, Davidson insists that '[n]o simple theory can put a speaker and interpreter in perfect agreement, and so a workable theory must from time to time assume error on the part of one or the other' (Davidson 1984:169). See also Tersman 1998b, where I discuss this further.

4 The Status of Observation Sentences

Let us turn to the thesis that observation sentences have a privileged epistemological role. Davidson's main reason for doubting this thesis seems to
be that he thinks that it relies on the view that the acceptance of an observation sentence could be justified by the stimulation that prompted it:

> In my view, erasing the line between the analytic and synthetic saved
> philosophy of language as a serious subject by showing how it could
> be pursued without what there cannot be: determinate meanings. I now
> suggest also giving up the distinction between observation sentences
> and the rest. For the distinction between sentences belief in whose
> truth is justified by sensations and sentences belief in whose truth is
> justified only by appeal to other sentences held true is as anathema [...]
> as the distinction between beliefs justified by sensations and beliefs
> justified only by appeal to further beliefs. (Davidson 1986:313)

His reason for rejecting the view that the acceptance of an observation
sentence could be justified by the stimulation that prompted it is, in turn,
that he finds it difficult to see what there *is* about the relation between the
stimulation and the belief that makes the former justify the latter. He acknowledges, of course, that there is a *causal* relation. But, according to
Davidson, 'a causal explanation of a belief does not show how or why it is
justified' (Davidson 1986:311. On the other hand, there cannot be a logical
relation, since stimulations 'are not beliefs or other propositional attitudes'
(ibid.). Davidson concludes that 'nothing can count as a reason for holding
a belief except another belief (Davidson' 1986:310), a view he accordingly
thinks is difficult to reconcile with the claim that observation sentences
have a privileged status.

However, whether this view *does* conflict with the thesis of the privileged role of observation sentences depends on what we take that thesis to
imply, more specifically. Let us assume that it at least involves the following two claims:

(A) A person's observational beliefs could be justified even if they obtain
no support from the rest of his beliefs.

(B) A person's non-observational beliefs are justified only to the extent that
they do obtain support from his observational beliefs.

Does (A) conflict with the view that nothing can count as a reason for
holding a belief except another belief? Well, if we assume that a person's
belief is justified only if he has some reason for it, then these views conflict. But nothing in Davidson's position commits him to this assumption.
Indeed, Davidson might even be said to have provided a kind of *justification* of the claim that observational beliefs can be justified in the absence of
supporting beliefs. As I noted earlier, Davidson's views on interpretation do
not rule out the possibility of observational mistakes, but they do–he ar-

gues–imply that they are rare. This means that each observational belief has a presumption in favor of its truth, which in turn might suffice to show that each of an individual's observational beliefs is justified, even if it obtains no support from the rest of his beliefs, at least unless it *conflicts* with the rest of his beliefs.

But it seems to me that (A) does not set empiricism apart from other epistemological views. What sets empiricism apart is rather (B). And (B) might seem less easy to reconcile with Davidson's position.

In assessing (B), it obviously becomes very important which beliefs we *count* as observational. To delimit these beliefs in a plausible way (that is, in a way such that the beliefs that come out as observational both carry a certain degree of certainty *and* can plausibly be held to provide the evidential basis for the rest of the individual's beliefs) might be difficult. For instance, Quine's views on the notion of observationality seem inadequate here.

Quine employs really two notions of observationality. He offers one definition of observationality for a single speaker, and another of observationality for a group. According to the first definition, in order for a sentence to be observational for a speaker, it is sufficient that he is disposed to assent to it (or dissent) immediately on the spot, when certain of his receptors are triggered. For example, Quine has recently said that 'what qualifies sentences [...] as observational, for a given individual, is just his readiness to assent outright on the strength of appropriate neural intake' (Quine 1993:108).[8] Thus, sentences such as 'It's raining', 'That's a rabbit', are likely to qualify as observational for many individuals.

Now, a problem in the present context is that the same probably holds for sentences such as 'He's a millionaire'. The obvious reason is that many individuals firmly *believe* that some men are millionaires while others are not, so that the appearance of any such man would command an immediate verdict. However, the belief that somebody is a millionaire does clearly not seem to be in *less* need of supporting evidence in order to be justified than many beliefs that are *not* observational given the present definition. So, Quine's definition of observationality for a single speaker does not by itself delimit a set of beliefs that may plausibly be held to be privileged in the indicated sense.

In order to exclude sentences such as 'He's a millionaire', however, Quine usually imposes a further, intersubjective condition. Thus, Quine is sometimes inclined to count as a person's observation sentences only those that are observational for the whole speech community to which he be-

---

[8] Notice that all observation sentences, according to Quine, are *occasion* sentences, where an occasion sentence is a sentence such that the speaker is disposed to accept it on some occasions and reject it on others, depending on how he is stimulated. See Quine 1960:35-6, and Quine 1981:3.

longs (Quine 1973:41; Quine 1969:88; Quine 1992:6), where this condition is met by a sentence only if it would, on any occasion, command the same verdict from all members of the community (Quine 1992:43).

In this way, we exclude sentences such as 'He's a millionaire' and 'He's a bachelor' but also, less plausibly in the present context, sentences such as 'There's mama' and 'I feel a nibble'. For these sentences do not satisfy the intersubjective condition for the whole speech community, or indeed for *any* substantial group. However, a person's belief that he feels a nibble seems clearly not to be in *more* need of supporting evidence in order to be justified than, say, his belief that some being is a rabbit. In other words, both Quine's notions of observationality are inadequate here. Neither of them substantiates the thesis that observational beliefs may be justified even if they obtain no support from other beliefs, while other beliefs are justified only if they obtain support from observational beliefs.[9]

In any case, independently of how a person's observational beliefs should be delimited more precisely, there is a general reason for thinking that Davidson's position is difficult to reconcile with the view that some subset of an individual's beliefs can provide the basis for the rest in the indicated sense.

I have argued that Davidson's views provide some justification for the claim that a person's observational beliefs may be justified even if they obtain no support from the rest of his beliefs, since they imply that each of his observational beliefs has a presumption in favor of its truth. However, it might be held that in so far as Davidson's views on interpretation lend themselves to a defense of this claim, they provide a similar justification for thinking that the same holds for *all* beliefs. For the claim that a person's observational beliefs can be justified even if they obtain no support from the rest derives from the view that we determine the meanings of observation sentences by interpreting them charitably. And this strategy applies, according to Davidson, not only to the speaker's observation sentences, but to *all* of his sentences ('across the board') (Davidson 1984:xvii). Accordingly, Davidson says that 'there is no belief without a presumption in its favor' (Davidson 1986:319).

However, there might be a difference in *degree* as to the presumption of truth that pertains to a given type of belief, at least in so far as it derives from the interpreter's duty to interpret a speaker's sentences charitably. Thus, Davidson often says that the Principle of Charity should *primarily* or *directly* be applied to sentences the speaker accepts depending on directly observable goings-on in his environment—i.e., what we normally count as observation sentences—and only *indirectly* to further sentences (Davidson 1986:318; Davidson 1989:164; Davidson 1991:160).

---

[9] For further discussion of Quine's definitions of observationality, see Tersman 1998c.

Moreover, Davidson has sometimes indicated that it is less plausible to attribute error at the observational level than at the theoretical level:

> Some disagreements are more destructive of understanding than others, and a sophisticated theory must naturally take this into account. Disagreements about theoretical matters may (in some cases) be more tolerable than disagreement about what is more evident; disagreement about how things look or appear is less tolerable than disagreement about how they are [...] (Davidson 1984:169).

This goes some way to meeting the claims made by empiricists. For it seems to indicate that in so far as Davidson's views on meaning do imply that our beliefs have a presumption in favor of their truth, they imply that observational beliefs have a stronger presumption than others. This in turn indicates that it would be wise for a person, in general, to let his theoretical rather than observational beliefs yield in case of conflict, which squares with the kind of priority empiricists attribute to observational beliefs. However, this advice is based on a difference in *degree*, and it might obviously be doubted if it is enough to justify (B). In other words, the justification for assigning a greater degree of confidence to our observational beliefs is going to be highly defeasible. This is possibly why Davidson says that even if beliefs that are directly caused by sensory experience 'often provide good reasons for further beliefs', this 'does not set such beliefs apart in principle or award them epistemological priority' (Davidson 1991:165).

5 Naturalized Epistemology

So, although it is possible to reconcile Davidson's position with a moderate version of the thesis that observation sentences have a privileged epistemological status, it does seem to conflict with this thesis if it is interpreted rather strictly. Does this mean that it conflicts also with *Quine's* version of this view? It seems not. Indeed, none of the claims that Quine makes on behalf of the epistemological status of observation sentences seems incompatible with Davidson's critical remarks.

That Quine does assign a special role to observation sentences is, of course, clear. Thus, Quine speaks of observation sentences as the 'checkpoints of science'.[10] In support of assigning this role to observation sentences, Quine cites primarily two considerations. First, observation sentences are (holophrastically construed) those of our sentences that are most closely connected with sensory stimulation. However, they are also (analytically construed) logically related to the rest of our theory of the world.

---

[10] See, e.g., Quine 1996:163, and Quine 1995:44. He has also said that observation sentences are 'the vehicle of evidence of the external world' (Quine 1993:108), and that it is through the responsiveness to observation sentences that science is something more than 'solely a quest for internal coherence' (Quine 1981:39).

Therefore, they may be seen as crucial links between our triggerings and our theory, and thus as relevant to the project by which Quine wants to replace traditional epistemology: To investigate how we arrive at our theory of the world merely from the triggering of our sensory receptors (Quine 1969). However, although the fact that observation sentences are closely linked to neural intake is what makes them relevant in this context, there seems to be no need to assume that such intake can somehow *justify* acceptance of observation sentences.

Second, observation sentences command, on any occasion, the same verdict from all competent speakers of the language.[11] This is, according to Quine, why the responsiveness of scientific theory to observation sentences explains why science is objective, or at least intersubjective, since the fact that such sentences command agreement means that the responsiveness of science to observation sentences ensures that there is a common ground on which scientists could meet when they disagree about theory (Quine 1960:44; Quine 1973:37). However, the claim that observation sentences have this function does not rest on some assumption to the effect that the acceptance of observation sentences could be justified by stimulation, or indeed by *anything*.

But notice that my point is not just that Quine does not make any *normative* claims about observation sentences. For instance, Quine would surely say that observation sentences are the checkpoints of science not only in the sense that scientists *do* assess theories on the basis of their conformity to such sentences, but also in the sense that they should assign this role to them.[12] Thus, Quine often suggests that a person should, normally, hold on to his verdict to an observation sentence rather than his theoretical beliefs in case of a conflict.

However, as I indicated above, it seems to me that this claim could also, to some extent, be reconciled with Davidson's position. For although his views on meaning and interpretation might be taken to imply that *each* of a speaker's beliefs has a presumption in favor of its truth, they seem to indicate that the presumption that pertains to observational beliefs are *stronger* than that which pertains to other beliefs, and thus that, generally, our theoretical rather than observational beliefs should be given up in case of conflict. This squares nicely, it seems to me, with Quine's version of the

---

[11] Obviously, I now assume that a sentence is an observation sentence in the relevant sense only if it is observational for the whole speech community.

[12] This latter claim is related to Quine's view that the test (and sometimes aim) of science lies in prediction of patterns of sensory stimulation, since observation sentences, given their close causal links to stimulation, may be looked upon as the 'means of verbalizing' such predictions (Quine 1992:4). However, notice that Quine does not seem to regard *this* claim in turn (i.e., the claim that the test of science lies in prediction of stimulation) as normative, but merely as 'defining a particular language game' (Quine 1992:20).

thesis of the privileged status of observation sentences, especially since Quine has stressed that such sentences are, in spite of their special role, revisable.[13]

6 Conclusion

In sum, then, I have tried to provide some support for Davidson's claim that the view that ties meaning to stimulation, or to any kind of subjective evidence, yields skepticism, and explain why his own view is not open to this objection. In my opinion, by bringing out these implications for skepticism of these different approaches to meaning, Davidson has made an important contribution, regardless of whether the proximal view could at any point be attributed to Quine.

I have also argued that Davidson's views allow him to accept many of the claims that empiricists tend to make about the epistemological status of observational beliefs, and, in particular, that nothing that Davidson has said is incompatible with Quine's views about the epistemological role of such sentences. So, in so far as these claims still comprise a distinctly empiricist position, Davidson's remark that we, by dropping the view on meaning that provides the main target of his criticism, are 'relinquishing what remains of empiricism after the two dogmas have been surrendered' (Davidson 1990a:68) appears premature, although the surviving empiricism might be somewhat watered down.

Moreover, this means that, in so far as Quine has given up the proximal view, or perhaps never even accepted it, the disagreement between Davidson and Quine appears less substantial than one might first think. This might not be surprising, in view of the deep kinship between Quine's and Davidson's philosophical outlooks. However, it has been challenged (see, e.g., Bergström this volume). Anyway, the mere fact that the conclusion is unsurprising will not discourage me, at least to the extent that it is correct.[14]

References

Bergström, L. 2001. Davidson's Objections to Quine's Empiricism. This volume.

Davidson, D. 1984. *Inquiries into Truth and Interpretation*. Oxford: Clarendon Press.

---

[13] Thus, Quine acknowledges that there may be extreme cases where a verdict to an observation sentence might have to be dismissed (*after* the event of stimulation) if it conflicts with 'a theory that has overwhelming support from other quarters' (Quine 1973:41). See also Quine 1981:71.

[14] I thank Lars Bergström, Peter Pagin, and Mike Ridge for valuable comments.

Davidson, D. 1986. A Coherence Theory of Truth and Knowledge. *Truth and Interpretation: Perspectives on the Philosophy of Donald Davidson*, ed. E. LePore, 307-19. Oxford: Blackwell.

Davidson, D. 1989. The Myth of the Subjective. *Relativism: Interpretation and Confrontation*, ed. M. Krausz, 159-72. Notre Dame: University of Notre Dame Press.

Davidson, D. 1990a. Meaning, Truth and Evidence. *Perspectives on Quine*, eds. R.B. Barrett and R.F. Gibson, 68-79. Oxford: Blackwell.

Davidson, D. 1990b. Epistemology Externalized. *Dialectica* 45:191-202.

Davidson, D. 1991. Three Varieties of Knowledge. *A.J. Ayer: Memorial Essays*, ed. Griffith, 153-66. Royal Institute of Philosophy (suppl. 30).

Davidson, D. 1994. On Quine's Philosophy. *Theoria* 60:184-92.

Davidson, D. 1996. The Folly of Trying to Define Truth. *Journal of Philosophy* 93:263-78.

Fodor, J. and LePore, E. 1992. *Holism: A Shoppers Guide*. Oxford: Blackwell.

Quine, W.V. 1960. *Word and Object*. Cambridge, MA: MIT Press.

Quine, W.V. 1969. *Ontological Relativity*. New York: Columbia University Press.

Quine, W.V. 1973. *The Roots of Reference*. La Salle, IL: Open Court.

Quine, W.V. 1981. *Theories and Things*. Cambridge, MA: Harvard University Press.

Quine, W.V. 1986. Reply to Nozick. *The Philosophy of W.V. Quine*, eds. L.E. Hahn and P.A. Shilpp, 364-67. La Salle, IL: Open Court.

Quine, W.V. 1992. *Pursuit of Truth*. 2nd ed. Cambridge, MA: Harvard University Press.

Quine, W.V. 1993. In Praise of Observation Sentences. *Journal of Philosophy* 90:107-16.

Quine, W.V. 1995. *From Stimulus to Science*. Cambridge, MA: Harvard University Press.

Quine, W.V. 1996. Progress on Two Fronts. *Journal of Philosophy* 93:159-63.

Quine, W.V. 1999. Where Do We Disagree? *The Philosophy of Donald Davidson*, ed. L.E. Hahn, 73-79. La Salle, IL: Open Court.

Tersman, F. 1998a. Stimulus Meaning Debunked. *Erkenntnis* 49:371-85.

Tersman, F. 1998b. Crispin Wright on Moral Disagreement. *Philosophical Quarterly* 48:359-65.

Tersman, F. 1998c. Quine on Ethics. *Theoria* 64:84-98.

15

Comments on Karlovy Vary Papers

DONALD DAVIDSON

The conference in Karlovy Vary at which precursors of many of the papers in this volume were delivered was a wonderful and deeply enjoyable experience for me. It was also sobering and educational, as I hope my replies reveal. I am grateful to those who organized the conference, those who attended, and especially to those who wrote the present papers, and edited this book.

1 The Rejection of Empiricism

When I have rejected empiricism, I have tried to make clear that what I oppose is the idea that there is an element in experience which serves as a basis and justification for empirical knowledge, an element which is private and subjective in the sense that it owes nothing to what is outside the mind. I don't doubt that experience is essential to our knowledge of the world, or that the senses mediate between the world and our knowledge of it. I have not, so far as I remember, ever questioned the existence of unconceptualized sensations. What I have criticized is the introduction of *epistemic* intermediaries between the world and our beliefs about it; by epistemic intermediaries I mean items that are given in experience and that provide the ultimate reasons for our take on the environment.

Some empiricists have thought that only such intermediaries can be known for certain. They were impressed with the claim that nothing can be

285

probable unless something is certain, and they thought that sense data, or something like them, would fill the bill in that they 'seem what they are and are what they seem' in Hume's cogent formulation. I have argued that if sense data are entities about which we can have knowledge, they must have properties unknown to us. I think there are general arguments against 'objects before the mind', and so hold that the quest for such objects as providing a sure foundation of knowledge is mistaken. This is not, of course, a general argument against every form of empiricism which looks to epistemic intermediaries to justify empirical beliefs. It is an argument against one form of empiricism.

Many empiricists have hoped general skepticism of the senses could be defeated by showing how our beliefs about the world can be constructed from, and justified by, intermediaries. I have maintained, on the contrary, that dependence on data which bear no logical relation to the outside world makes skepticism inevitable. If the argument is sound, then an empiricism that intends to circumvent skepticism, but actually entails the contrary, is self-defeating. This leaves open the possibility that empiricism as I construe it and skepticism are both viable. So it is clear that even if empiricism entails skepticism, the entailment does not prove skepticism false.

If the foundation of all empirical knowledge is an unconceptualized given, we are apt to accept the idea that there might be radically different ways of organizing the 'data'. Empiricism (as I think of it) leads to the dichotomy of scheme and content and hence to conceptual relativism. Since conceptual relativism is not (I think) intelligible, this has provided another reason (to my mind) for holding empiricism unacceptable.

But the central argument for rejecting empiricisms that base knowledge on something unconceptualized is that nothing that is unconceptualized can serve as a reason for an empirical belief, or for anything else, since the relation of a reason to what it supports is conceptual and so demands that the reason have a propositional content. John McDowell recognizes that I was clear about this, and it seems to me that a reader of 'A Coherence Theory of Truth and Knowledge' (Davidson 1983) cannot miss the emphasis I put on this point.

There are, then, at least two general kinds of empiricism I have rejected. Both kinds depend on epistemic intermediaries, but they differ in that one is relatively clear that the intermediaries are unconceptualized, while the other is not. It is likely that in making the case against empiricism I have often failed to distinguish these two sorts of empiricism and the arguments against them.

2 Skepticism

John McDowell, Bjørn Ramberg, and Folke Tersman all suppose that my chief reason for rejecting empiricism is that it leads to skepticism, but this is not so. I did always consider that it was a serious count against any theory that it entailed skepticism, but I realized that this in itself was not an argument against either skepticism or empiricism. Here, in rough outline, is how I arrived at my present position. As a graduate student I was convinced by Quine's case against reductive empiricism. Quine was mainly concerned with Carnap's *Der Logische Aufbau der Welt* (Carnap 1928), probably because it was the most ambitious and detailed attempt to show how knowledge of an objective world could be constructed from certain qualitative aspects of experience. The case was equally convincing against the empiricism of C. I. Lewis or what was more or less suggested by Hume, Mill, Russell, and others. Quine's argument could be considered as an attack on an empiricism based on unconceptualized phenomena or as an attack on an empiricism based (deductively) on sentences that reported these phenomena. Quine did not, of course, then or ever give up an empiricism based *nondeductively*, that is, holistically, on the 'testimony of the senses'. But I did abandon the attempt to make sense of any such empirical foundations, probably convinced by Wilfrid Sellars's 'Empiricism and the Philosophy of Mind' (Sellars 1956) with its powerful attack on the 'myth of the given'. In 1958 Quine invited me to read the manuscript of *Word and Object* (Quine 1960). I had been trying to teach philosophy of language and had been rereading Quine's earlier articles, but *Word and Object*, when I finally took it in, changed my thinking forever. It now seems absurdly simple, something I ought to have found in Wittgenstein, but it took Quine's account of radical translation to make me see that learning a language is not a matter of attaching the right meanings to words, but a process in which words are endowed with a use. I resisted Quine's notion of stimulus meaning, which seemed to me to suffer from much the same ills as sense data as the basis for meaning and knowledge. But if from the start one took Quine's radical translator as sharing an external world with his interlocutors, then language, and with it epistemology, would be ineluctably externalized.

It took time to appreciate what was for me the revolutionary power of this way of viewing language and thought and their relation to the world, and longer still to realize that if one accepted this view, general skepticism of the senses and skepticism about other minds would be seen to be futile before they could be formulated. I did not set out to discredit skepticism, nor did I give up empiricism because it led to skepticism. It is the form of externalism that developed from my concern with how thoughts and utterances come to have the content they do which discredits skepticism. Given the considerations and arguments which resulted in my dismissing skepticism, how should I describe my present attitude? Do I think I have refuted skepticism (shown it to be false) or, as Rorty puts it, told it to get lost (a non-problem)? Skepticism says we do not have knowledge of one sort or another. I argue that if we have doubts, we have thoughts, and if we have thoughts, it follows that we know there are other people with minds and that there is an environment we share with them. Granted that we do have doubts (or beliefs), and the subsequent argument, it follows that skepticism is false. But the skeptic starts with doubts, so (given the argument) the skeptic is not in a position to raise the question.

A number of philosophers, among them Ramberg and Peter Pagin in the present volume, have pointed out that I have no knock-down argument against skepticism. Of course not; note the provisos above. Some of the assumptions are empirical and so could (in one sense of 'could') be false. There are a number of questionable steps in the argument, and at least one large leap, for I accept the Wittgensteinian view that interpersonal communication can explain the fact that our thoughts and utterances can be true or false, and then claim that *only* social exchange can explain this fact.

3   Experience

John McDowell thinks I fail to take account of the legitimate role of experience in empirical knowledge, a role he allows may have been distorted by many historical versions of empiricism, but which ought to be recognized and correctly described. He is concerned to 'relieve the specific philosophical discomfort' that arises, at least for some philosophers, when they try to reconcile the idea that what is given in experience is unpolluted by the conceptual with the demand that this given provide reasons for our empirical beliefs. The hopeless struggle to accomplish this reconciliation I have described at some length (Davidson 1982; Davidson 1983). McDowell is critical of my description for having emphasized that the appeal of the unconceptualized was partly prompted by a desire for an epistemic base that was immune to doubt. But worse, he holds that I have shown, by my endorsement of a sort of coherentism, and therefore my rejection of what to his mind is valid in empiricism, that I am 'immune to the philosophical discomfort' he has tried to relieve. On this last point he is right. I have not been tempted by the idea that anything unconceptualized can provide reasons for beliefs, and I have also rejected empiricisms that interject epistemic intermediaries between the mind and the world. I think many of our beliefs are directly connected to the world they purport to be about. So neither horn of McDowell's dilemma appeals to me. What separates us (aside from the appropriate philosophical anxiety) is in how we think the world provides us with reasons to support our empirical beliefs.

I think the world causes us to perceive and believe things, and that this is the direct source of the 'friction' between world and mind that McDowell wants to accommodate. I get the impression that McDowell thinks that because our beliefs are 'free', such causality is out of place; it is an essential aspect of his dilemma that the world of the natural sciences is dominated by causality, but the life of the thinking mind is not. This is why it seems to him so hard to understand how the natural world can 'constrain' our thinking. This is a problem that does not arise in this form if one rejects such a dualism with respect to causality. Thinking, perceiving, remembering, and voluntary action characterize certain physical objects, and (in my view) causality does not 'constrain' these activities, but enables them. Kant thought there could be no conflict between the sort of autonomy judgment and action sometimes enjoy and universal causality, and he was right. Laws of nature, so-called, are another matter. Sharply defined laws are part of the point of a way of describing and explaining events which belongs to the domain of natural science, and this is a conceptual domain to which the vocabulary of psychology is not reducible. Causal talk spans the domains.

Perhaps it is to bridge what McDowell may see as an ontological chasm that he introduces a novel propositional attitude. The attitude has one foot in the world, in that we have no direct control over its occurrences; nature simply produces (causes?) it in us. It has the other foot in the mental world; it is fully conceptualized, and so has logical relations with other attitudes. The occurrence of one of these attitudes might be called an 'appearance', an appearance *that* things are a certain way. An appearance is not tinged with belief, since we are free to form beliefs as we please, but its manifestations can serve as reasons for beliefs, and so justify them. If we accept this account, McDowell holds, we will be relieved of the discomfort that results from the search for an unconceptualized justification of our beliefs. Thus there is a source of justification, it is provided independent of our will, but it is conceptualized, and so can be logically related to our beliefs.

How does my view of the relation between the world and our beliefs about it differ? We agree that in experience we are presented with fully conceptualized thoughts which serve as reasons for our beliefs about the world. The difference is this: I hold that the thoughts with which we are presented by nature are beliefs. We look, hear, feel, smell, and touch, and we are caused to believe there is an elephant before us. Where McDowell introduces epistemic intermediaries between nature and belief, what I have called 'appearances', I do not. For him, first there are the appearances and then we decide whether things are as they appear; for me, there is no distinction between things appearing to me to be a certain way and my taking them to be that way. I cannot see what McDowell requires of experience that I have left out. Where he has appearances I have perceptual beliefs. For him and for me, these presentations are not willed; this provides the 'friction' between world and mind he wants. He wants his concepts to have content. Perceptual beliefs provide this as surely as his appearances. It is essential for him, as it is for me, that what is given in experience supplies a rational justification for our settled beliefs. There does, however, remain one difference: for me, perceptual beliefs are not freely chosen. They can, however, be rejected, often in an instant, on the basis of further perceptions, memory, and general knowledge of the world.

McDowell describes a position whose aim is 'that there not be a mystery in the very idea of objective import' (McDowell 1998). I am mystified by his suggestion. I do not understand how a propositional attitude which is totally devoid of an element of belief can serve as a reason for anything. We take it in, he says. If this means we *know* what we have taken in, then we must believe that we have taken it in, and this belief can be a reason. But an attitude that carries no conviction would be inert. I also wonder why an appearance that has been taken in should be assumed to represent an objective world. It cannot be an adequate response to say that the content of an appearance purports to concern an objective world, since this is equally true of my perceptual beliefs, which McDowell rejects.

McDowell has objected to my view that perceptual beliefs are unmediated that this would make those beliefs mysterious; we would just have them, but *they* would be unjustified. It would, he says, be like what chicken-sexing is said to be. The chicken-sexer (we are told) cannot give a reason why he believes a chicken is male or female; he looks and feels, and believes. This seems to me just the way perception works. Of course we can often justify a judgment by saying, 'It looks and feels that way', but this either adds nothing more than the information that it was sight and feel that prompted the belief, or it expresses the belief that it looks and feels the way a female chicken looks and feels, which is another belief, and one that can be a reason to believe the chicken is of one sex rather than the other. My misleadingly called 'coherentism' comes just to this: only a belief can be a reason for another belief. McDowell thinks this implies that 'experience' has no input. But not so: to have an experience in the cases in which we are interested is just to be caused by our sense organs to have an empirical belief. I do not see how interjecting an appearance between sense organs and belief imbues thought with *more* content. Finally, I am baffled by the idea that beliefs are not caused. Of course if we are justified in accepting our perceptual beliefs as providing reasons for further beliefs, this needs to be explained. I will come to this point presently.

4   Quine and Empiricism

McDowell says I am wrong in holding that Quine's empiricism makes the basis of empirical knowledge private. Here McDowell misunderstands me. I did not mean that Quine depends on something mental whose content is grasped by only one person, but that he makes the content of empirical knowledge depend on something that is not shared with others. As Quine put it in one of his last publications, 'I remain unswerved in locating stimulation at the neural input, for my interest is epistemological, however naturalized. I am interested in the flow of evidence from the triggering of the senses to the pronouncements of science' (Quine 1990, p. 3). It is the 'evidence' Quine mentions here that is private.

Both Folke Tersman and Lars Bergström think I have failed to appreciate features of Quine's empiricism. Tersman is generally sympathetic to my criticism of Quine's individualistic empiricism, and gives a good account of my misgivings. But he holds that empiricism is right in awarding observation sentences a privileged role, and he reads me as denying this. The matter is a little complicated. In *Word and Object* observation sentences were the key to translation and hence to understanding communication, but I thought their tie to stimulus meaning unsuited them both for this task and as a key to the foundations of empirical knowledge. Over the years Quine abandoned stimulus meaning as the key to explaining linguistic communication, and in the end decided that what I called the distal stimulus was the external, shared, causal factor in the case of meaning (Quine 1996). Stimulus meaning was further demoted when Quine came to characterize observation sentences as commanding, on occasions when the external situation was shared, the same verdict from all competent speakers of the language. At this point our differences might have dwindled to zero, except for the empiricist doctrine from which he did not swerve. At this last stage, I could interpret his philosophy of language as a form of externalism with which I was happy, but I found his epistemology incongruously internalist (Davidson 1995). I am pretty sure, though, that Quine did not see it this way; he did not accept the externalism I thought his view of language implied.

I have always embraced Quine's idea that there are sentences the use of which is learned in ostensive situations, and the learning of which is essential to learning the use of all other sentences. These are the perceptual sentences a radical interpreter would probably understand first, and among the first sentences a beginner would learn. Thus there is a perfectly good sense in which certain perceptual sentences are for me epistemically prior: they are an entering wedge into language, and perceptual sentences generally are what connect empirical thought and talk to the world. I agree with Tersman that this important element in my epistemology and philosophy of language is similar to Quine's appeal to observation sentences (I consciously adapted it from Quine) and that it is one traditional feature of empiricism. Following Quine I have, of course, abandoned the idea that the empirical content of each empirical sentence can be tracked back to a definite stock of observation sentences. I also do not characterize observation sentences in terms of the sort of social agreement on which Quine has recently depended, for I do not think of successful ostensive learning as requiring that a learner use the same sounds or signs his teacher or teachers do in response to shared occasions. Where I differ from the spirit of empiricism most clearly, however, is in taking ostensive learning to infuse language and thought from the start with an objective relation to the world.

It is this last point that I think Lars Bergström has failed to appreciate. If, as Bergström says, 'Quine identifies sensory evidence with the triggering of sensory receptors', then Quine remained the internalist I long took him to be. But unlike Bergström Quine realized that it made no sense to take the triggering of sensory nerves literally as evidence. In his 'Comment on Davidson' (Quine 1990), in response to my complaint that sensory promptings could not be evidence (Davidson 1990), Quine wrote 'I agree that in my theory of evidence the term "evidence" gets no explication and plays no role', and he repeats the point (Quine 1990, p. 2). So the question what justifies our empirical beliefs remains. Quine and I both think the triggering of sensory nerves plays an essential (causal) role in what we believe, and we both think that (in Bergström's words) 'our beliefs about the world are, and should be, based on experience'. Where Quine and I differ, if we do, is in the details, and perhaps in our use of the word 'experience'.

5 Triangulation

Ramberg is right that an important change came over my thinking as the import of ostensive learning and teaching sank in. When it did I generalized the idea to what I called 'triangulation'. The elements had been there from the start. What was needed was Quine's account of radical translation with modifications which mainly involved substituting Tarski's semantic structure for Quine's emphasis on translation, and locating the key to ostension in the shared situations which provide the content of perceptual beliefs. These two moves were related, since the first demanded relating predicates to an ontology and the second tied the ontology to the world.

I have, as Peter Pagin complains, described triangulation in a number of ways and from several points of view. I do not see these descriptions and points of view as inconsistent. There is, first, the primitive situation, which does not require intensional attitudes. It involves two (or, as always, more than two) creatures reacting to the same scene, event, or object, and correlating the other's reactions with the observed external stimulus. This description is obviously a description that can be made only by someone with the concepts I have just used, but nothing in what I have described implies that the interacting creatures are capable of describing what they are doing. Nor does it imply that the creatures are capable of describing anything at all; I am talking here about interactions among creatures which well may lack concepts. I distinguish between having a concept and reacting, perhaps in complex and learned ways, to the environment. Having a concept, as I understand the word, consists in classifying events, objects, or features of the world, and being aware that misclassification is possible; no conceptualization without predication.

My thesis is that the triangular arrangement I have described is a necessary condition of speech and thought. It is not sufficient. If it, or it in addition to any other non-intensionally described conditions, were sufficient as well as necessary, we could reduce the intensional to the extensional, and this is not, in my opinion, possible. Pagin, if I understand him, thinks that if reduction is not possible, then it cannot be the case that there are philosophically interesting necessary conditions that can be stated extensionally, but I cannot see why this should be the case. Memory, perception, and voluntary action have conditions that must (usually) be stated in non-intensional terms, and it is the position of externalists like me that propositional thought and speech are in this respect like memory, perception, and voluntary action.

A *second* application of the idea of triangulation is to the learning situation where one creature is not yet into thought and language, but the social environment provides teachers or perhaps just appropriate verbal stimulation. The purpose of this exercise is not to explain in detail how the process works, for to do this would amount to reducing the intensional to the extensional. The purpose is to indicate how the triangular arrangement makes the process possible. It does this, I have urged, by conditioning the learner to associate the teacher's behavior with specific features of the world that the learner already discriminates, and by providing (as I have cautiously put it) a 'space' in which awareness of the possibility of error can take root. Pagin says this is sheer armchair empirical speculation, not philosophy. Since I am not enamoured of the analytic/synthetic distinction, neither am I sharp on the sheer-armchair-empirical-speculation/empirical-speculation distinction. It certainly is speculation, and just as surely is not proven to be the sole source of our sense of objectivity. It does not explain thought or language nor does it, if I understand the concept, 'explicate' them.

Implicit in the claim that triangulation is a necessary condition of propositional thought and language are two further claims. The first is that language and thought are mutually dependent; neither can exist without the other and so they must develop, no doubt by steps, together. The second is that for someone to think or say that the cat is on the mat there must be a causal history of that person that traces back, directly or indirectly, to triangular experiences, often ostensive in character. Pagin thinks this is an unsupported, or anyway philosophically uninteresting, hypothesis. I won't try to guess what is philosophically interesting, but the view that a history of encounters with some of the things we speak about and have beliefs about is necessary if we are to refer to and form attitudes towards those objects is at the heart of the sort of externalism I embrace. On this view, aspects of our interactions with others and the world are partially constitutive of what we mean and think. There can not be said to be proof of this claim. Its plausibility depends on a conviction which can seem either empirical or *a priori*; a conviction that this is a fact about what sort of creatures we are. Empirical if you think it just happens to be true of us that this is how we come to be able to speak and think about the world; *a priori* if you think, as I tend to, that this is part of what we mean when we talk of thinking and speaking. After all, the notions of speaking and thinking are ours.

I will try to say briefly how I think triangulation bears on the determination of the contents of our perceptual beliefs. In the *first* situation I described, in which interacting creatures do not have propositional thoughts or language, all we can say is that signaling can take place (what some are pleased to call animal communication). Even in the absence of a shared stimulus, a creature may react as it would if it were similarly stimulated. The *second* situation begins like the first for the novice, and evolves, given the intentional or unintended rewards and punishments of life, into speech and propositional thought. The learner, taking advantage of the space created by triangulation, becomes aware of the possibility of error, and so of the distinction between what is believed or seems to be the case and what is objectively so. Triangulation does not pretend to explain, explicate, or describe this process. There is a *third* situation in which two participants are equipped with thought and a language, but lack a common language. The problem is for each to learn to understand the other: the problem of radical interpretation. There seems, given how and what we are, no way this problem can be solved that does not involve something like ostensive learning. Only at this stage can we say that the shared cause helps determine the content of utterances, and this is because there is a shared understanding of the nature of ostension and general agreement about the main features of the world. Though radical interpretation cannot, of course, explain or describe how a first language is learned, it is hard to believe it does not throw light on what helps make that accomplishment possible.

6   Truth

'Beliefs', Bjørn Ramberg quotes me as saying, 'represent nothing. It is good to be rid of representations, and with them the correspondence theory of truth'. He then worries that, having thrown out representations as 'before' the mind because they would serve as epistemic intermediaries, I have (inadvertently?) made it impossible to say that our beliefs can 'stand in a truth-relation to the world'. In the passages he quotes, and others, I may have encouraged him, and maybe Richard Rorty, to conclude that I think it is a mistake to suppose there is a real world independent of our thoughts and to which our thoughts bear an epistemic relation. Fortunately Stephen Neale has, in his essay in this volume, expressed my views on truth and representation with great clarity, and has emphasized distinctions I apparently have not adequately stressed. When I have written about Quine, I have described him as having a theory of meaning in spite of the fact that he wants no truck with meanings. He agreed: meaning was all right, it was meanings to which he was opposed. I might have said representation, properly understood, is all right, but not representations. What I have inveighed against is the idea that true sentences and, by extension, propositional attitudes, represent, refer to, stand for, or correspond to, distinct situations or facts. My reasons are essentially semantical and derive from Frege's view (and Church's and Gödel's arguments) that if sentences correspond to anything, all true sentences correspond to the same thing. So we can say, if we please, that true sentences and beliefs correspond to, or represent, The World. But if it does please us to talk this way, we should be clear that we have not said anything more than that these sentences and beliefs are true; we have not explained truth. (For a detailed statement of the argument, and its limits, see Neale 1995.)

Both Ramberg and Neale note that I have two objections to representations. One I have just rehearsed: the only possible 'truth-maker' is the world, and so there are no interesting entities to stand in the representing relation. The other objection is to 'objects before the mind' which some have invoked as the basis for epistemology. If these objects are sense data or the like, the point is unrelated to the first argument and has nothing to do with representations. But when the objects are propositions, the arguments converge. If there are no things to represent, there can be no mental propositional representers.

7   Norms

Ramberg suggests that it may be worth paying the price of being a skeptic in order to salvage 'the explanatory force and the regulative function that the idea of truth as correspondence with reality appears to offer'. I don't see that my anti-representational stance entails or is entailed by skepticism or its rejection, and I have explained above that if correspondence with reality means no more than being true of the world, i.e., true, I have no objection. But does correspondence or truth have a 'regulative' function? I suppose this is the same as asking whether truth is a norm, the issue Pascal Engel pursues. Engel points out that I have always claimed that psychological terms like intention, belief, desire, memory, and perception, are normative. They are, because these are propositional attitudes or entail them, and such attitudes apply only to rational creatures, and the attribution of these attitudes requires the attributor to make use of his or her norms of rationality. But truth is not a psychological concept nor does it entail one. It is, or so I have argued, a concept we make essential use of in understanding the attitudes, but that is another matter.

Engel remarks that truth is a norm of assertoric practice, that is, the making of assertions. I agree, because someone who makes an assertion represents himself as believing what he says and so gives others the right to believe he believes what he says. But the norm attaches to the representing, not the belief. Of course anyone who has a propositional attitude knows, at least tacitly, what the truth conditions of the propositional content of the attitude are. But this does not make truth a norm. Engel classifies me as a sort of deflationist because I do not think truth is a norm, but I certainly do not hold that it is a mistake to 'read more into the concept of truth than the familiar formal features'. Rorty may be a deflationist, and Rorty and I agree that truth is not a norm, but we have disagreed repeatedly in print and in person over the question whether truth has further essential features. Much that I have written on truth is intended to describe these features, including two pieces that Engel lists (Davidson 1990; Davidson 1997); but also see (Davidson 1999; Davidson 2000).

Engel agrees with me that truth is not a goal. He explains the sense in which he thinks truth is a norm this way: 'That a belief is justified is a *prima facie* reason for thinking it true'. Justification and the notion of a reason are, as he correctly remarks, normative notions. Thus normative concepts are linked to truth. But does it follow that truth is a norm? Thinking something is true is believing it. We have reasons for believing things and our reasons, we often think, justify our beliefs. We aim to justify what we think. It is a goal of inquiry to be justified. We pursue this goal by replicating our experiments, studying the literature, checking our statistics, asking others to review our work, and reflecting that we may, in the bowels of Christ, be mistaken. None of this, as far as I can see, shows that truth is a norm. Unless, of course, we mean no more by saying truth is a norm than that being justified is a norm. Engel seems close to saying this in his antepenultimate sentence.

Kathrin Glüer's discussion of conventions and norms in the use of language is also pertinent to the question whether truth is a norm. Some philosophers, she points out (including Boghossian, whom she quotes), have claimed that every use of a meaningful predicate is normative because it is 'correctly' applied only to those things of which it is true. But as she explains, this is not a norm in any interesting sense: it cannot mean that we ought to say only what is true. And though it may be a moral norm that we ought to assert only what we believe to be true, this is not a norm of correct linguistic usage. I applaud Glüer's entire treatment of the nest of confusions permeating much talk of norms, conventions, and language games as these words or concepts have been brandished in the discussion of language; what she says I have not said as well myself. She gently scolds me for saying that 'meaning something requires that by and large one follows a practice of one's own, a practice that can be understood by others', because 'practice' is a loaded Wittgensteinian word, but she rightly sees that all I meant was that a considerable degree of consistency in the use of words is no doubt empirically necessary if we are to be understood. The only relevant norm is practical and follows from the fact that usually we want to be understood.

Glüer, like Engel, wonders why, if I do not think appeal to norms or conventions illuminates the notions of meaning and truth, I insist that concepts like belief, desire, intention, and meaning something are irreducibly normative. She thinks this is just a way of describing a feature of these concepts, and implies no prescriptions. I agree. What I have argued is that propositional psychological concepts are different from the concepts of the natural sciences in that they can be used to attribute attitudes only by the employment of the norms of the attributor. No matter what the subject matter, we use our own norms, of course, but in the case of attributing attitudes there is an essential twist: the attitudes we attribute, since they are constituted in part by rational considerations, are also norm-determined. Glüer is right that this does not impose any obligation on the user of psychological concepts: it is a description of a feature of their application. What I have called 'charity' in interpreting others is not a virtue.

8   Indeterminacy and Mind

I had hoped to defuse the excitement and counter the hostility Quine's doctrine of the indeterminacy of translation has aroused by comparing indeterminacy with the unexciting fact that we can represent various forms of measurement in the numbers in numberless ways. To those unhappy with indeterminacy, it is largely irrelevant that much of the indeterminacy Quine finds unavoidable can be reduced by appeal to evidence of the general sort to which he appeals. For example, Quine's method for detecting the pure sentential connectives can be utilized to detect quantificational structure, with the accompanying identification of singular terms, predicates, and quantifiers. Further reduction can result if one turns from translation to interpretation, as I call it, which involves the semantics of truth, which then requires the introduction of a form of reference (satisfaction) and an ontology. A further option can put decision theory, with its ability to extract both subjective probabilities and relative degrees of desire (utilities) from simple choices, into the mix of belief and meaning already implicit in Quine's approach. This step does much to constrain the indeterminacy attached to predicates, especially the more theoretical ones. If I am right, these modifications of Quine's method of radical translation take much of the sting out of the doctrine of indeterminacy: in my version, the clear remaining indeterminacy attaches to how predicates and singular terms are related to particular entities in the ontology. This is what Quine calls the 'inscrutability of reference'. There are, of course, algorithms for converting one system of reference to another, Quine's 'proxy functions' (Quine 1969). I had such cases very much in mind when I introduced the analogy with measurement. But reducing the indeterminacy does not quiet the complaints, nor does the analogy with measurement.

Piers Rawling concentrates on two features of the analogy that he finds troubling.

The first is that in the case of measurement, there is an 'algorithm' (specified by a uniqueness theorem) which tell us how we are allowed to convert one numerical measure into another (feet into meters, acres into hectares), whereas, he says, there is no such algorithm in the case of interpretations. Proxy functions, which apply in the cases I emphasize, are just such algorithms. And Tarski, whose methods I am following, proves a uniqueness theorem which says that if there are two ways of defining truth for a given language which satisfy his constraints, they are equivalent. I think there are other cases of indeterminacy which are equally harmless. There is an area in the continuum of hues where I say 'green' and others say 'blue'. You may decide either that I am wrong about the color or that I use the words differently: according to how you interpret what I mean you adjust my beliefs to suit. Although the change in your interpretation of my 'green' affects an infinity of possible further interpretations, it may be that there is no reason to choose between the interpretations. Again there is a simple algorithm. If I am wrong about this, it doesn't affect the main point, which is that there are endless ways in which the predicates and singular terms of a language may be mapped onto the same ontology which yield equivalent truth conditions for all the sentences of that language. Rawling does not dispute my (not particularly idiosyncratic) claim that both the evidence for and the output of a theory of meaning concern what (the utterances of) sentences mean. Frege's dictum that it is only in the context of a sentence that words have a meaning I interpret as saying that semantic theories can postulate what they please about words as long as what they yield for sentences is correct.

I am not quite clear whether the supposed absence of algorithms carries the entire burden of Rawling's case against the measurement analogy. There seems to be an independent point which depends heavily on the question what the entities are to which interpretations are assigned. He is right that in my view there are no such states of mind as belief states, but only because I am uncertain whether there are such *entities* as states, minds, or beliefs. But I am firmly convinced that when we make such remarks as 'Alphonse believes that Lisbon is in Portugal' what we say about Alphonse is objectively true or false. Statements like this attribute a genuine psychological property to a person. *People* believe, want, intend, and mean, this and that. Actually, I don't want to invoke properties at this point either: attributing a property is done by using a predicate, and the semantics of predicates don't need or want properties (unless, of course, for predicates, if such there be, that are true of properties). Having banished properties, states, beliefs, and so on, from my explanatory machinery, I will now continue to allow myself to use words that superficially seem to refer to such things, on condition that I be understood to hold that such talk can be exchanged at boring length for talk that doesn't use these words as referring to entities. It should be clear that my ontological scruples are due only to my suspicion that these entities do not help explain what I want to explain. I freely accept lots of abstract objects, among them sets, numbers, shapes, words, and sentences.

Our justifying evidence for attributions of attitudes to others is their behavior, sometimes observed, but more often correctly assumed or inferred from context. Our attributions do not constitute or create the attitudes. There are endless attitudes people keep to themselves and even when they don't we are apt to get them wrong. The only necessary connection between the existence of attitudes and attributions of attitudes is that a person must have come to understand others (not perfectly, of course) and be understood by them in order to have any attitudes.

Radical interpretation is based on observed speech, either utterances of sentences that are taken by the interpreter to be held true by the speaker under the circumstances, or cases where one sentence is taken to be preferred true to another. It is these sentences (relativized to the context) which are interpreted, not only semantically, but as sentences the utterances of which reveal the attitudes of belief and desire. Rawling elegantly explains how it is supposed to work. The story about radical interpretation depicts the interpreter as using his or her own sentences to interpret the speaker. This mirrors my semantic analysis of how we verbally express our attributions of attitudes: pinning a belief that Lisbon is in Portugal on Alfonse, I say, 'Alphonse believes this: Lisbon is in Portugal'. If what I say is true, I have specified an objective characteristic of Alphonse. The sentence following the colon is mine. In the measurement analogy, what serve as the 'numbers' are the interpreter's sentences, which can serve to keep track of everything propositional in the speaker which the resources of the interpreter can represent.

Rawling will still object that since there are in theory many ways the interpreter can use his sentences to accommodate the evidence, and indeed all possible evidence, of the sort allowed the interpreter, the speaker's attitudes will still not be determined uniquely. This objection is independent of any difficulties raised by the measurement analogy; it is an objection to any indeterminacy thesis. But it misses the point. Indeterminacy doesn't entail that, for all the interpreter can tell, the speaker may 'mean' any number of completely different things. The thesis is rather that one can capture exactly the same attitudes in systematically different ways. Rawling does not base his criticism of indeterminacy and the measurement analogy on arguments to show that a Tarski-style characterization of truth for a language is inadequate as an account of what would suffice for understanding that language. So suppose we have such an account. A defined notion of satisfaction tells us what entities satisfy each predicate of the language (that is, what entities each predicate is true of). Satisfaction can be extended, as Neale points out, to assign to each singular term the entity it names. Assume we have an acceptable characterization of truth and satisfaction. There will be endless proxy functions that map each entity in the ontology one-to-one onto another entity in the same ontology in a specified way (the 'algorithm'). Use any one of these functions to redefine satisfaction. The result will be that the truth conditions of every sentence are preserved, and so all logical relations among sentences, and the relations of each sentence to the world. There is no theoretical or empirical reason to choose one of these interpretive schemes rather than another, no way to tell which of the 'languages' various schemes attribute to a person that person is speaking, for there is no difference in what we are attributing. I have discussed indeterminacy and the accusation of antirealism about the attitudes in Davidson 1997b.

I had not thought of myself as arguing for first person authority, as Fredrik Stjernberg suggests in his interesting paper. I assumed that we know it exists, and I set out to explain the asymmetry between our knowledge of our own minds and our knowledge of other people's minds in a way that does not lead to skepticism. Stjernberg reminds me that I have also maintained that failing the presumption that people know what they believe a person could not come to understand someone else. One reason for saying this is that, absent the presumption, an interpreter could not get started making sense of what she takes to be honest assertions. The other is that unless the interpreter knew what she believes, she would be at a loss to use aspects of her own thought to keep track of the thoughts of someone else. I outline the reasoning for the first in (Davidson 1984) and for the second in (Davidson 1991) and (Davidson 1995). I was not arguing for the existence of first person authority, but for its necessity for communication. (Someone may believe in the existence of first person authority in the sense that if one has a belief about one's own attitudes, such beliefs are generally true without holding that we must have such beliefs about our own beliefs.) I don't know if Stjernberg will find that the reasoning in the last two pieces I refer to closes the gap he finds in the first. In any case, I agree that only those who have communicated with others have thoughts, and so both interpreter and interpretee must know what they think.

It has seemed obvious to many philosophers that what follows an expression like 'Alphonse believes that' must be the object of the belief, and that such objects are entirely mental; they are 'objects before the mind'. Since the identity of such an object determines the contents of a thought, we must be able to distinguish the appropriate object from others if we know what we think. I was willing to grant that if this thesis is correct, there would be a conflict between first person authority and externalism. I had both an argument against such entities, and an alternative suggestion which accommodates the view (which for semantic reasons must be right) that belief sentences and the like are relational. But the entity to which the thinker is related by an attribution of an attitude is not in any sense 'before the mind' of the thinker. It is, in my view, an utterance or sentence of the attributor, which the attributor uses to give the 'measure' of the speaker's thought.

Stjernberg wonders whether there may not be cases where ignorance of the external history or causes that partially determine the contents of my thought (twin-earth cases) make me wrong about what I think. Not in my opinion. Transplanted to twin-earth, I will (according to Putnam), be wrong about what I see, and I will be wrong if I think what I see is what gives my thoughts the content they have. But I will not be wrong about what I think.

When I attribute attitudes to myself, I do not treat myself as authoritative except in the sense that if someone questions my attribution, I assume I know better (except, maybe, on the analyst's couch). First person authority means no more than that I normally know what I think without seeking or needing evidence, and without interpretation. But *how*, Stjernberg asks, do I know it? What kind of answer could there be? In this respect, anyway, Wittgenstein was right: 'The language-game simply is the way it is'. What sets our knowledge of our own minds apart from other forms of knowledge is that there is no answer to the question how we know what we think.

9 Logical Form

Ernie Lepore and Kirk Ludwig are certainly right that the concept of logical form, as applied to natural languages, warrants much more attention than it has received. Many, including me, have been pretty cavalier in making claims about logical form when we have never tried very hard to define it. Lepore and Ludwig approach the task by way of formal semantics, and I do not know of a better method. It turns out that they don't attempt to define the logical form of a sentence, but rather the relation of sameness of logical form. In order to do this they require a formal characterization of truth for languages under consideration which satisfies the clause of Tarski's Convention T which says in effect that the theory that characterizes truth for a language L must entail, for every sentence s of L, a theorem of the form 's

is true in L iff p', where 'p' is replaced by a translation of s. Such theorems they call T-sentences. They assume a way of specifying when a proof is canonical, and define two sentences (of the same or different languages) to have the same logical form if and only if they have proofs that are, in sharply specified ways, similar.

Because of Tarski's requirement that the sentence of the metalanguage *translate* the sentence of the object language in T-sentences, truth theories are what Lepore and Ludwig call *interpretive*. Because of the obscurity of the concept of translation, I have dropped this requirement in favor of other constraints on a theory of truth which are modeled on, but distinct from, Quine's demands on radical translation. These constraints do not pretend to the uniqueness that sameness of meaning does. This difference will obviously make a considerable difference to how we think of logical form, particularly when we ask when sentences in different languages have the same logical form. (It is interesting that Tarski, in a footnote to the formulation of Convention T, says that it would present 'no great difficulties' to give an exact formulation of the phrase 'the translation of a given sentence (of the language studied) into the metalanguage'. But he is, as he insists, thinking only of extensional formal languages for which the interpretation is specified.)

The notion of sameness of semantic form plays an essential role in determining when the logical form of two or more sentences are the same, but I find I am unclear how sameness of semantic form is determined. The distinction between the forms of the axioms of a truth theory is clear enough, and we can read off the semantic form from the character of the axioms. But Lepore and Ludwig insist that in constructing the truth theory we must pay close attention to the actual semantic forms of expressions in the natural language being studied. How are we supposed to tell? They give us a number of examples, but no clear criterion as far as I can see. Yet on this point depends their case for freeing ourselves from 'overly simple models of the logical form of natural language sentences'. Exercising this freedom, they show how they think we should handle restricted quantifiers like 'some men', complex demonstratives, and words like 'most', 'many', 'big', 'slow'. All of these except the first have been recognized as problems for those who would like to stick to ordinary first-order quantificational logic, and I welcome the thought that Lepore and Ludwig have shown how these idioms can be accommodated in a clearly understood semantics. Their hints of how the appropriate axioms in the theory of truth would go do not convince me one way or the other: I would like to see proofs of T-sentences deduced from a formally satisfactory characterization of truth. There is certainly good reason to suppose the crude tools I have used will not do the necessary work.

I like Lepore and Ludwig's development of the idea, which I had casually suggested years ago, that at least for the purposes of discussing formal semantics and logical form, we draw a line between the logical terms for which we must give a recursive account and those for which we don't. We can then declare, if we want to, that the recursively defined terms are the true logical constants. The criterion has the merit of being clear, at least when applied to some logical domains. But it fails, as Lepore and Ludwig point out, to eliminate modal operators. Since allowing modal operators in the metalanguage will certainly open up new possibilities for the treatment of logical form, my remark (which Lepore and Ludwig refer to at the end of section 2) that logical form is relative to the logic of the metalanguage may seem more justified than they allow. But here, as with my other doubts about features of this ambitious paper, my admiration and approval of the attempt are undimmed.

Samuel Guttenplan raises a number of questions about the logical form of sentences about actions containing the word 'by' such as:

(1)   Jones ruined his suit by washing it.

(2)   Smith sank the *Bismark* by pushing a button.

(3)   Susan signaled by raising her arm..

He thinks I have not really discussed such sentences, and that the resources I have mustered will not do the job. It seems to me that I have said quite a lot that is directly relevant to the problems he raises, though I agree that the single essay he lists in his references, 'The Logical Form of Action Sentences', is only a first step. I took several more steps in 'Causal Relations', 'Agency' (all reprinted in Davidson 1980), 'Adverbs of Action' (Davidson 1985), and 'Problems in the Explanation of Action' (Davidson 1987).

Some of the problems posed by (1)–(3) arise in a much simpler form which lacks the word 'by', for example:

(4)   Bill killed the tyrant.

Suppose Bill stabs the tyrant, and as a consequence the tyrant dies a month later. The stabbing takes only a moment, the dying later. How then can the stabbing and the killing be one action, since they apparently occupy different time intervals? My original response was to brazen it out by saying the death is simultaneous with the stabbing. ('You've killed me' breaths the tyrant. Aria by tyrant follows.) I gave up on this line. There are clearly two *events*, a stabbing and a dying; one causes the other. Only one is an *action*, and it is both a stabbing and a killing. Actions, as I pointed out in 'Agency', can be characterized by their effects as well as in other ways; it was, after all, the point of introducing an ontology of events that they can be characterized in endless ways. What is special about a description of an action as having a certain effect is that the characterization doesn't apply until the effect occurs. One and the same stabbing may not at first be a killing, and then become one, just as Bill may at one time be an infant and at a later time be a slayer of tyrants and a grandfather. Guttenplan is right when he says 'by' suggests amplification and precisification. Bill killed the tyrant by stabbing him. Here both events are made more precise, one by having its cause specified, the other by having an effect specified. I have been talking as if these events were picked out by singular terms, but of course that is not so in these sentences. Bill may have stabbed the tyrant seven times and the tyrant have died nine deaths for all 'Bill killed the tyrant' tells us. So let us make this much explicit by giving the following as suggesting the logical form of (4):

(4')   There exist two events, e and f, such that Bill is the agent of e, e is a stabbing of the tyrant, f is a death of the tyrant, and e caused f. (I ignore tense.)

Here 'caused' does the work of 'by', and the stabbing can be modified to be with a knife without the dying being so modified. I suggest that (1) has essentially the same logical form. There is no difficulty about qualifying the washing, but not the ruining of the suit, as vigorous. In each case there is one action and two events.

There are other cases, however, such as (3), that have seemed to many philosophers to be different. (3) entails that Susan did raise her arm, and that by raising her arm she did signal. Was the signaling an *effect* of the Susan's arm going up? It surely was an outcome, a consequence, a result, of Susan's action. These words distinguish between action and consequence only if the relation is causal, and so not symmetrical. But there seem to be many cases where it is right to say that an action described in one way just is (identical with) doing something else, given the conventions or other conditions that obtain. We want to say writing one's name in a certain place is (identical with) signing a check, given certain conventions, a clear mind, and so forth. But we do not want to say that Smith wrote his name by signing the check or that Susan raised her arm by signaling. The problem is actually the same as in the other cases. There is a difference between Susan's signaling and a signal having been made, just as there is a difference between Jones's ruining of his suit and the suit being ruined. The point is that in (1) we did not try to pry apart Jones's washing of his suit and Jones's ruining of his suit: these are the same action twice described. The first description tells us there was an action of Jones's which was a washing; the second description tells us there was an action of Jones's which caused his suit to be ruined; the 'by' in (1) tells us one of the washings caused one of the ruinings. Note that this does *not* mean that one of Jones's washings of his suit caused one of his ruinings of his suit. When Susan raised her arm, she did, given the circumstances, cause a signal to be made.

Paul Horwich raises a fundamental question about the concern of people like Lepore, Ludwig, Guttenplan, and me, with logical form. He claims that we do not need a serious semantic theory to explain how the semantic properties of sentences depend on the semantic properties of the unstructured expressions of the language. He backs up this claim by describing a 'deflationary' approach to compositionality that 'involves no explication of meaning (e.g. in terms of truth conditions) and hence no explanation of why the principle of compositionality holds'. I have never asked for an explanation of why compositionality holds; like Horwich, I assume that compositionality must hold, for reasons on which we might agree. Nor do I think it is generally true that a knowledge of the syntax of a language plus a knowledge of what the words mean does not add up to knowledge of what sentences mean, though Horwich quotes me (correctly) as having said this. The context of my remark makes clear what I had in mind: knowledge of syntax and word meanings does not tell *how* this knowledge works to yield the meanings of sentences, even if one means by 'meanings' only the extensional features of words and sentences.

Horwich's deflationary account of compositionality is couched in terms of translation. I have criticized such accounts on the ground that someone who knows and understands a translation manual may not learn the meaning of a single word or sentence of a translated language. The reason is simple: a translation manual tells us how one language, say Italian, is to be translated into another, perhaps Japanese, but since the manual may be in English, it will not help anyone to understand either Italian or Japanese unless that person already knows one of them. As Horwich says, one needs to know that 'Marte' in Italian means (or, better, refers to) Mars, which is a semantic, not a translational, fact. One may confuse the two if one assumes that one's own language is both the metalanguage and one of the languages for which we are given a translation manual.

How well does Horwich account for compositionality? He introduces names of the meanings of the basic terms of the language for which compositionality is to be construed. Thus 'MARS' names the meaning of 'Mars' and 'ROTATES' names the meaning of 'rotates'. Horwich tries a quasi-Fregean move by saying we can apply the meaning of 'rotates' (which Horwich tells us is a function) to the meaning of 'Mars', which is said to yield the meaning of 'Mars rotates'; this is a plausible interpretation of Frege's view. But Horwich doesn't stay with it, for it loses the point of Frege's semantics to take the meanings of predicates to be the sort of objects that can be named. Frege appreciated the fact that combining a name with a predicate must yield a unit of some sort both on the level of reference and on the level of sense (meaning). Yet Horwich's rules of composition tell us that 'Mars rotates' means MARS ROTATES. Frege may have made a mistake when he said sentences are names, but Horwich outdoes him: for him the meaning of a sentence is named by a string of names. How can two names in a row combine to refer to a single object? 'Albert Einstein' names one person, but not because 'Albert' names one thing and 'Einstein' another. 'Andy's spouse' names or refers to one person, but only because what follows 'Andy' *isn't* a name. Frege treated predicates as functional expressions, as I have here treated what follows 'Andy'(spurning for a moment the theory of descriptions).

Like Horwich, I don't think it is worth looking for a deep characterization of the meanings of words. But our reasons are different. He thinks we can just assume we understand the notion of a meaning while explaining compositionality. I don't think the concept has been shown to help explain how language works.

References

Carnap, R. 1928. *Der Logische Aufbau der Welt*. Leipzig: Felix Meiner Verlag.

Davidson, D. 1980. *Essays on Actions and Events*. Oxford: Oxford University Press.

Davidson, D. 1982. Empirical Content. *Grazer Philosophichen Studien* 16/17:471-89.

Davidson, D. 1983. A Coherence Theory of Truth and Knowledge. *Kant oder Hegel*, ed. D. Henrich, 423-38. Stuttgart: Klett-Cotta.

Davidson, D. 1984. First Person Authority. *Dialectica* 38:101-11.

Davidson, D. 1985. Adverbs of Action. *Essays on Davidson: Actions and Events*, eds. B. Vermazen and M. Hintikka, 230-41. Oxford: Oxford University Press

Davidson, D. 1987. Problems in the Explanation of Action. *Metaphysics and Morality: Essays in Honour of J. J. C. Smart* eds. P. Pettit, R. Sylvan and J. Norman, 35-49. Oxford: Blackwell.

Davidson, D. 1990a. Meaning, Truth and Evidence. *Perspectives on Quine*, eds. R. B. Barrett and R. F. Gibson, 68-79. Oxford: Blackwell.

Davidson, D. 1990b. The Structure and Content of Truth. *The Journal of Philosophy* 87:279-328.

Davidson, D. 1991. Three Varieties of Knowledge. *A.J. Ayer Memorial Essays: Royal Institute of Philosophy Supplement 30*, ed A. P. Griffiths, 153-66. Cambridge: Cambridge University Press.

Davidson, D. 1995a. Could There Be a Science of Rationality? *International Journal of Philosophical Studies* 3:1-16.

Davidson, D. 1995b. Pursuit of the Concept of Truth. *On Quine* eds. P. Leonardi and M. Santambrogio, 7-21 Cambridge: Cambridge University Press.

Davidson, D. 1997a. The Folly of Trying to Define Truth. *The Journal of Philosophy* 94:263-78.

Davidson, D. 1997b. Indeterminism and Antirealism. *Realism/Antirealism and Epistemology*, ed C. B. Kulp, ed. Lanham, 109-22. Maryland: Rowman & Littlefield.

Davidson, D. 1999. The Centrality of Truth. *The Nature of Truth*, ed. J. Peregrin, 3-14. Dordrecht: Kluwer.

Davidson, D. 2000. Truth Rehabilitated. *Rorty and His Critics*, ed. R. B. Brandom, 65-74. Oxford: Blackwell.

McDowell, J. 1998. Précis of *Mind and World*. *Philosophy and Phenomenological Research* 58:365-68.

Neale, S. 1995. The Philosophical Significance of Gödel's Slingshot. *Mind* 104:761-825.

Quine, W. V. 1960. *Word and Object*. Cambridge, M.A.: MIT Press.

Quine, W. V. 1969. *Ontological Relativity and Other Essays*. New York: Columbia University Press.

Quine, W. V. 1990a. Comment on Davidson. *Perspectives on Quine*, eds. R. Barrett and R. Gibson, 81. Oxford: Blackwell.

Quine, W. V. 1990b. *Pursuit of Truth*. Cambridge, M.A.: Harvard University Press.

Quine, W. V. 1990c. Three Indeterminacies. *Perspectives on Quine*, eds. R. Barrett and R. Gibson, 1-16. Oxford: Oxford University Press.

Quine, W. V. 1996. Progress on Two Fronts. *The Journal of Philosophy* 93:159-63.

Sellars, W. 1956. Empiricism and the Philosophy of Mind. *The Foundations of Science and the Concepts of Psychology and Psychoanalysis*, eds. H. Feigl and M. Scriven, 1:253-329. Minneapolis: University of Minnesota Press.

Index

A

B

309

U

V

W